T0398757

Participatory Culture and the Social Value of an Architectural Icon: Sydney Opera House

This book develops new and innovative methods for understanding the cultural significance of places such as the World Heritage listed Sydney Opera House. By connecting participatory media, visual culture and social value, Cristina Garduño Freeman contributes to a fast-growing body of scholarship on digital heritage and the popular reception of architecture.

In this, her first book, she opens up a fresh perspective on heritage, as well as the ways in which people relate to architecture via participation on social media. Social media sites such as YouTube, Pinterest, Wikipedia, Facebook and Flickr, as well as others, become places for people to express their connections with places, for example, the Sydney Opera House. Garduño Freeman analyses real-world examples, from souvenirs to opera-house-shaped cakes, and untangles the tangible and intangible ways in which the significance of heritage is created, disseminated and maintained.

As people's encounters with World Heritage become increasingly mediated by the digital sphere there is a growing imperative for academics, professionals and policymakers to understand the social value of significant places. This book is beneficial for academics, students and professionals of architecture.

Cristina Garduño Freeman is emerging as a leader in the participatory culture and social value of iconic architecture. Her interdisciplinary work sits at the intersection of heritage, architecture and digital media. Currently, she is a Postdoctoral Research Fellow in the Australian Centre for Architectural History, Urban and Cultural Heritage (ACAHUCH) at the University of Melbourne, Australia. This is her first book.

'This is an important and timely book that proposes novel ways of understanding social value, identity and engagement with world heritage sites in the digitally mediated age. It will undoubtedly progress thinking and practice on the conception, representation and management of heritage.'

Hannah Lewi, Professor Architecture, University of Melbourne, Australia

'Focusing on the Sydney Opera House, Cristina Garduño Freeman's first monograph explores the persistent issue of "social value". In addition to providing a sustained exploration of heritage engagements within the context of the Opera House, her book also makes astute observations that are transferable well beyond those specifics, offering fresh empirical evidence and insight into the emerging relationships between heritage, online technologies and their associated modes of communication. The result is a strongly theorized monograph that will no doubt make an impactful and important contribution to the literatures supporting heritage and conservation studies.'

Emma Waterton, Associate Professor, Western Sydney University, Australia

Participatory Culture and the Social Value of an Architectural Icon: Sydney Opera House

Cristina Garduño Freeman

Routledge
Taylor & Francis Group

LONDON AND NEW YORK

First published 2018
by Routledge
2 Park Square, Milton Park, Abingdon, Oxon OX14 4RN

and by Routledge
711 Third Avenue, New York, NY 10017

Routledge is an imprint of the Taylor & Francis Group, an informa business

British Library Cataloguing-in-Publication Data
A catalogue record for this book is available from the British Library

Library of Congress Cataloging-in-Publication Data
A catalog record for this book has been requested

ISBN: 9781472469892 (hbk)
ISBN: 9781315599496 (ebk)

Typeset in Sabon
by Swales & Willis Ltd, Exeter, Devon, UK

Printed in the United Kingdom
by Henry Ling Limited

Contents

Figures

Preface

I was born in Mexico but emigrated to Australia when I was nine-and-a-half years old. Coming to Australia meant losing extended family and part of myself, too. At 15, as part of my high school's careers programme, I undertook work experience within the publicity department at the Sydney Opera House, and performed there the next year as part of a State Music Camp. I undertook much of my undergraduate education in Sydney.

I began to research the Sydney Opera House because I was curious about what the myriad of representations of this place could reveal. But, as with any major project, there is always something unconscious that motivates one. In the end, what I found was not just a fascinating phenomenon that evidenced the way other people engaged with this place on a grand scale, but a more personal connection.

Jørn Utzon travelled to Mexico in 1949 and visited archaeological sites in the Yucatan Peninsula. In his 1962 article for *Zodiac* he describes through text and drawings three significant indigenous sites: Chichen Itza, Uxmal and Monte Alban, all places I have visited myself. While I might not concur with Utzon's romantic notion that these places are primitive and unauthored architectures, it was nonetheless significant that links to Mexico were embedded in the platforms of the Sydney Opera House. In a way, this reinforced my sense that people made personal connections with works of iconic architecture, connections that while on their own might not be unique or significant at a national level were important to their own memories and identity. The Sydney Opera House, and the many representations I have collected over the course of this research, are now part of my professional and personal identity, and this connection serves as but one instance of the social value of this place.

Acknowledgements

Writing a book can be a lonely experience. Yet it takes the support of many to complete such an endeavour. Here, I thank those individuals and organisations that have contributed to its completion.

Naomi Stead, Kate Sweetapple and Kirsten Orr supervised the doctoral research that forms the major part of this book. Their encouragement, critical appraisal and articulate feedback have influenced my research and approach to academia. I would like to thank Sheridan Burke, Chris Johnston, Bronwyn Hanna, Paul Ashton, Emma Waterton, Hannah Lewi, Terry Smith and José van Dijck for their valuable feedback. The opportunity to be part of the 2009 Oxford Internet Institute Summer Doctoral Program, with Marcus Foth and Jean Burgess, gave direction to the value of the research within the emerging field of Internet Studies. Sasha Baroni, Vicki Leibowitz, Antonia Fredman, Lucila Carvalho, Fiona Gray, Karen Soldatic, Zoe Sadokierski and Jennifer Preston all contributed in various ways to the completion of this book.

Part of Chapter 5 was originally published in the *International Journal of Heritage Studies*, (16) 4 (2010), pp. 352–368 and part of Chapter 6 was originally published in the *Architecture Theory Review*, (18) 3 (2013), pp. 325–339.

Finally, I thank my immediate and extended family for their ongoing support. In particular, my husband Nicholas has listened, provided feedback, read and edited drafts, all the while providing unswerving emotional support and raising with me two curious, creative and confident digital-native children.

Introduction

How can the special attachment people feel towards the Sydney Opera House be understood? In what way can this attachment, which inspires people to visit the building, retell its story and intertwine this place with their own memories, be made evident and therefore analysed? The images in Figure I.1 are curious: why do people post photographs online, collect snowdomes and make cakes in the shape of this building?

Social value is defined as the attachment that people and communities have for places, which is expressed through people's interactions and engagements with each other and with the place itself. Iconic works of architecture hold special symbolic and aesthetic associations for specific groups of people. Typically, they are famous landmarks that are used to represent places or countries at a global level. The Sydney Opera House, designed by Jørn Utzon, is one such place. In 2007, this work of architecture was inscribed onto the United Nations Educational, Scientific and Cultural Organization's (UNESCO) World Heritage List as a 'world-famous iconic building'. Whilst the significance of this place is widely acknowledged, describing and substantiating its social value has until now been difficult and challenging and no comprehensive study, either within the field of architecture or of heritage, has been carried out.

The substantial body of existing academic research on the Sydney Opera House has already established its significance as a masterpiece of 20th-century architecture and the building's role as a symbol for Sydney, and more broadly for Australia, is widely recognised. The Sydney Opera House is a place that holds special meanings and associations for people at a national and an international level. Assessing the social value of such a landmark is challenging because its community, that is the individuals and groups of people who are attached to this place, are geographically dispersed across Australia as well as other countries. Here, popular culture practices such as collecting snowdomes, taking tourist photographs, or making cakes, are explored to investigate how they connect with concepts of social value and intangible heritage as set out in heritage discourse. Such forms of popular culture, which have long been practised but only recently been made accessible and visible through online forms of participatory media, offer a method for the analysis of the social value of the Sydney Opera House and of other works of architecture and sites of heritage.

Heritage, as an academic and professional field, has long sought to assess and articulate the value of architecture. Heritage listing implicates processes to determine the nature and the degree of significance of places within established legal frameworks. The discussion centres on one such framework, namely UNESCO's *Convention Concerning*

Figure I.1 Representations of the Sydney Opera House.

Sources: top left, Sydney Opera House souvenir snowdome; top right, Sydney Opera House (Opera) Cake (© Heather Baird, 2010); bottom left, Sydney Opera House scene from the musical adaptation of *Finding Nemo* by Disney (© Jennifer Fortwengler, 2008); bottom right, photograph of the Sydney Opera House posted on Flickr.com titled 'Not so big hu?' (© Mary-Pierre Serveaux and Fabien Hoareau, 2005).

the Protection of the World Cultural and Natural Heritage, 1972 (World Heritage Convention). Frameworks are important because they operate to define not only 'which' places, but the reasons 'why' a place becomes recognised as 'heritage'. Defining the significance of places is complex and for this reason the field of heritage draws on a wide range of disciplines to substantiate claims for the inscription and protection of sites and their listed values. The interdisciplinary nature of the field of heritage studies offers theoretical and practical frameworks that intersect with architecture and its social significance. The research draws on architecture, heritage studies and media studies. Publications that focus on the architecture of the building inform the discussion on its history and its value as an iconic building, while in heritage, critiques of legal inscription frameworks, such as the *World Heritage Convention*, and more generally the discipline of heritage, contextualise the discussion and analysis of the building's 2007 World Heritage inscription. Media studies approaches inform the way communities and audiences engage with popular culture and thereby provide a theoretical lens through which the significance of popular culture practices can be observed online.

Social value has been included as a form of place-significance in Australia's best-known heritage practice instrument *The Burra Charter: The Australia ICOMOS Charter for Places of Cultural Significance* (*Burra Charter*), since its initial adoption in 1979. A more comprehensive definition of the concept of social value, however, was not established until over a decade later. Interest in the concept of social value emerged from the work of Australian heritage practitioners Chris Johnston, Meredith Walker and Marilyn Truscott, in collaboration with the Australian Heritage Commission's representative Sandy Blair.[1] In 1992, the Australian Heritage Commission appointed Johnston to carry out the first formal investigation on social value.[2] The report, titled *What is Social Value?*, sought to offer a practical definition for the sense of attachment that communities have for particular places.[3] In the report, Johnston notes that social value was seen at the time as a means for describing forms of significance that fell outside of the existing professional frameworks.[4] Johnston's 1992 report exemplifies the increasing interest in recognising community perspectives as valid reasons for inscribing places as cultural heritage.[5]

Valuing buildings and places because they are significant to communities has gained much traction since Johnston's 1992 discussion paper. Workshops[6] and publications[7] in the following years continued to develop the idea of social value and methods for its assessment. At an international level, concepts such as cultural landscapes within World Heritage and instruments such as the *Nara Document on Authenticity* adopted by the International Council on Monuments and Sites (ICOMOS) in 1994, have emerged.[8] These concepts and instruments, like social value, are part of the larger movement in heritage to take account of, and recognise, forms of culture that are significant for communities, rather than forms more readily recognised as valuable by professional heritage practitioners. By the end of the 20th century the discussion on community attachment had shifted towards the concept of intangible heritage, which rather than inscribing places, seeks to recognise cultural practices, such as cuisine or dance, for their value to communities. Whilst the UNESCO *Convention for the Safeguarding of the Intangible Cultural Heritage* (*Intangible Heritage Convention*) that was adopted in 2003 signifies the importance of connecting heritage to communities, its central concern is not architecture.[9] Social value has more recently been the focus of international instruments such as the *Council of Europe Framework Convention on the Value of Cultural Heritage for Society* (*Faro Convention*) and in Australian research on the emotional connection to landscapes.[10] This interest in the valuation of contemporary culture exemplifies larger shifts in the focus of heritage: away from fixed ideas of preservation towards managing conservation, and the recognition that the present is just as significant as the past. All of these concepts aim to take account of the significance of heritage in relation to present-day communities; not just as historic or artistic exemplars of past culture.

The idea of community attachment to place, fundamental to social value, is broad and therefore informed by many academic discourses, including cultural studies, memory studies, critical tourism studies, cultural geography, sociology and anthropology. However, heritage has predominantly been addressed from within the disciplines of architecture, history and archaeology until the second half of the 20th century, when an influx of scholarship from the social science disciplines motivated the recognition of community-centred values.[11] Whilst the interest in social value is increasing, listings that include this value remain under-represented both at an international and national level.[12] Investigating the social value of an already recognised

World Heritage site might not seem necessary, after all the inscription requires the Australian government's plans for its conservation. Unlike other values for which places are listed, such as aesthetic, historic or scientific reasons, social value is not bound to the site itself, but exists in the way people use, engage with and express their attachment to such places. Exploring the social value of the Sydney Opera House offers an opportunity for developing ways to evidence and to analyse and to comprehend social value at an international level. This book makes a case for understanding how popular culture practices, such as dressing up as the Sydney Opera House, make a contribution to its broader social and cultural significance.

In 2007, when this research commenced, major shifts in the communication structure of the internet had taken place. The second generation of the internet, or Web 2.0,[13] made the frequent depiction of the Sydney Opera House in visual culture readily accessible. At the same time it also made visible some of the activities that were occurring around representations of this place, particularly on participatory media platforms. That the World Heritage inscription occurred at a time when the participation was being enabled by the internet became an opportunity for the research to develop a new means for the investigation of the social value of iconic architecture. This task was undertaken by collecting representations posted online and analysing the activities of communities around them in order to investigate the building's social value.

The assessment of social significance or social value has to date been carried out using methods established in the social sciences, such as interviews, questionnaires, focus groups, workshops and community consultation, in conjunction with more traditional heritage methods such as historical research and physical site analysis. Between 2001 and 2003, the aforementioned social value expert, Chris Johnston, was appointed by the Australian Heritage Commission to develop a defensible assessment methodology for the concept of 'inspirational landscapes' which describes the 'profound emotional response' Australians express for natural environments.[14] The project's emphasis on the emotional response to landscape is another way of describing people's attachment to place, where the focus of the report is on landscapes rather than iconic architecture, as is the case in this book. In the project report Johnston states that the assessment of places is complex and should include multiple forms of data, including many of the traditional social science methods mentioned above. Notably the report makes use of the opportunities afforded by the internet by including an online conference.[15] The report also mentions that 'research into historical and contemporary images and expressions' should be part of the assessment process.[16] The project's use of online means for participation in addition to its recognition of images as a means for research confirms the approach undertaken in this book. However, the methods in Johnston's report invite public participation through formal research, intentionally set up to gather such responses, whereas here, representations posted online through participatory forms of media are used as a means for investigating community attachment. While the research extends existing visual sociological methods of inquiry into the online realm, it also takes a different approach; it seeks to make observations of activities that are already occurring, independently of any form of academic inquiry

The discourse on World Heritage and its central instrument the *World Heritage Convention* is brought to bear on the 2007 inscription of the Sydney Opera House and the previous attempts at inscription in 1980 and 1996/1999. The 2007 inscription demonstrates the increasing recognition of contemporary works of architecture as heritage and of the broadening remit of values for which places are inscribed.

The *World Heritage Convention* is the legacy of the intellectual and political conditions in 1972, when it was written and adopted, before the discourse on social value had gained momentum. As a result, the convention is unable to directly account for social value. The 2007 inscription recognises the Sydney Opera House as a 'world-famous iconic building'.[17] This is intriguing as the inscription explicitly recognises the building's iconic status, as well as its *world-famous* regard, therefore bringing its *popularity* to bear within its heritage significance. However, the nomination documents that support the inscription reveal a discrepancy; while the inscription recognises the building's value as an icon is evident in the popular attention it receives, it accounts for this value purely in terms of its architecture. To address this discrepancy the concept of *socio-visual value* is proposed, as a means for describing the particular kind of attachment that people have for iconic works of architecture. Socio-visual value comprises an aesthetic or visual component and the research investigates how this might be evidenced in the online activities and representations associated with this place. By examining this aspect of the inscription, wider questions about the social value of the Sydney Opera House can be brought to light. The other instruments within UNESCO's cultural program, namely the *Intangible Heritage Convention* and the *Charter on the Preservation of the Digital Heritage* (*Digital Heritage Charter*) are explored as alternative means to recognise the social value of iconic works of architecture.

Discussions on the Sydney Opera House as a work of architecture concentrate on those texts, which frame it as an example of iconic architecture. Whilst one of the earliest applications of the term *iconic* to the Sydney Opera House appears in the 1977 publication by architectural historian Charles Jencks titled *The Language of Post-Modern Architecture*,[18] the discussion demonstrates that its symbolic and social value dates back to 1959 at the beginning of the building's realisation.[19] In later editions of this book, Jencks describes the way some works of architecture have both popular appeal and critical acclaim.[20] For the Sydney Opera House this is evident in the substantial body of academic and popular publications; there are some two hundred monographs, articles, book chapters and many hundred more media stories about the building. However, much of this research addresses the political issues around its architectural realisation,[21] its place within the Modernist architectural canon,[22] or its contribution as a major engineering and building project, rather than its popular appeal.[23] Recent literature by Leslie Sklair, Terry Smith and Richard Weston that cites the Sydney Opera House discusses the way certain buildings become popular aesthetic symbols, connecting iconicity with representations and popular appeal.[24] Building on the work of these scholars the socio-visual value of the Sydney Opera House can be evidenced through the representations and online instances of participation centred around this place.

This research will be of interest to architectural and heritage scholars and practitioners as well as the communities of the Sydney Opera House. Those who specialise in assessing the community values of places, may find the online methods explored here of value. Online forms of participation are new discursive spaces where socially contextualised values can be observed and assessed. Research on heritage and digital culture has largely been addressed within museum studies,[25] but research specifically focused on social media and participatory culture is beginning to emerge. This new area of research is exemplified by the publication of Elise Giaccardi's 2012 edited collection, *Heritage and Social Media: Understanding Heritage in a Participatory Culture*.[26] Scholars in media studies and internet studies already acknowledge the significance of such online cultural practices.

Framing these as contributing to the heritage value of iconic architecture offers a new perspective on these activities. Further, World Heritage purports to inscribe places that are of outstanding universal value to all of humankind.[27] Yet while places are inscribed for the benefit of all, World Heritage is not yet able to account for the ways that places, such as the Sydney Opera House, are significant to people. This research recognises the important contribution that people make through their popular culture practices to the iconic status and socio-visual value of this place.

Reframing the online representations of the Sydney Opera House as significant makes a contribution to existing research on heritage and interpretation, which is usually addressed as part of the interpretation of heritage sites.[28] The role of representations as social mediators that can influence popular and academic understandings of architecture, and by extension heritage, is exemplified by another recent publication by Emma Waterton and Steve Watson. Their edited collection, *Culture, Heritage and Representation: Perspectives on Visuality and the Past*, emphasises the way in which visual and material culture is critical in developing public perceptions of places.[29] Understanding architecture from this perspective will not only be of interest to heritage scholars, but to architectural theorists and practitioners too. The representation of architecture in broader culture is arguably a form of popular critique that operates as a potential dialogue between architects and architectural scholars and the communities interested in their creative endeavours.

The inability of other UNESCO instruments to accommodate social value indicates the need for legal frameworks which can recognise all the ways in which landmarks, such as the Sydney Opera House, are significant. The challenge that the rapid development of internet communication technologies poses for the field of heritage, both as exemplars of culture themselves and as vehicles for understanding the significance of other tangible and intangible forms of culture, is presented here. Such a gap in the frameworks through which architecture is evaluated will be of interest to scholars in these areas. The ability to observe and understand how and why places, such as the Sydney Opera House, are significant to people will also be of interest to those managing these venues. Visitor facilities are often in conflict with conservation plans, where retail and tourism are seen to impinge on heritage significance. Recognising these activities as important engagements that actively contribute to the iconic character of places, for example, photography or collecting souvenirs, reframes often-dismissed popular culture practices as evidence of the building's social value. By documenting the diverse ways the building infiltrates many aspects of everyday life, as a hat, as a lamp, or as a serviette, the ways in which the activities of individuals and groups are integral to the present-day cultural significance of the Sydney Opera House are articulated.

Collecting, analysing and ordering representations

The inquiry is undertaken through a visual analysis of collected representations of the Sydney Opera House, which leads to a proposed series of practices of participatory culture. These are explored through further studies that broadly describe instances of these practices and then explore one example in detail.

Between 2007 and 2012 around 900 popular representations of the Sydney Opera House were collected from the internet. The representations were gathered through proprietary search engines on sites such as Flickr and eBay as well as internet-wide engines such as Google and Google Images. Using the terms 'sydney', 'opera' and 'house' simultaneously, such searches undertaken returned images and websites that featured, referred to, or were in some way associated with the Sydney Opera House. The representations collected during this period formed the primary data for this book.

The collection comprises images that were gathered over two stages. Initially, only photographs retrieved from the website Flickr were included in the collection of representations. These photographs were retrieved using the terms 'sydney', 'opera' and 'house' in Flickr's search engine in mid 2007. Some 30,000 images posted to the site between 2004 when Flickr was launched and April 2007 were returned. From these over 3,000 photographs were viewed and a series of representative sets of 5–10 images were selected. These sets sought to describe the many different ways in which the Sydney Opera House features in photographs on Flickr. For example, one set was of photographs of the building taken from the giraffe enclosure at Taronga Zoo, whilst another was of close-up photographs of the tiles that cover the building's shells (Figure I.2). In total 300 images were gathered into 36 sets that featured the Sydney Opera House from an aerial perspective through to tourist snapshots.

This initial search for representations revealed that representations of the Sydney Opera House were not limited to photographs, but were in fact far more diverse. This prompted a second ongoing search for representations, carried out using the same search terms, 'sydney', 'opera' and 'house', but through Google and Google Images, and on the website eBay. Many more representations were retrieved, including: objects such as homewares, toys and jewellery, other images such as drawings, paintings and cartoons, logos, souvenirs, maps, films, performances, events, visual analogies, archival material and even other buildings, all associated in some way

Figure I.2 Results from Flickr search.

Sources: top left, 'Giraffe and Sydney Opera House' (© Laurie Wilson, 2011); top middle, 'Giraffe and Sydney Opera House' (© Denise Penney, 2007); top right, 'On Safari!' (© Nick Richards, 2006); bottom left, 'Opera House Roof Tiles' (© Anthony Agius, 2007); bottom middle, 'Sydney Opera House' (© Thomas Rotte, 2014); bottom right, 'Sydney opera house tiles' (© Jimmy Harris, 2006).

with the Sydney Opera House (Figure I.3). Like the first search that was limited to Flickr, the examples were ordered into sets to create a representative series of the diverse ways in which the Sydney Opera House features in visual culture and popular practices, such as the making of things. In most cases 5–10 examples of each type were gathered. Using the same criteria as in the initial search on Flickr, representations were selected because they clearly featured, depicted or were associated with the architecture of the Sydney Opera House. In order to control the material gathered, performances, concerts or recordings made at the venue were excluded from the collection. Overall over 600 representations were gathered into 39 sets describing how the Sydney Opera House is diversely depicted as costumes, in LEGO and even on cars, to name some examples.

The research method thus involved collecting images of the Sydney Opera House from the internet, analysing the relationship of these images to the original building and categorising the images in order to understand how these could evidence the building's socio-visual value. This process resulted in a schema of six socio-visual practices, that are presented in pairs in Chapters 4, 5 and 6. The six practices of participatory culture and the argument that underpins their significance is a key finding of the research.

Figure I.3 Results from internet search.

The practices are more fully discussed after a case has been made that socio-visual value can be evidenced in examples of participatory culture.

At the beginning of this research, scholarship on the subject of online visual methodologies was still emerging. For this reason the method of analysis was initially open and exploratory, whilst drawing on visual methods to unpack the significance of these examples. Such an approach to examining visual and material culture is evident in José van Dijck's *Mediated Memories in the Digital Age*. In this book, van Dijck takes personal memory artefacts, such as photographs, diaries, music collections and videos, and explores how these items mediate relationships at both a personal and collective level, articulating how their new digital counterparts offer both continuities to existing practices, as well as transformations.[30] Her conceptual tool of 'mediated memories' becomes increasingly useful and central to understand the way in which participatory culture is not simply tangible, but implicated in intangible and digital forms of culture.

Images sourced from the internet are referred to as representations. Using the term representations is a way of describing their significance, which critically is their *connection* to the Sydney Opera House. To represent something or someone is to 'stand in for' a thing or person.[31] The research collected images of the Sydney Opera House because they stand in for the physical building and facilitate social interaction between people. While a representation might be considered a copy, a lesser version of the original, the value of the representations here is not as images themselves, but as things that re-present the building from a social perspective. Further, although many of the examples that depict the Sydney Opera House are indeed images, others are films, websites, performances about the building and textual accounts. Describing these as representations allows the bringing together of divergent ways in which the Sydney Opera House is part of visual culture.

Two other publications have informed the way the representations in the collection have been analysed: Gillian Rose's *Visual Methodologies* and David Gauntlett's *Making is Connecting*.[32] Rose's text offers a framework for the critical analysis of visual representations where their meaning can be understood in relation to their production, the image itself and in relation to how and by whom it is exhibited to audiences. Looking at the representations of the building from these three perspectives informed what they could reveal about the way people use the Sydney Opera House in a variety of ways. The second text, by Gauntlett, observes how in the era of Web 2.0, making things, such as cakes, or taking photographs are a means for social connection. Thinking of the representations in this way reveals their significance as more than depictions of the Sydney Opera House; instead they can be understood as a kind of currency for social interaction.

Whilst Rose and Gauntlett's work was useful for questioning and framing the significance of individual representations of the Sydney Opera House, working with a large and unwieldy collection demanded a system of organisation. Initially the representations were ordered intuitively; although imperfect, these initial attempts revealed that the process of ordering, as much as the resultant taxonomy, was a means to interrogate the body of representations from multiple perspectives.[33]

Unexpectedly, a breakthrough in the process of ordering the representations came in 2011 with the launch of a participatory media platform called Pinterest.[34] This platform operates as an online pinboard, where members can 'pin' images from websites, and organise them on 'boards'. Pinterest facilitated the process of ordering the collection within an online context, storing the original location of each image as a live link.[35] Not only did this accelerate the process of ordering, it facilitated the organisation of these images under various themes. During the research, the collection was organised in various ways: by type (photograph, cake, painting, hat), by source (Flickr, eBay, Pinterest, Blogger), by author (individual, group, commercial enterprise or institution) and by date of creation. Whilst these explorations offered insights, none could fully account for all the representations or reveal the socio-visual value of the Sydney Opera House. Organisation by source indicated where representations clustered at online locations; by type gave clues as to the way the Sydney Opera House infiltrates everyday activities such as eating, or official uses such as stamps or Olympic branding; by author revealed that the Sydney Opera House features in the sites of institutions and participatory media platforms alike; by date revealed that such popular representations were not new but had existed since the building was first designed. The significance of the representations, as Gauntlett's work proposed, was as a kind of visual currency for social interactions.

Theoretical reframing: participatory culture

The term participatory media emerged within the field of media studies as an evolution of Henry Jenkins' concept of participatory culture. In coining this term, Jenkins aimed to challenge older ideas that framed audiences as passive spectators and to reconceive fan culture as creative, active and engaged.[36] Participatory media is also described as: social media, Web 2.0, user-based media, user content and amateur media. The extension of Jenkins' concept has been applied to the new generation of websites characterised by the way they facilitate 'many to many' communication. Participatory media allow even unskilled individuals to self-publish and publicly share their content outside of traditional institutional boundaries and are founded on active communities and individual participation through posting content on the internet.

The socio-visual value of iconic architecture is investigated through the online activities and representations associated with the Sydney Opera House. Participatory media is a means for investigating this because it makes participatory culture public. However, the focus is not on media (although it is implicated), but rather on the underlying participatory culture. The culture is the driver of the building's popularity and its representation, whereas participatory media is merely the location where participatory culture takes place. Jenkins' work on participatory culture is theoretically useful because it connects socio-visual value to the public participation that occurs around an iconic building, such as the Sydney Opera House.

The social and visual contributions on participatory media test the proposition that socio-visual value is made evident in online instances of participatory culture. The instances explored in Chapters 4, 5 and 6 are unsolicited contributions on websites such as Wikipedia, Blogger, Flickr and YouTube. They are examined by drawing on José van Dijck's conceptual tool of mediated memories to understand how intangible, intangible and digital intertwine. The investigations on the representations are contextualised within social interactions, and through their analysis it is possible to evidence something of the socio-visual value of the Sydney Opera House. The collection of representations are ordered in terms of the kinds of participation that they evidence. Rather than categorising the representation in terms of what it is, such as a hat, or a photograph, this process considers the practice implicated in the representation, such as *wearing* or *making* a hat, or *visiting* to *capture* the building through a photograph.

These practices are ways in which the representations can be understood as evidence of people's participation with the building. Blog entries recounting the building's history are practices of *telling* stories or experiences to others; visual metaphors both sublime and ridiculous are ways of *critiquing* the building. *Making* the Sydney Opera House out of cake or LEGO is a way of understanding the formal qualities of the building, while *trading* on the symbolic value of the Sydney Opera House by featuring it in logos and stamps is a way of employing its cultural capital.

The findings are then applied in Chapter 7 where an official part of the website of the Sydney Opera House, hosted at the time of Utzon's death, is examined. Together, these instances of participatory culture confirm that audiences and communities of the Sydney Opera House are engaged participants, where making representations, posting or sharing them is evidence of the attachment felt for this place. Yet, unlike the representations collected in the earlier part of the research, participatory culture is not a tangible form of culture. How might it be recognised as part of the building's cultural heritage? The examples of participatory culture may be digital traces, but the underlying activities that constitute the participatory culture of the Sydney Opera House are complex social practices that involve both offline and online activities.

The book concludes by considering how socio-visual value and its manifestation in participatory culture might be recognised within UNESCO's existing suite of heritage instruments. Specifically, the discussion investigates Criterion (vi) from the *World Heritage Convention*, as well as the *Digital Heritage Charter* and the *Intangible Heritage Convention*. The ideas centred on the Sydney Opera House are extended to other iconic works of architecture that have been recognised as heritage, for example the Eiffel Tower or the Taj Mahal. What becomes clear is that heritage frameworks are yet to offer a straightforward means to recognise the practices of participatory culture through which the social value of World Heritage sites is played out at an international level. They are yet to take account of the way people engage through tangible, intangible and digital forms of culture to draw meaning and maintain attachments with these places. The social significance of places is entangled, complex and dynamic, and it is implicated in individual and collective identity and memory. Until heritage is framed, both conceptually and legally as a network of significance, the challenges to recognise and maintain such forms of significance will remain.

Notes

1 In 2004 Australia restructured its national heritage system, and the Australian Heritage Commission became the Australian Heritage Council.
2 Chris Johnston (1992) *What Is Social Value? A Discussion Paper*. Canberra: Australian Government Publishing Service.
3 Johnston, *What Is Social Value?*, p. 4.
4 In 2003 Marilyn Truscott referred to a paper she wrote with Sandy Blair in 1987 as sparking interest in social value. Marilyn Truscott (2003) 'Intangible Values as Heritage in Australia'. Presented at the *Proceedings of the International Scientific Symposium Place, Memory, Meaning Preserving Intangible Values in Monuments and Sites*, Victoria Falls, Zimbabwe, 27–31 October. Retrieved: 10/07/2012, from: www.international.icomos.org/victoriafalls 2003/truscott_eng.htm, paragraph 13; Sandy Blair and Marilyn Truscott (1988) *Places of Social Significance*. Australian Heritage Commission. In 1992 Chris Johnston cites that the interest in social value was due to ideas contained within a report she completed with Meredith Walker and Carmel Boyce in 1986. Johnston, *What Is Social Value?*, p. 1; Meredith Walker, Chris Johnston and Carmel Boyce (1986) *Heritage Issues and Strategies: Western Region Cultural Heritage Study*. Braybrook: Melbourne Western Region Commission.

5 Chris Johnston (1992) 'Whose Views Count? Achieving Community Support for Landscape Conservation'. *Historic Environment*, 7 (2), pp. 33–37.
6 'Assessing Social Values: Communities and Experts – a Workshop Held by Australia ICOMOS' (1996) Sydney.
7 Ken Taylor (1999) 'Reconciling Aesthetic Value and Social Value: Dilemmas of Interpretation and Application'. *APT Bulletin, Landscape Preservation Comes of Age*, 30 (1), pp. 51–55; Meredith Walker (1998) *Protecting the Social Value of Public Places*. ACT: Australian Council of National Trusts.
8 ICOMOS (1994) *Nara Document on Authenticity*. Retrieved: 26/04/2013, from: www. icomos.org/charters/nara-e.pdf.
9 UNESCO (2003) *Convention for the Safeguarding of the Intangible Cultural Heritage*, 32nd Session: The General Conference of the United Nations Educational, Scientific and Cultural Organization. Paris. Retrieved: 29/11/2010, from: www.unesco.org/culture/ich/index.php?lg=en&pg=00022.
10 Council of Europe (2005) *Council of Europe Framework Convention on the Value of Cultural Heritage for Society (Faro Convention)*. Retrieved: 01/03/2013, from: http://conventions.coe.int/Treaty/en/Treaties/Html/199.htm; Chris Johnston, Libby Riches, Ann McGregor and Kristal Buckley (2003) 'Inspirational Landscapes. Volume 4: Assessment Method Report'. Canberra: Australian Heritage Commission, p. 1.
11 Laurajane Smith (2007) 'General Introduction'. In *Cultural Heritage: Critical Concepts in Media and Cultural Studies*. London: Routledge, p. 2.
12 Shaun Canning and Dirk Spenneman (2001) 'Contested Space: Social Value and the Assessment of Cultural Significance in New South Wales, Australia'. In *Heritage Landscapes: Understanding Place and Communities*, edited by Maria Cotter, Bill Boyd and Jane Gardiner. Lismore: Southern Cross University Press, pp. 457–468; Chris Johnston (2012) 'Swimming Upstream, with Crocodiles: Social Value and the Prevailing Heritage Discourse'. Presented at the *ACT and Region Annual Australian Heritage Partnership Symposium. Valuing Heritage: Advocating for Community Attachment in Planning*, Canberra, 28 July; Olwen Beazley (2004) 'Inspirational Landscapes as World Heritage: Problems of Identification and Management'. Presented at the *World Heritage Cultural and Ecological Landscapes, US ICOMOS*, Natchitoches, Louisiana, 25–27 March. Retrieved: 28/03/2011, from: www.usicomos.org/symp/archive/2004/docs/beazley-4780; Olwen Beazley and Harriet Deacon (2007) 'The Safeguarding of Intangible Heritage Values under the World Heritage Convention: Auschwitz, Hiroshima and Robben Island'. In *Safeguarding Intangible Cultural Heritage: Challenges and Approaches*, edited by Janet Blake. Builth Wells: Institute of Art and Law, pp. 93–107; Olwen Beazley (2009) 'Protecting Intangible Heritage Values through the World Heritage Convention?' *Historic Environment*, 22 (3), pp. 8–13.
13 Tim O'Reilly (2005) 'What Is Web 2.0: Design Patterns and Business Models for the Next Generation of Software'. Retrieved: 27/09/2007, from: www.oreillynet.com/lpt/a/6228.
14 Johnston *et al.*, 'Inspirational Landscapes. Volume 4', p. 1.
15 Chris Johnston, Libby Riches, Ann McGregor and Kristal Buckley (2003) 'Inspirational Landscapes. Volume 3: Overview of the On-Line Conference Inspirational Landscape – Heritage Places? (6–7 Nov 02)'. Canberra: Australian Heritage Commission, pp. 2–3.
16 Johnston *et al.*, 'Inspirational Landscapes. Volume 4', p. 27.
17 UNESCO (2007) 'Sydney Opera House (Australia) No 166 Rev: Advisory Body Evaluation'. World Heritage Centre. Retrieved: 27/04/2013, from: http://whc.unesco.org/archive/advisory_body_evaluation/166rev.pdf.
18 Charles Jencks (1977) *The Language of Post-Modern Architecture*. New York: Rizzoli, p. 46.
19 Arthur Drexler and Wilder Green (1959) *Architecture and Imagery: Four New Buildings*. New York: MOMA.
20 Charles Jencks (1981) 'Introduction'. In *The Language of Post-Modern Architecture*. New York: Rizzoli, p. 6.
21 Philip Drew (2001) *The Masterpiece: A Secret Life*. 2nd edn. South Yarra: Hardie Grant Books; Peter Murray (2004) *The Saga of the Sydney Opera House: The Dramatic Story of the Design and Construction of the Icon of Modern Australia*. New York: Spon Press; Ken Woolley (2010) *Reviewing the Performance*. Boorowa: The Watermark Press.

22 Philip Drew (2007) 'Romanticism Revisited: Jørn Utzon's Sydney Opera House'. *Architectural Theory Review*, 12 (2), pp. 121–145; Philip Goad (1997) 'An Appeal for Modernism: Sigfried Giedion and the Sydney Opera House'. *Fabrications*, 8, pp. 129–145.

23 Peter Jones (2006) *Ove Arup: Masterbuilder of the Twentieth Century*. New Haven: Yale University Press; Om Prakash Kharbanda and Jeffrey K. Pinto (1996) *What Made Gertie Gallop? Lessons from Project Failures*. New York: Van Nostrand Reinhold; Paolo Tombesi and Andrew Martel (2005) 'Vessels of Expression and Flows of Innovation on the Connection between Toilets and Architecture'. *Journal of Architectural Education*, 59 (2), pp. 43–52.

24 Leslie Sklair (2017) *The Icon Project: Architecture, Cities, and Capitalist Globalization*. New York: Oxford University Press. Terry Smith (2002) 'The Political Economy of Iconotypes and the Architecture of Destination: Uluru, the Sydney Opera House and the World Trade Center'. *Architectural Theory Review*, 7 (2), pp. 1–43; Richard Weston (2006) 'Monumental Appeal: Reflections on the Sydney Opera House'. In *Building a Masterpiece: The Sydney Opera House*, edited by Anne Watson. Aldershot: Lund Humphries, pp. 20–37.

25 Fiona Cameron and Sarah Kenderdine (2007) *Theorizing Digital Cultural Heritage*. Cambridge, MA: The MIT Press; Yehuda Kalay, Thomas Kvan and Janice Affleck (2008) *New Heritage: New Media and Cultural Heritage*. New York: Routledge; Katherine Jones-Garmil (1997) *The Wired Museum*. Washington, DC: American Association of Museums.

26 Elisa Giaccardi (ed.) (2012) *Heritage and Social Media: Understanding Heritage in a Participatory Culture*. London: Routledge.

27 UNESCO (1972) *Convention Concerning the Protection of the World Cultural and Natural Heritage*. Retrieved: 26/11/2012, from: http://whc.unesco.org/archive/convention-en.pdf, Article 1.

28 Freeman Tilden (1977) *Interpreting Our Heritage*. Chapel Hill: University of North Carolina Press; David Uzzell (2007 [1998]) 'Interpreting Our Heritage: A Theoretical Interpretation'. In *Cultural Heritage: Critical Concepts in Media and Cultural Studies*, vol. 4, edited by Laurajane Smith. London: Routledge, pp. 74–84; John Urry. (2007 [1990]) 'Gazing on History'. In *Cultural Heritage: Critical Concepts in Media and Cultural Studies*, vol. 3, edited by Laurajane Smith. London: Routledge, pp. 306–338.

29 Emma Waterton and Steve Watson (2010) *Culture, Heritage and Representation: Perspectives on Visuality and the Past*. Surrey: Ashgate.

30 José van Dijck (2007) *Mediated Memories in the Digital Age, Cultural Memory in the Present*. Stanford: Stanford University Press.

31 Tony Bennett, Lawrence Grossberg and Meaghan Morris (2009) *New Keywords: A Revised Vocabulary of Culture and Society*. Oxford: Blackwell, pp. 306–307.

32 Gillian Rose (2007) *Visual Methodologies: An Introduction to the Interpretation of Visual Materials*. 2nd edn. London: Sage; David Gauntlett (2007) *Creative Explorations: New Approaches to Identities and Audiences*. London: Routledge; David Gauntlett (2011) *Making Is Connecting: The Social Meaning of Creativity, from Diy and Knitting to Youtube and Web 2.0*. Cambridge: Polity Press.

33 Brenda Danet and Tamar Katriel (1994) 'No Two Alike: Play and Aesthetics in Collecting'. In *Interpreting Objects and Collections*, edited by Susan M. Pearce. London: Routledge, pp. 253–277.

34 Pinterest.com

35 All the thumbnail images in the book can be viewed on Pinterest under the book's own account: https://au.pinterest.com/cristinagardunofreeman.

36 The term participatory culture was first coined in: Henry Jenkins (1988) 'Star Trek Reread, Rerun, Rewritten: Fan Writing as Textual Poaching'. *Critical Studies in Mass Communications*, 5 (2), pp. 171–204.

1 World Heritage inscription and social value

The inscription of the Sydney Opera House in 2007 as a World Heritage site was a significant milestone for the World Heritage program. News headlines reported that the Sydney Opera House had won 'top status', and that the inscription was 'a standing ovation', finally recognising the building as 'masterpiece of mankind'.[1] The inscription was significant because, at the time, the Sydney Opera House was, at 34 years of age, the youngest site to be listed and only the second site inscribed during the lifetime of its architect, Jørn Utzon (1918–2008).[2] The recognition of the Sydney Opera House as World Heritage marks the broadening scope of the World Heritage programme to include Modern Architecture.

In 1957 when the Sydney Opera House project was first commissioned, Sydney aspired to be an international city.[3] The Sydney Opera House project was closely followed and the progress and costs of its realisation were frequently publicised in the media. The technical and political difficulties during construction, as well as issues of authorship, affected both public and expert opinions on its significance and contribution to culture. This public scrutiny during the realisation of the Sydney Opera House lays the ground for the way in which the inscription of the Sydney Opera House also served to formally establish the building's importance at a global level. Gaining World Heritage status was a key event in the history of the Sydney Opera House, one that not only offered legal protection for the building's preservation, but also publicly signalled its value as an exemplar of Modern Architecture. This international recognition, in the form of World Heritage inscription, can be seen as a way to quell ongoing contestation on its significance as a work of architecture; a response to the way this place has been publicly described both as the greatest building of the 20th century and as a flawed masterpiece.[4]

While the *1972 Convention Concerning the Protection of the World Cultural and Natural Heritage* (*World Heritage Convention*) has been highly successful as the central legal instrument of UNESCO's World Heritage program it has also been criticised.

The *World Heritage Convention* is the highest level of protection and recognition of heritage places and provides an accepted approach to preservation by bringing together the international community. However, the *World Heritage Convention* embodies Western notions of cultural heritage, thereby excluding more recent forms of culture or those of less wealthy and developed nations. Further, while World Heritage purports to speak for all the convention does not recognise social values. This chapter situates the 2007 inscription of the Sydney Opera House within the contemporary discourse of heritage and discusses its significance within the canon of Modern Architecture through the history of the Sydney Opera House and its nomination as a World Heritage site. The chapter argues that the inscribed World Heritage values are significant as they institutionalise the building's architectural values for a public audience and present a challenge to social values.

Coming together through World Heritage

Heritage has its roots in the 19th-century historical and architectural practices concerned with the preservation of ancient monuments and historic buildings. For much of the 20th century, heritage was the buildings (and objects) *inherited* from our predecessors, a definition that has its roots in the French concept of patrimony and which emerged in Europe (particularly in Britain, France and Germany) as part of modernity.[5] As the conditions of the 19th century gave rise to a middle class and the aristocracy was destabilised, 'new devices to ensure or express social cohesion and identity and to structure social relations' came into play.[6] For example, the museum as a heritage institution took on a regulatory role through its collecting and exhibiting practices, acting as a custodian of the past at the same time as informing present identity. The museum served as a repository of desirable civic, social and national identities and aspirations. Just as the museum strove to protect and regulate artefacts deemed as culturally significant, European nations began developing ways of conserving and protecting historic buildings. The second half of the 19th century saw the rise of charters and legal instruments that sought to protect ancient monuments or religious, historically or architecturally important buildings.[7]

According to Jukka Jokilehto, the principles of building conservation first arose at the end of the 19th century in the scholarship of John Ruskin, William Morris and Emmanuel Viollet-le-Duc.[8] There were two main approaches that have influenced the practice, recognition and theorisation of heritage over the last century. On one hand, Viollet-le-Duc was an advocate of 'romantic restoration', which proposed that buildings be reinstated to a state of completeness, even if they had never existed in this state in living memory. Romantic restoration emphasised unity in the architectural whole, instead of being concerned with architectural interventions made at different times. On the other hand, Ruskin and Morris championed the approach of the 'conservation movement', which in contrast to romantic restoration was concerned with protecting the fabric of buildings as an embodiment of technical skill and aesthetic expression, or as evidence of particular historical events. According to Jokilehto, the modern approach to conservation as delineated by the *World Heritage Convention* is a synthesis of these two approaches.[9] In contemporary practice of heritage conservation, sites gain authority and significance with age and authenticity is interpreted in terms of historical accuracy, as determined by expert sources. This combined approach is embedded in the earliest documents that attempt to regulate and articulate methods and principles for the preservation of buildings. The best known of these is the *1964 Venice Charter*, which provides the conceptual foundation for the *World Heritage Convention*.[10]

The legacy of these early approaches to conservation is important as they have become embedded in the legal instruments, which are used in practice to define and decide what is, and what is not, considered heritage. However, as David C. Harvey observes, 'every society has had a relationship with its past, even those which have chosen to ignore it'.[11] This challenges the definitions of heritage purported by Ruskin, Morris and Viollet-le-Duc as the foundation of heritage and resituates heritage in the present. Harvey argues that by

> extending the temporal scope of heritage both backwards and forwards, it becomes possible to conceive of a history of heritage – or 'heritage of heritage' – that has more power; heritage heroes such as William Morris, for instance, can be placed not as elements of an inevitable sequence of growing heritage concern, nor even in the context of their own time, but in the context of our needs and yearnings for a specific past and our desires for a particular future.[12]

Harvey's position is important for the overall discussion on World Heritage and social value because it situates heritage, not as an immutable and inherent quality that can be discovered, but rather as a status assigned to places that is defined by society. Jokilehto overcomes this issue by acknowledging that all societies have altered and repaired monuments and buildings, but that heritage is distinguished by the development of the principles of conservation.

World Heritage formalised the notion of the global significance of places. Prior to the adoption of the *World Heritage Convention* in 1972 no international instruments existed. The convention states in the preamble 'that parts of the cultural or natural heritage are of outstanding interest and therefore need to be preserved as part of the world heritage of mankind as a whole'.[13] Listing provides a means for distinguishing places with exemplary cultural significance from the rest of our physical world, and offers visible means for publicising inscribed sites alongside the concept of World Heritage. World Heritage status brings opportunities for new projects and international collaborations and financial assistance from the World Heritage Fund. Because of these geopolitical and financial consequences, as well as the cultural value of having sites acknowledged on an international stage, World Heritage is significant in terms of cultural, social and political identity.

The *World Heritage Convention* is interpreted through the *Operational Guidelines for the Implementation of the World Heritage Convention*, which are revised every few years to ensure 'new concepts, knowledge and experiences' are incorporated.[14] Properties are inscribed onto one of two World Heritage lists: as a representative example, or because it is considered to be in danger of destruction.[15] The World Heritage Centre is the organisational body that manages the programme, and the World Heritage Committee is the representative body of the programme's members (Figure 1.1).

Inscription onto the World Heritage list requires membership and ratification. To participate and benefit from the World Heritage programme, countries must first become Member States of UNESCO and then subsequently ratify the *World Heritage Convention*. At present 205 countries are Member States or Associate Members of UNESCO. Of these, 191 Member States have ratified the *World Heritage Convention*.[16] The wide acceptance of the *World Heritage Convention* at an international level means it forms 'an almost universally accepted set of principles and framework of action' for built and environmental forms of heritage at an international level.[17] Although UNESCO has adopted several other conventions[18] aimed at

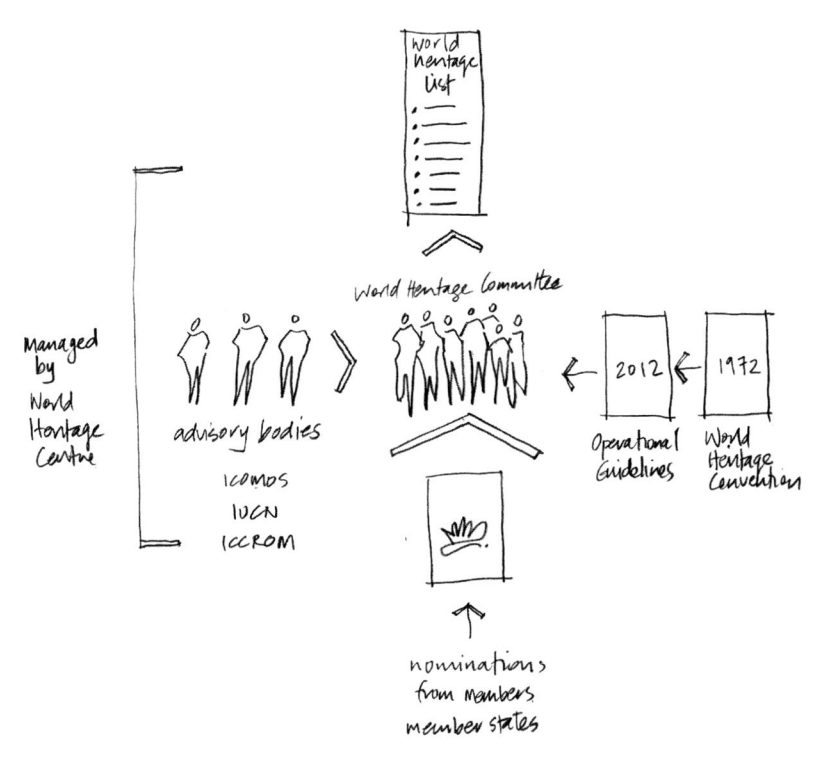

Figure 1.1 The relationship between the parts of the World Heritage programme. The *World Heritage Convention* is the legal instrument that is interpreted through the current edition of the *Operational Guidelines*. Nominations are produced using the guidelines, then assessed for inscription onto the World Heritage List by the World Heritage Committee, and its advisory bodies, ICOMOS, IUCN and ICCROM. The World Heritage Centre manages this process.

developing an intercultural dialogue around the protection of other kinds of cultural heritage, the *World Heritage Convention* is considered to be one of the most successful of all these international agreements[19] due to the involvement of State Parties in the nomination and subsequent protection and management of sites. World Heritage status also offers nations a means for establishing and promoting particular national and cultural identities[20] through the protection of heritage, whilst endorsing these sites as significant to an international audience.

The inscription of sites as World Heritage involves several other professional organisations. The *World Heritage Convention* recognises two main forms of heritage: natural sites, such as landscapes, and cultural sites, such as buildings or townships. Member States (State Parties) to the convention put forward places for inscription through a Nomination Dossier. These documents are evaluated by the World Heritage Committee in collaboration with international heritage organisations that provide expert advice.

The International Council on Monuments and Sites (ICOMOS) advises on matters of cultural heritage, while the International Union for Conservation of Nature and Natural Resources (IUCN) advises on matters of natural heritage. The International

Centre for the Study of the Preservation and Restoration of Cultural Property (ICCROM) provides expertise in conservation practices for both movable and immovable heritage.[21] The interconnection between these organisations and World Heritage is important because each of these professional organisations has national chapters, in addition to international representation who play key roles in the development of national charters and heritage legislation, thereby extending the influence of the *World Heritage Convention* beyond sites inscribed onto the list. Concepts move between national and international heritage discourse, and while the terminology between levels differs, the influence of World Heritage on Australia's heritage framework exemplifies the way these discourses interact.[22]

In 2004 Australia restructured its national heritage system with the intention of developing a clearer, more rational and integrated approach towards the protection of cultural heritage. Previously Australian heritage was inscribed onto the Register of the National Estate, a list established in 1975 under the *Australian Heritage Commission Act 1975*.[23] At the time these were the only legal mechanisms in Australia for the protection of places of cultural significance, but over time many other legal measures were developed and implemented, both at a local and a state level, resulting in sites inscribed on multiple lists and subject to multiple and/or conflicting protection and planning laws. The new system adopted in 2004 makes each tier of government responsible for the protection of heritage within its jurisdiction. The Australian Heritage Commission was replaced with the Australian Heritage Council, under the *Australian Heritage Council Act, 2003*,[24] and responsibility for sites of national significance is now enacted through the *Environment Protection and Biodiversity Conservation Act, 1999*.[25] In 2007, inscriptions onto the Register of the National Estate ceased and two new national lists replaced the register: the National Heritage List and the Commonwealth Heritage List. The National Heritage List is a register for places of outstanding national significance with mixed or discrete, natural, indigenous or historic value. The Commonwealth Heritage List provides recognition and protection to places owned or controlled by the Australian government. The Australian Heritage Council is now the expert body that provides advice to the Australian government's Minister for the Environment and Heritage on nominations. The Register of the National Estate survives only as a database and record of previously listed cultural heritage, used mainly for educational and promotional purposes and places inscribed on the register have been transferred to other lists.

Alongside the Australian national heritage legislation and lists are the guiding documents for best practice. *The Burra Charter: The Australia ICOMOS Charter for Places of Cultural Significance 2013* (*Burra Charter*) adopted by ICOMOS Australia is used for cultural heritage and the *Australian Natural Heritage Charter 2002* by IUCN is used for natural heritage,[26] in a parallel structure to the World Heritage programme. These charters are not legal instruments, like the *World Heritage Convention*, but rather embody guiding principles and best-practice processes intended to assist communities and heritage professionals in the assessment of cultural significance. The effect of the *Burra Charter*, in particular, goes beyond simply a non-legal guideline. The charter is used internationally as a precedent for the inclusion of community values in the processes of heritage assessment and conservation.[27]

The *Burra Charter* has influenced the discourse on heritage nationally and internationally. The document can be conceptualised as Australian version of the *1964 Venice Charter*, and represents the philosophical and theoretical framework for heritage assessment and definition in national legislation.[28] The *Australian Natural Heritage Charter 2002* is similarly structured to the *Burra Charter*, but is written with a focus on natural sites. The professional bodies responsible for these charters, ICOMOS Australia and the Australian Committee of IUCN respectively, have members who are practitioners, experts and academics, many of whom are also government advisors or are commissioned to produce specific reports that influence legislation and reform.[29] In this capacity these professional bodies tend to be unfettered by governmental regulations and therefore more progressive in their approach.

Barbara Kirshenblatt-Gimblett argues that distinguishing some places and not others though lists, such as the World Heritage list, decontextualises heritage sites from their communities.[30] Lists raise questions of whether sites should be 'the best of the best' or be 'representative',[31] especially in view of the way World Heritage inscription offers State Parties a vehicle for their own national agendas,[32] by contributing or creating tourist destinations.[33] The effect of World Heritage inscription in promoting and distinguishing places as national 'icons' has implications for the ownership and use of culturally significant places.[34] Conceptually for the idea of social value, World Heritage is important because it creates a universal tier of heritage significance. This was one of its innovations alongside the formation of an intellectual relationship between natural sites and cultural sites as heritage.[35] This was a response to the political and intellectual climate of the early 1970s, the period in which the *World Heritage Convention* developed, where there was a rising awareness of environmental issues and a developing sense of global responsibility.[36] Bringing together natural and cultural heritage as the 'common heritage of mankind' was a means for UNESCO to fulfil its aims in fostering intercultural dialogue, peace and cooperation. Some of the contemporary criticisms of the programme arise as consequences of this aim. In particular, the assumption of the programme that heritage is a universal notion and that places are of equal importance to all peoples is an outcome that has been increasingly recognised as rooted in the European understanding of heritage to the exclusion of other cultures.[37] World Heritage status is inherently political.[38]

World Heritage is a complex international programme that recognises places of universal significance. It offers nations a vehicle for establishing and promoting their cultural identity to an international community. This programme has been highly successful; it was innovative both in practical and intellectual terms. However, the remit of World Heritage, and its discourse, influences national heritage programmes through scholarship and professional bodies, such as ICOMOS, IUCN and ICCROM. The influence of World Heritage at an international and national level makes it an important and widely accepted framework for the recognition of works of architecture, such as the Sydney Opera House and other built forms of culture.

Significance of World Heritage inscription for the Sydney Opera House

The 2007 inscription of the Sydney Opera House as a site of World Heritage was the culmination of almost three decades of seeking recognition through two unsuccessful nominations.[39] The first nomination was prepared in 1980, but was withdrawn during the initial period of evaluation. The second, prepared in 1996, was far more comprehensive than the first, but was never submitted for evaluation, as a result of lack of support from the Howard Liberal government that was in power in Australia at the time. In 1999, a further attempt to submit a partially revised version of the 1996 nomination was made, but again this did not receive government support.[40]

The quest for World Heritage status for the Sydney Opera House must be understood in relation to the building's history. The commissioning of the Sydney Opera House was an aspirational project for Sydney, a city perceived as a British outpost in the Antipodes for much of its history. Sydney was a British settlement founded in 1788. Sydney City, and Bennelong Point, where the Sydney Opera House is situated, lie within Indigenous lands known as the Eora nation, whose traditional owners are the Cadigal people. In the 1950s Sydney had little to claim as unique at an international level apart from the Sydney Harbour Bridge and its natural harbour features. Building an opera house was seen, both nationally and internationally, as a way for Sydney to graduate as a metropolis.[41] Such a cultural facility was described as essential, like a parliament, a city hall, a stock exchange or a cathedral. The Sydney Opera House project emerged at a time when 'a new international view of Australia began to emerge', as mass travel became commonplace and international communication systems developed as post-Second World War globalisation gained momentum.[42] The proposal for an opera house stimulated public debate on the cost of such a project in light of the post-war shortage of housing, the building's potential location, its procurement and the nationality of its architect.

The site chosen was Bennelong Point, where Francis Greenway's Fort Macquarie had stood since 1817, until it became a tram depot around the turn of the 20th century. However, before Australia's British colonisation in 1788, Bennelong Point had been a significant meeting place for local Aboriginal people. The site was named after Bennelong, a local Wangal man who built a hut on the point. He was an important cross-cultural mediator in early colonial times. Bennelong Point remains significant to Indigenous communities today.[43]

The project to build an opera house in Sydney was the focus of political and public debate before it had even been commissioned and these debates were regularly published in the *Sydney Morning Herald*.[44] In 1956 an international competition for the design of the Sydney Opera House was held, and in January 1957, a young Danish architect named Jørn Utzon was announced the winner.[45] The next day the scheme was published on the front page of the *Sydney Morning Herald* and its selection by the judging panel became a contentious issue.[46] Utzon's competition entry had breached some of the competition rules and was sketchy and incomplete, so much so that the sketch featured in the *Sydney Morning Herald* was not Utzon's, but an interpretive perspective drawing prepared by Arthur Baldwinson.[47] The winning scheme was unusual and highly sculptural, and did little to quell debate.

The proposal for the Sydney Opera House was a unique architectural form. Utzon's design comprised a series of interlocking vaulted shells that were set upon a stepped platform. The design was highly original and therefore controversial; but the judges were convinced of its merit.[48] It had a distinctive silhouette, unlike other contemporary performing arts centres, which provoked analogies with 'flowers unfolding' and 'sails on the harbour'. The reaction of the architectural community and the public was mixed and there was pressure to begin construction quickly.[49] The scheme was described as a 'poetic solution' and an 'outstanding piece of art', as well as being publicly ridiculed and compared to a 'danish pastry' and 'a collection of abandoned umbrellas'.[50] These factors, alongside Utzon's unresolved scheme, made the building a controversial and widely debated subject throughout the 14-year history of its realisation.

The history of the Sydney Opera House is punctuated by its architect's resignation. Utzon's scheme proposed a series of thin concrete shells that could not be built.[51] The project was technically challenging and construction began before the design was fully resolved. Another Dane, Ove Arup, was commissioned to provide engineering services; the early years of the building's realisation were filled with difficulties as a structural solution for its expressive forms was sought. But because of the public focus on the project and its frequent representation in the media, it seemed the silhouette had been set in the public's mind and Utzon would not change the profile of the building or compromise on his Modernist principles that dictated the integration of material, structure and form.[52] This resulted in ever-increasing costs and delays. In 1962, Utzon declared that he had found a solution to the structural problems by deriving the geometry of the building from a single sphere, even though this decision changed the profile of the building that he had steadfastly held onto because it was imprinted in the public mind.[53] As circumstances became more difficult, Utzon's role and the construction of the Sydney Opera House became the centrepiece of battles between Australia's two major political parties. Seven years after construction works on the Opera House began in 1959, there was a change of government in New South Wales (NSW), from Labor to Liberal, bringing the situation to a climax. Utzon needed funds for prototypes and to prepare the final drawings, but the NSW government demanded the drawings before paying his fees. In 1966, Utzon felt forced to resign from the project and left Australia. He never saw the completed building and never returned to Australia. His resignation divided the profession and the community of Sydney.[54] Supporters claimed the building would fail to be a masterpiece without Utzon's continuing input and vision, while his opponents, tired of increasing costs and delays, supported the appointment of a new Australian team of architects. In 1973, Peter Hall, Lionel Todd and David Littlemore completed the Sydney Opera House commenced by Utzon almost a decade and a half earlier.[55]

The controversial realisation of the Sydney Opera House is documented in many publications. More than two hundred monographs, articles, book chapters and many hundreds of news stories have been published about this building. These include popular books, historical accounts, academic research, fictions, photographic works and debate in the media to such an extent that 'the building is already its own literary genre'.[56] Early histories of this work of architecture by John Yeomans, Michael Baume and Elias Duek-Cohen are pleas for Utzon's reinstatement or accusations about his professional misconduct.[57] As time has passed, less polemical accounts of the history of the building have provided a more balanced version of events, especially after 1997, when the NSW government released all documents from the building's construction.[58]

In 2001, Philip Drew published *The Masterpiece: Jørn Utzon and the Sydney Opera House*, an extensive joint biography of the architect and the building; in 2002 Richard Weston published *Utzon: Inspiration, Vision, Architecture*, the only account written with Utzon's input. In 2004, Peter Murray published *The Saga of the Sydney Opera House*, an account of the events that considers both Drew's and Weston's versions in light of the archival documents available at the time. In 2006, Peter Jones published the first account from the perspective of the building's engineers, in which Ove Arup's contribution is brought to the fore. Although these accounts differ at times on the details and interpretation of events, they concur that the history of the Sydney Opera House was filled with political difficulties, that the design was ambitious, the cost of the works had been inadequately estimated and the project was mismanaged.

The nomination of the building as a site of World Heritage must be understood in light of this controversial history. The 1980 nomination, submitted only seven years after the building was completed in 1973, attempted to gain World Heritage status for a then very young and aesthetically contemporary structure. The Sydney Opera House was part of a larger nomination that included the Sydney Harbour Bridge and the surrounding waterways from Bradley's Head to McMahons Point.[59] In contrast, the 2007 inscription is only for the Sydney Opera House site.[60] At this time the World Heritage programme had only been in operation for three years with 84 sites already inscribed – however, none were works of Modern Architecture.[61] The attempt to inscribe such a contemporary building during the initial years of the World Heritage programme is indicative of the value that this status can bring to architecture. Whilst the 1980 nomination was for the larger harbour area, the claim for inscription is mostly focused on the Sydney Opera House. World Heritage status would have helped to formally establish the significance of the Sydney Opera House at an international level, increase tourism, and promote the inscribed values through visitor interpretation and marketing.

Sixteen years after the first nomination in 1996, a second attempt was made to inscribe the Sydney Opera House onto the World Heritage List.[62] Like the earlier attempt, this nomination sought to inscribe the Sydney Opera House as part of the larger area of Sydney Harbour. By this time the World Heritage programme had been in operation for almost 20 years and the significance of the Sydney Opera House as a work of architecture was much more established. Architectural historians such as Charles Jencks, William Curtis, Dennis Sharp and Kenneth Frampton had included the Sydney Opera House in their publications on Modern Architecture.[63] Special issues of *World Architecture* and the *Architecture in Detail* series by Phaidon Press, accounts on the building's engineering, as well as popular versions of the building's history, emerged during this period.[64] Utzon had been awarded a number of international awards and prizes.[65] In comparison to the 1980 nomination dossier, the 1996 version was a 'lavishly illustrated monograph' indicating the increase of resources and sophistication of the nomination process.[66] However, issues around the practical management of the Sydney Opera House at a state level, coupled with the increasing public pressure to reinstate Utzon's unrealised designs for the interiors, potentially fuelled by the exhibition of these in *Unseen Utzon*,[67] meant that the nomination was never signed off by the Howard Liberal government at the time.[68]

As Patricia Hale and Susan Macdonald have argued, the 'interest in the opera house's heritage significance [during the 1990s] turned the spotlight back on Utzon's role in its creation'.[69] This manifested in a quest to re-engage Utzon as a way of ensuring maintenance and upgrade works were in keeping with his original vision. The 1996 nomination was revised in 1999, but then abandoned. The federal government was concerned 'not to become legally responsible for a site currently administered by the NSW State Government, or to become a target for Utzon supporters who regularly demanded his interior scheme to be realised'.[70] Although it was more than 30 years since Utzon's resignation from the project, the legacy of his incomplete vision lived on. In 1999, after much negotiation Utzon, was re-appointed to write the *Utzon Design Principles*, a guide for the future development of the Opera House.[71] In 2003 Utzon was awarded the prestigious Pritzker Prize, the equivalent of architecture's Nobel Prize. In the same year the building was inscribed onto the *State Heritage Register of New South Wales*. Two years later in 2005, after substantial changes to the Australian heritage system, the Sydney Opera House was inscribed onto the National Heritage List in preparation for the 2006 nomination. Recognition as a site of World Heritage was a means to reconcile the building's controversial history.

Significance of recognising Modern Architecture as World Heritage

Heritage as a distinct academic discipline did not formally arise until the late 20th century,[72] and was dominated by practitioners and academics from the disciplines of archaeology, architecture and history. However, during the first half of the 20th century public interest in the concept and practice of heritage grew, as Indigenous and community activism around culture in the 1960s and 1970s gained prominence. These groups criticised the practice and conceptualisation of heritage for the way it emphasised expert perspectives over those of communities.[73] This was exacerbated by the increasing accessibility of travel, which resulted in heritage sites being subsumed into commercial entertainment practices implicated in mass tourism. In the last two decades (1990–2010) scholars working within cultural studies, anthropology and sociology have turned their attention to these issues, broadening the field of heritage, its practice and it implications, as well as cementing its academic standing as a field of theoretical inquiry.[74]

The critical perspectives contributed by the humanities and social sciences have opened discussion on the inherent biases of the World Heritage programme. While the *World Heritage Convention* has successfully brought the international community together to safeguard places of cultural significance, its mandate is also a double-edged sword; for while it provides protection it simultaneously acts to define what is recognised as heritage through the inscription and listing process. Many of the cultural properties inscribed on the World Heritage list are cathedrals and palaces or places already recognised as national symbols, such as the Taj Mahal or the Eiffel Tower. The over-representation of such (usually) Western examples is problematic because it reinforces that heritage is inherently built forms and that these symbols are representative of grand nationalistic narratives,[75] resulting in an under-representation of sites on the list from nations whose heritage does not take this form.[76]

The concept of heritage embodied in the *World Heritage Convention* is not impartial. Eminent scholar Laurajane Smith states that this 'highlight[s] the common sense assumption that "heritage" can unproblematically be identified as "old", grand, monumental and aesthetically pleasing sites, buildings, places and artefacts'.[77] Whilst these assumptions are shifting, at the time of the Sydney Opera House's first nomination in 1980, heritage was still primarily understood as the practice of conserving historic sites. The Sydney Opera House was a contemporary structure, considered at the time as an avant-garde example of Modern Architecture[78] and despite Australia's support for the convention, and the national significance of the building, this nomination was not well received by the Committee.[79] Their response stated 'that modern structures should only be accepted when there was clear evidence that they had established, or were outstanding examples of, a distinctive architectural style'.[80] The nomination was withdrawn after the Committee advised that the legacy of the Sydney Opera House was untested.

Henry Cleere argues that the disparity in listings between Western and non-Western countries, and arguably between traditional and newer examples of culture, as was the case for the Sydney Opera House, could be simply due to the frequency of nominations.[81]

However, he also suggests that Western nations may be more likely to consider their heritage to be of universal significance. His analysis of the 630 World Heritage sites listed in 2000 finds that 55 per cent were located in European nations, compared with less than 15 per cent on each of the other continents.[82] By 2005 the proportion of World Heritage sites in Europe had dropped to 49 per cent, and in 2010 remained at a substantial 47 per cent.[83] With such imbalance, the *World Heritage Convention* fails to create a balanced representation of heritage, in which all nations and all forms of heritage are equally acknowledged. Although there are now programmes to address this issue, World Heritage remains predominantly Western and European.

Concerted efforts since 1980 have been made to gain recognition for works of Modern Architecture as sites of World Heritage in response to the destruction and demolition of significant works.[84] In 1988 the International Committee for Documentation and Conservation of Buildings Sites and Neighbourhoods of the Modern Movement (DOCOMOMO) was formed. A major shift occurred in 1994 with UNESCO's adoption of the *Global Strategy for a Credible, Balanced and Representative World Heritage List*,[85] which was a response to the over-representation of cultural sites and the high number of inscribed properties from Europe.[86] The strategy also sought to ameliorate the emphasis on ancient and historic sites, by recognising 'less-represented categories of heritage' such as 'Modern Heritage, which comprises the architecture, town planning and landscape design of the 19th and 20th centuries'.[87] By 1996 several sites of Modern Architecture finally gained World Heritage recognition: Antonio Gaudi's Parque Güell in 1984, the City of Brasilia in 1987 and the Cemetery of Skogskyrkogården in 1994.[88] But none of these were as young and untested as the Sydney Opera House in the 1980 or the 1996 nominations.

The recognition of the need to consider Modern Architecture as heritage in the mid 1990s demonstrates how the 1980 nomination of the Sydney Opera House heralds an 'emerging interest, at an international level, in the recognition of 20th century places as culturally valuable'.[89] The recognition of modern works of architecture as sites of World Heritage, particularly relatively young buildings, such as the Sydney Opera House, is not just indicative of the changes in the programme but also changes in the definition of heritage not only beyond ancient and historic structures, but also beyond built and material forms of culture. In the last decade (2000–2010) UNESCO has adopted a new definition of heritage, embodied within the *2003 Convention for the Safeguarding of the Intangible Cultural Heritage (Intangible Heritage Convention)*.[90] This new definition of heritage is emblematic of a larger movement for recognising all forms of culture as heritage, not only from the past but also of the present day. The discourses on *Intangible Heritage Convention* and related concepts in World Heritage such as associative values and contemporary definitions of authenticity emphasise the need to better understand the social value of works of architecture at an international level.

The *World Heritage Convention* promotes a universal concept of heritage that implies listed sites are equally important to everyone. Yet Cleery's analysis of the number of inscribed sites per region challenges this assertion. Instead World Heritage is perhaps better understood as a form of 'soft-power', a way for nations to project and 'communicate their cultural, social and even environmental credentials to the world'.[91] This suggests that part of the convention's concept of universality is at times appropriated by State Parties for their own nationalistic ends.[92]

Although the idea of universally significant sites of heritage was intended as a means to draw nations together around a common cause, its effect has also been to reinforce embedded narratives of nationhood. Laurajane Smith describes this as the 'Authorised Heritage Discourse'[93] where heritage is framed as an inherent quality. Smith and other scholars within the discourse of critical heritage studies argue that this is not immutable, but rather can be viewed as 'a process of meaning making – it is a list that not only identifies, but also creates or recreates sites as universally important and meaningful'.[94] This makes World Heritage, and the concept of universal significance, a vehicle for endorsing forms of culture to both national and international audiences. Whilst the programme protects significant sites, it also defines what counts as heritage and defines why it is significant.

World Heritage both recognises and articulates what constitutes heritage and the values for which such forms of culture can be inscribed, thereby defining these in relation to its criteria. David Lowenthal argues that perhaps 'too much is asked of heritage. In the same breath, we commend national patrimony, regional and ethnic legacies and a global heritage shared and sheltered in common. We forget that these aims are usually incompatible'.[95] These criteria are the products of the era in which they were written, before concerns about Modern Architecture and social value came to the fore. While the *World Heritage Convention* is highly successful not all sites are equally valuable to all people, not all values are accounted for and not all forms are included as heritage.

Conclusion

The 2007 inscription of the Sydney Opera House was significant for Australia because it reframed the building as 'cultural heritage'. Prior to this, Australia had only one other example of cultural heritage on the World Heritage list, although it had 15 natural heritage sites listed.[96] The inscription of the Sydney Opera House was part of a national desire for the recognition of cultural accomplishment.

The recognition of the Sydney Opera House as World Heritage, even in light of the critiques of the *World Heritage Convention*, remains significant. The significance of the Sydney Opera House is established in the academy as well as in the public sphere. The recognition of the Sydney Opera House at an international level as a site of World Heritage served to formally endorse its contribution to the development of Modern Architecture and more broadly to culture. At the same time, the inscription is also significant as an indicator of the broadening scope of the World Heritage programme.

Understanding the consequences and implications of World Heritage inscription provides the context for the next chapter where the values under which the Sydney Opera House was inscribed as a World Heritage site are discussed in detail.

Notes

1 Newspaper headlines on the day the Sydney Opera House was inscribed on to the World Heritage List: Joyce Morgan (2007) 'Opera House Wins Top Status'. *Sydney Morning Herald*, 28 June. Retrieved: 26/06/2012, from: www.smh.com.au/news/travel/opera-house-wins-top-status/2007/06/28/1182624058781.html; APP (2007) 'Opera House Wins Top Status'. *The Age*, 28 June. Retrieved: 26/06/2012, from: http://news.theage.com.au/national/opera-house-wins-top-status-20070628-kxi.html; Simon Ferguson (2007) 'Opera House Has Heritage'. *Daily Telegraph*, 28 June, p. 15; 'Masterpiece for All Mankind' (2007) *Hobart Mercury*, 29 June, p. 5; 'Opera House Gets a Standing Ovation' (2007) *Geelong Advertiser*, 29 June, p. 16.

2 Sydney Opera House (circa 2007) 'World Heritage Listing'. Retrieved: 26/11/2012, from: www.sydneyoperahouse.com/the_building/world_heritage.aspx; Peter Lewis (2007) 'Opera House Makes World Heritage List'. *ABC News*, 28 June. Retrieved: 26/06/2012, from: www.abc.net.au/news/2007-06-28/opera-house-makes-world-heritage-list/83814; Morgan, 'Opera House Wins Top Status'.

3 John Connell (2000) *Sydney: The Emergence of a World City*. Melbourne: Oxford University Press.

4 In 2006 academics Philip Drew and Anne Watson, along with writer Sylvia Lawson and librettist Dennis Watkins, spoke with the late Alan Saunders on the ABC radio programme *By Design*. Apart from Watkins, all interviewees agreed that the Opera House was a 'flawed masterpiece'. Alan Saunders, Philip Drew, Sylvia Lawson, Dennis Watkins, Anne Watson and Alan John (2006) 'By Design: Writing the House' [Radio Broadcast]. Sydney: ABC Radio National, 3 June. Retrieved: 23/11/2012, from: www.abc.net.au/radionational/programs/bydesign/writing-the-house/3326266. Later that year former prime minister of Australia, Paul Keating, gave a speech at the launch of Anne Watson's edited collection titled *Building a Masterpiece*. Anne Watson (2006) *Building a Masterpiece: The Sydney Opera House*. Aldershot: Lund Humphries. This speech was later reprinted in *After Words: The Post-Prime Ministerial Speeches*. Keating, who has an avid interest in architecture, described the Sydney Opera House in this speech not only as the 'greatest building of the twentieth century' but as one of the 'greatest of all history'. Paul Keating (2011) 'Building a Masterpiece: The Sydney Opera House. Sydney 10 August 2006'. In *After Words: The Post-Prime Ministerial Speeches*. Crows Nest: Allen & Unwin, p. 3.

5 David C. Harvey (2007 [2001]) 'Heritage Pasts and Heritage Presents: Temporality, Meaning and the Scope of Heritage Studies'. In *Cultural Heritage: Critical Concepts in Media and Cultural Studies*, vol. 1, edited by Laurajane Smith. London: Routledge, p. 26; David C. Harvey (2008) 'The History of Heritage'. In *The Ashgate Research Companion to Heritage and Identity*, edited by Brian Graham and Peter Howard. Hampshire: Ashgate, p. 21.

6 Eric J. Hobsbawm (1983) 'Mass-Producing Traditions: Europe, 1870–1914'. In *The Invention of Tradition*, edited by Eric J. Hobsbawm and Terence O. Ranger. Cambridge: Cambridge University Press, p. 263.

7 For example, see frequently cited early texts such as: William Morris (2007 [1877]) 'Manifesto of the Society for the Protection of Ancient Buildings (Spab)'. In *Cultural Heritage: Critical Concepts in Media and Cultural Studies*, vol. 1, edited by Laurajane Smith. London: Routledge, pp. 111–113. Alois Riegl (2007 [1903]) 'The Modern Cult of Monuments: Its Character and Its Origin'. In *Cultural Heritage: Critical Concepts in Media and Cultural Studies*, vol. 1, edited by Laurajane Smith, translated by Kurt W. Foster and Diane Ghirardo in 1982 from German. London: Routledge, pp. 94–110.

8 This is significant because it distinguishes the idea of heritage, as understood by scholars such as David Harvey, who see it as a relationship to the past, and Jokilehto's definition of heritage as the practice and principles of architectural conservation. Jukka Jokilehto (2005 [1999]) *A History of Architectural Conservation*. Oxford: Elsevier Butterworth-Heinemann.

9 Jukka Jokilehto (1986) *A History of Architectural Conservation: The Contribution of English, French, German and Italian Thought Towards an International Approach to the Conservation of Property*. PhD thesis, Institute of Advanced Architectural Studies, University of York, p. 8.

10 Laurajane Smith (2006) *Uses of Heritage*. London: Routledge, pp. 88–95; Marilena Vecco (2010) 'A Definition of Cultural Heritage: From the Tangible to the Intangible'. *Journal of Cultural Heritage*, 11 (3), p. 322. Emma Waterton, Laurajane Smith and Gary Campbell (2006) 'The Utility of Discourse Analysis to Heritage Studies: The Burra Charter and Social Inclusion'. *International Journal of Heritage Studies*, 12 (4), pp. 339–355.

11 Harvey, 'Heritage Pasts and Heritage Presents', p. 26.

12 Harvey, 'The History of Heritage', p. 21.

13 UNESCO (1972) *Convention Concerning the Protection of the World Cultural and Natural Heritage*. Retrieved: 26/11/2012, from: http://whc.unesco.org/archive/convention-en.pdf. Preliminary Comments, p. 1.

14 At the time of writing, 2016, the most current revision of the *Operational Guidelines* is the 2015 revision. In this study I use the 2011 revision. Where the *Operational Guidelines* are used in reference to the 1980 and 1996 nominations of the Sydney Opera

House the editions referred to are those that were current at the time the nominations were prepared. UNESCO Intergovernmental Committee for the Protection of the World Cultural and Natural Heritage, Paris (2012) *Operational Guidelines for the Implementation of the World Heritage Convention*. Retrieved: 26/11/2012, from: http://whc.unesco.org/archive/opguide12-en.pdf. All the revisions can be found at: UNESCO, 'The Operational Guidelines for the Implementation of the World Heritage Convention', *World Heritage Centre*. Retrieved: 26/11/2012, from: http://whc.unesco.org/en/guidelines.

15 UNESCO, *Convention Concerning the Protection of the World Cultural and Natural Heritage*, Article 1.

16 UNESCO, 'State Parties: Ratification Status'. *World Heritage Centre*. Retrieved: 31/12/2015, from: http://whc.unesco.org/en/statesparties/. UNESCO has 195 Member States and ten Associate Members. UNESCO (2011) 'Member States'. *UNESCO*. Retrieved: 31/12/2015, from: http://en.unesco.org/countries/member-states.

17 Sophia Labadi and Colin Long (eds) (2010) *Heritage and Globalisation*. London: Routledge, p. 6.

18 There are seven conventions pertaining to culture. The *World Heritage Convention* was the fourth to be adopted. This chapter focuses on the *World Heritage Convention*, and Chapter 8 discusses the *Intangible Heritage Convention* and the *Digital Heritage Charter*, both adopted more recently in 2003. More information on UNESCO's other conventions on the UNESCO website. UNESCO, 'UNESCO: Culture', *World Heritage Centre*. Retrieved: 26/06/2012, from: www.unesco.org/new/en/culture.

19 Michael C. Hall (2006) 'Implementing the World Heritage Convention: What Happens after Listing?' In *Managing World Heritage Sites*. Oxford: Butterworth-Heinemann, p. 22; Colin Long and Sophia Labadi (2010) 'Introduction'. In *Heritage and Globalisation*, edited by Sophia Labadi and Colin Long. London: Routledge, p. 6.

20 Marc Askew (2010) 'The Magic List of Global Status: UNESCO, World Heritage and the Agenda of States'. In *Heritage and Globalisation*, edited by Sophia Labadi and Colin Long. London: Routledge, p. 23.

21 The international websites of these organisations are: ICOMOS (2011) 'International Council on Monuments and Sites (ICOMOS)'. Retrieved: 26/06/2012, from: www.icomos.org/en/; IUCN (2013) 'International Union for Conservation of Nature and Natural Resources (IUCN)'. Retrieved: 25/04/2013, from: www.iucn.org/; ICCROM (2013) 'International Centre for the Study of the Preservation and Restoration of Cultural Property (ICCROM)'. Retrieved: 25/04/2013, from: www.iccrom.org/.

22 Each nation has developed its own heritage legislation; although they differ somewhat between nations, there are many commonalities and often they are underpinned by the same international documents. There is a complex interdependent relationship between international heritage and a country's national legislation and charters.

23 Australian Government (2012) 'Register of the National Estate – Archive'. *Department of Environment* [Federal government department information portal]. Canberra. Retrieved: 31/12/2015, from: www.environment.gov.au/topics/heritage/heritage-places/register-national-estate; Australian Government (1975) *Australian Heritage Commission Act 1975*. Retrieved: 31/12/2015, from: www.austlii.edu.au/au/legis/cth/num_act/ahca1975311/.

24 Australian Government (2003) *Australian Heritage Council Act 2003*. Retrieved: 31/12/2015, from: www.austlii.edu.au/au/legis/cth/consol_act/ahca2003262/.

25 Australian Government (1999) *Environment Protection and Biodiversity Conservation Act 1999*. Retrieved: 31/12/2015, from: www.austlii.edu.au/au/legis/cth/consol_act/epabca 1999588/.

26 ICOMOS Australia (2013) *The Burra Charter: The Australia ICOMOS Charter for Places of Cultural Significance 2013*. Retrieved: 31/12/2015, from: http://australia.icomos.org/publications/charters/; IUCN (2002) *Australian Natural Heritage Charter*. Retrieved: 31/12/2015, from: www.environment.gov.au/system/files/resources/56de3d0a-7301-47e2-8c7c-9e064627a1ae/files/australian-natural-heritage-charter.pdf.

27 Waterton *et al.*, 'The Utility of Discourse Analysis to Heritage Studies'.

28 ICOMOS (1964) *Venice Charter*. Retrieved: 31/12/2015, from: www.icomos.org/charters/venice_e.pdf. Yahaya Ahmad (2006) 'The Scope and Definitions of Heritage: From Tangible to Intangible'. *International Journal of Heritage Studies*, 12 (3), p. 297.

29 For example Chris Johnston, founder and director of Context Pty Ltd, a heritage consultancy established in 1984, is an expert in the assessment of social value. In 2006 she wrote a report on strategies for a more integrated heritage system in Australia. Chris Johnston, Lorraine Cairnes and Kathy Eyles (2006) *An Integrated Approach to Environment and Heritage Issues*. Retrieved: 26/11/2012, from: http://laptop.deh.gov.au/soe/2006/publications/integrative/heritage/pubs/heritage.pdf.

30 Barbara Kirshenblatt-Gimblett (2004) 'Intangible Heritage as Metacultural Production'. *Museum International*, 56 (221–222), pp. 56–65.

31 Christina Cameron (2008 [2005]) 'Evolution of the Application of "Outstanding Universal Value" for Cultural and Natural Heritage'. In *The World Heritage List: What Is Ouv? Defining the Outstanding Universal Value of Cultural World Heritage Properties*, edited by Jukka Jokilehto. Paris: ICOMOS, pp. 71–74.

32 Askew, 'The Magic List of Global Status'.

33 Michael A. Di Giovine (2009) *The Heritage-Scape: UNESCO, World Heritage, and Tourism*. Lanham: Lexington Books.

34 Stuart Hall takes up this issue in: Stuart Hall (2007 [1999]) 'Whose Heritage? Un-Settling "the Heritage", Re-Imagining the Post-Nation'. In *Cultural Heritage: Critical Concepts in Media and Cultural Studies*, vol. 2, edited by Laurajane Smith. London: Routledge, pp. 87–100.

35 Francesco Francioni (2008) 'The 1972 World Heritage Convention: An Introduction'. In *The 1972 World Heritage Convention: A Commentary*, edited by Francesco Francioni and Federico Lenzerini. Oxford: Oxford University Press, p. 5; Lucas Lixinski (2008) '"Spaces of Normativity" World Heritage and the Heritage of the World – Book Review; F. Francioni and F. Lenzerini, the 1972 World Heritage Convention: A Commentary'. [Book Review] *European Journal of Legal Studies*, 2 (1), pp. 371–386.

36 Janet Blake (2000) 'On Defining the Cultural Heritage'. *International and Comparative Law Quarterly*, 49 (1), p. 62.

37 Smith, *Uses of Heritage*, pp. 95–102. Henry Cleere (2001) 'The Uneasy Bedfellows: Universality and Cultural Heritage'. In *Destruction and Conservation of Cultural Property*, edited by Robert Layton, Peter G. Stone and Edward Thomas. London: Routledge, pp. 22–29.

38 Cleere, 'The Uneasy Bedfellows'; Askew, 'The Magic List of Global Status'.

39 Nominations are submitted to the World Heritage Committee the year before they are evaluated. Thus the 2006 nomination of the Sydney Opera House resulted in its inscription in 2007.

40 The document was prepared by the Australian Heritage Commission on behalf of the Australian Government. Parliament of New South Wales (1998) *Sydney Opera House World Heritage Listing*. Retrieved: 27/11/2012, from: www.parliament.nsw.gov.au/prod/parlment/hansart.nsf/V3Key/LA19980506030.

41 The *Sydney Morning Herald* reported from *The Times* (New York): 'Praise for Opera Move' (1955) *Sydney Morning Herald*, 22 May, p. 3.

42 Peter Spearritt (1999) *Sydney's Century: A History*. 1st edn. Sydney: UNSW Press, p. 259.

43 Melinda Hinkson discusses the Aboriginal significance of Bennelong Point in: Melinda Hinkson (2002) 'Exploring "Aboriginal" Sites in Sydney: A Shifting Politics of Place?' *Aboriginal History*, 26, p. 65. The 1996 nomination of the Sydney Opera House describes the Aboriginal history of Bennelong Point. It states that a midden (a sacred site) was located here. Australian Government (1996) *Sydney Opera House in Its Harbour Setting*. Glebe: Historic Houses Trust of NSW for the Commonwealth Department of the Environment, Sport and Territories and NSW Department of Urban Affairs and Planning, p. 140. Deborah Cheetham, a well-known Indigenous artist, describes Bennelong Point as a meeting place where song, dance and ritual have been performed for more than 70,000 years of Aboriginal inhabitance. Sam Doust (2012) 'Bennelong Point: Indigenous Heritage'. *The Opera House Project, the Story of an Australian Icon* [Online Multimedia Documentary]. ABC Innovation and Sydney Opera House Trust. Retrieved: 27/11/2012, from: http://theoperahouseproject.com/#!/bennelong-point.

44 For example, see Letters to Editor sections and the following articles from 1955: Morton Herman (1955) 'Interpret Own Age: Plea to Architects'. *Sydney Morning Herald*, 5 July, p. 11; 'Praise for Opera Move', p. 3.; 'Letters to Editor' (1955) *Sydney Morning Herald*, 6 August, p. 2.

45 Utzon's entry was No. 218. The competition was prepared and managed by the Department of Public Works of the NSW government in conjunction with the Sydney Opera House Executive Committee. The committee comprised Stan Haviland, the Under Secretary for Local Government, Ingham Ashworth, Professor of Architecture at the University of Sydney, Sir Charles Moses, the General Manager of the Australian Broadcasting Commission (ABC) and Sir Bernard Heinze, the Conductor of the Sydney Symphony Orchestra (SSO). Sir Eugene Goossens, predecessor to Heinze as the Director of the NSW Conservatorium of Music, and Conductor of the Sydney Symphony Orchestra, was also instrumental in the development of the project of the Opera House. The competition booklet is also known as the 'Brown Book' and it can be viewed online at the website of the NSW Government State Records. NSW Government (1955) *An International Competition for a National Opera House at Bennelong Point, Sydney, New South Wales, Australia: Conditions and Program (Brown Book)*. Sydney: Booklet printed by A.H. Pettifer, Government Printer. Australian Government (1955) *Sydney Opera House: The Brown Book*, NSW Government State Records. Retrieved: 27/06/2012, from: http://gallery.records.nsw.gov.au/index.php/galleries/sydney-opera-house/sydney-opera-house-the-brown-book/.

46 Anne Watson (2006) 'An Opera House for Sydney: Genesis and Conclusion of a Competition'. In *Building a Masterpiece: The Sydney Opera House*, edited by Anne Watson. Aldershot: Lund Humphries, pp. 38–55.

47 'Dane's Controversial Design Wins Opera House Contest' (1957) *Sydney Morning Herald*, 30 January, front page.

48 The judges of the competition were Sir Leslie Martin, Professor of Architecture, Cambridge University, Eero Saarinen, American architect, Cobden Parkes, Government Architect (1935–1958) and Henry Ingham Ashworth, Professor of Architecture, University of Sydney. 'Dane's Controversial Design Wins Opera House Contest', front page.

49 The Premier of NSW, Joe Cahill, had concerns that support for the project would be lost if the Labor Party did not win the 1959 State elections. This provided the impetus to begin construction on the project before it had been fully resolved.

50 'Poetry or Pastry? Argument on Opera House Plans' (1957) *Sydney Morning Herald*, 30 January, p. 3. 'Opera House Design Be a Lively Topic' (1957) *Sydney Morning Herald*, 2 February, p. 2.

51 Mexican architect Felix Candela commented on Utzon's scheme. He was an expert in thin concrete shells, however, Utzon's scheme did not follow the structural principles Candela's buildings used. Shell structures rely on being either a complete sphere or a half-sphere for their strength, so that the load is borne on the centre of the cross-sectional arch. Utzon's scheme comprised 1/8th sections of a sphere, where the structural load was unevenly distributed. Georges Molnar (1957) 'Candela: Authority on Shapes'. *Sydney Morning Herald*, 23 March, p. 11. Peter Murray (2004) *The Saga of the Sydney Opera House: The Dramatic Story of the Design and Construction of the Icon of Modern Australia*. New York: Spon Press, p. 13.

52 Utzon's design could not be built, the thin shell structures could not support themselves. At the same time he would not change the profile of the building, or accept a composite structure for the shells, as it went against his Modernist principle of material authenticity. The situation arose because Utzon had failed to take any engineering advice before submitting his design in the competition. This lack of rigour was openly criticised by architects such as Felix Candela from Mexico who were specialists in thin self-supporting concrete shells. Peter Jones (2006) *Ove Arup: Masterbuilder of the Twentieth Century*. New Haven: Yale University Press, pp. 173–236. Molnar, 'Candela', p. 11. Murray, *The Saga of the Sydney Opera House*, p. 13.

53 The change in profile is documented in the Yellow Book, accessible online at Jørn Utzon (1962) *The Yellow Book: Sydney National Opera House*. Sydney: State Records of NSW. Retrieved: 27/04/2013, from: http://gallery.records.nsw.gov.au/index.php/galleries/sydney-opera-house/sydney-opera-house-the-yellow-book/.

54 Ronald A. Gilling (2002) 'Utzon, the Institute and the Sydney Opera House: A Narrative of How the Resignation Affected the Profession and the Part Played by the Royal Australian Institute of Architects, 2002', Mitchell Library.

55 Hall, Todd and Littlemore made efforts to complete the building sympathetically, but the client brief kept changing. There was a major revision of the two performance halls, and their purposes were swapped (the large space became the Concert Hall, and the smaller the Opera Theatre). This 'move' has been blamed for the lack of facilities in the Opera Theatre, one of the major criticisms of the Opera House from a performer's and audience member's perspective. The original estimate for the cost of the building was GBP£3.5 million (AUD$7 million). The final bill was AUD$102 million. Murray, *The Saga of the Sydney Opera House*, pp. xii–xiii.

56 Elizabeth Farrelly (2010) 'Reviewing the Performance'. *Sydney Morning Herald*, 11 June. Retrieved: 18/05/2011, from: www.smh.com.au/entertainment/books/reviewing-the-performance-20100611-y2oi.html.

57 Michael Baume and Peter Hall (1967) *The Sydney Opera House Affair*. Melbourne: Nelson. John Yeomans (1968) *The Other Taj Mahal: What Happened to the Sydney Opera House.* London: Longmans, Green; Elias Duek-Cohen and Philip Drew (1998 [1967]) *Utzon and the Sydney Opera House: Statement in the Public Interest (with Additional Text by Philip Drew).* Sydney: Morgan Pubs.

58 On 28 March 1997, the Premier of NSW, and Minister for the Arts, Bob Carr, announced that all construction records of the Sydney Opera House were to be made public, regardless of their age. NSW Government (2012) 'Archives in Brief 28: A Brief History of the Sydney Opera House'. *NSW Government State Records*. Retrieved: 26/10/2012, from: www.records. nsw.gov.au/state-archives/guides-and-finding-aids/archives-in-brief/archives-in-brief-28. Historical accounts by Peter Murray, Ken Woolley, Philip Drew and Peter Jones incorporate these documents as primary research material and are therefore more balanced. Murray, *The Saga of the Sydney Opera House*; Ken Woolley (2010) *Reviewing the Performance.* Boorowa: The Watermark Press; Philip Drew (2001) *The Masterpiece: A Secret Life.* 2nd edn. South Yarra: Hardie Grant Books; Jones, *Ove Arup*.

59 The document was prepared by the Australian Heritage Commission on behalf of the Australian Government. Australian Government (1980) *Nomination of the Sydney Opera House in Its Harbour Setting with the Sydney Harbour Bridge and the Surrounding Waterways of Sydney Harbour from Bradley's Head to Mcmahon's Point for Inclusion in the World Heritage List.* Canberra: Australian Heritage Commission.

60 Australian Government (2006) *Sydney Opera House: Nomination by the Government of Australia for Inscription on the World Heritage List.* Canberra: Department of Environment and Heritage and NSW Heritage Office. Retrieved: 28/11/2012, from: http://whc.unesco. org/uploads/nominations/166rev.pdf, p. 9. See Fig. 1.3

61 Although the *World Heritage Convention* was adopted in 1972, the first inscriptions to the World Heritage list did not take place until 1978, when it had been ratified by enough Member States and came into force. Australia was the seventh country to ratify the World Heritage Convention on 22 August 1974. 'State Parties: Ratification Status'. *World Heritage Centre* [Website]. The only 20th century structure inscribed before 1980 was Auschwitz Birkenau, which was inscribed in 1979, but for its association with the Nazi movement rather than its architecture. However, it was inscribed under Criterion (vi) for being 'directly or tangibly associated with events or with ideas or beliefs of outstanding universal significance', as opposed to Criterion (i) which states 'represent a unique artistic achievement, a masterpiece of the creative genius' under which the 1980, 1996 and 2007 nominations sought inscription of the Opera House. UNESCO Intergovernmental Committee for the Protection of the World Cultural and Natural Heritage, Paris (1980) *Operational Guidelines for the Implementation of the World Heritage Convention.* Retrieved: 26/11/2012, from: http://whc.unesco.org/archive/opguide80.pdf.

62 The 1996 nomination was led by Joan Domicelj and included essays by Philip Drew and Christian Norberg-Schultz. This earlier nomination dossier is the foundation for the 2006 submission for the World Heritage inscription of the Sydney Opera House. The 1996 dossier is frequently cited in the 2006 dossier and many of the arguments used in the 1996 dossier are also used in the 2006 dossier. Australian Government (1996) *Sydney Opera House in Its Harbour Setting*; Australian Government (2006) *Sydney Opera House: Nomination by the Government of Australia for Inscription on the World Heritage List.*

63 Charles Jencks (1984) *The Language of Post-Modern Architecture*. 4th edn. London: Academy Editions; William J.R. Curtis (1987) *Modern Architecture since 1900*. 2nd edn. Oxford: Phaidon; Dennis Sharp (1991) *The Illustrated Dictionary of Architects and Architecture*. London: Headline; Kenneth Frampton and John Cava (1995) *Studies in Tectonic Culture: The Poetics of Construction in Nineteenth and Twentieth Century Architecture*. Cambridge, MA: The MIT Press.

64 Monographs: Tobias Faber, Dennis Sharp and Christian Norberg-Schulz (1991) 'Jørn Utzon: Special Issue'. *World Architecture*, 15, pp. 32–35; Philip Drew (1995) *Sydney Opera House: Jorn Utzon*. London: Phaidon Press. Popular accounts: James Sim (1983) *The Sydney Opera House*. Sydney: View Productions; Ava Hubble (1983) *The Sydney Opera House: More Than Meets the Eye*. Sydney: Lansdown Press, p. 48; Michael Pomeroy Smith (1984) *Sydney Opera House: How It Was Built and Why It Is So*. Sydney: Collins; Ava Hubble (1988) *The Strange Case of Eugene Goossens and Other Tales from the Opera House*. Sydney: Collins; Jill Sykes (1993) *Sydney Opera House: From the Outside In*. Pymble: Playbill. Engineering: Alan Holgate (1986) *The Art in Structural Design*. New York: Oxford University Press; Jack Zunz (1988) 'Sydney Revisited'. *The Arup Journal*, 23; Max Anderson and Pierre Cochrane (1989) *Julius Poole & Gibson: The First Eighty Years from Tote to Cad*. Sydney: Julius Poole & Gibson; Peter Rice (1989) 'A Celebration of the Life and Work of Ove Arup', *RSA Journal*, June; David Dunster (1996) *Arups on Engineering*. London: Ernst & Sohn.

65 In 1985, Utzon received the Companion of the Order of Australia (AC) (Honorary Award) for achievements in the field of Architecture. In 1992 Utzon was awarded the Wolf Foundation Prize in Arts (Architecture), recognising 'qualities existing well beyond the range of passing fashion, qualities that enhance use, transform construction and liberate the mind'. Australian Government (2006) *Sydney Opera House: Nomination by the Government of Australia for Inscription on the World Heritage List*, p. 103.

66 Peter Proudfoot (1997) 'Operatic Recitative: Nomination of Sydney Opera House in Its Harbour Setting for Inscription on the World Heritage List by the Government of Australia, 1996'. *Fabrications*, 8, p. 154.

67 In 1994, Utzon's drawings for the interiors of the Sydney Opera House from the Utzon collection of the NSW State Library were shown in *Unseen Utzon*, a jointly mounted exhibition between these institutions. In the exhibition, Philip Nobis digitally modelled the interiors proposed by Utzon, as part of his dissertation. Philip Nobis (1994) *Utzon's Interiors for the Sydney Opera House: The Design Development of the Major and Minor Hall 1958–1966*. Bachelor of Architecture thesis, University of Technology, Sydney; Philip Nobis, 'Unseen Utzon'. *YouTube* [Animation of Original Interiors of the Sydney Opera House as Designed by Jørn Utzon, between July 1965 and February 1966]. Retrieved: 02/07/2012, from: www.youtube.com/watch?v=aU6oQpHfDz8; Philip Nobis and John Murphy (1994) 'Unseen Utzon' [Exhibition]. Sydney Opera House and NSW State Library, 1 November. A year earlier the interiors were also the focus of another dissertation by Peter Georgiades, a fellow UTS architecture student. Jørn Utzon (1956–1967) 'Jorn Utzon Sydney Opera House Collection, 1956–1967'. *State Library of NSW*. Retrieved: 02/07/2012, from: http://acms.sl.nsw.gov.au/item/itemdetailpaged.aspx?itemid=41166; Theodore Peter Georgiades (1993) *Utzon's Unseen Work: A Search to Discover the Design Intentions of Jørn Utzon for the Interior Auditoria of the Sydney Opera House*. Bachelor of Architecture thesis, School of Architecture, University of Technology, Sydney.

68 The Liberal Party was in power at the time, with John Howard as prime minister. Parliament of New South Wales (1998) *Sydney Opera House World Heritage Listing*.

69 Patricia Hale and Susan Macdonald (2005) 'The Sydney Opera House, an Evolving Icon'. *Journal of Architectural Conservation*, 11 (2), p. 16.

70 'Headlines: New South Wales', *Architecture Australia*, May/June 1996.

71 Jørn Utzon and Sydney Opera House Trust (2002) *Utzon Design Principles*. Sydney. Retrieved: 27/04/2013, from: http://sohweb.cdnl.sydneyoperahouse.com/uploadedFiles/About_Us/The_Building/Content_AboutUs_UtzonDesignPrinciples.pdf.

72 Laurajane Smith (ed.) (2007) *Cultural Heritage: Critical Concepts in Media and Cultural Studies*, 4 vols. London: Routledge; Jukka Jokilehto (1998) 'International Trends in Historic Preservation: From Ancient Monuments to Living Cultures'. *APT Bulletin, Historic Structure Reports (1997)*, 29 (3/4).

73 Smith, *Uses of Heritage*; D. Fairchild Ruggles and Helaine Silverman (2009) *Intangible Heritage Embodied*. London: Springer.

74 Smith, *Cultural Heritage*, p. 1; Susan Macdonald (2009) 'Materiality, Monumentality and Modernism: Continuing Challenges in Conserving Twentieth-Century Places'. Presented at the *(Un)Loved Modern: Conservation of 20th Century Heritage Conference*, Sydney, 7–10 July 2009.

75 Dawson Munjeri (2004) 'Tangible and Intangible Heritage: From Difference to Convergence'. *Museum International*, 56 (1–2), p. 16.

76 Cleere, 'The Uneasy Bedfellows', pp. 22–29.

77 Smith, *Uses of Heritage*, p. 11.

78 Arthur Drexler and Sigfried Giedion both wrote about the aesthetic innovations of the Sydney Opera House. Sigfried Giedion (1965) 'Jørn Utzon and the Third Generation: Three Works by Jørn Utzon – a New Chapter of Space Time and Architecture', *Zodiac*, 14, pp. 36–47; Arthur Drexler and Wilder Green (1959) 'Architecture and Imagery – Four New Buildings'. *Museum of Modern Art* [Press Release]. MOMA, February 10. Retrieved: 27/11/2012, from: www.moma.org/docs/press_archives/2448/releases/MOMA_1959_0014.pdf?2010; Arthur Drexler and Wilder Green (1959) *Architecture and Imagery – Four New Buildings*. New York: MOMA.

79 UNESCO (1981) 'Bureau of the World Heritage Committee, Fifth Session, Paris, 4–7 May 1981: Report of the Rapporteur'. *World Heritage Centre*. Retrieved: 27/11/2012, from: http://whc.unesco.org/archive/1981/cc-81-conf002-4e.pdf.

80 UNESCO, 'Bureau of the World Heritage Committee, Fifth Session, Paris, 4–7 May 1981'.

81 The preparation of nomination dossiers requires both financial and intellectual resources. For example, the preparation of the 1996 nomination of the Sydney Opera House is recorded by Mr Knowles as having cost the Commonwealth of Australia AUD\$200,000. Parliament of New South Wales (1998) *Sydney Opera House World Heritage Listing*.

82 Cleere, 'The Uneasy Bedfellows'.

83 Author's analysis of updated figures in 2010.

84 UNESCO (2003) *Identification and Documentation of Modern Heritage: World Heritage Papers 5*, World Heritage Centre. Retrieved: 11/04/2012, from: www.whitr-ap.org/themes/69/userfiles/download/2012/3/5/f8psqtlnnavqjro.pdf, p. 4.

85 UNESCO, *Identification and Documentation of Modern Heritage*, p. 4.

86 UNESCO. 'Global Strategy'. *World Heritage Centre*. Retrieved: 27/04/2013, from: http://whc.unesco.org/en/globalstrategy.

87 UNESCO, *Identification and Documentation of Modern Heritage: World Heritage Papers 5*, p. 4.

88 Jukka Jokilehto (2002) 'Great Sites of Modern Architecture'. *World Heritage*, 25, pp. 4–21. Further, it is interesting to note that the examples cited are older than the Sydney Opera House, revealing the long-standing disagreement on the definition of Modern Architecture, between European working parties of DOCOMOMO and 'new world' parties such as Australia and the United States. These 'new world' parties have deliberately included examples from the 1960s and 1970s to gain listings. This demonstrates the way in which World Heritage listing is seen as a tool for social and political advancement on an international stage.

89 Macdonald, 'Materiality, Monumentality and Modernism', p. 1.

90 UNESCO (2003) *Convention for the Safeguarding of the Intangible Cultural Heritage*, 32nd Session: The General Conference of the United Nations Educational, Scientific and Cultural Organization. Paris. Retrieved: 29/11/2010, from: www.unesco.org/culture/ich/index.php?lg=en&pg=00022.

91 Labadi and Long, *Heritage and Globalisation*, p. 6.

92 Askew, 'The Magic List of Global Status', p. 6; Long and Labadi, 'Introduction'.

93 Smith, *Uses of Heritage*, p. 98.

94 Smith, *Uses of Heritage*, p. 99. This view is also held by Barbara Kirchenblatt-Gimblett and Dawson Munjeri. Kirshenblatt-Gimblett. 'Intangible Heritage as Metacultural Production'; Munjeri, 'Tangible and Intangible Heritage'.

95 David Lowenthal (1998) *The Heritage Crusade and the Spoils of History*. Cambridge: Cambridge University Press, p. 227.

96 Before the 2004 inscription of the Royal Exhibition Building and Carlton Gardens (Melbourne, Victoria) Australia had 15 sites on the World Heritage List, none of which were inscribed for their cultural value. Notably there were four sites inscribed for Mixed Cultural and Natural value, but all of these were inscribed for their cultural value to Indigenous peoples. Uluru-Kata Tjuta National Park – for its significance as part of a traditional belief system of the Anangu Aboriginal People (1987), Tasmanian Wilderness – for its significance as a site of ancient human occupation 20,000 years ago (1982), Kakadu National Park – for its significance to the traditional Indigenous owners still residing there (1981), Willandra Lakes Region – for its significance in terms of human evolution (1981).

2 Social value and iconicity

The Sydney Opera House is inscribed as a World Heritage site for its outstanding universal value as a work of architecture, as a work of engineering and because of its value as a world icon. All heritage inscriptions require the formal establishment of a property's significance. For World Heritage, this is defined by a statement that sets out the property's outstanding universal value, which forms 'the key reference for the future effective protection and management of the property'.[1] This statement justifies inscription and guides conservation. It is part of the legally binding agreement forged between UNESCO and the nominating State Party and if the values described in the statement are not maintained, the property may be removed from the World Heritage List.[2] The statement of outstanding universal value for the Sydney Opera House frames the significance of this place in three broad ways:

> The Sydney Opera House is a great architectural work of the 20th century. It represents multiple strands of creativity, both in architectural form and structural design, a great urban sculpture carefully set in a remarkable waterscape and a world famous iconic building.[3]

Primarily the Sydney Opera House is significant because of its contribution to the development of Modernism in architecture. In particular the building is evidence of a creative synthesis between sculptural form and programmatic function. Secondarily, it is significant in the context of engineering, evidenced in the methods and innovative techniques used for its realisation. The value of the Sydney Opera House in these fields of professional practice and academic knowledge is extensively documented in academic and popular forms of literature. The building's significance within the modern canon of architecture has been established through the work of international architectural historians such as Sigfried Giedion, Kenneth Frampton, Christian Norberg-Schulz and Australian academics such as Philip Goad and Philip Drew.[4] The contribution of the Sydney Opera House as evidence of innovative building methods and advances in structural engineering systems is documented in the work of scholars such as Yuzo Mikami and Osamu Murai, Peter Jones, Jack Zunz, John Nutt, David Taffs and Paolo Tombesi.[5] However, the inscription also recognises a third form of significance for this place; it cites the Sydney Opera House as a 'world-famous iconic building'. The iconic value of the Sydney Opera House is usually discussed from the perspective of the building's architecture. But world fame is a term usually used to describe something or someone that has become widely known and globally familiar, suggesting that there is a value in the building's popularity. What does this mean?

Inscribed for its value as a 'world-famous iconic building'

The concept of values forms a central aspect of the World Heritage system, conservation processes and heritage theory.[6] Traditionally, heritage buildings have been preserved for their historic and aesthetic values, harking back to the work of Alois Riegl.[7] An Austrian art historian, Riegl explored the complexities of evaluating monuments and built heritage and was one of the first scholars to make 'a systematic analysis of heritage values and of a theory of restoration'.[8] For Riegl, buildings are the embodiment of technical skills and aesthetic expression, or they are evidence of particular historical events. Authority comes with age, and authenticity is interpreted in terms of historical accuracy, as determined by reliable (expert) sources. Such principles continue to be embedded in present-day legal instruments, such as the *World Heritage Convention*, which defines monuments as:

> architectural works, works of monumental sculpture and painting, elements or structures of an archaeological nature, inscriptions, cave dwellings and combinations of features, which are of outstanding universal value from the point of view of history, art or science.[9]

Since the adoption of the *World Heritage Convention* in 1972, the discipline has come to recognise the importance of social and community values. Sophia Labadi argues that values are subjective and 'based on changes in time and particular cultural, intellectual, historical and psychological frames of reference held by specific groups'.[10] Yet the *World Heritage Convention* only recognises the value of a work of architecture with regard to established fields of knowledge, namely, art, history and science, and does not include social values. Which makes the inscription of the Sydney Opera House as a *world-famous iconic building* a curious inclusion worthy of further investigation.

The theory on iconic architecture hints at a social component to such a status. Sociologist Leslie Sklair offers an insightful explanation of the increasing use of the term 'iconic' in regards to architecture. In his publication titled 'Iconic Architecture and Urban, National, and Global Identities', Sklair makes a distinction between past and contemporary uses of the term 'icon'.[11] Historically the term has been used to describe sacred representations that are honoured, worshipped and adored.[12] This definition underpins theory on iconology and iconography within art history, which focuses on representative art.[13] In this historic sense, the term icon is theorised in relation to representation, symbolism and expression.[14] According to Sklair, the more common contemporary usage of the term iconic, particularly in reference to world fame and to architecture, is linked to globalisation and identity.

The inscription of the Sydney Opera House for its value as a *world-famous* iconic building is an acknowledgement of the way such examples of architecture have gained popular value and recognition, in contrast to acclaim gained within its disciplinary field. It is interesting to note that the Statement of Outstanding Universal Value of the Sydney Opera House describes the building as 'a great artistic monument and an icon, accessible to society at large'.[15] Whilst the primary significance of the Sydney Opera

House in terms of its inscription is its contribution to the fields of architecture and engineering, its social significance to communities is confirmed by the description of the building as an icon that is readily appropriated and appreciated. The inscription of the Sydney Opera House for its value as a world-famous iconic building indicates a desire to acknowledge the importance of the building for people. But how are the traditional ideas around the symbolic value of icons connected with contemporary ideas of popularity?

Sklair theorises the relationship between past and contemporary uses of the term iconic as it relates to certain characteristics of architecture. He proposes that iconic in the past is indicative of a different, but related condition than that which is intended in contemporary discussions of iconic buildings. He argues that in the past, iconic was used to describe stereotypical form. For example, common city landmarks, such as gothic churches, were understood as iconic because they conformed to the stereotype of gothic church architecture. Sklair argues, however, that since the advent of the global era, which took force after the 1950s, the term iconic has been 'more often used in an entirely opposite sense'.[16] In more recent years the term iconic has come to be used as a way of describing buildings that challenge stereotypes through the use of unique aesthetic propositions. The contemporary description of buildings as iconic is suggestive of a kind of fame that has arisen from the controversy around their aesthetic departure from established forms. Both past and contemporary uses of the term imply that community recognition is part of the significance of such places. However, Sklair argues that in this contemporary use of the term, iconicity arises because of the *participation of a community* who discuss the controversial aesthetic strategy such buildings deploy; unusual forms are often described in popular culture in terms of their ability to suggest more familiar objects – a gherkin, sails or even a scrunched-up paper bag.[17] Understood through Sklair's theorisation of architectural iconicity the value of the Sydney Opera House as a world-famous icon of architecture is connected to its visual popularity and formal distinctiveness.

The World Heritage inscription of the Sydney Opera House as a *world-famous iconic building* is possibly indicative of the inclusion of social values in the Australian heritage discourse. The Australia ICOMOS *Burra Charter* is distinct from the *World Heritage Convention* in two significant ways; it uses the term 'place' instead of 'monument' and it includes social and spiritual values as part of cultural significance.[18] The charter states that '*Cultural significance* means aesthetic, historic, scientific, social or spiritual value for past, present or future generations'.[19] The use of the term 'place' in the *Burra Charter* is connected to the broadening conception of heritage in Australia in the 1970s and 1980s. The *Burra Charter* was first adopted in 1979 and the use of the term 'place' instead of 'monument' was intended to account for Australia's very different sense of heritage compared with that of Europe; for example, white settlement in Australia that was evidenced as built fabric was only 200 years old, whilst Aboriginal culture which emphasised a connection to country (the landscape) had existed for 40,000 years.[20] The term monument was thought to be inappropriate to describe the qualities of Australia's cultural heritage. The idea that buildings can have social or spiritual value is related to the use of the term place. The concept of place is central to discourse in geography, where it is used to differentiate sites that have special meaning or significance for communities.[21] The term place inherently accommodates subjective values such as social or spiritual value; it activates sites and includes people as active entities within them. The use of 'place' and the inclusion of social value within the *Burra Charter* is indicative of the broadening scope of heritage. How has this been addressed in World Heritage?

In 1972, when the *World Heritage Convention* was initially adopted, the concept of 'outstanding universal value' lacked specific definition. The term is both a quantitative and qualitative indicator of significance. It describes the level of significance – global – as well as describing the specific values (aesthetic, historic or scientific) for which a property is inscribed. Determining outstanding universal value has been the subject of much debate throughout the programme's operation.[22] To address this, the World Heritage Committee has developed criteria and conditions to describe how outstanding universal value may be evidenced in the *Operational Guidelines for the Implementation of the World Heritage Convention* (*Operational Guidelines*). This means that while all properties on the World Heritage List have outstanding universal value, their inscribed values may differ greatly.

The current *Operational Guidelines* provide six criteria for the interpretation of outstanding universal value. They define how a property may be recognised as significant enough for inscription. Two criteria are pertinent to the inscription of the Sydney Opera House as a 'world famous iconic building', namely Criterion (i) under which the building is inscribed and Criterion (vi) which is a vehicle for the potential inclusion of social values.[23] Criterion (i) states that a site has outstanding universal value if it 'represents a masterpiece of human creative genius'.[24] The inscription of the Sydney Opera House attributes this outstanding universal value to 'Utzon's original design concept and his unique approach to building [which] gave impetus to a collective creativity including architects, engineers and builders'.[25] The inscription of the building under this criterion is built entirely upon Utzon and his authorship of the building. It frames the significance of the Sydney Opera House as a work of architecture that is the result of Utzon's creative capacity to synthesise the structural and programmatic requirements into a spectacular urban sculpture. Criterion (i) only recognises the value of works of architecture that have been established by experts who have the skills to distinguish ordinary examples from masterpieces. Jukka Jokilehto paraphrases this criterion as:

> an outstanding example (or the peak) of a style evolved within a culture, having a high intellectual or symbolic endowment, and a high level of artistic, technical or technological skills.[26]

The use of Criterion (i) for the inscription of the Sydney Opera House accords with its recognised contribution to the canon of Modern Architecture and its contribution in terms of structural engineering and technological innovation. However, the use of this criterion to frame the building's value as a world-famous iconic building is inconsistent with the criterion's dependence on expert analysis. Sklair's observation that the term iconic, in contemporary use, is related to a building's aesthetic popularity frames the significance of the Sydney Opera House from the perspective of its communities.

Iconic value, understood as a social and visual kind of popularity is more appropriately understood through Criterion (vi),[27] which recognises that outstanding universal value can be indicated by associated culture, rather than for aesthetic or technical distinction in its field. Criterion (vi) states that a site has outstanding universal value if it is:

directly or tangibly associated with events or living traditions, with ideas, or with beliefs, with artistic and literary works of outstanding universal significance. (The Committee considers that this criterion should preferably be used in conjunction with other criteria.)[28]

The description of the Sydney Opera House as an iconic building for 'society at large' is readily recognised through this alternative criterion. A sense of attachment suggests that a place embodies particular ideas or beliefs held for a community. The popularity of a symbol, such as the Sydney Opera House, or for that matter an icon in the original sense of a religious image, is implicated in the symbol's widespread acceptance.

The earlier nominations of the Sydney Opera House, prepared in 1980 and 1996/1999, demonstrate the difficulty of including social forms of significance as part of World Heritage inscription. The withdrawn nomination of 1980 sought to inscribe the Sydney Opera House with the Sydney Harbour Bridge as part of the larger area of the harbour.[29] The nomination justified the listing through Criterion (i), Criterion (iv) and Criterion (v).[30] Similarly the 1996/1999 nomination, which was never approved by the Australian government, sought to list the Sydney Opera House and Sydney Harbour Bridge in the context of the harbour, again under Criterion (i) and (iv), but used Criterion (vi) instead of Criterion (v).[31] This nomination sought to include the value of people's associations with the Sydney Opera House and surrounds, arguing that the greater harbour area is significant because it is associated with:

> the eighteenth century encounter between Aboriginal and European people, an event epitomising a human drama of universal dimensions, and the site's association with outstanding literary, artistic, engineering and architectural works.[32]

The 1996/1999 claims for inscription under Criterion (vi) are framed both in terms of the value of the harbour for people and in terms of the way this place, and the Sydney Opera House in particular, serves as inspiration for acclaimed visual representations.[33] Revising the earlier unsuccessful nomination of the Sydney Opera House suggests that the 2007 inscription as a world-famous iconic building was not a newly recognised value, but rather one that has been historically complex and difficult to implement.

The interpretation and application of Criterion (vi) for World Heritage inscription has been a point of substantial debate. The 2015 *Operational Guidelines* recommendation is that it be used with other criteria because Criterion (vi) recognises subjective values. This has been controversial and the autonomous use of this criterion has been modified many times over the 40-year lifetime of the World Heritage programme.[34] The recognition of iconic value as a World Heritage value is not straightforward.

To evaluate the claims made by a State Party about the outstanding universal value, and the values of nominated sites, the World Heritage Committee has developed two further conditions that a property must meet:

> to be deemed of Outstanding Universal Value a property must also meet the conditions of integrity and/or authenticity and must have an adequate protection and management system to ensure its safeguarding.[35]

Integrity and particularly authenticity are significant concepts in the discourse on World Heritage. Integrity is defined in the *Operational Guidelines* as:

> a measure of the wholeness and intactness of the natural and/or cultural herit-age and its attributes.[36] [This is achieved by ensuring that:] the physical fabric of the property and/or its significant features should be in good condition, and the impact of deterioration processes controlled [and] relationships and dynamic functions [of] living properties ... should be maintained.[37]

For integrity to be maintained the physical fabric of the building and its use must be preserved, implying that a site's significance is located in its material features. Without being in a complete and unchanged state a site's values are unable to be recognised or preserved. Places, and buildings, however, can be significant in immaterial ways. This was exemplified when the Sydney Opera House was used as a visual space for political messages in 2003, when two protestors against the war in Iraq scaled the sails and wrote 'NO WAR' in five-metre-high red painted letters. The event was widely publicised in the official media as well as documented and commemorated in photo-graphs, further acts of graffiti and souvenirs (Figure 2.1). While the architectural-scale graffiti was removed the following day, the event continues to be remembered. Sylvia Lawson writes that although government officials and the management of the building admonished this act, many in the public domain lauded it, yet had the red paint marks been permanently rendered on the white Modernist monument, the building's integrity could have been substantially affected.

In contrast to the interpretation of integrity the concept of authenticity in the World Heritage literature is more contested and less straightforward. The acceptance that values are subjective, as Labadi asserts, has been more readily applied in relation to authenticity and a more subjective definition has been accepted. In 2005, at the time of the 2006 nomination for the Sydney Opera House, the *Operational Guidelines* stated that the authenticity of a property depended on the:

> design, material, workmanship or setting and ... that reconstruction is only accept-able if it is carried out on the basis of complete and detailed documentation on the original and to no extent on conjecture.[38]

Figure 2.1 Defacing the sails.

Sources: left, photograph posted on Flickr.com 'No War' (© Deborah Pitt, 2006); middle, photograph posted on Flickr.com 'Image 456' No War stencil (© Chris Adkins, 2005); right, 'No War' Sydney Opera House salt and pepper shakers gifted to director James Searle by the cast of 'Word Space', a short play by Elizabeth Bennett staged in 2007 at *Short and Sweet, Sydney* Festival.

As late as 2005, authenticity, like integrity, was clearly located within the material extent of a building or site. By 2008 the definition of authenticity contained within the *Operational Guidelines* had changed to be dependent on the:

> degree to which information sources [as cited in the nomination document] about this value may be understood as credible or truthful.[39] [However,] Judgments about value attributed to cultural heritage, as well as the credibility of related information sources, may differ from culture to culture, and even within the same culture.[40]

The change from understanding authenticity as a material characteristic to an intellectual and cultural one is attributable to the argument posed by the *1994 ICOMOS Nara Document on Authenticity* (*Nara Document on Authenticity*).[41] While this document was adopted by ICOMOS, rather than the signatories to the *World Heritage Convention*, it demonstrates the strong affiliation of such an international organisation with UNESCO's World Heritage programme. The *Nara Document on Authenticity* explains its connection with World Heritage in its preamble, which states the:

> World Heritage Committee's desire to apply the test of authenticity in ways which accord full respect to the social and cultural values of all societies, in examining the outstanding universal value of cultural properties proposed for the World Heritage List.[42]

The *Nara Document on Authenticity* was adopted in response to criticisms of World Heritage for its universalising notions of cultural heritage as 'old, grand, monumental and aesthetically pleasing sites',[43] as discussed in Chapter 1. The *Nara Document on Authenticity* acknowledged that authenticity is not implicit or stable; it is not permanent 'truth'. In other words, authenticity is subjective and can shift between cultures, between historical periods, or between present-day groups and individuals. For example, authenticity may be defined in very different ways for an academic expert and a tourist. For an architectural historian, such as Philip Drew, who has written extensively on the Sydney Opera House, the building's authenticity as a masterpiece of 20th-century architecture is marred by its dual authorship that resulted from Utzon's resignation and the completion of the building by Hall, Todd and Littlemore.[44] Their work has largely been overlooked and dismissed as diminishing the value of Utzon's genius vision. Yet, Hall's real contribution to the completion of the Opera House has recently come to light through the work of architectural historian Anne Watson, and Peter Webber's recent biography.[45] Drew's concerns were that the interiors of the building were completed outside of Utzon's holistic architectural vision, making the building a 'flawed masterpiece' affecting the building's recognition as contributing to the modern canon. In contrast, authenticity for a tourist may involve being able to circumnavigate the building, take photographs, attend a performance and describe their close experience of the place. If authenticity is to be culturally determined, whose authenticity is represented?

The formal acknowledgement of the subjectivity in assessments of authenticity by the *Nara Document on Authenticity* provided an avenue for deeming continually changing structures as eligible for World Heritage inscription. As D. Fairchild Ruggles and Helaine Silverman state:

the acknowledgement of impermanence and renewal had an impact that far exceeded that of monument preservation because it admitted the human being as integral to the construction of meaning and the ongoing creation of material culture. If a building or a work of art is to be ritually renewed, then the actors who effect the renewal become essential elements in the preservation process.[46]

This is an important intellectual shift in the conceptualisation of World Heritage because it displaces significance from its previous conception as inherently embodied in the materiality of buildings to a value attributed to places *by people*. Including people in the definition of heritage challenges existing ideas that privilege built fabric over associations and uses, tangible over intangible, and sites over people. The *Nara Document on Authenticity* indicates the desire to include socially constructed perspectives in the recognition of World Heritage. Like the inscription of the Sydney Opera House for its value as a world-famous iconic building, this new way of understanding authenticity is indicative of the desire to include, in some form or another, the concept of social significance within the World Heritage framework.

The development of the Sydney Opera House as an icon

Historically the iconic value of the Sydney Opera House has been understood in terms of the building's architecture. This was first formally recognised in 1959.[47] Arthur Drexler and Wilder Green included Utzon's concept drawings of the Sydney Opera House in an exhibition titled *Architecture and Imagery: Four New Buildings*, held at the Museum of Modern Art (MoMA), New York.[48] The exhibition presented four works of architecture considered at the time to be at the forefront of Modern Architecture. In an essay published in the accompanying catalogue, Drexler observes that the formal expression of these works of architecture goes beyond expressing programmatic function to 'evoke images of natural or man-made objects'.[49] Drexler quickly reframes this quality as connected to the building's structural and functional requirements, rather than the result of artistic expression. Nonetheless, he asserts that these qualities are significant because:

> some forms are inherently richer in overtones – are more provocative of associations – than the purely geometric forms of abstract architectural composition. The images such forms evoke become part of a building's ultimate value whether or not the architect sought or anticipated them.[50]

This observation is the first formal articulation of the iconic value of the Sydney Opera House. Drexler highlights the iconic quality as significant and asserts that the building's power to suggest other images or forms is an important contribution. In 1965 Sigfried Giedion wrote an extensive article in the Italian architecture magazine *Zodiac*, on Utzon and his relationship to the 'third generation of modernist architects'.[51] Here he lauded Utzon for introducing the 'right of expression above pure function', asserting that this was a departure from the approach of the previous generations of Modernist architects from the 1920s.[52] He also praised Utzon for creating an architecture that was sculptural and that created a connection with anonymous historic forms.[53] The referential framing of the Sydney Opera House in relation to historic forms connects it with the traditional interpretation of 'icon' as a stereotype. Simultaneously, its expressive form is an aesthetic rupture with Modernism, setting the stage for controversy. Giedion, like Drexler, saw that the building's form was an important part of its contribution to the development of Modern Architecture.

After Utzon's resignation in 1966, the way the building's iconic value was framed, changed. Instead, the sculptural and evocative form of the building drew criticism from architectural scholars. In 1972, Philip Drew condemned the building's 'permissive expression' because it 'frequently degenerates into arbitrary sensationalism of idiosyncratic forms which devalue architectural integrity'.[54] In 1973 Charles Jencks disparaged the Sydney Opera House as an example of 'individual creativity' becoming 'functionally and politically "fantastic"'.[55] The same sculptural forms that had been praised by Giedion almost a decade earlier were now framed as pure spectacle.

By 1977 Jencks began to frame the 'fantastic' and 'evocative' forms of the Sydney Opera House as 'iconic'. In *The Language of Post-Modern Architecture*, Jencks uses a theoretical derivation of semiotic theories of communication[56] to propose that architecture can be read as a language; a system of signs able to be interpreted.[57] Jencks defines an 'iconic' work of architecture as an 'enigmatic' sign, one that can elicit a 'superabundance of metaphorical associations'.[58] Situated within Jencks' semiological interpretation of architecture, the enigmatic sign is another way of describing Giedion's 'right of expression' and Drexler's initial articulation of the 'associations' evoked by this building. However, Drexler notes that this is an unintentional attribute of the architecture, whereas Giedion frames it as expression, implying that architecture is a medium, while Jencks argues that this make the building a sign that can be interpreted.

Like Jencks, Christian Norberg-Schulz theorises the iconic value of the Sydney Opera house in terms of its meaning. In 1980 Christian Norberg-Schulz published an essay in a special edition of the *Global Architecture* series.[59] In this publication he discusses the value of the Sydney Opera House in terms of his broader phenomenological reading of architecture. Norberg-Schulz rejects Jencks' proposition that architecture can be understood as a series of signs, and, instead, argues that the 'meaning' of architecture is to create holistic experience that can offer a sense of spirituality:

> A work of architecture does not express its contents by means of a language of 'signs', but by how it stands on the ground, how it rises up, how it extends in space and how it opens and closes. This defines how it 'is' between earth and sky, constituting a *place* where human life can take place. (Original emphasis)[60]

Norberg-Schulz conceives of architecture as a greater project than Jencks' system of signs. He seeks a 'meaningful' architecture that can heal the 'split of thought and feeling' by ascribing to universal forms rooted in the cosmos and nature.

The discourse on the iconic value of the Sydney Opera House has primarily been framed in terms of its ability to evoke visual associations or its spiritual meaning. That both Jencks and Norberg-Schulz appropriate the building's 'image-value' for the purpose of furthering the Post-Modern project for architecture is perhaps a consequence of the shifts that occurred in the discipline during the period of the building's construction. In the late 1950s and early part of the 1960s the limitations of Modernist approaches to architecture became evident. The 14-year lag between the design and completion of the Sydney Opera House is one potential reason for the uptake of this work of architecture into the Post-Modern project. The shifts in the theorisation of the Sydney Opera House evidence how the building was used to frame larger theories on iconicity and phenomenology in architecture. For example, Norberg-Schulz reiterates his phenomenological reading in his evaluative essay in the 1996 World Heritage nomination of the building,[61] whereas Jencks' position remains unchanged in his later editions of *The Language of Post-Modern Architecture*.[62] These discourses centre on the aesthetic value of the building within the context of the development of the field of architecture. The building's recognition of the *world-famous* iconic status as an inscribed World Heritage value evidences a further shift; iconicity becomes framed within popular culture. It demonstrates a social rather than a purely architectural approach. How has this been accounted for in the nomination dossier?

To better understand the anomalies implied in the inscription of the Sydney Opera House as a world-famous iconic building it is worthwhile revising the 2006 nomination documents. The arguments and expert sources cited reveal a discrepancy between a desire to recognise its social value and the way this value is accounted for as a self-evident quality of the architecture. A State Party must include in the nomination dossier a section titled 'The Justification for Inscription' that provides evidence for the Statement of Outstanding Universal Value and, more broadly, the inscription.[63] This part of the 2006 nomination dossier has four distinct headings that State Parties must address: the criteria and justification for inscription, the proposed statement of outstanding universal value, a comparative analysis for each of these outstanding universal values and a statement of integrity and authenticity. In the 'Justification for Inscription' within the 2006 nomination dossier for the Sydney Opera House, it states the building is 'instantly recognised by people around the globe',[64] and affirms that it is an 'image of great beauty' and that the building 'achieved iconic status even before its completion'.[65] The arguments presented in the dossier inadvertently reveal that the building's value includes a social component. This is interesting, since the Sydney Opera House is inscribed under Criterion (i), which argues that the value of the building is its architectural value, whereas, these statements situate the value of the Sydney Opera House in relation to *people* and, significantly, *to representations*. While the inscription is under Criterion (i) the arguments in the dossier acknowledge the connection between the iconic character of the Sydney Opera House and its recognition by audiences and communities as an image that is widely acknowledged as sublime. That the nomination dossier states that iconic value of the Sydney Opera House was evident before the building was completed, is intriguing. It suggests that this is not only a characteristic of the building, now physically realised, but is connected with its initial existence as a series of drawings and models. This is a significant fact, as the materialisation of buildings is generally preceded by a process of design, in which architecture is investigated *through* drawings and models, that is *through representations*.[66]

The dossier goes on to describe the Sydney Opera House as a 'multifaceted public monument that is simultaneously "high-brow" and "low-brow", captivating the hearts and minds of everyone who experiences it'.[67] Here, part of the value of the Sydney Opera House is explicitly located in the *sense of attachment that communities have with this place*. The use of the term 'low-brow' describes the building's significance for people and alludes to its place in popular culture. The expert sources used to support the inscription of the Sydney Opera House as a world-famous icon of architecture in the dossier demonstrate a disparity between its recognition as a social value and the ability to account for it in this way. This raises questions around how this sense of attachment, the perspective of the ordinary person can be revealed? Examining the representations of the Sydney Opera House circulating in popular culture may offer some insight.

The dossier uses academic sources that recognise the Sydney Opera House as a world-famous iconic building to substantiate this claim. In comparison to the dossier's justification of the building's contribution to architecture and engineering, its iconic value is treated as a *self-evident quality of the architecture*. The dossier makes statements about the building's recognition by people all over the world, but then accounts for this by referring to the 'transformative experience' designed by Utzon, and to its 'visceral and optical more than cerebral' appeal, where its power lies in its 'primitive roots'.[68] The justification fails to evidence how audiences and communities come to recognise the Sydney Opera House, nor does it describe in what way the building is significant to them. The arguments made imply that the building's iconic value is an inherent part of the architecture and, reasonably, this is the way iconic architecture has been framed within the discipline. However, it fails to recognise that iconic status, as Sklair articulates, is also connected to architecture's reception and representation in popular culture.

The justification substantiates the claim for iconicity through the work of Richard Weston, Terry Smith and Charles Jencks published prior to submission, the Pritzker Prize citation by Bill Lacey, as well as two essays especially commissioned for the nomination by Philip Goad and Dennis Sharp.[69] As discussed above, Jencks frames his discussion on the iconic character of the Sydney Opera House through architectural semiology, whilst Weston's position follows Giedion's analysis where the expression of the building is described in terms of its appropriation of universal forms derived from primitive architectures. The nomination also cites Terry Smith's 2002 essay, but does not employ the thesis of the essay, instead selectively quoting from it in a cursory manner.

Smith has published several articles that explore iconicity with regards to architecture.[70] In 'The Political Economy of Iconotypes and the Architecture of Destination: Uluru, the Sydney Opera House and the World Trade Center', Smith describes the relationship between iconic architecture and its representation in culture. He explores the way in which the Sydney Opera House, among other architectural examples, circulates in the form of images in a 'global cultural economy'. Smith questions:

> How did they achieve this status? How do ideas of destination work within their representational lives? How do they fit within the larger circuitry of potent visual imagery in symbolic exchange, within this economy of icons, this iconomy?[71]

In this article Smith coins the term 'iconomy' specifically in reference to architecture.[72] He uses it to describe how the iconic value of architecture can be dislocated from the edifice itself through its representation and converted into an economy of cultural exchange, that is, he reveals the way iconic architecture has a parallel existence in the global exchange of representations. Smith frames his notion of 'iconomy' in terms of cultural capital used in the interactions between groups of people for whom such representations of iconic architecture offer a sense of identity. Yet the justification for the inscription of the Sydney Opera House as a world-famous iconic building does not acknowledge this core idea of Smith's theoretical premise. The nomination dossier only cites Smith's observation in terms of the architecture of the Sydney Opera House. The extract from the essay cited in the dossier notes:

> That the Sydney Opera House was immediately, and radically, novel is self-evident: it was instantly spectacular, and remains so for all those who see it for the first time (and for many of us who see it often).[73]

In this context, Smith's observation of the relationship between iconic architecture and its circulation as images that have cultural currency is omitted. The extract quoted above from the nomination dossier confirms that the Sydney Opera House is iconic, but does not offer an account of how this is evidenced. However, Smith does acknowledge that architecture recognised as iconic is also widely disseminated through its representations, and that these representations have value for those engaged with them. In other words, Smith acknowledges the social and subjective components of the condition of iconicity.

The relationship between iconic architecture and its widespread representation is also part of Charles Jencks' semiological reading of architecture as a 'sign'. In his oeuvre on Post-Modern Architecture and iconic buildings, Jencks observes that the Sydney Opera House has been described as many different things; shells, petals unfolding, sails on the harbour and even a scrum of nuns! These metaphors are acknowledged in the nomination, but not as part of its value as world-famous iconic building, instead as a characteristic of its aesthetic value in terms of the architecture.[74] This is significant because it fails to acknowledge the way in which, like Smith, Jencks somewhat unknowingly implies that the iconicity of architecture is located in its reception. Jencks describes the way the Sydney Opera House is a mixed metaphor where:

> the shells have symbolised flowers unfolding, sailboats in the harbour, fish swallowing each other ... As with the Eiffel Tower, ambiguous meanings have finally transcended all possible functional considerations and the building has simply become a national symbol. This rare class of sign, like a Rorschach test, provokes [a] response[,] *which focuses interest on the responder*, not the sign. (Emphasis added)[75]

Jencks' statement, published in 1977, establishes the possibility that people see other familiar forms in the building, forms that break away from architectural stereotypes. It is not that the building itself figuratively depicts flowers unfolding or fish swallowing one another, but rather that its forms are suggestive and open and therefore enable these interpretations. Importantly, however, it is not the building but *individuals*, who through their imaginative mental processes associate such images with the architectural form of this building. These kinds of metaphors occur as part of the building's reception, rather than being a quality of its production. While Jencks recognises that works of architecture, such as the Sydney Opera House (and the Eiffel Tower), are iconic because of the responses they provoke he does not articulate this phenomenon in terms of the engagement of audiences with the building or acknowledge that people's responses may also occur around, and be influenced by, representations of this place.

The nomination dossier justifies the inscription of the Sydney Opera House for its value as a world-famous iconic building in terms of its recognition as an acknowledged image of beauty by its audiences and communities. The justification does not accord with the way in which this is argued as a self-evident quality of the architecture. This disparity, between the recognition of audience reception and its justification through architecture, offers means to open up wider questions about how the social value of iconic works of architecture might be evidenced. This is not to challenge that the building's architectural value is an important part of its iconic value. But rather that there is another less acknowledged part of its iconic value that recognises the connection between the social life of the Sydney Opera House, in and through its representations. This phenomenon will be described here as *socio-visual value*. This newly conceptualised and more specific value describes the building's iconic value from a social perspective, and will now be developed further in this chapter through a discussion of recent literature that addresses the Sydney Opera House as an exemplar of iconic architecture along with literature from within heritage studies that focuses on the concept of social value. These two areas offer theoretical support for the term I propose here.

Socio-visual value: social value through representations in mass media

Social value has been included as a form of place-significance in Australia's best-known heritage practice instrument, *The Burra Charter: The Australia ICOMOS Charter for Places of Cultural Significance* (*Burra Charter*), since its initial adoption in 1979. However, the heritage discourse on *social value* emerged within Australia in the 1990s as recognition for community values grew, following the reaction to the professionalisation of heritage during the 1980s. This was the same period that saw the international adoption of the *Nara Document of Authenticity*, which recognised that values are socially and cultural embedded. Social value explicitly seeks to recognise the significance of heritage for communities, groups and individuals. The definition for social value was established by Chris Johnston's seminal report, titled *What is Social Value?*, commissioned in 1992 by the Australia Heritage Commission.[76] In this report Johnston states that:

> our surroundings are more than their physical form and their history. Places can be the embodiments of our ideas and ideals. We attach meanings to places – meanings known to individuals and meanings shared by communities.[77]

The discourse on social value can be framed as challenging expert interpretations of heritage.[78] Denis Byrne has argued that its marginalisation is 'a poor fit for the reality of the way communities value and interact with their heritage places'.[79] During the 1980s professional architects, archaeologists and historians dominated heritage practice. Their expertise in aesthetic and historic concerns resulted in an emphasis and bias towards these values within heritage listings at this time.[80] The lack of recognition of community perspectives on places deemed as heritage was seen as problematic, particularly as one of the remits of heritage is conservation for the community.

Social value argues for the formal recognition of community values alongside those assessed from a professional perspective. The influence of the discourse on social value resulted in the substantial revision of the *Burra Charter* in 1999 to reflect this shift:

> to reflect the current concern of heritage and conservation in Australia, including conservation of intangible values. It recognises social and aesthetic values as part of cultural significance, as well as intangible values or intangible cultural heritage referred to by UNESCO as an integral aspect of heritage significance.[81]

Where previously the *Burra Charter* defined cultural significance solely in terms of aesthetic, historic, scientific or social value, the 1999 revision added spiritual value and articulated that 'cultural significance is embodied in the *place* itself, its *fabric, setting, use, associations, meanings*, records, *related places* and *related objects*' (original emphasis).[82] The explicit articulation of spiritual value as part of social value is indicative of the shift towards recognising less easily defined and more subjective values as an important part of heritage significance. In addition, the recognition that these values exist, not only in the place itself, but also in its use, associations, meanings, related places and related objects, implies a broader understanding of the way significance is embodied. This revision was preceded by revisions in 1987 of the 1981 *Burra Charter* with a set of guidelines on cultural significance that expanded on several issues including social value, adopted in 1984. Subsequently the guidelines were incorporated and integrated into later revisions.[83]

The most recent version of the *Burra Charter*, which was revised in 2013, positions social value as more closely aligned with intangible heritage.[84] While Australia is yet to ratify the UNESCO *Convention for the Safeguarding of the Intangible Cultural Heritage*[85] and the definition of intangible heritage at an instrumental level is distinct from social value, the *Burra Charter*'s inclusion of the 'intangible dimensions' of places implies that cultural significance is embodied within and across complex and diverse forms of culture.

The ongoing revisions to the *Burra Charter*, as outlined so far, are indicative of the increasing attention towards recognising that the way people use places, for ceremonial or pragmatic activities, are ways in which such places *gain* significance. It is through such activities that communities develop important associations and meanings that are not necessarily inherent within the materiality of the places themselves. In including social values and the intangibility of places, the *Burra Charter* recognises that significance extends beyond the physical limits and material components of sites, situating related places and related objects as elements that can embody and contribute to the overall significance of places of heritage.

Whilst the *Burra Charter* is not a legal instrument, but a best-practice guide, its influence on the Australian heritage framework is evident in the criteria used at a national level. The Sydney Opera House was inscribed onto the National Heritage List on 12 July 2005.[86] The inscription states that the Sydney Opera House fulfils the threshold of 'outstanding heritage value to the nation' in six of the nine criteria for the National Heritage List.[87] Two of the nine criteria specifically position the value of places in relation to communities. The first is Criterion (e), 'Aesthetic Characteristics', which states that a place fulfils this criterion for its 'importance in exhibiting particular aesthetic characteristics valued by a community or cultural group'.[88] The second is Criterion (g), 'Social Value', which states that a place is valued for the 'strong or special association with a particular community or cultural group for social, cultural or spiritual reasons'.[89] Socio-visual value incorporates both these criteria, and the Sydney Opera House is already recognised for both of these in its inscription on the National Heritage List. However, while recognised, these values are not well justified through evidence.

The way in which the inscription of the Sydney Opera House on the National Heritage List states that the building fulfils Criterion (e) 'Aesthetic Characteristics' and Criterion (g) 'Social Value' demonstrates the way these values are closely intertwined. Under Criterion (e) 'Aesthetic Characteristics' the inscription describes the social attachment that people have with this place as 'the building's ability to *emotionally move people* and invoke a strong aesthetic response', while under Criterion (g) 'Social Value' it describes how the building's role as a national emblem inspired 'the *logo* used to promote the 2000 Olympic Games held in Sydney' (emphasis added).[90] The National Heritage listing clearly brings the building's aesthetic value together with its social value, where both of these values are understood to be ways in which communities hold esteem for and engage with places of heritage significance.

The interconnection of social and aesthetic values as part of community-held perspectives on heritage has already been observed in scholarly literature. Both Haig Beck and Ken Taylor explore the connection of these values to communities and argue that aesthetics should be conceived in terms of human perception and emotional attachment rather than 'design appreciation'.[91] The National Heritage List, however, defines community in relation to these two criteria in a specific way. A community or cultural group is defined through their 'shared social organisation, culture and spiritual values' and can include the Australian community as a whole.[92] While community is often thought of as geographically based, it can also be formed through common beliefs or shared cultural backgrounds. This appears to be a common-sense approach for places of significance at a national level. But how can the community be defined for a World Heritage site, such as the Sydney Opera House, where those who feel a sense of attachment to this place are not solely located in Australia, or are likely to be part of other cultures? And while it is possible to use national emblems, such as an Olympic logo as evidence of the building's social value in terms of an Australian community, how do representations at an international level evidence the social value of the Sydney Opera House?

The assessment and recognition of social value is not straightforward.[93] To address this Australia ICOMOS held a workshop in 1994 to discuss the development of methods for the assessment of social value. Heritage practitioners, scholars and representatives of the Australian Heritage Commission attended the workshop. The overarching theme in the papers presented at the workshop was the idea of community involvement in the assessment process. Chris Johnston advocated careful observation, interviews and nuanced research,[94] while others such as Gregory Young proposed cultural mapping as a method.[95] All of these methods are predicated on the idea that a community is invited to participate in the assessment process, and that evidence of social value is often intangible and must be drawn out through consultation and participation.

In spite of efforts to develop methodologies to assess and document social value during the 1990s, research by Shaun Canning and Dirk Spenneman in 2001 demonstrated that listings were under-represented in this category. They argue that this is because:

> the methodologies currently employed in Australian cultural heritage management … cannot assess social value in anything but a cursory manner. The established (and dominant) methods of quantifiable measurement, such as those used in the physical or natural sciences, are in no way appropriate for the assessment of social value. These dominant positivist techniques cannot accurately determine the depth of community feeling and attachment to cultural or natural environments – the very attributes that create a sense of place or identity.[96]

Canning and Spenneman articulate the difficulty in producing reliable empirical methods for the evaluation of highly subjective values, such as a 'sense of attachment'. Whilst there is an increasing desire to recognise social value as a reason for the inscription of places as heritage, the development of defensible tools for their assessment is still needed. More recently, about 40 of the 104 places on the National Heritage List are inscribed for their social value (Criterion (g)) and only one is exclusively listed under this criterion.[97] This confirms that while social value is acknowledged, its use as a primary criterion for inscription is still not commonplace.

Social value is aligned with other heritage concepts. For example, Johnston's report on the evaluation of inspirational landscapes is arguably a methodology for a specific type of social value.[98] The term 'inspirational landscapes' is used in heritage discourse to describe the 'profound emotional response' that people have to places. Johnston's methodological tool cites stories, art, images, creative expressions, visitations, actions and cultural practices as indicative of social value.[99] Although the focus is on natural environments, rather than works of architecture such as the Sydney Opera House, the proposed indicators listed point to the importance of representations in evidencing the social value. Forms of culture such as stories, art and creative expressions exist independently of other methods for assessing social value such as interviews and workshops. Such forms of culture are ways in which social value is evidenced in people's everyday lives. At the same time, they are representations, an aspect that is central to iconicity. The discourse of social value offers clues for how the sense of visual attachment that people feel for places, such as the Sydney Opera House, might be evidenced at an international level through representations, and the literature on iconic architecture that has emerged since the 2006 World Heritage nomination of the Sydney Opera House makes valuable observations for understanding iconic value from a social perspective.

The first part of the chapter described the work of Terry Smith and Leslie Sklair in terms of contemporary conceptualisations of iconic architecture. Key to this discussion was Sklair's assertion that the contemporary use of the term iconic is more usually associated with a sense of fame or popularity and frequent representation, than with traditional associations with a religious image. The chapter also situated Smith's idea of the iconomy, which he uses to describe the global flow of representations and expand upon the relationship between iconic architecture and its representation in mass media. Importantly, both Sklair and Smith acknowledge social interaction and representations in their conceptualisation of iconic architecture. This connection is not just evident in the work of Sklair and Smith, but also in the observations of others who consider the role of representations for the Sydney Opera House, and architecture more generally.

In 2006, Richard Weston wrote a book chapter for an edited collection published to celebrate the 50-year anniversary of the Sydney Opera House competition. In 'Monumental Appeal: Reflections on the Sydney Opera House', Weston writes about the iconic value of the Sydney Opera House and connects the ubiquity with which the building is represented with its dissemination in mass media. Although not explicitly like Sklair and Smith, Weston recognises that buildings become iconic, rather than being inherently so. He understands that iconicity is not simply a factor of the architecture and questions:

> what combination of intrinsic properties and extrinsic circumstances can it be, then, that has elevated [only these] buildings to the status of 'world monuments'?[100]

Weston's explanation is that:

> to achieve such almost universal recognition they [buildings] must, by definition, be ubiquitous in the mass media ... figure almost *ad nauseum* in advertising generally, and in the world of travel in particular ... and to achieve this they, or rather a recognisable image of them must be reducible to the scale of a postage stamp and reproducible as almost anything from a key fob to bar of soap, to paperweight, mantelpiece ornament or pencil sharpener.[101]

For Weston the 'instant recognition' of the Sydney Opera House by its communities and audiences is the result of the building's repeated and frequent representation *ad nauseum* in the mass media. Sklair, too, notes that iconicity and the dissemination of representations are connected. For Sklair, 'the importance of drawings and photography in establishing the iconic status of buildings or spaces is obvious in the history of architecture'.[102] Although Sklair's statement is a generalisation, it raises an important and under-addressed area of research in the field of architecture, namely its reception in mass media.[103] The field of architecture has generally been more focused on questions of production than those of reception.[104] The study of representation in the field of architecture has been far more concerned with its role in the process of design, rather than its role after its construction in mass media. Kester Rattenbury takes up this subject in her edited collection, *This is Not Architecture*. Here she explores the way representations of architecture work to frame our understandings of the built objects themselves:

> Architecture's relationship with its representation is peculiar, powerful and absolutely critical. Architecture is driven by belief in the nature of the real and the physical: the specific qualities of one thing – its material, form, arrangement, substance, detail – over another. It is absolutely rooted in the idea of 'the thing itself'. Yet it is discussed, illustrated, explained – even defined – almost entirely through its representations.[105]

For Rattenbury, the representation of architecture is a powerful force in the way that buildings are understood, at both an academic and popular level. She asserts that the representation of architecture in the media is critical because it 'affects how we interpret and value architecture. At the level of discussion, publication and reference, representation arguably surpasses the architecture itself'.[106] She makes a critical distinction between the practice of architecture, the edifices created and the way in which representations circulating in mass media, in the iconomy, are a means through which our understandings of buildings and the built environment are developed. Rattenbury articulates the important role that representations play *post factum*, after the building has been realised. She asserts that representations in the media inform our notions about the significance of particular works of architecture by making certain buildings familiar to us through the picturing of actual built edifices.

   The references made by Weston, Sklair, Smith and Rattenbury to the role representation in mass media plays in constructing our ideas about architecture, connects the popularity of the Sydney Opera House with its representation and circulation in mass media. The iconic value of this place is not simply an attribute of the architecture, it is also a marker of social value (Figure 2.2). Representations offer a means to investigate socio-visual value, understood as the particular aesthetic attachment that people have to iconic works of architecture.

Figure 2.2 World-famous iconic buildings comprise architectural value and social value.

Scholars within the field of Critical Heritage Studies consider social value as a central issue for contemporary definitions of cultural heritage. In *The Uses of Heritage*, Laurajane Smith's seminal text, she proposes that heritage is not a material artefact, but instead a cultural process of where meaning is constructed.[107] She argues that places become culturally significant because of the way in which we ascribe value to them. The concept coined here, that is social value, is underpinned by this argument. Rather than accepting that iconic value is simply a characteristic of a work of architecture, socio-visual value expands this to include the way people use representation to express, exchange or hold on to the value that the Sydney Opera House has for them. The intellectual shift towards understanding the value of heritage from the perspective of people is exemplified by Dawson Munjeri's often cited assertion that:

> Cultural heritage should speak through the values that people give it and not the other way around. Objects, collections, buildings, etc. become recognized as heritage when they express the value of a *society* and so the tangible can only be understood and interpreted through the intangible. *Society and values* are intrinsically linked. (Original emphasis)[108]

The result of the growing emphasis on social perspectives of heritage is that heritage is increasingly being characterised as a dynamic social and cultural process located within society rather than abstracted from it.[109] Smith's provocative position asserts that the material fabric of heritage is not inherently significant; instead, she argues that it becomes significant through what people's activities, uses and associations with it. In other words, it is the meanings assigned to material forms of culture that make them heritage. Following on from this position, Smith also makes a case for privileging heritage from the perspective of the present day, rather than the past. Importantly, this positions heritage in relation to communities where significance, and what is recognised as heritage, is determined by cultural processes. This position resituates the concept of social value at the centre of contemporary understandings of heritage.

Conclusion

Understood within the contemporary discourses on iconic architecture and World Heritage inscription, social value can be connected with widespread representation of the Sydney Opera House in the mass media. The recognition of this place for its value as a 'world-famous iconic building' reveals a desire to recognise the social value of this place and a discrepancy in the way it is accounted for as a self-evident quality of the architecture. The chapter makes a case for a more explicit term to describe the social value of iconic works of architecture. The widespread representation of the Sydney Opera House is linked together with its social value through the original concept of socio-visual value. The remainder of the book explores how representations can evidence socio-visual value.

Notes

1 UNESCO Intergovernmental Committee for the Protection of the World Cultural and Natural Heritage, Paris (2008) *Operational Guidelines for the Implementation of the World Heritage Convention*. Retrieved: 26/11/2012, from: http://whc.unesco.org/archive/opguide08-en.pdf, Article 51.

2 In 2006 the Arabian Oryx Sanctuary was removed from the World Heritage List due to Oman's failure to preserve the outstanding universal value of the Sanctuary. UNESCO (2007) 'Twenty-Two New Sites Inscribed on Unesco's World Heritage List, and One Deleted During Committee Meeting in Christchurch'. *World Heritage Centre*. Retrieved: 26/06/2012, from: http://whc.unesco.org/en/news/365.

3 UNESCO (2007) 'Sydney Opera House'. *World Heritage Centre*. Retrieved: 26/06/2012, from: http://whc.unesco.org/en/list/166rev.

4 Philip Drew (2007) 'Romanticism Revisited: Jørn Utzon's Sydney Opera House'. *Architectural Theory Review*, 12 (2), pp. 121–145; Kenneth Frampton and John Cava (1995) *Studies in Tectonic Culture: The Poetics of Construction in Nineteenth and Twentieth Century Architecture*. Cambridge, MA: The MIT Press; Sigfried Giedion (1965) 'Jørn Utzon and the Third Generation: Three Works by Jørn Utzon – a New Chapter of Space Time and Architecture', *Zodiac*, 14, pp. 36–47; Philip Goad (1997) 'An Appeal for Modernism: Sigfried Giedion and the Sydney Opera House', *Fabrications*, 8, pp. 129–145; Christian Norberg-Schulz and Yukio Futagawa (1980) 'Jørn Utzon: Sydney Opera House, Sydney, Australia, 1957–73', *Global Architecture*, 54, pp. 54–58.

5 Peter Jones (2006) *Ove Arup: Masterbuilder of the Twentieth Century*. New Haven: Yale University Press; Yuzo Mikami and Osamu Murai (2001) *Utzon's Sphere: Sydney Opera House: How It Was Designed and Built*. Tokyo: Shokokusha; John Nutt (2006) 'Constructing a Legacy: Technological Innovation and Achievements'. In *Building a Masterpiece: The Sydney Opera House*, edited by Anne Watson. Aldershot: Lund Humphries, pp. 104–121; David Taffs (2006) 'Computers and the Opera House: Pioneering a New Technology'. In *Building a Masterpiece: The Sydney Opera House*, edited by Anne Watson. Aldershot: Lund Humphries, pp. 84–103; Paolo Tombesi (2005) 'Iconic Public Buildings as Sites of Technological Innovation'. *Harvard Design Magazine*, 21; Jack Zunz (1988) 'Sydney Revisited'. *The Arup Journal*, 23, pp. 2–11.

6 Sophia Labadi (2007) 'Representations of the Nation and Cultural Diversity in Discourses on World Heritage'. *Journal of Social Archaeology*, 7 (2), p. 148.

7 Alois Riegl (2007 [1903]) 'The Modern Cult of Monuments: Its Character and Its Origin'. In *Cultural Heritage: Critical Concepts in Media and Cultural Studies*, vol. 1, edited by Laurajane Smith, translated by Kurt W. Foster and Diane Ghirardo in 1982 from German. London: Routledge, pp. 114–142.

8 Jukka Jokilehto (2005 [1999]) *A History of Architectural Conservation*. Oxford: Elsevier Butterworth-Heinemann, p. 215.

9 UNESCO (1972) *Convention Concerning the Protection of the World Cultural and Natural Heritage*. Retrieved: 26/11/2012, from: http://whc.unesco.org/archive/convention-en.pdf, Article 1.

10 Labadi, 'Representations of the Nation', p. 148. In this article Sophia Labadi is building on the work of Timothy Darvill and Ian Hodder Timothy Darvill (1995) 'Value Systems in Archaeology'. In *Managing Archaeology*, edited by Malcolm A. Cooper, John Carman, Anthony Firth and David Wheatley. London: Taylor & Francis, p. 40; Ian Hodder (1985) 'Postprocessual Archaeology'. *Advances in Archaeological Method and Theory*, 8, pp. 1–26.

11 Leslie Sklair (2011) 'Iconic Architecture and Urban, National, and Global Identities'. In *Cities & Sovereignty: Identity Politics in Urban Spaces*, edited by Diane E. Davis and Nora Libertun De Duren. Bloomington: Indiana University Press, pp. 179–195. Leslie Sklair has more recently undertaken an extensive exploration on iconic architecture in: Leslie Sklair (2017) *The Icon Project: Architecture, Cities, and Capitalist Globalization*. New York: Oxford University Press.

12 'Icon, N.' (1993) In *The New Shorter Oxford English Dictionary*, vol. 2, edited by Leslie Brown. Oxford: Clarendon Press.

13 For example, see the work of Ernst Hans Gombrich for a traditional perspective and the work of William J. Thomas Mitchell for a literary perspective. Ernst Hans Gombrich (1972) *Symbolic Images*. London: Phaidon; William J. Thomas Mitchell (1986) *Iconology: Image, Text, Ideology*. Chicago: University of Chicago Press.

14 Leslie Sklair cites Gombrich in this article. I acknowledge that there is a vast literature on icons from the fields of visual studies and art theory; however, my intention here is to remain focused on its use in regard to architecture, and to apply this literature to the concepts embedded within the *World Heritage Convention*. Sklair, 'Iconic Architecture', p. 181; Gombrich. *Symbolic Images*, p. 124.

15 UNESCO (2007) 'Sydney Opera House'. *World Heritage Centre*.

16 Sklair, 'Iconic Architecture', p. 181.

17 Foster and Partners' 40-storey tower in London at 30 St Mary Axe is known as the Gherkin. Utzon's Sydney Opera House is often described as sails on the harbour and the Dr Chau Chak Wing in Sydney by Frank Gehry has been described as a brown paper bag. Elizabeth Farrelly (2014) 'Frank Gehry's UTS Building Is No Opera House'. *Sydney Morning Herald*, 13 January. Retrieved: 06/01/2016, from: www.smh.com.au/comment/frank-gehrys-uts-building-is-no-opera-house-20140709-zt144.html#ixzz3wRZaPioR.

18 Yahaya Ahmad traces the evolution of national and international heritage instruments, noting their contribution to the discourse and to the development of future instruments, in: Yahaya Ahmad (2006) 'The Scope and Definitions of Heritage: From Tangible to Intangible'. *International Journal of Heritage Studies*, 12 (3), pp. 292–300.

19 Here I reference the version of the *Burra Charter* current at the time the nomination document was being prepared. The 2013 *Burra Charter* is the most current version at time of writing. ICOMOS Australia (1999). *The Burra Charter: The Australia ICOMOS Charter for Places of Cultural Significance 1999*. Retrieved: 31/12/2015, from: http://australia.icomos.org/publications/burra-charter-practice-notes/burra-charter-archival-documents/, Article 1.2.

20 Graham Brooks (1992) 'Australia's Methodology for Conserving Cultural Heritage'. *Places*, 8 (1), p. 84.

21 The term 'place' is widely used in geography, and also in sociology, architecture and philosophy. According to Tim Cresswell it became a central concept for humanistic geographers such as Edward Relph and Yi Fu Tuan in the late 1970s and early 1980s. Tim Cresswell (2005) *Place: A Short Introduction*. Malden, MA: Blackwell, p. 12. It was around this time that Norberg-Schulz developed his ideas on architecture and phenomenology that were highly influenced by the philosophy of Martin Heidegger. Christian Norberg-Schulz (1996 [1976]) 'The Phenomenon of Place'. In *Theorizing a New Agenda for Architecture: An Anthology of Architectural Theory 1965–1995*, edited by Kate Nesbitt. New York: Princeton Architectural Press, pp. 412–428.

22 In this book chapter, Marc Askew elaborates on Christina Cameron's 2005 paper cited below. Marc Askew (2010) 'The Magic List of Global Status: UNESCO, World Heritage and the Agenda of States'. In *Heritage and Globalisation*, edited by Sophia Labadi and Colin Long. London: Routledge, p. 30. Christina Cameron (2008 [2005]) 'Evolution of the Application of "Outstanding Universal Value" for Cultural and Natural Heritage'. In *The World Heritage List: What Is Ouv? Defining the Outstanding Universal Value of Cultural World Heritage Properties*, edited by Jukka Jokilehto. Paris: ICOMOS, pp. 71–74.

23 UNESCO (2007) 'Sydney Opera House'. *World Heritage Centre*.

24 In Chapter 7, I also discuss the use of Criterion (vi). UNESCO Intergovernmental Committee for the Protection of the World Cultural and Natural Heritage, Paris (2011) *Operational Guidelines for the Implementation of the World Heritage Convention*. Retrieved: 26/11/2012, from: http://whc.unesco.org/archive/opguide11-en.pdf, paragraph 77.

25 UNESCO (2007) 'Sydney Opera House (Australia) No 166 Rev: Advisory Body Evaluation'. *World Heritage Centre.* Retrieved: 27/04/2013, from: http://whc.unesco.org/archive/advisory_body_evaluation/166rev.pdf.

26 Jukka Jokilehto (2008) *The World Heritage List: What Is Ouv? Defining the Outstanding Universal Value of Cultural World Heritage Properties.* Paris: ICOMOS, p. 18.

27 Iconic value as a World Heritage value has also been the focus of research by Mario Gabriele Roberto Rimini. In his doctoral thesis he draws together the concepts of 'outstanding universal value' from the *World Heritage Convention* with broader notions around the term 'wilderness' where both are conceptualised as ways of describing iconicity. However, his focus here is natural landscapes and the way inscription onto the World Heritage List increases global attention on places, rather than the inscription of places for their already existing value as iconic works of architecture. Mario Gabriele Roberto Rimini (2010) *Iconic Lands: Wilderness as a Reservation Criterion for World Heritage.* PhD, Institute of Environmental Studies, University of New South Wales, Sydney.

28 UNESCO Intergovernmental Committee for the Protection of the World Cultural and Natural Heritage (2011) *Operational Guidelines for the Implementation of the World Heritage Convention,* paragraph 77(vi).

29 Australian Government (1980) *Nomination of the Sydney Opera House in Its Harbour Setting with the Sydney Harbour Bridge and the Surrounding Waterways of Sydney Harbour from Bradley's Head to Mcmahon's Point for Inclusion in the World Heritage List.* Canberra: Australian Heritage Commission, p. 11.

30 The 1980 *Operational Guidelines* defines Criterion (iv) as 'an outstanding example of a type of structure which illustrates a significant stage in history' and Criterion (v) as 'an outstanding example of a traditional human settlement which is representative of a culture and which has become vulnerable under the impact of irreversible change'. UNESCO Intergovernmental Committee for the Protection of the World Cultural and Natural Heritage, Paris (1980) *Operational Guidelines for the Implementation of the World Heritage Convention.* Retrieved: 26/11/2012, from: http://whc.unesco.org/archive/opguide80.pdf, Article 16a.

31 Australian Government (1996) *Sydney Opera House in Its Harbour Setting.* Glebe: Historic Houses Trust of NSW for the Commonwealth Department of the Environment, Sport and Territories and NSW Department of Urban Affairs and Planning, p. 97.

32 Australian Government (1996) *Sydney Opera House in Its Harbour Setting,* p. 97.

33 The nomination cites two paintings by the Australian artist, Lloyd Rees. Australian Government (1996) *Sydney Opera House in Its Harbour Setting,* p. 108.

34 Between 1980 and 1996 the autonomous use of Criterion (vi) was limited to 'exceptional circumstances'. It could however, be used in conjunction with another criterion. The result was that only four sites were listed autonomously under Criterion (vi) in comparison to 100 listed through other criteria. During 1996 to 2005 the autonomous use of Criterion (vi) was completely removed. Currently this restriction has been softened: there is a preference for the use of Criterion (vi) in conjunction with another criterion. In March 2011, 200 of 911 properties were listed under Criterion (vi) but only 11 under its autonomous use. For a more detailed report on the use of this criterion see the UNESCO 2001 report cited below. Olwen Beazley (2009) 'Protecting Intangible Heritage Values through the World Heritage Convention?' *Historic Environment,* 22 (3), p. 8; Jokilehto, *The World Heritage List,* p. 32; UNESCO (2001) *Information Document: Analysis of the Application of Cultural Criterion (Vi).* Retrieved: 27/04/2013, from: http://whc.unesco.org/uploads/events/documents/event-827-9.pdf.

35 UNESCO Intergovernmental Committee for the Protection of the World Cultural and Natural Heritage (2011) *Operational Guidelines for the Implementation of the World Heritage Convention,* paragraph 78.

36 UNESCO Intergovernmental Committee for the Protection of the World Cultural and Natural Heritage, Paris (2015) *Operational Guidelines for the Implementation of the World Heritage Convention.* Retrieved: 01/01/2016, from: http://whc.unesco.org/document/137843, paragraph 88.

37 UNESCO Intergovernmental Committee for the Protection of the World Cultural and Natural Heritage (2015) *Operational Guidelines for the Implementation of the World Heritage Convention,* paragraph 89.

38 UNESCO Intergovernmental Committee for the Protection of the World Cultural and Natural Heritage, Paris (1999) *Operational Guidelines for the Implementation of the World Heritage Convention*. Retrieved: 26/11/2012, from: http://whc.unesco.org/archive/opguide99.pdf, paragraph 24 (b) (i).

39 UNESCO Intergovernmental Committee for the Protection of the World Cultural and Natural Heritage (2008) *Operational Guidelines for the Implementation of the World Heritage Convention*, paragraph 80.

40 UNESCO Intergovernmental Committee for the Protection of the World Cultural and Natural Heritage (2008) *Operational Guidelines for the Implementation of the World Heritage Convention*, paragraph 81.

41 ICOMOS (1994) *Nara Document on Authenticity*. Retrieved: 26/04/2013, from: www.icomos.org/charters/nara-e.pdf.

42 ICOMOS (1994) *Nara Document on Authenticity*, Preamble, paragraph 2.

43 Laurajane Smith (2006) *Uses of Heritage*. London: Routledge, p. 11.

44 Alan Saunders, Philip Drew, Sylvia Lawson, Dennis Watkins, Anne Watson and Alan John (2006) 'By Design: Writing the House' [Radio Broadcast]. Sydney: ABC Radio National, 3 June. Retrieved: 23/11/2012, from: www.abc.net.au/radionational/programs/bydesign/writing-the-house/3326266.

45 Anne Watson (2013) *Peter Hall and the Sydney Opera House: The 'Lost' Years 1966–70*. Sydney: Sydney University; Ben Cheshire, Greg Hassall and Kieran Ricketts (2015) 'ABC Australian Story: The Man Who Fixed the "Plain Illegal" Sydney Opera House'. Retrieved: 15/03/2016, from: www.abc.net.au/news/2016-01-31/peter-hall-architect-who-fixed-opera-house-after-utzon-departed/7127160; Peter Webber (2013) *The Phantom of the Opera House*. Boorowa: Watermark Press; Anne Watson (2012) 'Divided Loyalties: Peter Hall, Philip Parsons and the Dilemma of Utzon's Return'. *Fabrications*, 22 (2).

46 D. Fairchild Ruggles and Helaine Silverman (2009) *Intangible Heritage Embodied*. London: Springer, p. 6.

47 Prior to this there had been many articles in newspapers and professional journals, but it took two years before the significance of Utzon's scheme was theorised in the academy.

48 Arthur Drexler was the Director, and Wilder Green the Assistant Director of the Department of Architecture and Design at the Museum of Modern Art (MoMA), New York. Wilder Green went on to become the Director of the MoMA's Exhibition Program. Three other works were part of the 1959 *Architecture and Imagery* exhibition. They were: Notre Dame de Royan in France (1958) by Guilliame Gillet, First Presbyterian Church in Stamford, Connecticut (1958) by Wallace Harrison and Max Abramovitz (known as Harrison and Abramovtiz), and the Trans-World Airlines Terminal at Idlewild Airport, New York (1956–1962) by Eero Saarinen & Associates. Arthur Drexler and Wilder Green (1959) 'Architecture and Imagery – Four New Buildings'. *Museum of Modern Art* [Press Release]. MOMA, 10 February. Retrieved: 27/11/2012, from: www.moma.org/docs/press_archives/2448/releases/MOMA_1959_0014.pdf?2010. The selection of Utzon's scheme became contentious as problems arose in the building's realisation. Interestingly, Eero Saarinen had been one of the judges on the Sydney Opera House competition. Philip Drew states that the popular myth that has circulated put forward that Saarinen, late to the assessment, retrieved Utzon's scheme from the pile of discarded entries, in the process implying the other judges, Henry Ingham Ashworth, Cobden Parkes and Leslie Martin, did not possess the acumen to distinguish 'the one worthy scheme'. Drew's account suggests Martin selected the winning scheme, and Peter Murray suggests that it was Martin and Saarinen. The essence of the story is that, apart from Saarinen, the other judges were unable to recognise architectural genius from mediocre schemes. Philip Drew (2001) *The Masterpiece: A Secret Life*. 2nd edn. South Yarra: Hardie Grant Books, p. 137. Peter Murray (2004) *The Saga of the Sydney Opera House: The Dramatic Story of the Design and Construction of the Icon of Modern Australia*. New York: Spon Press, p. 10.

49 Drexler and Green, 'Architecture and Imagery – Four New Buildings'.

50 Drexler and Green, 'Architecture and Imagery – Four New Buildings'.

51 The Sydney Opera House had previously appeared in *Zodiac* in 1959, as part of an article on emerging Danish architects, where Keld Helmer-Petersen wrote on Utzon and reported on Utzon's winning scheme and its progress. In 1962 Utzon published an article that discussed his ideas on the 'plateau' as an architectural type, in reference to the Sydney Opera

House. However, neither of these articles specifically theorise on the value of the Sydney Opera House to the development of Modern Architecture. Keld Helmer-Petersen and Jørn Utzon (1959) 'A New Personality: Jørn Utzon'. *Zodiac*, 5, pp. 70–105; Jørn Utzon (1962) 'Platforms and Plateaus: Ideas of a Danish Architect'. *Zodiac*, 10, pp. 112–140.

52 Giedion. 'Jørn Utzon and the Third Generation', p. 36.

53 Utzon had travelled to Mexico in 1949. There he visited the ruins of Monte Alban (in the state of Oaxaca), Uxmal and Chichén Itzá (in the state of Yucatan), three examples of Mayan architectural complexes. Drew, *The Masterpiece*, pp. 73–76; Giedion. 'Jørn Utzon and the Third Generation', p. 39. The presumption that ancient ruins are 'anonymous' when in fact they are Indigenous is indicative of the way these forms are unproblematically incorporated into the design of the Sydney Opera House. This theme is taken up in Philip Goad's excellent journal article, 'An Appeal for Modernism', where he argues that Giedion used the Sydney Opera House as means to continue the Modernist project by framing the building's value through its use of primitive typologies from exotic cultures (Mexico) and the use of technology. Giedion's *Zodiac* article of 1965 became a chapter in *Space Time and Architecture* two years later. Giedion's text on Modernism had almost canonic status at the time. Goad, 'An Appeal for Modernism', p. 130.

54 Philip Drew (1972) *Third Generation: The Changing Meaning of Architecture*. London: Pall Mall Press, p. 37.

55 Charles Jencks (1973) *Modern Movements in Architecture*. Garden City: Anchor Press, p. 66.

56 Semiotic theories of communication were part of Linguistic Theory. These ideas were later developed in cultural studies in the work of Stuart Hall. Stuart Hall (1997) *Representation: Cultural Representations and Signifying Practices*. London: Sage, in association with The Open University.

57 Charles Jencks (1977) *The Language of Post-Modern Architecture*. New York: Rizzoli, p. 42.

58 Jencks, *The Language of Post-Modern Architecture*, p. 42.

59 Christian Norberg-Schulz (1926–2000) was an architectural historian who developed the ideas embedded in the third generation of Modernism, around humanising architecture, using phenomenology. He was influential in the development of discourses on 'sense of place' and 'genus loci', which emphasise the experience of architecture. In 1980 he co-wrote a book on the Sydney Opera House with Utzon, with whom he had a social connection through a mutual friend, Arne Korsmo. Norberg-Schulz and Futagawa, 'Jørn Utzon'.

60 Christian Norberg-Schulz, Jørn Utzon and Yukio Futagawa (1980) *Sydney Opera House: Sydney, Australia, 1957–73*. Tokyo: A.D.A. Edita, unpaginated

61 Christian Norberg-Schulz (1996) 'The Sydney Opera House: International Comparison, an Evaluation of Its Position in the History of Modern Architecture'. In *Sydney Opera House in Its Harbour Setting, Unpublished World Heritage Nomination by the Government of Australia*, edited by Government of Australia. Glebe: Historic Houses Trust of NSW for the Commonwealth Department of the Environment, Sport and Territories and NSW Department of Urban Affairs, pp. 161–173.

62 This book was republished in 1977, 1978, 1980, 1984, 1988 and 1991. The same position is reiterated in his 2005 book on iconic architecture. Charles Jencks (2005) *The Iconic Building*. New York: Rizzoli.

63 Australian Government (2006) *Sydney Opera House: Nomination by the Government of Australia for Inscription on the World Heritage List*. Canberra: Department of Environment and Heritage and NSW Heritage Office. Retrieved: 28/11/2012, from: http://whc.unesco.org/uploads/nominations/166rev.pdf, pp. 25–56. UNESCO (2011) *Preparing World Heritage Nominations (Second Edition)*. World Heritage Centre. Retrieved: 27/04/2013, from: http://whc.unesco.org/uploads/activities/documents/activity-643-1.pdf, p. 8.

64 Australian Government (2006) *Sydney Opera House: Nomination by the Government of Australia for Inscription on the World Heritage List*, p. 42.

65 The nomination dossier in this instance is citing Richard Weston and the Pritzker Prize 2003 Statement. Australian Government (2006) *Sydney Opera House: Nomination by the Government of Australia for Inscription on the World Heritage List*, p. 42; Richard Weston (2002) *Utzon: Inspiration, Vision, Architecture*. Hellerupis: Edition Bløndal, p. 185; Bill N. Lacy (2003) 'Jorn Utzon 2003 Laureate: Jury Citation'. *The Pritzker Architecture Prize*. Retrieved: 27/04/2013, from: www.pritzkerprize.com/2003/jury.

66 Stan Allen and Diana Agrest (2000) *Practice: Architecture, Technique and Representation.* Amsterdam: Gordon and Breach, p. XXI; Robin Evans (1997) *Translations from Drawing to Building and Other Essays.* London: Architectural Association.

67 Here the nomination dossier is citing Philip Goad's unpublished written statement. Philip Goad (2005) 'Unpublished Written Statement Commissioned for the World Heritage Nomination for Sydney Opera House'. Australian Department of the Environment and Heritage and the New South Wales Heritage Office; Australian Government (2006) *Sydney Opera House: Nomination by the Government of Australia for Inscription on the World Heritage List*, p. 43.

68 The quotes cited in the nomination dossier are from the work of Richard Weston. Weston, *Utzon*, p. 186; Australian Government (2006) *Sydney Opera House: Nomination by the Government of Australia for Inscription on the World Heritage List.*

69 Weston, *Utzon*, pp. 33–51; Terry Smith (2003) 'The Dialectics of Disappearance: Architectural Iconotypes between Clashing Cultures'. *Critical Quarterly*, 45 (1–2), pp. 1–2; Jencks. *The Iconic Building*; Goad, 'Unpublished Written Statement Commissioned for the World Heritage Nomination for Sydney Opera House'; Dennis Sharp (2005) 'Unpublished Written Statement Commissioned for the World Heritage Nomination for Sydney Opera House'. Australian Department of the Environment and Heritage and the New South Wales Heritage Office.

70 Terry Smith (2002) 'The Political Economy of Iconotypes and the Architecture of Destination: Uluru, the Sydney Opera House and the World Trade Center'. *Architectural Theory Review*, 7 (2), pp. 1–43; Smith, 'The Dialectics of Disappearance', pp. 33–51; Terry Smith (2006) *The Architecture of Aftermath.* London: The University of Chicago Press; Terry Smith (2008) 'Spectacle Architecture before and after the Aftermath: Situating the Sydney Experience'. In *Architecture between Spectacle and Use*, edited by Anthony Vidler. Williamstown: Sterling and Francine Clark Art Institute, pp. 3–24.

71 Smith, 'The Political Economy of Iconotypes', p. 10.

72 The term iconomy has been used previously in reference to religious icons, rather than works of iconic architecture. The discussion of icon in relation to architecture within philosophy and aesthetics is discussed in: Dimitris Vardoulakis (2009) 'Between Logos and Icons: Notes Towards a Transfigurative Culture'. *Empedocles: European Journal for the Philosophy of Communication*, 1 (2), pp. 175–186.

73 Smith, 'The Political Economy of Iconotypes', p. 19, quoted in Australian Government (2006) *Sydney Opera House: Nomination by the Government of Australia for Inscription on the World Heritage List*, p. 42.

74 Australian Government (2006) *Sydney Opera House: Nomination by the Government of Australia for Inscription on the World Heritage List*, p. 32.

75 Jencks, *The Language of Post-Modern Architecture*, p. 42.

76 In 2003, Marilyn Truscott stated that the discussion paper titled 'Places of Social Significance', which she prepared with Sandy Blair for the Australian Heritage Commission, triggered the exploration of social value in 1987. Citations are offered below. Chris Johnston (1992) *What Is Social Value? A Discussion Paper.* Canberra: Australian Government Publishing Service. Sandy Blair and Marilyn Truscott (1988) *Places of Social Significance.* Australian Heritage Commission. Marilyn Truscott (2003) 'Intangible Values as Heritage in Australia'. Presented at the *Proceedings of the International Scientific Symposium Place, Memory, Meaning Preserving Intangible Values in Monuments and Sites*, Victoria Falls, Zimbabwe, 27–31 October. Retrieved: 10/07/2012, from: www.international.icomos.org/victoriafalls2003/truscott_eng.htm.

77 Johnston, *What Is Social Value?* p. iii.

78 Annie Clarke and Chris Johnston (2003) 'Time, Memory, Place and Land: Social Meaning and Heritage Conservation in Australia'. Presented at the *Proceedings of the International Scientific Symposium Place, Memory, Meaning Preserving Intangible Values in Monuments and Sites*, Victoria Falls, Zimbabwe, 27–31 October 2003. Retrieved: 13/11/2007, from: www.international.icomos.org/victoriafalls2003/papers/B3-7%20-%20Johnston.pdf.

79 Denis Byrne, Helen Brayshaw and Tracy Ireland (2003) *Social Significance: A Discussion Paper.* Sydney: Research Unit, Cultural Heritage Division, NSW National Parks and Wildlife Service. Retrieved: 07/10/2010, from: www.environment.nsw.gov.au/resources/cultureheritage/SocialSignificance.pdf, p. ix.

80   Clarke and Johnston, 'Time, Memory, Place and Land'.
81   Ahmad, 'The Scope and Definitions of Heritage', p. 297.
82   ICOMOS Australia (1984) *Guidelines to the Burra Charter: Cultural Significance*; ICOMOS Australia (1999) *The Burra Charter: The Australia ICOMOS Charter for Places of Cultural Significance 1999.*
83   ICOMOS Australia (1984). *Guidelines to the Burra Charter: Cultural Significance.*
84   ICOMOS Australia (2013) *The Burra Charter: The Australia ICOMOS Charter for Places of Cultural Significance 2013.* Retrieved: 31/12/2015, from: http://australia.icomos.org/publications/charters/.
85   As at December 2015.
86   Places inscribed onto the National Heritage List are protected under the Environment Protection and Biodiversity Conservation Act 1999 (*EPBC Act*) as described in Chapter 1.
87   Australian Government (2005) 'Place Details: Sydney Opera House, 2 Circular Quay East, Sydney, Nsw, Australia'. *Department of Sustainability, Environment, Water, Population and Communities.* Australian Heritage Database. Retrieved: 13/03/2013, from: www.environment.gov.au/cgi-bin/ahdb/search.pl?mode=place_detail;place_id=105738.
88   Australian Government (2009) *Guidelines for the Assessment of Places for the National Heritage List.* Canberra: Australia Heritage Council & Department of the Environment, Water, Heritage and the Arts, p. 34.
89   Australian Government (2009) *Guidelines for the Assessment of Places for the National Heritage List*, p. 42.
90   Australian Government (2005) 'Place Details: Sydney Opera House, 2 Circular Quay East, Sydney, Nsw, Australia'. *Department of Sustainability, Environment, Water, Population and Communities.*
91   Haig Beck (1995) 'Social and Aesthetic Values: New Assessment Methodologies for Involving the Community'. *In Place: A Cultural Heritage Bulletin*, 1, pp. 15–18; Ken Taylor (1999) 'Reconciling Aesthetic Value and Social Value: Dilemmas of Interpretation and Application'. *APT Bulletin, Landscape Preservation Comes of Age*, 30 (1), pp. 51–55.
92   Australian Government (2009) *Guidelines for the Assessment of Places for the National Heritage List*, p. 43.
93   In 2003 Chris Johnston completed a report, which developed methodologies for the assessment of Inspirational Landscapes, which overlaps with social value. One of the aims of this project was to develop methods for assessment; however, this was carried out within an Australian context. Chris Johnston, Libby Riches, Ann McGregor and Kristal Buckley (2003) *Inspirational Landscapes.* Canberra: Australian Heritage Commission, pp. 1–4.
94   Chris Johnston (1996) 'Corner Shops and Well-Trodden Ways'. In *Assessing Social Values: Communities and Experts – a Workshop Held by Australia ICOMOS*. Canberra: Australian Heritage Commission, pp. 8–11.
95   Gregory Young (1996) 'Cultural Mapping: Capturing Social Value, Challenging Silence'. In *Assessing Social Values: Communities and Experts – a Workshop Held by Australia ICOMOS*. Canberra: Australian Heritage Commission, pp. 12–17.
96   Shaun Canning and Dirk Spenneman (2001) 'Contested Space: Social Value and the Assessment of Cultural Significance in New South Wales, Australia'. In *Heritage Landscapes: Understanding Place and Communities*, edited by Maria Cotter, Bill Boyd and Jane Gardiner. Lismore: Southern Cross University Press, p. 459.
97   Search of the Australian National Heritage Register on 15 April 2016. Australian Government (2016) 'Australia's National Heritage List'. Department of the Environment. Retrieved: 08/04/2016, from: www.environment.gov.au/heritage/places/national-heritage-list.
98   Chris Landorf has also addressed the concept of social value as applied to historic environments. She approaches social value from the perspective of social sustainability and economic and social well-being indicators for a community, rather than understanding what a place might affectively means for a group of people. Chris Landorf (2011) 'Measuring the Social Value of Heritage: A Framework Based on the Evaluation of Sustainable Development'. Presented at the *Audience: Proceedings of the 28th Annual Conference of the Society of Architectural Historians, Australia and New Zealand*, State Library of

Queensland, Brisbane, Queensland, Australia, 7–10 July, pp. 1–18; Chris Landorf (2011) 'Evaluating Social Sustainability in Historic Urban Environments'. *International Journal of Heritage Studies*, 17 (5), pp. 463–477.

 99 Chris Johnston, Libby Riches, Ann McGregor and Kristal Buckley (2003) 'Inspirational Landscapes. Volume 4: Assessment Method Report'. Canberra: Australian Heritage Commission, p. 16.

100 Richard Weston (2006) 'Monumental Appeal: Reflections on the Sydney Opera House.' In *Building a Masterpiece: The Sydney Opera House*, edited by Anne Watson. Aldershot: Lund Humphries, p. 21.

101 Weston here refers to a pencil sharpener his friend Martin Schwartz possesses. Schwartz is also an architect and writer. See footnote no. 6 in: 'Monumental Appeal: Reflections on the Sydney Opera House', p. 22.

102 Sklair, 'Iconic Architecture', p. 180.

103 Sklair is a sociologist, rather than an architectural theorist or historian. My research into the area of architecture and representation reveals that much of this area focuses on representation in terms of the production of architecture, rather than in terms of its dissemination in the mass media. Notable exceptions here include the work of Beatriz Colomina and Kester Rattenbury. Kester Rattenbury (2002) *This Is Not Architecture: Media Constructions*. New York: Routledge. Colomina explores the relationship between Modern Architecture and its engagement with mass media where its representation becomes a new context for architectural production. Although Colomina's work is seminal in exploring the relationship of architecture and its representation in mass media, it is nonetheless framed in terms of the design and production of architecture, rather than its dissemination and iconicity. Beatriz Colomina and Joan Ockman (1988) *Architectureproduction*. New York: Princeton Architectural Press; Beatriz Colomina (1994) *Privacy and Publicity: Modern Architecture as Mass Media*. Cambridge, MA: The MIT Press; Beatriz Colomina (1999) 'The Private Site of Public Memory', *The Journal of Architecture*, 4 (4), pp. 337–360; Beatriz Colomina (2002) 'Architectureproduction'. In *This Is Not Architecture: Media Constructions*, edited by Kester Rattenbury. New York: Routledge, pp. 207–221. Ari Seligmann also completed a PhD dissertation on this topic in 2008. Ari D. Seligmann (2008) *Architectural Publicity in the Age of Globalization*. PhD thesis, Architecture and Urban Design, University of California Los Angeles.

104 Naomi Stead and Cristina Garduño Freeman (2013) 'Architecture and "the Act of Receiving, or the Fact of Being Received": Introduction to a Special Issue on Reception'. *Architectural Theory Review*, 18 (3).

105 Kester Rattenbury (2002) 'Introduction'. In *This Is Not Architecture: Media Constructions*, edited by Kester Rattenbury. New York: Routledge, p. xxi.

106 Rattenbury, 'Introduction', p. xxii.

107 *Uses of Heritage*, p. 2.

108 Dawson Munjeri (2004) 'Tangible and Intangible Heritage: From Difference to Convergence'. *Museum International*, 56 (1–2), p. 13.

109 This position is also held by Denis Byrne. Byrne *et al.*, *Social Significance*, p. 7.

3 Participatory culture and socio-visual value

Like many cultural icons, a myriad of representations of the Sydney Opera House exist. The popularity of the building sees it referenced and depicted in almost every shape and form. So how might this 'iconomy' offer a way to evidence and understand what the building's socio-visual value is?

The centrality of participation to new online media platforms offers a means to understand how the representations of the Sydney Opera House can be interpreted as evidence of participatory practices that embody the building's socio-visual value. Richard Weston posits 'universal recognition' is synonymous with ubiquity in mass media. He argues that buildings, such as the Sydney Opera House, must be recognisable in miniature and reproducible as 'as almost anything from a key fob to bar of soap, to paperweight, mantelpiece ornament or pencil sharpener'.[1] This points to the central role that representations play in the reception of architecture. At the time of the 2007 inscription of the Sydney Opera House onto the World Heritage list, the internet was developing rapidly from a read-only to a read-write paradigm. Many representations of the Sydney Opera House, including those that Weston describes (Figure 3.1), became available online. Searches for representations of the Sydney Opera House conducted from 2007 onwards revealed that this building appears in many different guises within popular culture (Figure 3.2). Airlines feature images of

Figure 3.1 The ubiquity of the Sydney Opera House according to Richard Weston.

Sources: left, plastic keyring purchased on eBay; middle, Sydney Opera House Soap, AUD$5.95, from their Corporate Gift Catalogue (Sydney Opera House trademark reproduced with permission of the Sydney Opera House Trust, photographer unknown, 2007); right, Sydney Opera House die cast pencil sharpener produced by Wilmot Harvey (© Wilmot Harvey, 2017).

it as a destination in travel advertisements, and the Australian Postal Corporation uses it as a national symbol on stamps. The building appears on pens and mugs and is the visual subject of a multitude of postcards. It is miniaturised and captured inside snowdomes, and sold 'by the fragment' as an authentic souvenir. The Sydney Opera House features on textiles, scarves, cushions, and as inspiration for homemade costumes as well as haute couture. The building is fashioned into hats, salt and pepper shakers, stereo speakers and campervans, while its silhouette is evident in logotypes, in artworks, and in graffiti. The Sydney Opera House is depicted in political cartoons; it provides a setting for feature films, fictional narratives, historical accounts and children's books. The illumination of the building for festivals and its defacement in the name of political activism are photographed. The form is evoked in a flower's unfolding petals, a stack of dirty dishes and an Ikea lampshade, while also rendered edible in cakes, large and small, to be shared and consumed in celebration. The building has even inspired an opera.[2]

Figure 3.2 Representations that depict the Sydney Opera House.

Collecting and ordering representations of the Sydney Opera House

The search for representations returned many examples and web pages that associate themselves in some way with the Sydney Opera House. However, as a collection of 'representations' they are not homogeneous. To begin with it is important to acknowledge that what had been collected was a set of digital images being displayed on a computer screen. Next, these are not simply images. Some are textual descriptions, some are illustrations or photographs of paintings, others are photographs of physical objects, such as a key ring. They are not all simply photographs of the building and they are not all the same. Take for example the two images in Figure 3.3. One is a *photograph* of the Sydney Opera House from the harbour, while the other is a photograph of a *paper serviette* folded to mimic the building's form. While both are images found online, the first directly depicts the building, where the second is a photograph of a three-dimensional depiction of the building. In other words, their relationship to the object – in this case the physical structure known as the Sydney Opera House – is not the same.[3] Although they are both images, what they reveal about the Sydney Opera House is not equivalent.

The work of English and Art Professor William J. Thomas Mitchell on representation explains how the term 'image' can be related to such a varied set of things. It offers a way to explain how the collection of representations of the Sydney Opera House may be understood in relation to the idea of an image. In his book, *Iconology: Image, Text, Ideology*, Mitchell explains that many things go by the name image, 'including pictures, statues, optical illusions, maps, diagrams, dreams, hallucinations, spectacles, projections, poems, patterns, memories, and even ideas' (Figure 3.4).[4]

Figure 3.3 A photograph and a serviette.

Rather than limiting images to pictorial depictions, Mitchell's literary analysis of the term reveals the way images are culturally conceptualised in ways that extend their remit to abstract forms such as a map or memory. If Mitchell's diagram of images is amended to describe representations, rather than images, the wide variety of forms in which the Sydney Opera House is represented can be organised from more tangible forms such as jewellery, clothing and toys to less tangible forms such as memories, analogies and descriptions (Figure 3.5).

Mitchell aligns terms such as 'likeness, resemblance and similitude' to the term image, words that align with ideas around *representations*.[5] To represent something or someone is to 'stand in for' a thing or person.[6] Building on Mitchell's analysis of the image, what is key about the examples collected is what connects these examples to each other and distinguishes them from those images that stand alone; their association with the Sydney Opera House. Calling these digital artefacts

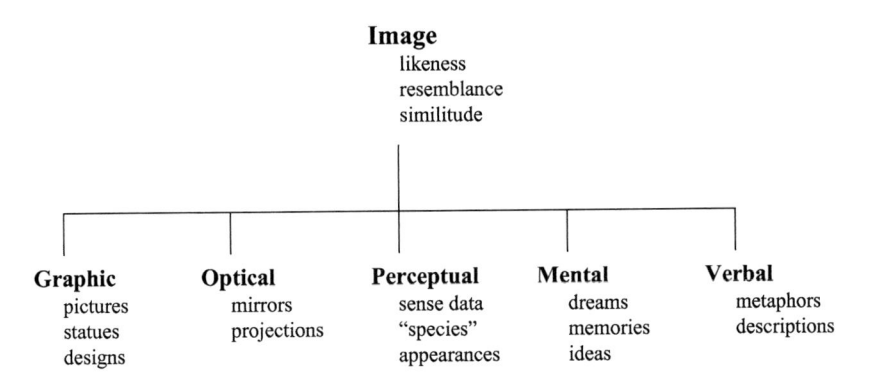

Figure 3.4 Mitchell's family of images.

Source: Diagram reproduced with permission of William J. Thomas Mitchell (1986).

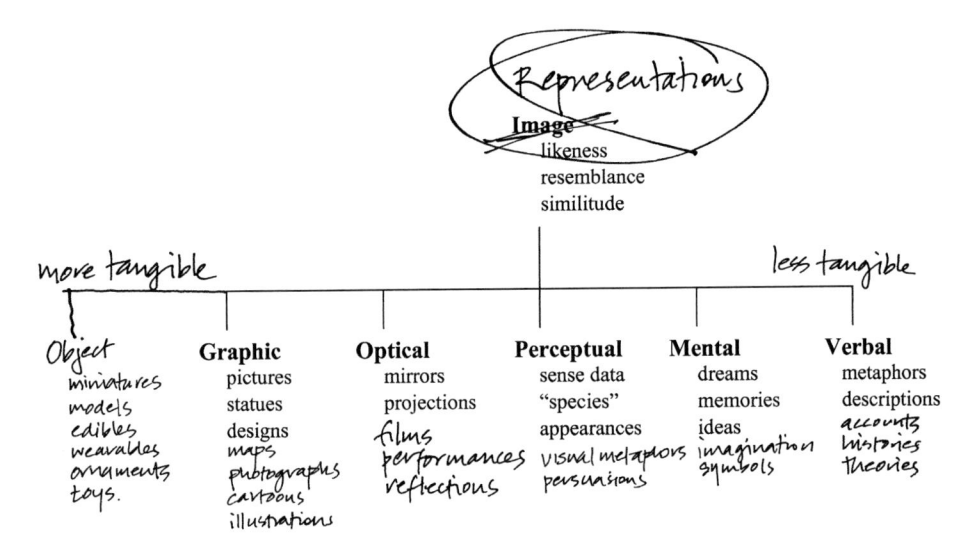

Figure 3.5 Types of representations gathered from the internet.

representations, rather than images, distinguishes their purpose in relation to the building, from their existence as digital media on the internet. The need to make such a distinction became clear through the process of collecting, analysing and ordering the found examples into a potential set of categories. Some examples are unproblematic. Depictions of the Sydney Opera House, such as photographs, are fairly straightforward. Others are less directly connected with the building They depict other things, such as flower petals or shells. Yet such examples were retrieved and included because they had textual descriptions or annotations that somehow connected them with the building.[7] The searches carried out retrieved images of other non-typical examples such as illustrations or digitally altered photographs, even images of other buildings that remind people of the Sydney Opera House. Understanding these nuanced differences between the collected representations is important because it demonstrates the wide and broad reach of the iconic value of this place.

The importance of representations in heritage is emerging. Emma Waterton and Steve Watson observe that while representation has been considered to be at the core of heritage, particularly in the sub-field of heritage interpretation and in museum studies, it is yet to be 'the dedicated focus of scholarship'.[8] In *Culture, Heritage and Representation* they make a case for representations and 'the visual' more broadly as active agents that participate in our negotiated relationship to the past. Waterton and Watson see that representations and visuality also bear upon questions of heritage as part of everyday life.[9] The authors in this edited volume emphasise the significance of representations in terms of a concept of heritage that is characterised as complex socio-cultural processes. Rather than focusing on representation as artefacts to be preserved, they examine instances where visual culture is used to represent the past in the present everyday. Watson and Waterton assert that 'the power of representation lies with few, yet the subjective response is owned by many'.[10] The collection of representations of the Sydney Opera House brings to the fore the critical role that representation plays in the way iconic works of architecture and World Heritage sites are perceived.[11]

The relationship between the representations and the original is central to the way the images of the Sydney Opera House replace the actual building in online forms of social life. In his canonical work, *Simulacra and Simulation*, French sociologist and philosopher Jean Baudrillard theorises the precession of simulacra, in which he describes the way copies (or representations) come to stand in for the original thing.[12] Unlike other more mobile forms of culture, buildings are anchored to a geographical site. Yet, released from architectural immobility as representations, the Sydney Opera House can be a form of visual currency that facilitates social interaction between people. Baudrillard's theory centres on the distinction between the copy and the real for a society where the copy is increasingly treated as the real thing. While he argues that the consequence of this is the loss of reality and the establishment of endless simulacra, the case of the Sydney Opera House as copy which might ordinarily be considered a lesser version of the original, has value specifically for the way it simulates or re-presents the building. Mitchell's expansive conceptualisation of images offers a means to understand how such a varied set of things can be brought together under one superordinate category, whilst Baudrillard's treatise on the role of these images as digital artefacts that stand in for the edifice offers a primary reason for their analysis.[13]

Working with a large and unwieldy collection of some 900 images demanded a system of organisation to understand their significance. Initially ordering the collection was executed manually and intuitively.[14] The resultant classification categories resembled those of the fictitious Chinese encyclopaedia cited by Michel Foucault in the preface to his book, *The Order of Things*.[15] Although these initial attempts were imperfect, they revealed that the process of ordering, rather than the resultant taxonomy, was also a way of interrogating the representations of the Sydney Opera House collected from multiple perspectives.[16]

Comparing the initial intuitive categories that resulted from ordering the representations to Foucault's reference to the Chinese encyclopaedia illustrates how such an imperfect process was valuable to the analysis of the collection on the Sydney Opera House. Foucault describes a passage from Jorge Luis Borges' 1952 essay titled 'The Analytical Language of John Wilkins'. In the passage Borges describes an apparently arbitrary system of animal classification described in the Chinese encyclopaedia known as the *Celestial Emporium of Benevolent Knowledge*:

(a) belonging to the emperor, (b) embalmed, (c) tame, (d) sucking pigs, (e) sirens, (f) fabulous, (g) stray dogs, (h) included in the present classification, (i) frenzied, (j) innumerable, (k) drawn with a very fine camelhair brush, (l) etcetera, (m) having just broken the water pitcher, (n) that from a long way off look like flies.[17]

Foucault employs Borges' essay on the arbitrary nature of ordering systems to argue that such ordering systems are revealing of cultural norms. He argues that although the taxonomy cited in the *Celestial Emporium of Benevolent Knowledge* might not appear to make sense to a Westerner, to a person from within the same intellectual culture it is perfectly logical. Foucault proposes that such apparently arbitrary systems are not incorrect but rather mirror the limitations of our own systems of thought.

While there is conjecture as to whether the ordering system cited by Foucault is real or an invention of Borges, it is Foucault's observation that the system appears erroneous because the Western reader is unable to form an obvious relationship between the categories, that is valuable here. The inability to find the similarities and differences between the categories of object, between animals that are 'fabulous' and those 'that from a long way off look like flies' demonstrates the importance of the relationship of the subcategories in the generation of knowledge.

The Sydney Opera House representations were collected in two stages: first, some 300 images from the website Flickr and then an additional 600 images were gathered from many websites on the internet. The initial classifications, like Borges' arbitrary system, offered no overarching order

Flickr-wide Search

(a) aerial, ambiguity, analogy, (b) -, (c) cockatoos, (d) -, (e) event, (f) flag, framed, (g) giraffes, graphic manipulation, graphic representation, (h) hair, harbourscape, hidden, (i) -, (j) -, (k) -, (l) land elevation, (m) mascot, (n) neighbouring buildings, no sails, not the Sydney Opera House, (o) object representations, (p) photographers, portrait colonnade, portrait detail, portrait elevation, postmodern, (q) -, (r) reflection, (s) sails, seagulls, ship, silhouette, sky elevation, (t) tiles, tour guide, (u) -, (v) veiled, (w) water elevation, working harbour, (x) -, (y) -, (z) -.

Internet-wide Search

(a) advert, analogy, art, australiana, (b) books, branded, buildings, (c) cake, caricature, construction, (d) dinnerware, drawings, designs, descriptions, (e) ebay, (f) fashion, film, furniture, (g) giraffes, (h) hats, (i) -, (j) jewellery, (k) -, (l) logotypes, (m) memorial, models, maps, (n) no war, (o) ornament, (p) pattern, photomontage, professional photographs, (q) -, (r) records, (s) souvenirs, stamps, (t) tourist, toys, (u) -, (v) views, vivid festival, (w) wedding, world youth day, (x) -, (y) -, (z) -.

Whilst categories such as (c) cockatoos, (f) flag and (m) mascot from the Flickr search indicate the way people photograph the building alongside other symbolic Australian objects, these are unrelated to categories such as (r) reflection and (v) veiled, which indicate the way people seek to photograph the building indirectly; in glazed façades and through blurred fences. Similarly, categories from the wider search that described the way objects are (b) branded and made more valuable by printing a Sydney Opera House logo bear no relation to the things sold on (e) eBay, or (p) professional photographs taken during the building's construction.

After these intuitive attempts to find an overarching order of categorisation attempts were made to develop an ordering system based on chronology and in terms of Baudrillard's precession of simulacra. Understanding the historical development of these representations in popular culture revealed that these are not new phenomena (Figure 3.6). In the days that immediately followed the announcement of Utzon's design in 1957 the form of the building was vividly described as like 'abandoned umbrellas'.[18] By 1962 Peter Morton's 'Sydney Opera House Hat' featured on the cover of *The Australian Woman's Weekly*, and Mrs B. Chard of Killara is noted as the first prizewinner of the most original cake at the Royal Easter Show described as a 'beautifully scaled model of the Sydney Opera House'.[19] And this is before the building had even been completed.

The representations that had been collected were also categorised using Baudillard's precession of simulacra. In considering representations, Baudrillard traces the dissolution of the separation between the original and the copy, which culminates in pure simulacrum. He devised a system of orders that describes the successive phases of the image:

> it is the reflection of a profound reality;
> it masks and denatures a profound reality;
> it masks the *absence* of a profound reality;
> it has no relation to any reality whatsoever:
> it is its own pure simulacrum. (Original emphasis)[20]

These definitions articulate the relationship of different kinds of representations, such as photographs or analogies, to the Sydney Opera House as the original edifice. Using this intellectual framework, spolia such as the fragments of roof tiles sold as souvenirs or embedded in the façade of the Chicago Tribune Tower in Chicago can be brought together as the order of reality (Figure 3.7). Photographs of the building form the first order of representation, as they reflect a profound reality since to produce them proximity to the building is required (Figure 3.8). Hats, cupcakes, Lego and logos that depict the Sydney Opera House can be thought

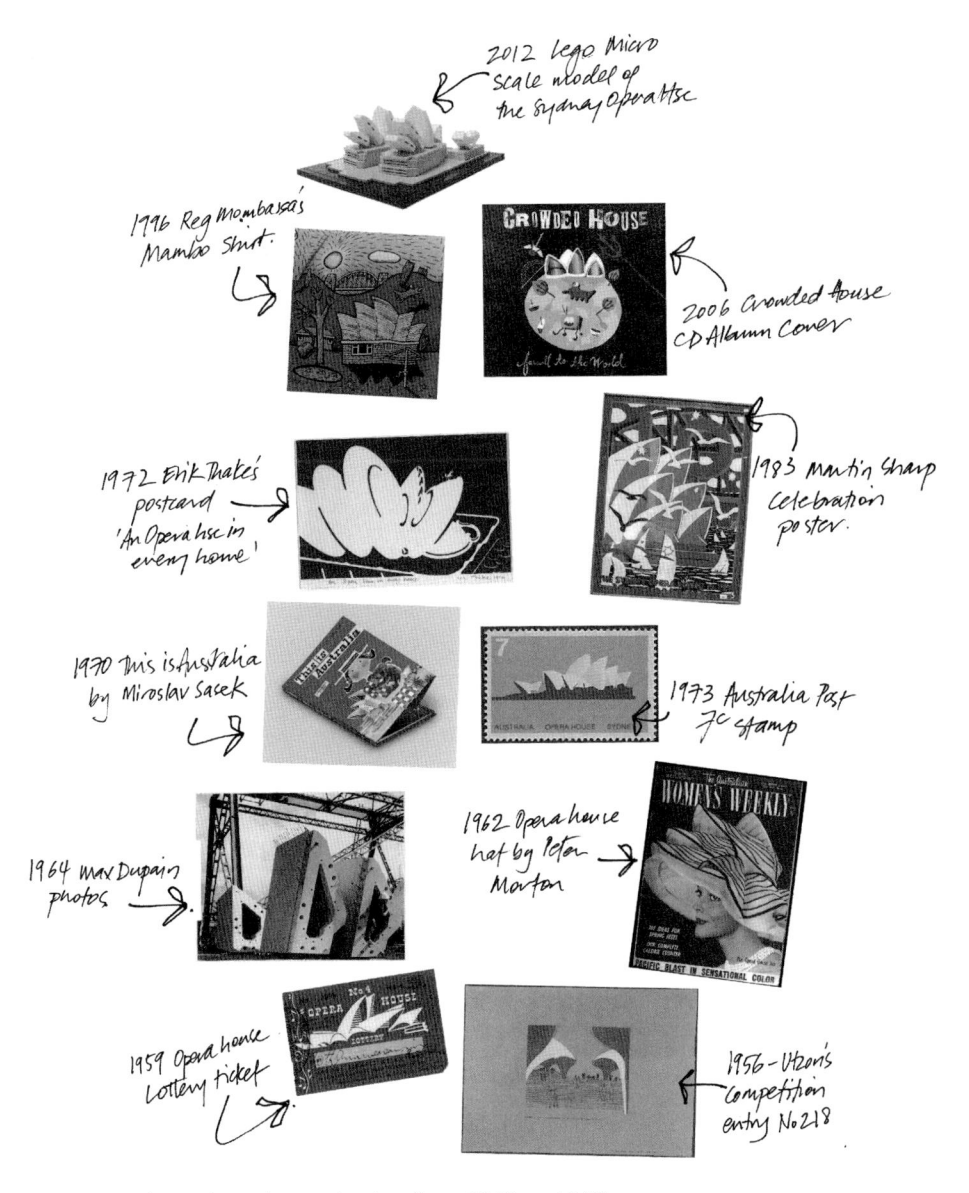

Figure 3.6 Chronological organisation from 2012 to 1957.

of as a second order, which masks and denatures a profound reality (Figure 3.9). These objects are not accurate representations of the Sydney Opera House; they distort the building, but remain recognisable. Models, drawings and historic photographs of the building's construction can also be framed as a second order of representation, however these mask the *absence* of a profound reality, and they are objects of times past (Figure 3.10). A third order includes objects such as the sails of a yacht, a nun's cornette wimple, or a photograph of dishes drying in a rack that has no relation to any reality whatsoever; these things are not the Sydney Opera

House but have become associated with this place (Figure 3.11). A fourth order of representation presents simulacra of the Sydney Opera House (Figure 3.12). Scaled versions of the building in themeparks such as Legoland, and subway entries in the Chinese city of Jiujiang, demonstrate how replicas of the building have become entities that attract their own tourists. Alongside these physical examples are digitally altered photographs that depict the Sydney Opera House in alternate locations and states of decay. While Baudrillard's precession of simulacra reveals the extent of influence that the Sydney Opera House has, from photographs and spolia, to copies in Lego that attract their own visitors, its focus on the relationship between the original and the copy does not account for the value of these artefacts for people.

Each of these initial attempts to create an ordering system that could evidence socio-visual value informed the possible kinds of knowledge that could be garnered from the collection as a whole. Neither ordering intuitively, by chronology, nor by Baudrillard's precession of simulacra could explain why these representations circulate in online instances of mass media, why people make opera-house-shaped cakes and hats, or what these activities mean collectively. A way to account for the representations as a social phenomenon is required.

Figure 3.7 Order of reality (real pieces of the Sydney Opera House).

Sources: left, pieces of glazed and non-glazed tiles from the Sydney Opera House gifted to the author; middle, tiles from the Sydney Opera House embedded in the south-western façade of the Chicago Tribune Tower in 2006 (© Wayne Lorentz/Artefaqs, 2013); right, souvenir fragment of a Sydney Opera House tile, AUD$135.00, from their Corporate Gift Catalogue (Sydney Opera House trademark reproduced with permission of the Sydney Opera House Trust, photographer unknown, 2007).

Figure 3.8 1st order: reflection of reality (photographs on Flickr.com of the Sydney Opera House).

Sources: left, 'Sydney Opera House' (© Jim Robinson, 2006); middle, 'Sydney Opera House' (© David Moggs, 2006); right, 'pink Opera House' (© Jong Soo (Peter) Lee, 2009).

Figure 3.9 2nd order: denatures reality (things in the shape of the Sydney Opera House).

Sources: left, collectable salt and pepper shakers offered in Virgin Australia Business Class since 2009; middle, Australia Day cupcakes sold at AUD$2 by Cupcakes on Pitt Street in 2009 (© Livia Cheng, Chamelle Photography, 2009); right, 'The Opera House Hat' designed by Peter Morton featured in the 25 July issue of the Australian *Women's Weekly* magazine in 1962. Archives of the publication held in the Trove digital collection at the National Library of Australia (© Bauer Media Pty Limited/The Australian Women's Weekly, 1962).

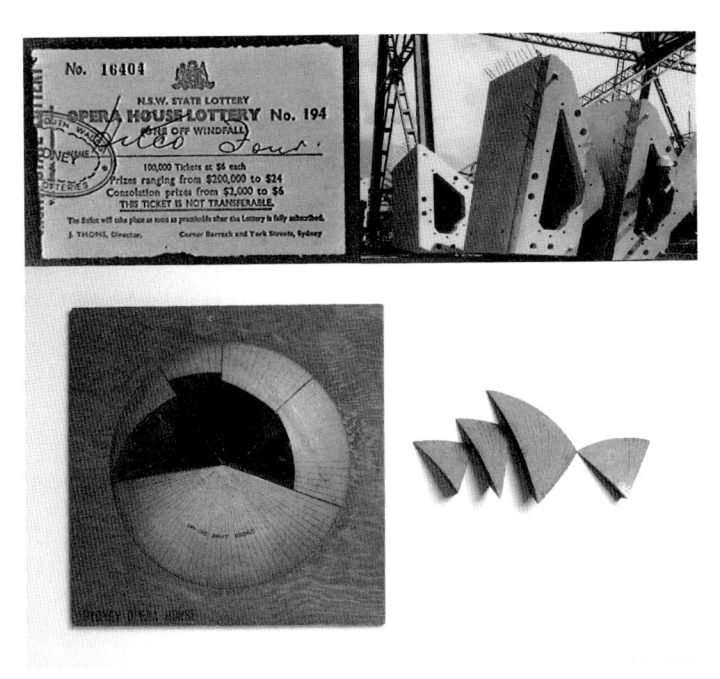

Figure 3.10 2nd order: absence of reality (artefacts that preceded the realisation of the Sydney Opera House).

Sources: left, 'APA studio photograph of Mr. Kentwell's Hitco Four syndicate winning Opera House Lottery ticket (lottery no. 194, ticket 16404) which won $200,000' (© unknown. IE868656 Collection: State Library of NSW); middle, 'Item 16: Jorn Utzon Sydney Opera House photographs: construction site, 1964 (© State Library of New South Wales and Max Dupain and Associates, 1964. IE976912 - Collection: State Library of NSW); right, model illustrating the origin of the roof geometry of the Sydney Opera House, Ove Arup and Partners/Jorn Utzon, England/Australia, 1961–1965 (© Arup. 2003 34 1 1 – Collection: Museum of Applied Arts and Sciences. Photograph: Alison Brennan).

Figure 3.11 3rd order: associative relationship (things inspired by the form of the Sydney Opera House).

Sources: left, photograph posted on Flickr.com of Ikea pendant lamp 'Knappa' with the title 'Shaping Up: Our Ikea pendant lamp that we finally put up reminds us of the Sydney Opera House. Or a beautiful white flower. (I turned the photo on its side)' (© Jenny Lamy, approx. 2009); middle, photograph posted on Flickr.com of dishes arranged in a washing up rack to look like the Sydney Opera House (© James Prince, 2012); right, Campervan inspired by the Sydney Opera House titled 'The Opera' (© Rob Vos, 2010).

Figure 3.12 4th order: simulacra (buildings that are like the Sydney Opera House).

Sources: left, photograph posted on Flickr.com of underground entries that mimic the Sydney Opera House with the title 'The JiuJiang opera houses' (© Brian Yap, 1992); middle, photograph posted on Flickr.com of the Lotus Temple in Dehli, India, design by Fariborz Sahaba, 1986 (© Travis Wise, 2014); right, photograph posted on Flickr.com of Clyde Auditorium (SEC Armadillo) in Glasgow, Scotland designed by Norman Foster, 1997 (© James Scantlebury, 2014).

Participatory culture, architecture and the internet

The idea of participation in the production of architecture was a prevalent ideology in the 1960s in the United Kingdom and United States.[21] Interest in this phenomenon has re-emerged recently, alongside emerging interest in the sociology of architecture.[22] Scholars such as Paul Jenkins, Lesley Forsyth, Peter Blundell Jones, Doina Petrescu and Jeremy Till have made important contributions that address how user participation can shift the normative power structures endemic within architectural production as well as in the consequent valuation of architecture.[23] This approach can, perhaps, be understood as a reaction to the power and cultural capital held by the elite architects that are commissioned to produce high-profile public buildings, since public participation in the design process side-steps the idea of the architectural genius, often connected with landmark buildings. Yet ideas on community participation in architecture are always framed as processes of direct consultation and engagement with the design of projects. Community consultation and participation is usually employed through traditional qualitative methods: interviews with residents, workers and local interest groups; workshops to brainstorm design ideas, receive feedback and resolve conflicts; surveys at a larger scale; discussion groups with stakeholders; and appointing advisory committees to provide impartial guidance to the design team.

Until recently, architecture's relationship to 'the social' has received little academic attention.[24] Yet scholars are increasingly recognising the social, cultural, economic and political contexts that are implicated in the production of architecture. For example, Paul Jones and Jeremy Till both address a prevalent contradiction. Architecture, unlike many other forms of culture, is dependent entirely on clients, government approvals, builders and users for its realisation. Yet the field of architecture operates as if it is autonomous of these societal contexts. In *The Sociology of Architecture* Jones states that much architectural theory focuses on understanding buildings in terms of 'nationalistic styles and traditions . . . within a hierarchy of entirely aesthetic objects'.[25] Jones adopts Pierre Bourdieu's sociological framework of 'social capital', the 'field' and the 'habitus', to offer an analysis of the production of architecture where significant civic projects are the exclusive terrain of elite 'starchitects'. He argues that the way this select group of architects legitimise their masculinised position of power is through the notion of the design 'genius'. Jones unravels the way such discourses maintain control over *what* is defined as architecture, *which* examples are to be lauded, the *values* for which they are recognised, and therefore *who* should be celebrated.

While Jones acknowledges that much of the built environment is made up of everyday examples of architecture that are designed by architects who do not necessarily belong or subscribe to the values espoused by the elite, he primarily draws on well-known works of architecture. His focus on iconic buildings is strategic: first, these buildings exemplify 'cultural capital' and therefore the social and cultural conditions pertinent to their production are more clearly implicated in the process their architects must negotiate. Second, Jones is also responding to the way the discipline of architecture tends to focus on a specific group of buildings that enter the architectural canon, via teaching, architectural press, media and politics.[26] These are the same elite examples that proliferate as representations online and are often discussed within architectural discourse in terms of their highly aestheticised forms. However, participation need not be a direct engagement with the formal processes of production to be meaningful to communities or to contribute to the way forms of culture are valued.

The concept of 'participatory culture' emerged in the late 1980s from within scholarship in media studies and cultural studies. The concept, defined by Henry Jenkins, aims to address the way established notions of 'audience' framed some social groups as passive spectators. Jenkins, as an avid participant in fan culture, knew audiences were not passive consumers. He was concerned that framing audiences in this way resulted in neatly defined readings of popular culture, when he knew otherwise. The manner in which groups of people participate in popular culture by drawing on mass media in everyday social life came to be understood as researchers like Jenkins found ways to make more nuanced accounts of audience reception.[27]

Media studies and audience reception studies are primarily concerned with the social effects of mass communication and mass media.[28] These areas of academic research developed out of the larger discipline of cultural studies, which seeks to construct a complex and rich account of popular culture. Audience reception studies particularly focus on low-brow forms of mass culture, such as television, popular fiction and newspapers, rather than privileging what are often defined as elite or high-brow forms of culture, such as art and architecture, that have their own established academic disciplines. Although media studies and audience reception studies do not directly address the concept of social value as understood within heritage, they are directly concerned with mass culture and popularity. In particular, the later generations of research within audience reception studies are concerned with understanding the value of mass culture from a social perspective, and therefore offer a theoretical grounding for investigating the concept of socio-visual value of architecture within mass media.

According to Pertti Alasuutari's analysis of the field of reception studies, Jenkins' concept of participatory culture belongs to the third generation of media audience research.[29] Alasuutari describes the development of the field in three phases or generations. Initially, audience research was premised on a straightforward model of 'producer-text-audience'. The first generation of research on audience reception was situated around television and took place in the 1970s. Stuart Hall was one of the main contributors during this period. Hall applied a semiotic model of communication to investigations of audience reception, where this process was framed as acts of encoding and decoding.[30] The second generation, like the first, was also largely focused on television audiences and developed in the mid 1980s. This second generation of research made a departure from Hall's semiotic framing and made use of ethnographic approaches to research audience reception. For example, rather than focusing on how the meaning of television programs was understood by audiences, Ien Ang's seminal research on the television soap opera *Dallas* used qualitative methods to understand *why* audiences found enjoyment in watching this melodrama.[31] Rather than simply trying to understand the content of the message (whether it was 'decoded' or not) Ang's research sought to investigate the basis of audience members' *emotional attachment* to this television programme. The ethnographic methods of the second generation of research resulted in richer and more detailed accounts of audiences' experiences than those documented using the semiotic approach of Hall and the first generation of researchers.

The third generation, to which Jenkins' concept of participatory culture belongs, is characterised by a departure from the model of 'producer-text-audience' employed by the first and the second generations. In the late 1980s scholars began to question the framing of audiences as neatly bounded entities. This generation of media scholars continues to be interested in understanding the significance of different kinds of media within the context of people's everyday lives and acknowledges that audiences are complex, mobile and dynamic entities. John Fiske's differentiation of mass culture, understood as products created for a mass market, and popular culture, understood as individuals' use and incorporation of these objects into everyday life, exemplifies this focus.[32] Fiske, along with Jenkins, acknowledges the way culture moves fluidly from a public domain to a personal one. The third generation of audience reception research is underpinned by Fiske's idea of popular culture, where audiences are not simply passive consumers of media such as television, but instead are recognised as groups who actively engage with objects of mass culture for their own social ends.

Jenkins defines participatory culture as a culture in which the individuals who make up an audience are understood to be 'active, critically engaged and creative' members of society. Rather than passively consuming mass culture these audience members appropriate, transform and extend its value.[33] Jenkins is specifically concerned with the activities and cultural artefacts produced *in relation* to objects of mass media, rather than the objects of mass media themselves. For example, he is interested in the way particular groups of fans extend television programmes by writing and making their own versions of these shows for use within their own particular community. Jenkins understands these kinds of 'fan culture' engagements as creative expressions and forms of civic engagement. At the core of the concept of participatory culture is the idea that the appropriation of collective forms of mass culture is significant, and the reinterpretation of these into the realm of popular culture and everyday life serves social needs. These kinds of active engagements involve the reinterpretation of mass culture as a means for creating and reinforcing social connections within communities and groups. The concept of participatory culture as defined by Jenkins is useful to the investigation of the socio-visual value of the Sydney Opera House, because it recognises the activities and artefacts produced by individuals and groups in relation to existing forms of culture. Whilst Jenkins and media scholars more generally use this concept to understand how mass culture, such as television or newspapers, infiltrates everyday life, this conceptualisation of audience engagement can also be used in relation to popular works of architecture. While the Sydney Opera House is regarded as a masterpiece of Modern Architecture and engineering, it too is an entity of mass culture. This is evident in its significance as a landmark and tourist destination, evidenced in its visitor numbers. Importantly, participatory culture defines audiences (and communities) through acts of engagement, rather than through shared geography, connections, beliefs or cultural background.[34]

In recent years, technological developments around the internet have made participatory culture highly visible. In the first years of the internet, audiences were generally unable to interact with the content published online, or with other users. Generally, the content on websites was 'read-only'. This is now referred to as Web 1.0. Around 2004 the structure of websites began to change from a 'read-only' model to a 'read-write' model. This new model of mass communication is also known as the 'participatory turn', or Web 2.0, a term coined by Tim O'Reilly in late 2005. As information and communication technologies have developed, websites that harness user-generated content have become commonplace; these websites are more aligned with the idea of 'platforms' or 'services' than with publications in a traditional sense.[35] These new websites or platforms allow individual users to engage and respond to online content, to post their own content, and to engage with each other in new and emergent ways. Commonly referred to as social media, participatory media, user-generated content or user-based platforms, these new media platforms are facilitating new forms of cultural engagement.

The concept of participatory culture has now become central to the discourse on Web 2.0.[36] The effects of widespread participation in public spaces of communication were initially characterised as having both utopian and dystopian repercussions. Utopian perspectives are exemplified by publications such as *Wikinomics*, in which business commentator Dan Tapscott and academic Anthony Williams put forward the benefits of the democratisation of culture through audience participation. Dystopian perspectives, exemplified by publications such *The Cult of the Amateur* by Andrew Keens, argue that these new forms of communication will destroy our institutions of knowledge.[37] However, the reality that has emerged with time is not as extreme as the polemical accounts by Tapscott and Williams or Keen suggest. In *Democracy and New Media*, Henry Jenkins and David Thorburn identify that such polarised reactions to new forms of media have also been evident during other historical shifts in communication systems, for example with the introduction of the printing press, photography and television.[38]

Internet technologies that facilitate audience participation have gained momentum and changed regularly in the first decade of the 21st century. The use of media platforms such as Wikipedia, Facebook, Blogger, Twitter, Flickr, Instagram, Tumbler, Pinterest and many others has become a part of everyday social and cultural life in Western societies. Engagement through these participatory media platforms is not limited to individuals; institutions and commercial organisations are increasingly employing these technologies to communicate and to engage with audiences too.

How can participatory media be identified? Media theorist Howard Rheingold suggests participatory media have three specific but interrelated characteristics.[39] First, they have a technical-structural characteristic – that facilitates 'many to many' production and consumption. Websites such as Flickr, Blogger and Wikipedia allow individuals to self-publish or post online and to access each other's self-publishing efforts. Second, they have a psychological and social characteristic. Participatory media derive their value from the active engagement of large numbers of people; without user-generated content, websites such as Blogger, Facebook or Flickr would be empty software platforms. Third, they have a political and economic characteristic. Participatory websites such as Twitter or Pinterest amplify existing, and generate new, social networks enabling a more efficient coordination of activities. Whilst participation is fundamental to the platforms named above, the characteristics of participatory media are also integrated into other proprietary websites. While all websites do not necessarily exemplify Rheingold's characteristics to the same extent, Jenkins' concept of participatory culture remains central to these new forms of internet media. Jenkins argues that audience participation has grown to such an extent it has become the norm:

> the concept of the active audience, so controversial two decades ago, is now taken for granted by everyone involved in and around the media industry. New technologies are enabling average consumers to archive, annotate, appropriate, and recirculate media content. Powerful institutions and practices (law, religion, education, advertising, and politics, among them) are being redefined by a growing recognition of what is to be gained through fostering – or at least tolerating – participatory cultures.[40]

The significance of participatory culture as a concept is increasing. The emergence of media technologies that enable participation has meant that this concept is presently more broadly applicable than solely to fan cultures.[41] However, it is important to recognise that participatory media platforms *enable* participation and, critically, make these activities and engagements *visible*. Before participatory media technologies became commonplace, the term 'audiences' described a group of people who watched a particular example of culture, such as a television show, where the interactions of the group around this example remained unobservable to the public. Social media platforms have changed this situation; audience activities and responses to particular forms of culture are now content on the internet. The interactions of audience members with organisations and with each other are now observable online. And some of these activities even attract *their own* audience.

Coupled with sophisticated search engines, participatory media platforms facilitate observations of the activities and engagements of audiences on specific subjects, such as the Sydney Opera House. Online, representations from different sources co-exist in ways that previously did not occur. Prior to participatory media, personal representations such as holiday snapshots or photograph albums tended to reside in shoeboxes within the private domain of people's lives. These artefacts were shared at private gatherings where people came together in groups within their own existing social networks. With new media platforms, some of the practices around these forms of culture have moved into the public sphere where they are posted and shared online through photosharing websites and blogging services.[42] These days, personal, commercial and professional representations reside together online, posted by one person or organisation, only to be appropriated and re-contextualised by another. The consequences of these shifts are that participatory media blurs the previously established divisions between the public and the private realms of social and visual engagement. The uptake of these forms of communication by institutions, commercial groups as well as individuals has also had the consequence of co-locating contributions from all these types of societal organisations in new and emergent ways.[43] Increasingly, organisations and institutions are establishing online presences through large-scale proprietary websites, as well as through membership on participatory media platforms such as YouTube, Twitter and Facebook (Figure 3.13).

Collecting representations of the Sydney Opera House from the internet was carried out using everyday online search engines, such as Google, along with Flickr and eBay's own proprietary engines.[44] These methods retrieved images from many

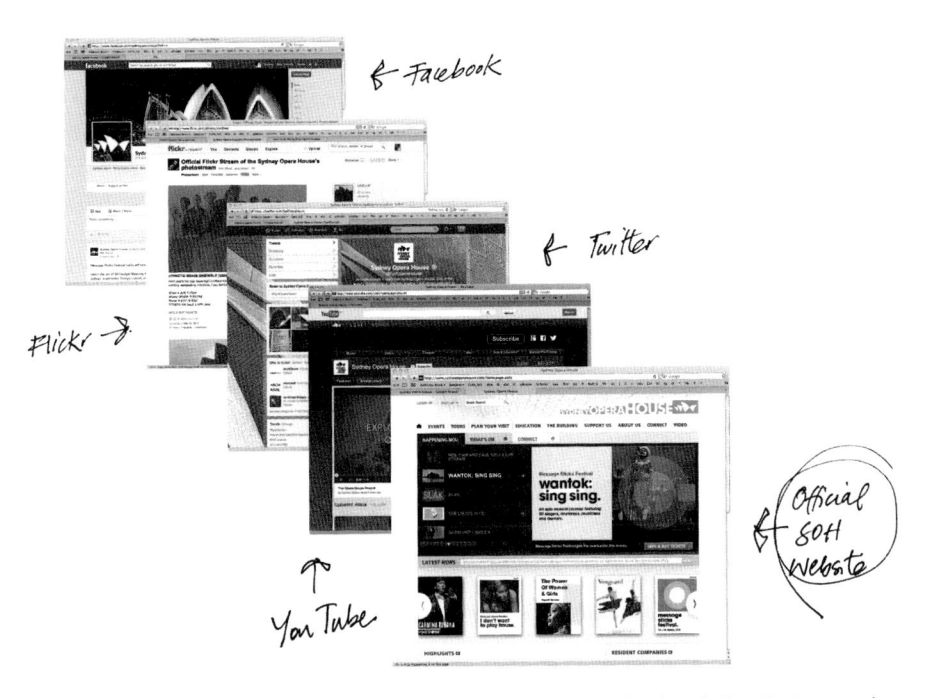

Figure 3.13 The Sydney Opera House and its presence on Facebook, Flickr, Twitter and YouTube.

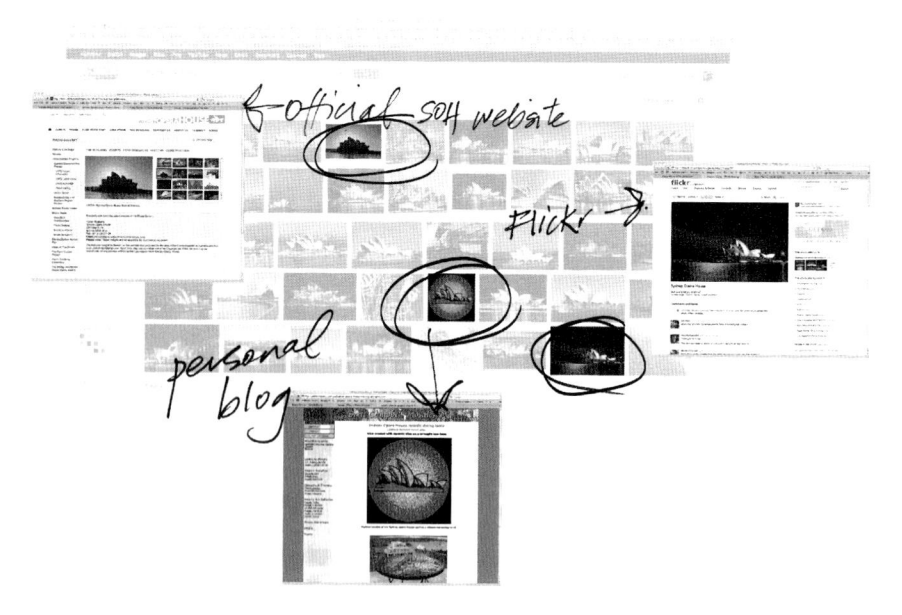

Figure 3.14 Google Images search 8 August 2012 using the terms 'Sydney', 'Opera' and 'House'.

different contexts.[45] For example, one search on Google Images returned the following representations of the building within the search engine's own interface (Figure 3.14). These images appear similar because of the way Google Images decontextualises them from their online source.

Each of the images shown in Figure 3.14 comes from a different context. The sunset scene (top) is in fact part of the institutional gallery of professional commissioned photographs from the official Sydney Opera House website. The night scene (bottom right) is a photograph posted by 'ShotsbyGun.com' on Flickr.[46] Although both representations are technically proficient photographs of the Sydney Opera House, the first is institutionally sanctioned, whilst the second is a personal work. The third representation (bottom left) shown in Figure 3.14 has a commercial imperative and has been posted by an individual. The representation is from Brett Campbell's website and depicts a dining table top featuring a handmade mosaic of the Sydney Opera House. Campbell has posted this image as an example of a professional commission.[47] Google Images does not discern who contributes images online with the result that images retrieved can come from any website.[48] Although all three representations come from distinct online sources they become co-located by search engines such as Google Images. This reveals that many different social entities contribute to the building's ubiquity in its visual culture online. As can be seen in Figure 3.15, institutions such as the Sydney Opera House, the State Records Authority of NSW, the Powerhouse Museum, as well as individuals on Flickr, eBay and Blogger, interest groups on architecture or philately, commercial organisations such as the Sydney Swans, the Sydney Writers Festival and the Sydney Gay and Lesbian Mardi Gras all contribute in some way to the widespread representation and corresponding recognition of this place. Participatory media not only facilitates individuals' engagements with each other, it also extends the way commercial and institutional organisations engage online.

Figure 3.15 Websites that contribute to the ubiquity of the Sydney Opera House in visual culture.

As online technologies develop, social media platforms are increasingly enabling content to be shared across multiple platforms; photographs can be hosted on Flickr and shared within the site's groups, whilst at the same time posted as an entry onto a separate weblog on Blogger. The consequences are that representations first published by an institution easily become incorporated into posts on personal blogs and, conversely, personal photographs on Flickr become part of institutional collections.[49]

Henry Jenkins describes this increased flow of content and the blurring of boundaries as a convergence of the media landscape that is both 'a top-down corporate driven process and a bottom-up consumer driven process. Corporate convergence coexists with grassroots convergence'.[50] Just as new media platforms offer a means for individuals to contribute content, so too it is a means by which formal institutions disseminate content and gather new audiences. This convergence demonstrates the way such organisations 'are learning how to accelerate the flow of media content across delivery channels to expand revenue opportunities, broaden markets, and reinforce viewer commitments'.[51] Large formal organisations are seeking to engage the participation of audiences by creating online presences on social media platforms. At the same time, Jenkins argues that 'consumers are learning how to use these different media technologies to bring the flow of media more fully under their control and to interact with other consumers'.[52] Just as institutions are finding ways to participate with their audiences, so too are individuals and consumers appropriating content from institutions and using it for their own purposes. Although much of Jenkins' research centres on the way that engaged audiences are challenging media such as television, books or games, the implications of these shifts in media technologies can be applied to architecture too. Jenkins' concept of convergence recognises that participatory culture is not discrete or bound to specific websites, but rather, is part of a much larger complex network of cultural and social interactions. The participatory culture of the Sydney Opera House is embodied within the dynamic and fluid engagements between people who contribute to the building's representation in culture.

The significance of participatory culture and representations for digital heritage

The interest in the concept of participatory culture and participatory media within the field of heritage is emerging and rapidly becoming established. Digital forms of heritage have been recognised for over a decade, marked by the international adoption of soft policy instruments such as UNESCO's *Charter for the Preservation of Digital Heritage* in 2003.[53] For much of this time digital heritage has mostly been the remit of museum scholarship, exemplified by the development and move towards digital archives, conservation of digitally native examples of culture and for use as part of visitor interpretation strategies.[54] Since UNESCO's charter was adopted the nature of internet communication technologies has undergone widespread and rapid change. This is particularly evident in the shift towards public participation and contribution of content to the internet. Alongside such socio-technological shifts, a movement towards recognising everyday activities as contributing to heritage has been growing.[55]

Heritage and Social Media: Understanding Heritage in Participatory Culture, edited in 2012 by Elisa Giaccardi, is one of the first publications to specifically explore the concept of participatory culture and its manifestation through social media in relation to heritage.[56] Giaccardi asserts that the essays contained within this publication explore the way 'social media reframes our understanding and experience of heritage by opening up more participatory ways of interacting with heritage objects and concerns'.[57] The contributions within this edited collection recognise the significance of the activities and interactions of audiences to the way heritage operates in society and culture, and rather than separating technological interaction and characterising them as somehow 'artificial' the essays all emphasise technology as a connected part of everyday life.[58]

In her introduction, Giaccardi characterises participatory culture enabled by social media as a 'complex set of social practices that interweave memories, material traces and performative enactments to give meaning and significance in the present to the lived realities of our past'.[59] Giaccardi, like Jenkins, recognises that participatory culture is not new. Rather it is a cultural phenomenon that was largely unrecognised. She notes, however, that the centrality of new media platforms in our lives has spurred many scholars in the publication to explore how social media offers new ways of engaging with heritage, and ways of extending existing forms of engagement. Further, it is possible that the research emerging around participatory culture and participatory media is revealing new ways of describing the value of heritage.

The essays in *Heritage and Social Media: Understanding Heritage in Participatory Culture* cover three thematic areas: social practice, public formation and sense of place. Essays on social practice discuss the ways in which participatory media is enabling new kinds of social and visual practices, where collecting images and making representations are considered significant elements of online communication, and personal accounts are legitimised in relation to community perspectives. The essays that focus on public formation specifically address the way in which social media is blurring existing ideas about community versus audiences, whilst also serving as a technical means for new types of group formation in the public realm. Essays that address sense of place explore the way social media is not only an online experience, but also a means for engendering and shifting 'real' experiences with places of heritage, thereby building on existing scholarship from the fields of architecture and cultural geography.[60] Importantly, these technologically enabled forms of participation are not seen to detract from the socio-cultural qualities essential to ideas of place, rather, as Jeff Malpas argues, these new technologies augment the significance by 'bring[ing] to the fore the character of place as the very matrix out of which human significance and meaning arise'.[61] In other words, while participatory and social media enable forms of engagement with heritage through technology, and have the potential to transform and augment these, they do not directly create them. It is important to recognise that participation occurs both online and offline.

The online instances of participatory culture explored in this book potentially augment rather than diminish the World Heritage value of the Sydney Opera House, by demonstrating the extent of influence this building has had in visual culture, both offline and online. Gillian's Rose's model for the critical analysis of visual materials helps explain how the representations collected of the Sydney Opera House can be framed as evidence of offline examples of participatory culture. In *Visual Methodologies: An Introduction to the Interpretation of Visual Materials*, Rose argues that visual culture is a socially situated phenomenon.[62] She states that the way we understand, create and use images is determined by context and culture. In this highly regarded book, Rose offers a condensed overview of theory on 'the visual' and 'visual culture' to propose a critical approach to the study of images using a variety of disciplinary approaches to the study of representations and images. She puts forward that the meaning of an image occurs at three different sites: images can be analysed in terms of their production, in terms of the content of the image itself, and in terms of the way they are viewed – their audiencing (Figure 3.16). Analysing the context, that is the type of webpage, in which each of the collected representations was found would be to observe the representations from the site of their *audiencing*. Focusing on the *content* of each of the representations, considering what it is, can tell us about the extent of the iconic value of the Sydney Opera House. But the content is also useful to interpret the practices that lead to their *production* (Figure 3.17). Such an approach enables an understanding of the production of these representations, in the first place as a response to, and a form of, engagement with the building. Reframed in this way, the collection of representations can then be ordered to explain a set of the socio-visual practices through which people appropriate, express and connect with the Sydney Opera House through its visual culture. How might the significance of such popular culture practices be understood as part of a larger cultural process of heritage?

The central aim of heritage practice and law is to conserve and protect inherited forms of culture for future generations. The *World Heritage Convention* explicitly

Figure 3.16 Rose's sites of meaning for images.

Source: Author's drawing based on Gillian Rose (2007) *Visual Methodologies: An Introduction to the Interpretation of Visual Materials.* London: Sage, p. 13.

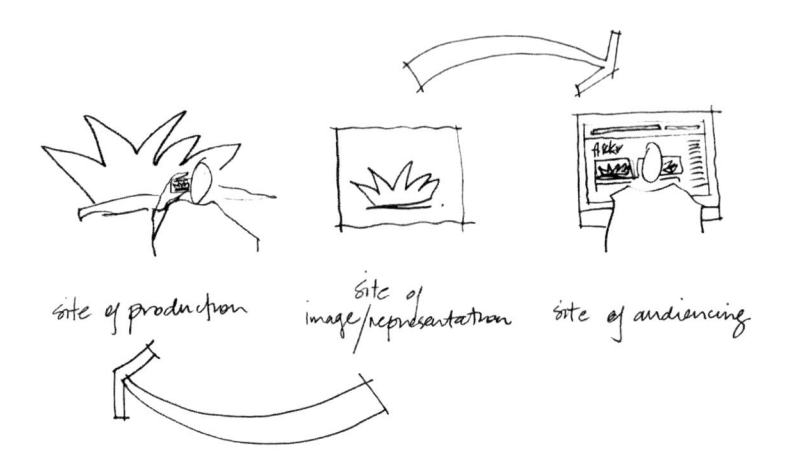

Figure 3.17 Representations as evidence of practices of participatory culture.

articulates that signatories to the convention have 'the duty of ensuring the identification, protection, conservation, presentation and transmission to future generations of the cultural and natural heritage'.[63] Heritage, framed by the convention, is a process whereby cultural artefacts of the past are deemed valuable in the present. Places of heritage can be conceptualised as forms of culture that mediate a sense of connection with the past and the future.[64]

In her 2007 book, titled *Mediated Memories in the Digital Age*, José van Dijck explores how everyday visual artefacts, such as photographs, diaries, music and video, and their online counterparts are implicated in personal and collective forms of memory. A key argument in her work is to frame both versions as technologies, to make visible their continuities and transformations. Van Dijck's theoretical work in this book unpacks the way such personal artefacts that arise as part of participatory culture can evidence social value. While her focus is not specifically on international heritage, its practice or inscription, this book offers insights into the ways in which popular online practices and their offline counterparts can be understood as culturally significant.

Van Dijck's analysis of everyday artefacts in *Mediated Memories* posits what she terms a 'conceptual tool' developed to articulate the way such objects serve to mediate the memories and identities of individual and groups (Figure 3.18). Van Dijck observes how everyday visual artefacts, such as those being examined here, situate 'a person in his or her contemporary culture'.[65] Van Dijck conceptualises such artefacts like the diary or the photograph (and by extension souvenirs, folded serviettes, logos, costumes, hats and other popular culture artefacts) as 'enabling technologies' instead of categorising them by their objecthood or format. She also argues that the function of such artefacts is to facilitate a connection of the past with our present-day experiences, and that by framing these artefacts as technologies, van Dijck dissolves the division between the 'real' physical world of printed photographs and handwritten diaries and the 'virtual' online realm of photosharing and blogging in order to better understand their social function.

Van Dijck's conceptual tool of 'mediated memories' aligns with the perspective of cognitive philosophy where memory is conceived as a relational process mediated by the brain's interaction with external objects.[66] Beginning from this premise van Dijck brings her own cultural scholarship to bear on the subject to embed these interactions between mind/brain and object/technology within socio-cultural forms and practices. Van Dijck's tool offers an analytical account of the interconnections between cultural practices, such as taking photographs at destinations such as the Sydney Opera House, the artefacts that emerge from these, and the personal forms of significance that these offer. Framed through van Dijck's concept of mediated memories, participatory culture practices and technologies can be understood to embody, facilitate and support remembering, identity and experience. The idea of mediated memories operates spatially on three axes: a horizontal axis that expresses relational identity, a vertical axis that articulates temporality and a third diagonal axis that accounts for embodiment (Figure 3.18).

The horizontal axis of relational identity mediates between a personal sense of self and a more collective social life with others. Using photographs posted online as an example, it is possible to connect the artefacts with the embodied action of creating

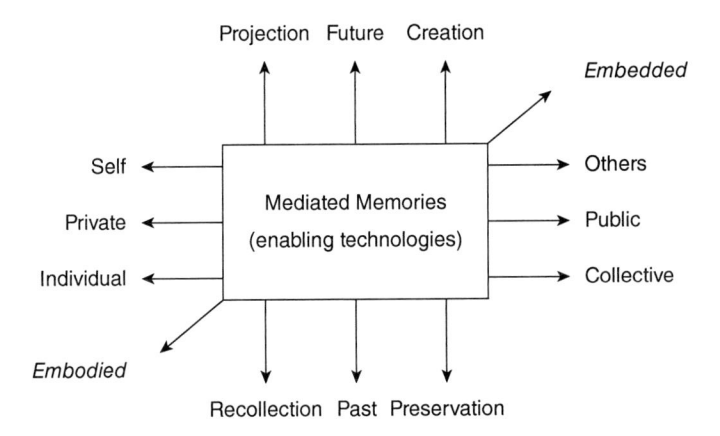

Figure 3.18 Mediated memories by José van Dijck.

Source: José van Dijck (2007) *Mediated Memories in the Digital Age*. Stanford: Stanford University Press, p. 50.

these representations. Scholarship from critical tourism studies frames photographic practices as ways in which people mediate experience and identity, both personal and collective. The idea of the 'looking' is central to John Urry's *The Tourist Gaze*.[67] The horizontal axis of the mediated memories tool acknowledges the way personal meanings are co-constituted with collective ones aligning with the work of Jonas Larsen and Jørgen Ole Bærenholdt where they describe the way everyday practices of holiday photography are performances through which people negotiate social relationships and reinforce idealised notions of family.[68] So, while these representations evidence the iconic status of the Sydney Opera House, they also evidence the building's participatory culture and using van Djick's conceptual tool can be argued to reveal the way their production, content and reception is implicated in the building's socio-visual value.

The vertical axis conceptualises temporality in terms of the way everyday objects assist in providing a sense of continuity for people. Photographs and diaries, among other artefacts including souvenirs, are ways to document present-day experiences for future remembering. Such personal artefacts help people to construct personal histories. As the technological traces of ageing fade photographs and turn diaries yellow, the materiality of such objects can remind of the passing of time and offer a relic of the former self. The idea that such artefacts mediate the past, present and future aligns with the assertion by David Harvey and Laurajane Smith that heritage is a cultural process of meaning making around practices, things and places.[69] Preserving cultural artefacts and places is motivated by a desire to provide a sense of history that operates in the present, alongside an intention to maintain continuity of the present in the future. The temporal axis of van Dijck's tool articulates the way artefacts provide a scaffold through which to articulate a present perspective of the past.

Van Dijck's third diagonal axis explores embodiment. She connects individual and personal experiences with broader embedded cultural practices. Taking photographs or buying a souvenir is often a personal endeavour, while sharing these either online, or once back home with the actual object itself is an embedded social custom. Some examples from the collection of representations of the Sydney Opera House are souvenirs and, similarly, the value of such artefacts is theorised by scholars such as Susan Stewart, Celeste Olalquiaga, Beverly Gordon, and Lisa Love and Nathaniel Kohn, who propose they can be understood as personal expressions of identity, implicated in people's ongoing performances of memory-making.[70] The importance of these artefacts is framed not only in terms of their material qualities, but in how their function is socially situated. The strength of van Dijck's model for understanding the participatory culture of architecture is its ability to connect such fleeting forms of popular culture or personal artefacts of the Sydney Opera House to practices, the mediation of time and a larger sense of public significance. Van Dijck observes that 'private collections tap into the much larger phenomenon of communal rites of storing and retrieving', thus underscoring the way representations can inform the social meanings of the Sydney Opera House for individuals and communities.[71]

The concept of socio-visual value established in Chapter 2 seeks to describe the attachment that people have towards the Sydney Opera House through representations. Participatory culture offers a way of defining widespread and contingent communities and audiences that exist globally, through their participation and online public engagement. Representations and textual contributions posted online are a form of evidence of both existing and new kinds of audience engagements. So how is the audience of the Sydney Opera House defined through its representations?

In their 2010 article, 'The Recognition and Misrecognition of Community Heritage', Waterton and Smith argue that the term 'community' has been so widely used that it defies specific definition. In particular they take issue with the idea of communities as homogeneous collectives with agreed viewpoints.[72] In the context of heritage, the term community is usually reserved to describe groups of people who are stakeholders in a particular site. This is central to the idea of social value and underpins the arguments made by scholars of this area such as Johnston and Byrne.[73] In contrast, the term audiences usually describes those groups of people, such as tourists, who come to visit places of heritage. The emphasis is on education and communicating the significance that places have for local communities to those who come from other places. Unlike communities, audiences are outsiders; it is assumed they do not have a prior connection with the site of heritage and that there is a need to 'educate' and instil the appropriate values of visited places. For example, Freeman Tilden, a seminal scholar of heritage interpretation, asserted that audiences would be more interested in preserving sites of cultural significance if they understood why they were valuable. A more contemporary perspective is offered by John Urry who proposes the idea of the 'historic gaze' to explain the significance of touristic practices at heritage sites.[74] But online audiences and communities are not clearly defined. Who is the community and who is the audience of the Sydney Opera House?

For objects of mass culture, such as a television melodrama, the audience can be clearly identified as those who watch the programme. For a building it is more complicated. One way to define the audience of a building is to count those who visit the actual edifice. Corporate documents relating to the Sydney Opera House certainly measure audiences in this way.[75] For example, from July 2010 to June 2011, the Sydney Opera House hosted 1,795 performances that were attended by 1.3 million people. The total number of visitors to the Sydney Opera House during the same period was 8.2 million, indicating that almost three-quarters of visitors do not attend a performance, but come to see the architecture. Are these visitors the audience of the Sydney Opera House?

Another way to define the audience of the Sydney Opera House would be to assume that it is the people of Sydney, the community that is geographically connected with this place. After all the Sydney Opera House is frequently used to represent Sydney, not only as a distinct place, but also in terms of its 4.61 million residents.[76] Yet in 2013, Deloitte assessed the economic impact of the Sydney Opera House, and specifically the building's digital footprint. This is one way in which online forms of participation with such places have been measured and determined to be of value. Deloitte estimated the building's digital audience at a reach of 128 million people, predominantly via Facebook.[77] This is almost 16 times the number of visitors to the Sydney Opera House building itself, estimated at 8.2 million,[78] and almost 90 times the 1.4 million people who attended a performance in the same year.[79] The Sydney Opera House is a well-known tourist destination as well as a performance venue. It is a landmark, which attracts visitors from other locations within Australia, as well as overseas. The audience of the Sydney Opera House is not only those who live in close geographical proximity, or those who visit within a particular year, but includes all those people who feel a sense of attachment to this place.

The Sydney Opera House is the locus of a widespread body of cultural activity. A diverse group of people engage with this place in many different ways. The architecture of the building serves as a symbol and is used to generate many other artefacts that are part of popular culture; some are objects of mass culture, such as snowdomes, while others are unique personal representations, such as a homemade child's hat. Both are shown in Figure 3.19.[80] These artefacts can be understood as representations made by members of the audience of the Sydney Opera House. They can be framed as responses to the architecture and therefore as evidence of people's engagement with this place. Such representations posted online are the result of complex everyday social interactions. For example, purchasing a snowdome as a souvenir is not just a commercial activity, but can be understood as a tangible memento that is used by the traveller to define, express and reinforce a social connection held with others still at home.[81] Trivial artefacts, such as a snowdome, can also serve as an object for cultural analysis that can reveal how places, such as the Sydney Opera House, are framed from particular perspectives.[82] What does the snowdome show? How is the building represented? How does this reveal whose story is being told?

In the same way, posting an image of a homemade children's hat online can be understood as a way of identifying with a particular place by demonstrating creative skill. Were the hat to be of some other less well-known work of architecture it would likely remain an obscure paper-plate piece of headwear, only discernible to a local community familiar with a local building. However, by employing the form of the Sydney Opera House in a homemade article both the mother (and author of the post) and child demonstrate their identification with the building, and implore its recognition. In his book, *Making is Connecting: The Social Meaning of Creativity, from DIY and Knitting to YouTube and Web 2.0*, David Gauntlett argues that people engage with the world by making things.[83] For Gauntlett, everyday creative outcomes are part of a participatory culture that is enabled by Web 2.0. People use these artefacts to connect with each other, both online and in their real-world lives.

Defining the audience of the Sydney Opera House through the online representations might appear too broad. Yet the relationship between audiences and

Figure 3.19 Homemade hat and commercial snowdome.

Sources: left, 'Sydney Opera House Hat made from paper plates' (© www.laughingkidslearn.com, 2016); right, Sydney Opera House souvenir snowdome.

communities is no longer clear. This distinction has been muddied by the advent of digital technologies. Whilst communities are usually understood to be those groups of people who have a strong connection through geography or common interest, audiences are characterised as groups to whom a message was broadcast. The way in which online participatory media platforms connect members of the same audience and make the structure of such groups more like communities means that these definitions are no longer as relevant or useful when considering online groups of people. Waterton addresses this problem in her article 'The Advent of Digital Technologies and the Idea of Community', wherein she makes a case for specifically revisiting the idea of communities that operate online in relation to heritage. Rather than define communities through their geographic or platform co-location, Waterton argues that online communities 'need not be considered in opposition to those created offline, but re-imagined as similar complexities of camaraderie and support forming in a new space, or place, where relationships are forged and new ways of being enacted and embodied'.[84] Building on Benedict Anderson's seminal work on 'imagined communities', Waterton makes a case for online activities and connections to be taken seriously.

Broader and more encompassing definitions of audience/communities align with the way the management of the Sydney Opera House envisages its goals for public engagement. Part of the 'Community Engagement and Access' programme of the Sydney Opera House seeks to extend opportunities for audience engagement with the organisation, both online and at external sites.[85] Representations, such as the snowdome or the homemade paper-plate hat also reveal the way the distinctions made between commercial objects and homemade things are more fluid than they might appear at first. The snowdome is a commercial object. Such an artefact is likely manufactured in China. Often snowdomes feature semi-accurate representations and strange compositions where the building features both inside the globe and as decoration on its base. However, as a souvenir the same snowdome anchors the ephemerality of a visit to the Sydney Opera House, gaining personal significance for its owner or recipient.[86] In a similar way the personal significance of the paper-plate hat changes if it becomes part of a children's craft e-book sold online. Now, the paper-plate hat, or its instructions, are a commercial product, deployed like the snowdome for economic gain.

Using representations to define the audience of the Sydney Opera House arguably extends audiences and communities even further. For example, the State Records Authority of NSW displays historical artefacts of the Sydney Opera House from its collections as a 'gallery' on its website (Figure 3.20). These images are the scanned pages of *The Red Book*, a set of architectural drawings prepared by Utzon's office during the construction of the building. Now that the building has been realised, these drawings serve a different purpose; as an online exhibition of archival material they attract audiences to the State Records Authority of NSW website. Perhaps people are keen to experience first-hand the changes in the profile of the building, a highly contested issue documented in the historical accounts of the building's realisation.[87] Such representations reveal how the communities that have a sense of attachment to the Sydney Opera House are not limited to those who reside in Sydney or Australia, or those who physically visit the site, but include the commercial entities involved in the design, manufacture and sales of objects of mass culture, the people who make things inspired by this place, the individuals and groups for whom the building holds personal memories, and the institutions who employ the popularity of the building as a point of interest.

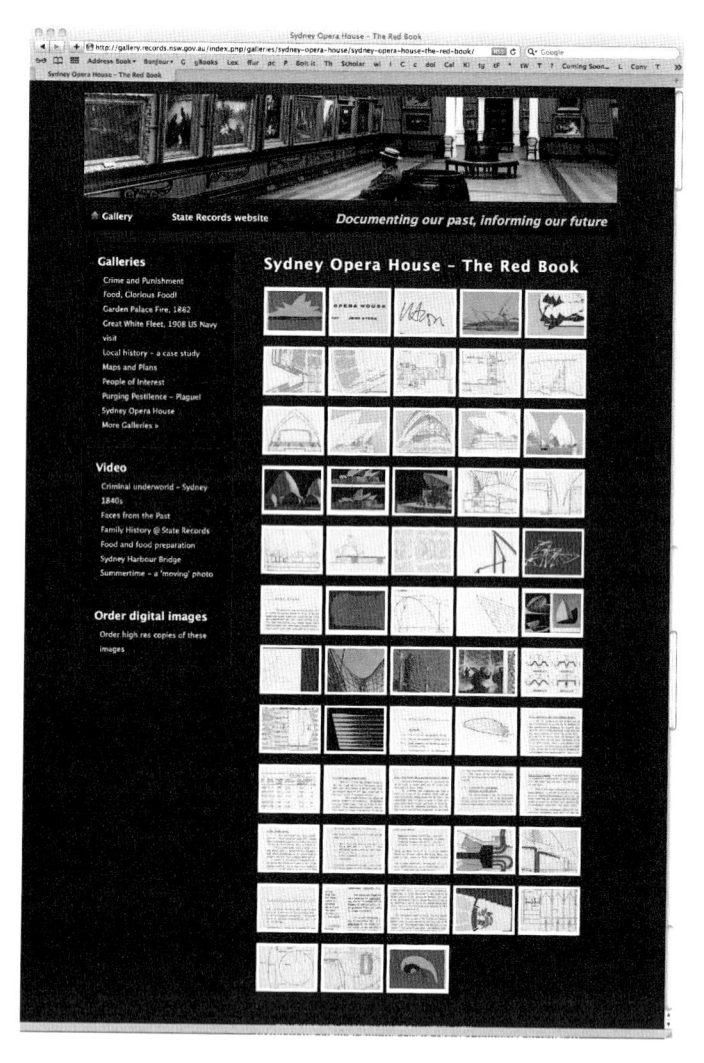

Figure 3.20 Scanned pages from *The Red Book* in a digital gallery.

Source: Screengrab showing pages from *The Red Book* posted as a gallery on the website of the State Records of NSW, 2017 (© Jørn Utzon, 1958. NRS 12707 [SZ107] – Collection: State Records of NSW).

The audience of the Sydney Opera House is best understood as a difficult to define social entity, comprising individuals, groups, commercial organisations and institutions, some which may be more appropriately characterised as communities, others as passive audience groups. As is exemplified by the snowdome, the child's hat and the gallery of architectural drawings, the social entities that engage with the Sydney Opera House through representations are not easily defined as communities. Each of these entities is actively involved in creating or disseminating representations of the place in the online sphere. Each of the examples discussed frames the Sydney Opera House differently: the snowdome is a link to experiences, the paper-plate hat a humorous costume for a child, and the scanned pages of *The Red Book* a connection

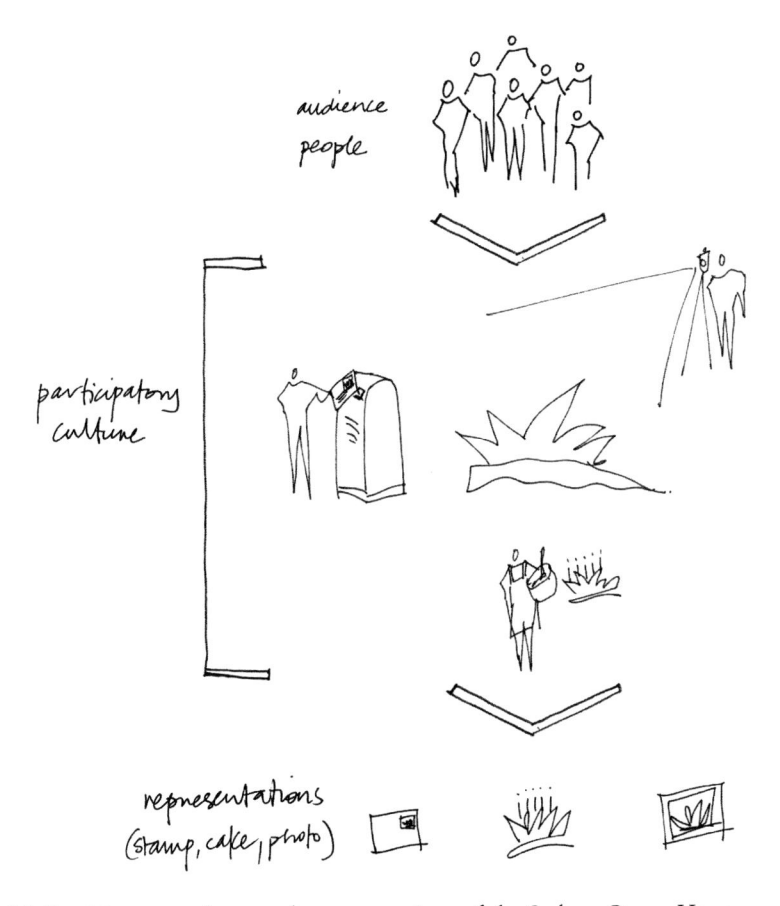

Figure 3.21 Participatory culture and representations of the Sydney Opera House. Representations show how communities-audiences connect with places, as active social groups, in a process that could also be described as participatory culture.

to the building as an historic object. Whilst the motivation for the use and consumption of representations of the Sydney Opera House differs for each of these entities, each contributes to the iconicity of the building, that is the frequency with which depictions of it appear in visual culture and become mentally embedded. Rather than privilege the significance of groups characterised as communities over those more akin to audiences the aim here is to understand the ways in which people engage and interact with the Sydney Opera House as evidenced in representations of the building (Figure 3.21).

Introduction to the observations and analysis of participatory culture

Having established the concept of participatory culture and the way it is manifest in participatory media, the collection of representations of the Sydney Opera House can be organised into a speculative schema by interpreting the practices that precede their production (Figure 3.22). The schema describes six socio-visual practices: *telling, critiquing, making, trading, visiting and capturing*. These categories emerged from the continuing process of ordering the collection of representations to try and find a meta-category, which could explain their relationship to each other and to the concept of socio-visual value. While both these instances are examples of participation through online media platforms, it is important to articulate that the focus is on participatory culture. The subsequent chapters offer more detailed descriptions of the significance of each socio-visual practice, elaborated upon through observation and analysis. Although the examples are to a greater and lesser extent examples of participatory media, it is important to articulate that these websites are not the same as participatory culture; the former is the site and enabler of the latter.

The social activities and visual contributions on these websites are closely connected and at times intertwined with these information and communication technologies. Therefore, while it is not possible to make a perfect distinction between participatory media and participatory culture, it is also important not to conflate them. Participatory culture is enacted both online and offline. While it is possible to observe those aspects of participatory culture posted publicly on the internet, some parts inevitably continue to remain private. At the same time participatory media platforms enable communication through the contribution of text and images where 'a set of

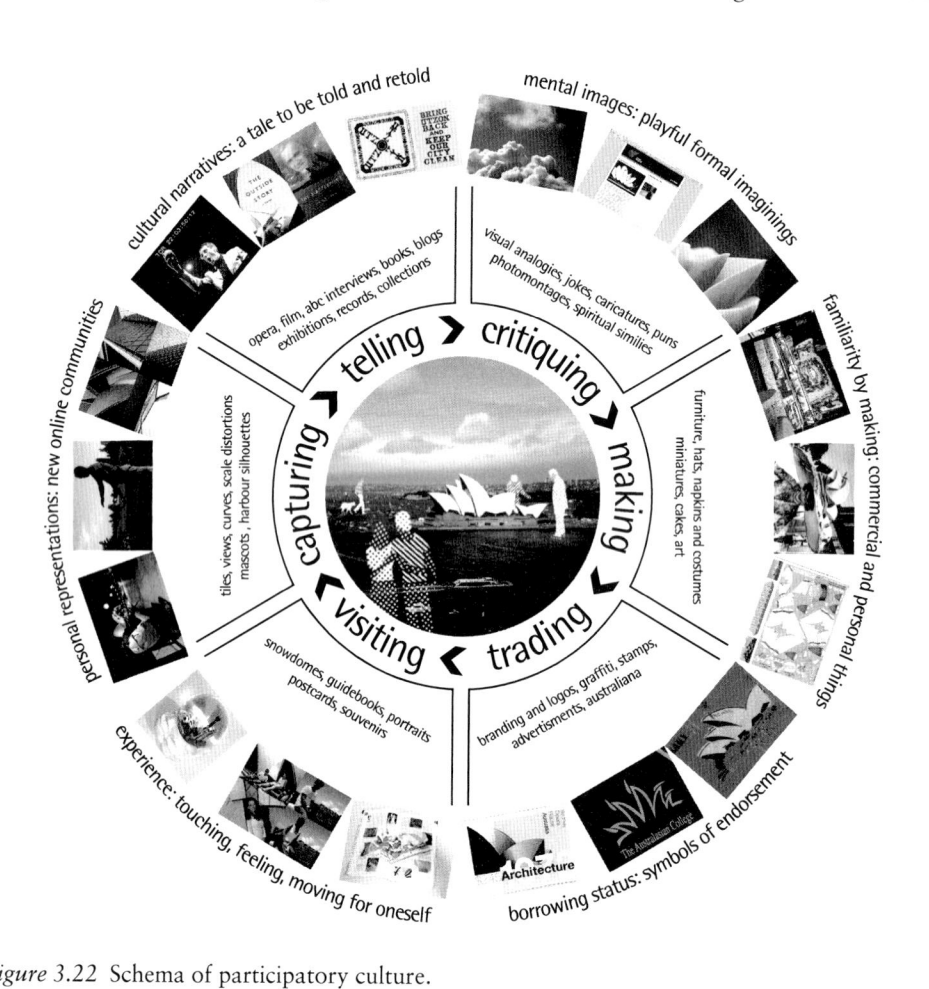

Figure 3.22 Schema of participatory culture.

associated "protocols" or social and cultural practices ... have grown up around that technology'.[88] So while it is valuable to distinguish between media and culture, acknowledging their co-constitution is also important, as participatory culture is an agglomeration of all of these: the images, the accompanying text, posting, sharing, the socio-visual practices that underpin them and the online technologies that facilitate them (Figure 3.23).

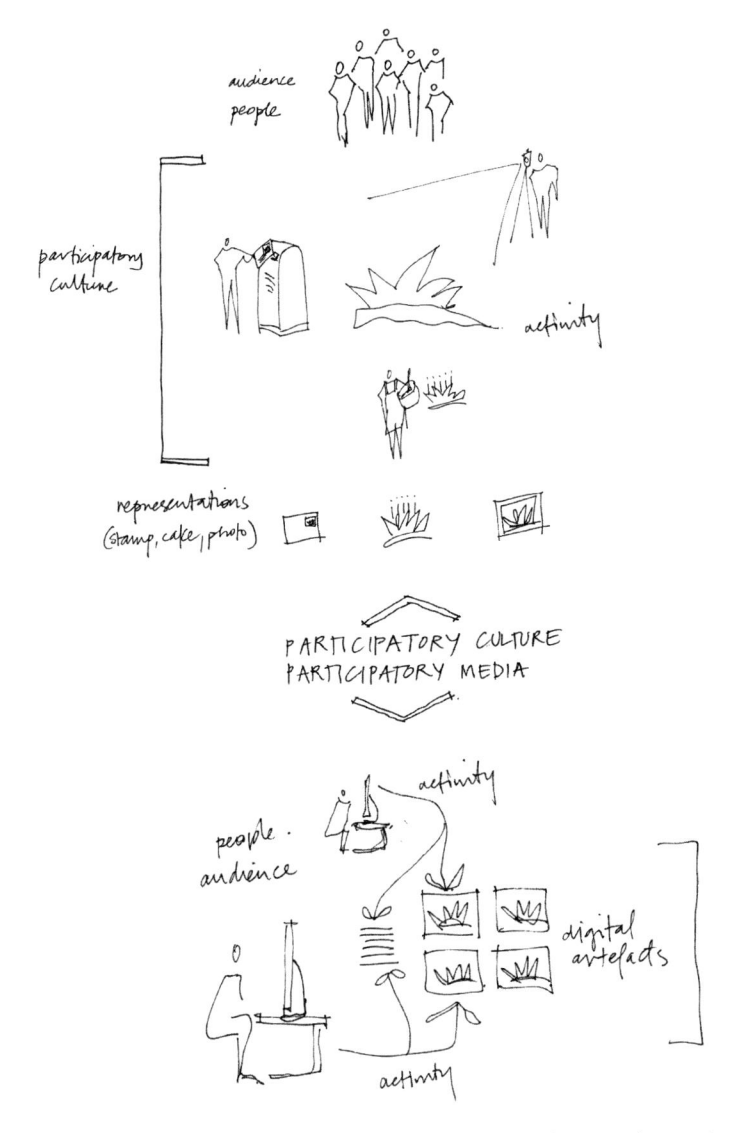

Figure 3.23 The relationship between artefacts, participatory culture and participatory media. Participatory culture can be conceptualised as people who come together as an audience, the activities that they engage in associated with the Sydney Opera House and the artefacts produced and used in these activities. Participatory media is a technological artefact that makes participatory culture visible in an online setting. Participatory media is also an artefact and in this way reveals how artefacts are both produced and in turn then structure examples of participatory culture.

Practices are central to the participatory culture that arises in response to objects of culture, such as the Sydney Opera House. Practices are forms of engagement that occur at both a personal and at a societal level. Objects such as an opera-house-shaped cake or a snowdome are the results of these practices; such artefacts in turn become images used online to extend and develop new kinds of engagements with the building. These representations and the activities around them are evidence of the building's participatory culture, documented and made visible through participatory media.

The initial question for this research asked how the representations of the Sydney Opera House posted online might evidence the building's social value. The literature on iconic architecture, introduced in Chapter 2, indicated that the relationship between iconicity and frequent representation in visual culture has already been recognised in the scholarly contributions of Leslie Sklair, Terry Smith, Richard Weston and Kester Rattenbury. This connection, however, has not been recognised in terms of the representations posted online and in terms of people's sense of attachment to iconic building's such as the Sydney Opera House. This attachment, as related to representation, was established as socio-visual value. Participatory culture, as conceptualised through the work of Henry Jenkins, provides the preliminary criterion to create a taxonomy that makes a meaningful system of relationships between the hundreds of examples gathered as part of the research. Michel Foucault asserts in *The Order of Things* that it is the overarching relationship between the categories of an ordering system that is key to the generation of knowledge. Foucault describes how any attempt at creating an ordering system relies on 'the result of a precise operation and the application of a preliminary criterion'.[89] Participatory culture offers a material and embodied conceptualisation of the socio-visual practices through which people make connection with, and express existing relationships with, the building. Reframed as the products of participatory culture, the representations posted online are significant evidence of the socio-visual value of the Sydney Opera House.

The preliminary criterion that makes sense of the collection of representations of the Sydney Opera House is participatory culture. Framed in this way, the representations evidence six socio-visual practices that together comprise the participatory culture of the building. While the representations and engagements are shared online these practices exist offline as part of everyday life. The schema of socio-visual practices informs existing understandings of the way in which the production of representations of the Sydney Opera House, like their sharing online, are implicated in mediating relationships, temporality and experience for individuals and communities.

Conclusion

The term participatory culture has been used in media studies to describe the cultural activities of individuals and groups around forms of popular culture,[90] but it has not been extended to describe the activities of people around works of architecture, or the centrality of representations to these practices.[91] Prior to Web 2.0 assessing the social value of places for audiences and communities required gathering evidence from the private realm of people's lives, through methods such as interviews, workshops and questionnaires. Participatory media connects audiences, participation and representations so that it is possible to observe how the creation and dissemination of representations, both online and offline, evidence the socio-visual value of the Sydney Opera House for such groups. Explored through van Dijck's conceptual tool of mediated memories, these online and offline artefacts are connected to the desire to mediate time, to mediate our personal and collective sense of identity and between individual experiences and embodied practices which underpin the value of the Sydney Opera House as a world-famous iconic building.

Notes

1 Weston here is referring to a pencil sharpener his friend Martin Schwartz possesses. Schwartz is also an architect and writer. See footnote no. 6 in Weston's essay. Richard Weston (2006) 'Monumental Appeal: Reflections on the Sydney Opera House'. In *Building a Masterpiece: The Sydney Opera House*, edited by Anne Watson. Aldershot: Lund Humphries, p. 22.

2 Alan John and Dennis Watkins (1995) 'The Eighth Wonder', Australian Opera.

3 These kinds of distinctions are central to the field of semiotics where authorities, such as Charles Peirce, theorise the structure of language and meaning. However, the intention here is not to enter into a semiotic discussion of these two representations, but to find a way of organising the collection of representations which might reveal the building's social value.

4 William J. Thomas Mitchell (1986) *Iconology: Image, Text, Ideology*. Chicago: University of Chicago Press, p. 9.

5 Mitchell, *Iconology*, p. 10.

6 Tony Bennett, Lawrence Grossberg and Meaghan Morris (2009) *New Keywords: A Revised Vocabulary of Culture and Society*. Oxford: Blackwell, pp. 306–307.

7 'Tagging' is a system of collaborative classification known as a folksonomy.

8 Steve Watson and Emma Waterton (2010) 'Introduction: A Visual Heritage'. In *Culture, Heritage and Representation: Perspectives on Visuality and the Past*, edited by Emma Waterton and Steve Watson. Surrey: Ashgate, p. 1; David Crouch (2010) 'The Perpetual Performance of Heritage'. In *Culture, Heritage and Representation: Perspectives on Visuality and the Past*, edited by Emma Waterton and Steve Watson. Surrey: Ashgate.

9 Crouch, 'Culture, Heritage and Representation'.

10 Watson and Waterton, 'Introduction', p. 4.

11 Two chapters that focus on digital examples of representation are: Jerome de Groot (2010) 'Historiography and Virtuality'. In *Culture, Heritage and Representation*, edited by Emma Waterton and Steve Watson. Surrey: Ashgate, pp. 91–104; Richard Voase (2010) 'Visualising the Past: Baudrillard, Intensities of the Hyper-Real and the Erosion of Historicity'. In *Culture, Heritage and Representation*, edited by Emma Waterton and Steve Watson. Surrey: Ashgate, pp. 105–123.

12 Jean Baudrillard (1994) *Simulacra and Simulation*. Ann Arbor: University of Michigan Press.

13 Brenda Danet and Tamar Katriel (1994) 'No Two Alike: Play and Aesthetics in Collecting'. In *Interpreting Objects and Collections*, edited by Susan M. Pearce. London: Routledge, p. 260.

14 David Gauntlett's work on creative methodologies makes a case for reflective and intuitive processes as part of formal research. He states that the process of working creatively allows for an iterative and reflective process to take place that results in a more considered and nuanced result, rather than more direct methods, such as interviews and surveys. David Gauntlett (2007) *Creative Explorations: New Approaches to Identities and Audiences*. London: Routledge; David Gauntlett and Peter Holzwarth (2006) 'Creative and Visual Methods for Exploring Identities'. *Visual Studies*, 21 (1), pp. 82–91.

15 Michel Foucault (2003 [1966]) *The Order of Things: An Archaeology of the Human Sciences*. London: Routledge.

16 Danet and Katriel, 'No Two Alike', pp. 253–277.

17 Jorge Luis Borges (1965) 'The Analytical Language of John Wilkins (El Idioma Analítico De John Wilkins)'. In *Other Inquisitions 1937–1952*, translated by Ruth L.C. Simms. Austin: University of Texas Press, p. 103.

18 'Opera House Design Be a Lively Topic' (1957) *Sydney Morning Herald*, 2 February, p. 2.

19 'Arts and Crafts' (1962) *Sydney Morning Herald*, 11 April, p. 6.

20 Baudrillard, *Simulacra and Simulation*, p. 6.

21 Paul Jenkins and Lesley Forsyth (eds) (2010) *Architecture, Participation and Society*. New York: Routledge, p. xv.

22 Paul R. Jones (2006) *The Sociology of Architecture: Constructing Identities*. Liverpool: Liverpool University Press.

23 Jenkins and Forsyth, *Architecture, Participation and Society*; Peter Blundell Jones, Doina Petrescu and Jeremy Till (eds) (2005) *Architecture and Participation*. New York: Taylor & Francis; Nishat Awan, Tatjana Schneider and Jeremy Till (2011) *Spatial Agency: Other Ways of Doing Architecture*. New York: Routledge.

24 Jones, *The Sociology of Architecture*, p. 1.

25 Jones, *The Sociology of Architecture*, p. 21.

26 Jones, *The Sociology of Architecture*, p. 3. Jones frames this observation around the work of Garry Stevens, Magali Sarfatti Larson, Kim Dovey and Deyan Sedjuc. Garry Stevens (2002) *The Favoured Circle: The Social Foundations of Architectural Distinction*. Cambridge, MA: The MIT Press; Magali Sarfatti Larson (1994) 'Architectural Competitions as Discursive Events'. *Theory and Society*, 23 (4); Deyan Sudjic (2005) *The Edifice Complex: How the Rich and Powerful Shape the World*. New York: Penguin Press; Kim Dovey (2009) *Becoming Places: Urbanism/Architecture/Identity/Power*. London: Routledge.

27 Henry Jenkins (1988) 'Star Trek Reread, Rerun, Rewritten: Fan Writing as Textual Poaching'. *Critical Studies in Mass Communications*, 5 (2), p. 88.

28 Pertti Alasuutari (1999) 'Introduction: Three Phases of Reception Studies'. In *Rethinking the Media Audience: The New Agenda*. London: Sage, p. 9.

29 Alasuutari, 'Introduction'.

30 Stuart Hall (1973) *Encoding and Decoding in the Television Discourse*. Birmingham: Centre for Contemporary Cultural Studies.

31 Ien Ang (1985) *Watching Dallas: Soap Opera and the Melodramatic Imagination*, translated by Della Couling. London: Routledge.

32 John Fiske (1989) *Understanding Popular Culture*. Boston: Unwin Hyman.

33 Henry Jenkins (2006) *Fans, Bloggers, and Gamers: Exploring Participatory Culture*. New York: New York University Press, p. 1. Jenkins, 'Star Trek Reread, Rerun, Rewritten', p. 103.

34 Australian Government (2009) *Guidelines for the Assessment of Places for the National Heritage List*. Canberra: Australia Heritage Council & Department of the Environment, Water, Heritage and the Arts, p. 43.

35 For example, see O'Reilly's 2005 definition here: http://oreilly.com/web2/archive/what-is-web-20.html. I am aware that the term Web 2.0 has been critiqued for its inconsistent use, and that O'Reilly has secured much of his economic gain by maintaining his position as 'founder' of the term. The term is ambiguous and academically contested, since websites such as eBay and Blogger, established in the late 1990s, also harness user-generated content. These two examples, a publishing platform and an auction service pre-date O'Reilly's definition. However, here I use it to ground the research broadly in terms that are familiar to readers. Matthew Allen (2009) 'Tim O'Reilly and Web 2.0: The Economics of Memetic Liberty and Control'. *Communication, Politics and Culture*, 42 (2), pp. 6–23.

36 Tim O'Reilly (2005) 'What Is Web 2.0: Design Patterns and Business Models for the Next Generation of Software'. Retrieved: 27/09/2007, from: www.oreillynet.com/lpt/a/6228.

37 Don Tapscott and Anthony D. Williams (2006) *Wikinomics: How Mass Collaboration Changes Everything*. New York: Portfolio. Andrew Keen (2007) *The Cult of the Amateur: How Today's Internet Is Killing Our Culture*. 1st edn. New York: Doubleday.

38 Henry Jenkins and David Thorburn (2004) *Democracy and New Media*. Cambridge, MA: The MIT Press, pp. 1–2.

39 Howard Rheingold (2008) 'Using Participatory Media and Public Voice to Encourage Civic Engagement'. In *Civic Life Online: Learning How Digital Media Can Engage Youth*, edited by W. Lance Bennett. Cambridge, MA: The MIT Press, pp. 97–118.

40 Jenkins, *Fans, Bloggers, and Gamers*, p. 1.

41 Aaron Delwiche and Jennifer Jacobs Henderson (2013) *The Participatory Cultures Handbook*. New York: Routledge.

42 José van Dijck (2005) 'From Shoebox to Performative Agent: The Computer as Personal Memory Machine'. *New Media & Society*, 7 (3), pp. 311–332; Flickr (2012) 'Welcome to Flickr'. Retrieved: 17/07/2012, from: www.flickr.com/.

43 Fiona Cameron (2008) 'Object-Oriented Democracies: Conceptualising Museum Collections in Networks'. *Museum Management and Curatorship*, 23 (3), pp. 229, 43; Fiona Cameron and Sarah Mengler (2009) 'Complexity, Transdisciplinarity and Museum Collections Documentation: Emergent Metaphors for a Complex World'. *Journal of Material Culture*, 14 (2), pp. 189–218; Powerhouse Museum (2012) 'Homepage'. Retrieved: 19/07/2012, from: www.powerhousemuseum.com/ (the Powerhouse Museum is now known as the Museum of Applied Arts Sciences: https://maas.museum).

44 Pinterest was launched in 2011. It is a media platform structured as an online 'pin-board' and was used to facilitate the process of gathering the representations of the Sydney Opera House from any website as it maintains a link to the original site.

45 Google is increasingly developing specific search engines, such as Google Images. However, I recognise that Google is not a neutral retriever of information. Sources are ranked using its proprietary ranking algorithm trademarked as *PageRank* where web pages are measure in terms of their relative importance. José van Dijck explores the implications of these algorithms in relation to the construction of academic knowledge. 'Pagerank' (2012) *Wikipedia*. Retrieved: 03/08/2012, from: http://en.wikipedia.org/wiki/PageRank. José van Dijck (2010) 'Search Engines and the Production of Academic Knowledge'. *International Journal of Cultural Studies*, 13 (6), pp. 574–592.

46 Sydney Opera House (2012) 'Photo Gallery'. Retrieved: 03/08/2012, from: www.sydney operahouse.com/about/media/photo_gallery.aspx; ShotsbyGun.com (2005) 'Sydney Opera House'. *Flickr*. Retrieved: 03/08/2012, from: www.flickr.com/photos/gunsydney/176222797/.

47 Brett Campbell, 'Sydney Opera House Mosaic Dining Table'. *Brett Campbell Mosaics*. Retrieved: 03/08/2012, from: www.mosaics.com.au/Sydney-Opera-House-mosaics-art-table.html.

48 If desired searches can be refined to specific websites.

49 National Library of Australia (2013) 'Picture Australia (Now Trove)'. National Library of Australia. Retrieved: 19/03/2013, from: http://trove.nla.gov.au/general/australian-pictures-in-trove.

50 Henry Jenkins (2006) *Convergence Culture: Where Old and New Media Collide*. New York: New York University Press, p. 18.

51 Jenkins, *Convergence Culture*, p. 18.

52 Jenkins, *Convergence Culture*, p. 18.

53 UNESCO (2003) *Charter on the Preservation of the Digital Heritage*. Retrieved: 11/04/2011, from: http://portal.unesco.org/en/ev.php-URL_ID=17721&URL_DO=DO_TOPIC&URL_SECTION=201.html.

54 Fiona Cameron and Sarah Kenderdine (2007) *Theorizing Digital Cultural Heritage*. Cambridge, MA: The MIT Press; Yehuda Kalay, Thomas Kvan and Janice Affleck (2008) *New Heritage: New Media and Cultural Heritage*. New York: Routledge.

55 Laurajane Smith (2006) *Uses of Heritage*. London: Routledge.

56 The publication was the outcome of a two-day workshop titled 'Heritage Enquiries: A Designerly Approach to Human Values', which was part of the Designing Interactive Systems Conference held in Aarhus, Denmark. Elisa Giaccardi and Ole Sejer Iversen (2010) 'Workshop: Heritage Enquiries a Designerly Approach to Human Values'. Presented at the *Designing Interactive Systems*, Aarhus, Denmark, 16–20 August. Retrieved: 24/09/2012, from: www.dis2010.org/index.php?Workshops+at+DIS+2010.

57 Elisa Giaccardi (2012) 'Introduction: Reframing Heritage in a Participatory Culture'. In *Heritage and Social Media: Understanding Heritage in a Participatory Culture*, edited by Elisa Giaccardi. London: Routledge, p. 1.

58 John McCarthy and Peter Wright (2004) *Technology as Experience*. Cambridge, MA: The MIT Press, p. 5.

59 Giaccardi, 'Introduction', p. 1.

60 For example, the work of Dolores Hayden and Yi-Fu Tuan. Tim Cresswell (2005) *Place: A Short Introduction*. Malden: Blackwell; Yi-Fu Tuan (1975) 'Place: An Experiential Perspective'. *Geographical Review*, 65 (2), pp. 151–165; Dolores Hayden (1997) *The Power of Place: Urban Landscapes as Public History*. London: The MIT Press.

61 Jeff Malpas (2008) 'New Media, Cultural Heritage and the Sense of Place: Mapping the Conceptual Ground'. *International Journal of Heritage Studies*, 14 (3), p. 207.

62 Gillian Rose (2007) *Visual Methodologies: An Introduction to the Interpretation of Visual Materials*. 2nd edn. London: Sage, p. 2.

63 UNESCO (1972) *Convention Concerning the Protection of the World Cultural and Natural Heritage*. Retrieved: 26/11/2012, from: http://whc.unesco.org/archive/convention-en.pdf. Article 4.

64 Smith, *Uses of Heritage*, p. 29.

65 José van Dijck (2007) *Mediated Memories in the Digital Age*. Stanford: Stanford University Press, p. 24.

66 van Dijck, *Mediated Memories in the Digital Age*, p. 38.

67 John Urry (2002) *The Tourist Gaze*. 2nd edn. London: Sage.

68 Jørgen Ole Bærenholdt, Jonas Larsen, John Urry and Michael Haldrup (2003). *Performing Tourist Places*. Aldershot: Ashgate; Jonas Larsen (2004) *Performing Tourist Photography*. PhD thesis, Department of Geography and International Development Studies, Roskilde University, Denmark.

69 Smith, *Uses of Heritage*, p. 2; David C. Harvey (2007 [2001]) 'Heritage Pasts and Heritage Presents: Temporality, Meaning and the Scope of Heritage Studies'. In *Cultural Heritage: Critical Concepts in Media and Cultural Studies*, vol. 1, edited by Laurajane Smith. London: Routledge, pp. 25–44.

70 Susan Stewart (1984) *On Longing: Narratives of the Miniature, the Gigantic, the Souvenir, the Collection*. Baltimore: Johns Hopkins University Press; Beverly Gordon (1986) 'The Souvenir: Messenger of the Extraordinary'. *The Journal of Popular Culture*, 20 (3), pp. 135–146; Celeste Olalquiaga (1999) *The Artificial Kingdom: A Treasury of the Kitsch Experience*. London: Bloomsbury; Lisa Love and Nathaniel Kohn (2001) 'This, That, and the Other: Fraught Possibilities of the Souvenir'. *Text and Performance Quarterly*, 21 (1), pp. 47–63.

71 van Dijck, *Mediated Memories in the Digital Age*, p. xii.

72 Emma Waterton and Laurajane Smith (2010) 'The Recognition and Misrecognition of Community Heritage'. *International Journal of Heritage Studies*, 16 (1–2), pp. 4–15.

73 Chris Johnston (1992) 'Whose Views Count? Achieving Community Support for Landscape Conservation'. *Historic Environment*, 7 (2), pp. 33–37. Chris Johnston and Annie Clarke (2001) *Taking Action: Involving People in Local Heritage Places Part of the Heritage and Community: Theory and Practice Project*. Australian National University, Environment Australia, Context Pty Ltd. Retrieved: 26/04/2013, from: http://contextpl.com.au/static/pdf/taking_action_guide.pdf. Jim Russell and Chris Johnston (2005) 'Community and Cultural Values: The Upper Mersey Valley and the Tasmanian Wilderness World Heritage Area'. *Historic Environment*, 18 (2), pp. 39–42. Chris Johnston (2006) *An Integrated Approach to Environment and Heritage Issues*. 2006 Australia State of the Environment Committee. Retrieved: 31/12/2015, from: www.environment.gov.au/system/files/pages/38cc94e0-6c03-41b2-af5d-c73a8268e6c9/files/heritage.pdf. Denis Byrne, Helen Brayshaw and Tracy Ireland (2003) *Social Significance: A Discussion Paper*. Sydney: Research Unit, Cultural Heritage Division, NSW National Parks and Wildlife Service. Retrieved: 07/10/2010, from: www.environment.nsw.gov.au/resources/cultureheritage/SocialSignificance.pdf.

74 Freeman Tilden (1977) *Interpreting Our Heritage*. Chapel Hill: University of North Carolina Press; John Urry (2007 [1996]) 'How Societies Remember the Past'. In *Cultural Heritage: Critical Concepts in Media and Cultural Studies*, vol. 2, edited by Laurajane Smith. London: Routledge, pp. 188–205; John Urry (2007 [1990]) 'Gazing on History'. In *Cultural Heritage: Critical Concepts in Media and Cultural Studies*, vol. 3, edited by Laurajane Smith. London: Routledge, pp. 306–338; Urry, *The Tourist Gaze*.

75 Sydney Opera House (2011) *Sydney Opera House Annual Report 2010/11: Imagination Lives Inside*. Sydney. Retrieved: 07/06/2012, from: www.sydneyoperahouse.com/uploaded Files/About_Us_(new_nav)/Sydney_Opera_House/Annual_Report/Annual%20Report%20 2011.pdf, p. 10.

76 Australian Bureau of Statistics (2011) 'Population Change in Greater Sydney'. Retrieved: 10/03/2013, from: www.abs.gov.au/ausstats/abs@.nsf/Products/3218.0~2011~Main+Featur es~New+South+Wales?OpenDocument#PARALINK1.

77 Ric Simes, John O'Mahony, Frank Farrall, Kate Huggins and David Redhill (2013) *How Do You Value an Icon? The Sydney Opera House: Economic, Cultural and Digital Value*, edited by Deloitte. Sydney: Deloitte, p. 2.

78 In 2013 visitors to the Sydney Opera House were estimated at 8.2 million. Simes *et al.*, *How Do You Value an Icon?* p. 3.

79 Simes *et al.*, *How Do You Value an Icon?* p. 11.

80 Snowdomes are also known as snow-globes and water-globes. For a general history on snowdomes see Nancy McMichael (1990) *Snowdomes*. New York: Abbeville Press.

81 Lisa L. Love and Peter S. Sheldon (1998) 'Souvenirs: Messengers of Meaning'. Presented at the *Advances in Consumer Research*, Provo. Retrieved: 26/04/2013, from: www.acrwebsite. org/volumes/display.asp?id=8149, pp. 47–63; Love and Kohn. 'This, That, and the Other'.

82 Erica Rand uses a snowdome as the central object of her research on Ellis Island, as a way of unpacking the way these objects reveal whose heritage is held as important and who heritage is neglected. Erica Rand (2005) *The Ellis Island Snow Globe*. Durham, NC: Duke University Press.

83 David Gauntlett (2011) *Making Is Connecting: The Social Meaning of Creativity, from Diy and Knitting to Youtube and Web 2.0*. Cambridge: Polity Press.

84 Emma Waterton (2010) 'The Advent of Digital Technologies and the Idea of Community'. *Museum Management and Curatorship*, 25 (1).

85 Sydney Opera House (2011) *Sydney Opera House Annual Report 2010/11: Imagination Lives Inside*, p. 38.

86 For example see the work of Celeste Olalquiaga on Kitsch and memory, and the work of Lisa Love and Nathaniel Kohn on souvenirs. Olalquiaga, *The Artificial Kingdom*; Love and Kohn, 'This, That, and the Other'.

87 Peter Murray (2004) *The Saga of the Sydney Opera House: The Dramatic Story of the Design and Construction of the Icon of Modern Australia*. New York: Spon Press, pp. 32–33; Philip Drew (2001) *The Masterpiece: A Secret Life*. 2nd edn. South Yarra: Hardie Grant Books, pp. 175–208.

88 Jenkins is paraphrasing Gitelman. Jenkins, *Convergence Culture*, p. 13; Lisa Gitelman (2006) *Always Already New: Media, History, and the Data of Culture*. Cambridge, MA: The MIT Press. The interdependent relationship between practices and artefacts/technologies is also central to José van Dijck's concept of 'Mediated Memories'. van Dijck, *Mediated Memories in the Digital Age*.

89 Foucault, *The Order of Things*, p. xxi.

90 Aaron Delwiche and Jennifer Jacobs Henderson (2012) *The Participatory Cultures Handbook*. New York: Routledge.

91 Kester Rattenbury (2002) 'Introduction'. In *This Is Not Architecture: Media Constructions*, edited by Kester Rattenbury. New York: Routledge.

4 Mediating identity
Telling and critiquing

The story of the Sydney Opera House is recounted through many different forms including publications such as: dedicated monographs, academic and historical accounts, on the Sydney Opera House website and as part of the Wolanski Archives, in souvenir books, travel guides, in official and unofficial tours, personal retellings on blogs, and communally on sites such as Wikipedia.[1] The story of the Sydney Opera House is also recounted through visual forms of culture too, in films, plays and even as an opera.[2] The story of this building has inspired so many iterations since its inception almost 60 years ago, that it has almost become mythical.[3] At the same time the Sydney Opera House is manifest through representations; both sublime and ridiculous. On one hand the building has been compared to petals unfolding, sails on the harbour, clouds in the sky, whilst on the other, it is described as a scrum of nuns, a dish rack full of crockery, and turtles caught copulating (Figure 4.1). Such visual analogies have always been part of the public discourse that surrounds this building; responses to the winning scheme published in the *Sydney Morning Herald* described Utzon's design both as a masterpiece and like 'an insect with a shell on its back that has crawled out from under a log'.[4] From its inception the scheme was compared to a 'Danish pastry', 'a collection of abandoned umbrellas, an unmade bed, and a circus tent', and there were suggestions that it be regarded as 'something funny' and never be built.[5]

This chapter explores two socio-visual practices of participatory culture, *telling* and *critiquing*. In the last chapter six practices of participatory culture around the Sydney Opera House were identified as contributing to the building's socio-visual value and iconic status. Chapters 4, 5 and 6 describe how each practice can be exemplified through various representations. A broad description of each practice is then followed by a more in-depth analysis of specific examples of participation that can be connected to aspects of van Dijck's conceptual tool of mediated memories. Specifically, the examples of *telling* and *critiquing* examined in this chapter demonstrate the way representations of the building support participation at both a personal and collective level.

Beginning with an historical account, an opera and a narration presented as part of an architectural walking tour, the chapter demonstrates how these examples evidence how *telling*, and retelling, the building's story is a form of participatory culture through which people engage with this place (Figure 4.2). Then it focuses on the communities of the Sydney Opera House Wikipedia page to discover how the narrative of the building, alongside the accepted facts of its realisation, continue

Figure 4.1 Critiquing: flowers, sails, clouds, dishes, nuns and turtles copulating.

Sources: top left, photograph of a flower's petals posted to Flickr.com titled 'Sydney Opera House – Ok. Not exactly, but that's what I first thought of through the viewfinder' (© Luke Olsen, 2007); top middle, 'Sydney nostalgia – When I first saw these traditional Dhow sailing boats on the beach at Nungwe, Zanzibar, it made me a bit nostalgic for the Sydney Opera House' (© Darren Cox, 2007); top right, photograph of clouds that are opera-house-shaped (© Árný Jóhanns, 2006); bottom left, 'Nun and Opera House' (© Nathalie-Margaux Jouenne, 2008); bottom middle, illustration by John Stanton featured on the back cover of *Architecture in Australia* in February 1974 (Vol. 63, Issue 1) which was produced by students and marked the creation of the Australasian Union of Student Architects (© Architecture in Australia, 1974); bottom right, Eric Thake (Australia, b.1904, d.1982) *An Opera House in Every Home* 1972. Linocut, printed in black ink on white cartridge paper folded as card, 13.7 x 21.2 cm. (© Estate of Eric Thake, 1972 7.1973 – Collection: Art Gallery of New South Wales Gift of Hal Missingham 1973. Photograph AGNSW).

to be contested territory for the page's 'watchers'. This collaborative encyclopaedia entry reveals how the story of the Sydney Opera House is an extension of the building and the way in which people engage with this place through textual narratives. While tracing the way the story of the Sydney Opera House is told and retold in various ways, an historical association between the Taj Mahal and the Sydney Opera House reveals *critiquing* as a form of engagement, where both sublime and ridiculous analogies offer a means for socio-visual connections. *Critiquing*, like *telling*, is positioned as an historically rooted form of participatory culture, one which continues in a variety of ways from visual depictions and imagined metaphors through to repurposing the Sydney Opera House from performance venue to salt and pepper shakers, cakes or a hat. The value of critiquing is then explored through one specific representation and its derivatives. By focusing on Eric Thake's 'An Opera House in Every Home', it is possible to understand how such subversive metaphors are ways in which the building becomes appropriated from the realm of high culture into everyday culture, both in the past and the present.

Figure 4.2 Telling: books, operas and tours.

Sources: left, photograph of John Yeoman's 1968 early history on the Sydney Opera House titled *The Other Taj Mahal: What Happened to the Sydney Opera House*, published by Longmans, Green in London; middle, video still of the moment where Utzon beholds an orange and conceptualises the solution for the modular construction of the Sydney Opera House taken from an ABC recording of Alan John and Dennis Watkins 'The Eighth Wonder' the staged by Opera Australia in 1995 and again in 2016; right, photograph of Eoghan Lewis during a Sydney Architecture Walk tour of the Sydney Opera House (© Craig Bentley Smith, 2006).

Telling the Sydney Opera House: a textual and performative practice

In 1968, John Yeomans recounted the story of the construction of the Sydney Opera House. His book, titled *The Other Taj Mahal: What Happened to the Sydney Opera House*, was a work of individual journalistic research and one of the first monographs on the subject.[6] Prior to Utzon's resignation in 1966, most public discussion on the Sydney Opera House took place in newspapers, such as the *Sydney Morning Herald*, or in professional magazines such as *Architecture Australia* (previously titled *Architecture in Australia*) and the Italian architecture journal *Zodiac: International Magazine of Contemporary Architecture*. The story of the Sydney Opera House is also recounted on Wikipedia, the online collaborative encyclopaedia. On Wikipedia members can create, review and edit encyclopaedia entries. Unlike Yeomans' monograph, the story of the Sydney Opera House on Wikipedia is subject to change and negotiation, something evident in discussions around changes to the page. The Wikipedia entry is a collaborative version of the story, but one that sits outside of official versions, while Yeomans' monograph is an individual account that has been endorsed by a publisher. These two examples demonstrate the way *telling* the story of the Sydney is not confined to a particular kind of social formation, and as is described next, neither is it confined to text-based publications.

In 1995, Opera Australia commissioned and staged an opera called *The Eighth Wonder* that recounted the political story of the construction of the building.[7] The libretto, by Dennis Watkins, is set in the 1950s and offers a 'sense of the development of national identity' in Australia during this period, whilst the score, by Alan Johns, is eclectic and popular.[8] Interestingly Opera Australia, the country's national opera company, emerged from the Elizabethan Theatre Trust, one of the companies to be housed in the initial brief for the design of the Sydney Opera House. It seems fitting that this company stage a performance about the edifice and institution that was instrumental in its development. In contrast to the grand performance of the story in *The Eighth Wonder*, Sydney architect Eoghan Lewis retells the story of the building through a different kind of performance; the walking tour.[9] In addition to practising as an architect,

Lewis runs Sydney Architecture Walks (SAW); one of which focuses on the Sydney Opera House. In these tours, Lewis takes groups of 15 or 20 people to several parts of the Sydney Opera House and its surrounds, offering an 'in-depth and textured portrait of enigmatic Danish architect Jørn Utzon as well as a narrative of perhaps the 20th centuries greatest architectural project' using his own perspective and his architectural experience to explain the building.[10] His engaging manner and extensive knowledge creates an intimate and often quite personal account of the realisation of this building.[11]

The manifestation of the story of this building in the form of a book, a collaborative web page, an opera and a guided tour indicates that the practice of *telling*, and by extension all the practices identified in the schema set out here, are not limited to specific forms of culture, or to individuals, groups, commercial organisations or institutions. Participatory culture does not only occur online, but can be analogue too. Although these examples vary widely in terms of their historical terms and disposition, together they offer a new way of understanding the iconic value and cultural significance of the Sydney Opera House.

Participatory culture, as defined by Henry Jenkins, is 'active, critically engaged and creative' members of society.[12] As the examples cited above demonstrate, the practice of *telling* the story of the Sydney Opera House is embodied in the activities it prompts. A more detailed observation of the Wikipedia page of the Sydney Opera House offers an example of the way in which 'curating' or 'maintaining' a non-authorised version of this story brings together a community of people who together engage in critical discussions on what should and shouldn't be included, as interwoven with the site's structure, editorial guidelines and principles.

Watching the Wikipedia article

Wikipedia is a participatory platform that supports a collaborative encyclopaedia holding over five million articles and growing at 800 new articles per day.[13] Unlike a traditional encyclopaedia, whose authority and reliability lay with the reputation of the publishing house, such as the *Encyclopaedia Britannica*, Wikipedia has emerged as a free online democratic knowledge space, created, edited and maintained collaboratively. Wikipedia has been central to conceptions of Web 2.0 open access and participatory technologies. While Wikipedia's participatory structure and collaborative content is often critiqued as inaccurate or unreliable – after all, everyone can claim to be an expert and write an article – comparisons between authoritative sources such as the *Encyclopaedia Britannica* and Wikipedia have found a similar level of erroneous information.[14] This similarity is perhaps because users resolve disputes about content accuracy through discussion.

Each Wikipedia entry created has a series of additional pages that sit alongside the main article page. The 'Article' page displays the most recently edited version. Information for the topic is displayed under a series of subheadings. For example, on the Sydney Opera House's Wikipedia page, these include: Description; Construction history; Jorn Utzon and his resignation; Architectural design role of Peter Hall; Opening; Performance firsts; Reconciliation with Utzon – building refurbishment; Public and commemorative events; Awards; See also; References; Bibliography; and External links (Figure 4.3).[15] Anyone can edit the article. People can choose to become Wikipedia members or to be unregistered users who contribute to the page.[16] However, there are two other pages for each Wikipedia entry. A 'Talk' page that is a discussion space to propose and debate improvements to the Wikipedia entry and 'View history'

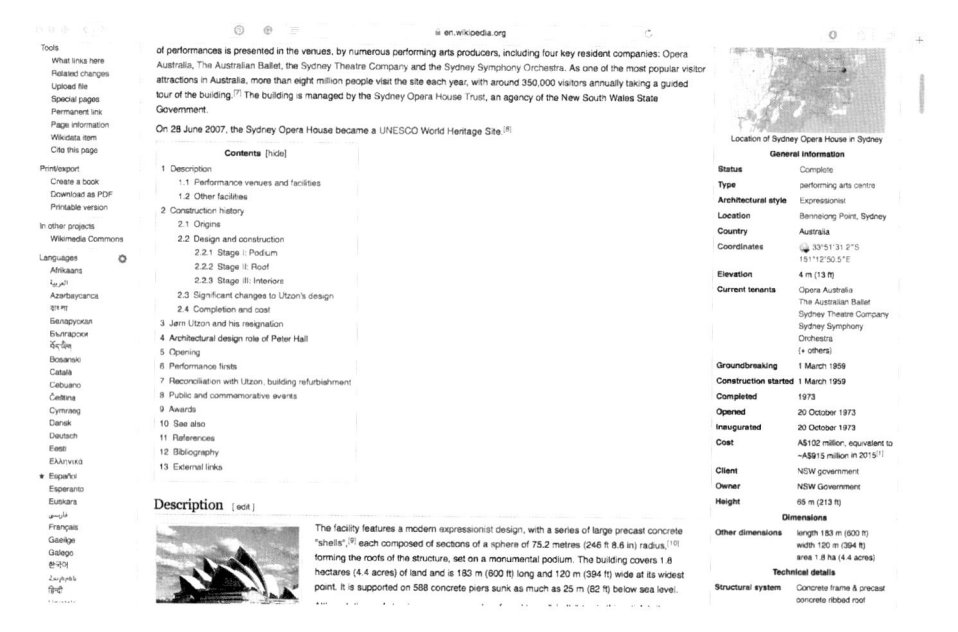

Figure 4.3 Wikipedia's Sydney Opera House page.

Source: Screengrab from Sydney Opera House Wikipedia Article Page (Wikipedia, 2016).

page that documents all the changes made to the page, when, by whom (either user-name or their IP address is shown) and a summary of the changes made. Changes can be small or major edits or even reversions back to a prior version of the Article page. If malicious changes appear or other incidents occur, the administrators of Wikipedia, who are higher in the social structure of the platform than members, have the facility of locking the edits on a page until future notice.

The Sydney Opera House article page on Wikipedia was created on 24 September 2001, during Wikipedia's first year of existence.[17] This page has been edited over 4,500 times during the last 15 years and receives an average of 2,500 views per day.[18] In terms of page views the page ranks at 8,842 from more than five million overall pages, making it a relatively popular page. About two-fifths of the edits of the Sydney Opera House article page on Wikipedia are by anonymous users rather than registered Wikipedia members and about a third of the edits are considered minor.[19] As a means of comparison the most edited pages on Wikipedia have about a million edits, but these pages are mostly Wikipedia's own information pages. The most edited page not about Wikipedia itself is the article about George W. Bush, which has almost 46,000 edits, demonstrating the popularity of the subject and, perhaps, the diverse views on what content should be included.[20] The edits on the Sydney Opera House article have been performed by about 2,000 different users, but like all social media sites, some users are more active than others.[21] Approximately 33 per cent of all the edits are the work of about 300 editors of the page, and about 15 per cent are by the top five editors.[22] Participation, like many online communities, is skewed to active users. Privileges are not uniform; developers and system administrators have the highest level of access while newly registered and anonymous users the lowest level of access.[23]

The Sydney Opera House article has 189 'watchers'. Watchers are members who request notification of any edits made on specific pages. On Wikipedia, participation is not solely carried out by contributing content, but can also involve developing, discussing and maintaining the article page. Any discussion about the article is documented on the 'Talk' page. Discussions on the Sydney Opera House talk page date from 2004 to the present day and are divided between issues about the content of the article and editorial issues, such as grammar, formatting and compliance with Wikipedia's manual of style.[24] Editorial issues are not only handled by Wikipedia members, but also by 'bots'. This is the shorthand name for software robots that search for vandalism and other introduced errors. Bots quickly correct vandalism within a few hours and the community usually corrects errors not picked up by them within a few days.[25] This means that while Wikipedia is a site of participatory culture, it is also structured by socio-technical interactions between the platform, its content management system and the people who frequent it.[26]

The current content on the Sydney Opera House article page describes the story of the building's realisation, Utzon's departure and reconciliation, Peter Hall's contribution, a small section on public and commemorative events, a bibliography and references. The inclusion or exclusion of this information is negotiated by members and watchers on the talk page and is assessed under Wikipedia's three core rules: 'verifiability', which requires content referencing existing publications and reputable sources;[27] 'no original research', which excludes unpublished material being included;[28] and 'neutral point of view', which requires information to be presented in an unbiased manner.[29] Of the 46 topics on the talk page 14 (30 per cent) are editorial posts by bots and members about maintaining Wikipedia's editorial and formatting standards. About nine posts (20 per cent) are discussions on technical aspects of the building, its construction, the acoustics of the performance venues, details on power supply or the definition of the form of the building's roof as a paraboloid or hyperboloid. Another nine posts (20 per cent) raise well-rehearsed controversies around the issues of Utzon's resignation and subsequent reconciliation or other interpretations of historical facts. Two posts are about visitor issues, such as the existence of a hot-dog stand or slippery steps and the remaining 12 posts focus on the lack of representation of the building's interiors, significant events such as the painting of 'No War' on the building's sails, the building's symbolism, influence on other works of architecture and its role in popular culture. The exclusion of any mention on the article page about the five-metre high 'No War' grafitti painted in red on the sails of the Sydney Opera House in 2003 is interesting because the section on 'Public and commemorative events' does include mention of its role as a venue for the 2000 Olympic Games, as inspiration for *Icon*, a large-scale music theatre piece by Constantine Koukias and REM in celebration of the building's 20th anniversary, and as a site for projections and New Year's Eve fireworks celebrations. The discussion around including the painting of 'No War' on the sails of the Sydney Opera House reveals the way in which some members envision the article page as a consensus history, whereby this event is simply newsworthy rather than a notable moment in the building's history. Yet, part of the value of Wikipedia is its ability to document aspects of culture normally excluded from more formally acknowledged histories. As has already been discussed in the previous chapters, the No War event is demonstrative of the way in which the sails of the Sydney Opera House are a semi-sacred space, venerated through events such as the Vivid Festival and desecrated by the No War graffiti. Further, there are posts on buildings that appear to have a similar form to the Sydney Opera House as well as the building's symbolism. These aspects are central to evidencing its iconic value. Yet, these are mostly sidelined in the article page where they appear as links in the 'See also' section without any information on why they are connected with the Sydney Opera House. The most revealing characteristic of the way in which members and watchers identify with maintaining an article's academic integrity is in their exclusion of a 'popular culture' section.

In 2007, a member who goes by the pseudonym of 'TheCoolestDude' asks why their popular culture section has been removed. Member 'JPD' notes that a year ago a similar section was deleted. Reviewing the changes through Wikipedia's historical capture of the article page reveals the popular culture section was created by an anonymous user (IP address is listed as 202.147.143.166) on 25 November 2005 (Figure 4.4). The section listed references to the building's iconic status through its appearance in logos, such as the 2000 Summer Olympics, the Australian Football League Sydney Swans team as well as its appearance in films such as *Independence Day* and *Finding Nemo*. The popular culture section remained part of the article page until 17 December 2006, when it was replaced by a similar section titled 'Symbolism' which existed until 8 July 2007. Then it became incorporated as a subsection of 'Importance as a building and landmark' and lasted until 14 July 2007 when a series of vandalism incidents took place which deleted the section and it was never reverted. In the talk page discussion on the popular culture section that took place between 28 February and 1 March 2007, member Merbabu, the fifth most active watcher of the article, states:

> Pop culture sections are rubbish. Generally they have nothing to do with providing information about or improving are understanding of the articles actual topic. What do we learn about the Opera House by the trivial information that it appear in the film Independence Day.[30]

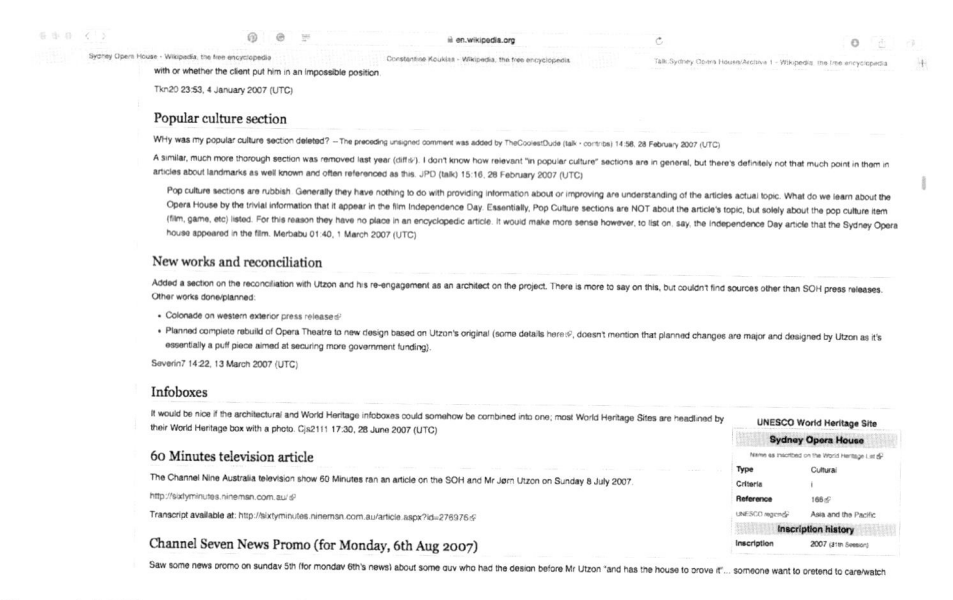

Figure 4.4 Why was my popular culture section deleted?

Source: Screengrab from the archived 'talk' page from the Sydney Opera House Wikipedia entry titled 'Talk:Sydney Opera House/Archive 1 (Popular Culture Section)' (Wikipedia, 2012).

What is important to understand here is not to whether the building's appearance in films, in logos or in other forms of popular culture is of value – this is the book's essential argument – but rather to demonstrate the way the building's significance is negotiated between watchers and members who have a connection with the Wikipedia Sydney Opera House page. In other words, the story itself, in its *telling* and *retelling*, whether through an architectural tour, an opera, a book or blog post is a site for engagement and participation in constructing its value in the 'public mind'. The history of the building is not a narrative of the past, but is made present through these retellings. And, furthermore, the discussions on the talk page demonstrate that audiences are not passive, but rather are critically engaged in this act, albeit one that is interwoven with the technological architecture and assistance of Wikipedia's software robots.

The other Taj Mahal

The title of Yeomans' book, *The Other Taj Mahal*, refers to the popular association between the Sydney Opera House and the Indian edifice referred to in Yeomans' title. This association emerged in the early years of the Sydney Opera House's history and appears common-sense; both buildings are large-scale white monuments, sculptural, curved and imposing, both are iconic destinations and are inscribed as World Heritage sites (Figure 4.5).[31] However, the programme for each building is quite different; the Taj Mahal is a mausoleum constructed at the order of Mughal emperor Shah Jahan in memory of his favourite wife, while the Sydney Opera House is a modern-day performing arts centre built by an aspirational city seeking to define its national identity. How did these two works of architecture become associated with each other?

The association between the Sydney Opera House and the Taj Mahal can be understood as a form of critique. As Leslie Sklair notes, iconic architecture is linked to some form of aesthetic judgement.[32] In the introduction to his book, Yeomans states that the Opera House 'gives off such an indestructible aura of magnificence, that it is hard not to think of it as another Taj Mahal'.[33] For Yeomans, the association is a form of praise, one that is tied to the use of architecture as a symbol of national identity. This is also

Figure 4.5 The Sydney Opera House and the Taj Mahal.

Sources: left, photograph posted to Flickr.com 'Sydney Opera House' (© Jim Robinson, 2006); right, photograph taken by Ross Garden Tours leader 'The Taj Mahal' (© Linda Ross, 2017).

evidenced in Lynd Nathan's 'Letter to the Editor' published in the *Sydney Morning Herald* in 1957, only days after Utzon's scheme had won the competition. Nathan makes a case for accepting Utzon's unique design even if its form seems unfamiliar:

> We do not live in an age of magnificent cathedral-building and our huge commercial structures are unlikely for many years to escape the utilitarian needs of the rectangular box. Nobody is likely to try and erect a Taj Mahal in Sydney, or a St. Mark's, Venice, or copy of the facade of the Paris Opera House. Nobody would want to.
>
> What then is left for us to do if we want to produce an architecture that will stimulate the mind?
>
> We must soar into the unimaginable future. And, if the result may seem to some of us to look like something out of the lunar world, Mars, science fiction, or the Missile Age, what is wrong with that? We are a young nation: where else have we to go but into the future? Where else can we look now for stimulus in architecture?[34]

Yet by 1962 the association between these two buildings was framed as derision. The *Sydney Morning Herald* reported the Opera House would be 'a beautiful building but quite useless except that it attracts tourists' like 'the Taj Mahal does' and concluded that the Opera House would be a 'memorial' and 'a marvellous ornament', rather than a great work of useable architecture.[35] This shift in the tone of the association with the Taj Mahal should be contextualised within the social changes occurring at the time. The 1950s saw the growth of mass tourism, accelerated by the advent of air travel, where destinations were framed as low-culture popular attractions, even though they offered status and presence for nations on a growing international stage.[36] The association between the Taj Mahal and the Sydney Opera House, both as a form of praise and as a form of criticism, reveals the dual role of the building as an icon of both high and low culture. This suggests that *critiquing* is also a practice that manifests the building's socio-visual value. This dual role surrounds and arguably contributes to the status of iconic architecture; as landmarks they offer international status but as popular places they are derided as superficial spectacles.

Critiquing: sublime and ridiculous

The second half of the chapter describes examples of participatory culture centred on the activity of *critiquing* of the Sydney Opera House. This predominantly takes place through metaphorical associations and visual analogies or through repurposing the building by transposing its scale or composition for an unrelated function. In this way, the Opera House has become something to be worn, something to be eaten, and even somewhere for roosters and chickens to reside! Serious representations repurpose the building as designer objects, speakers, a mobile camper trailer and jewellery. Some analogies elevate the significance of the Sydney Opera House by likening its form to natural and celestial objects, while others liken its form to more commonplace things like hats, chickens, cakes and dirty dishes. These critiques, positive and negative, do not detract from the significance of the Sydney Opera House; rather they offer a means to re-appropriate this monument into the personal and domestic realm, with satire and humour.

In 1976, three years after the building was opened, Australian comedian Barry Humphries dressed himself in the character of his widely loved Australian housewife Dame Edna Everage (Figure 4.6). As Dame Edna, Humphries attended the race meet at Royal Ascot, in England, toting a spectacular hat that featured the Sydney Opera House rendered from satin and curved wire. The hat, made by milliner Lorraine McKee, featured a 'sea of net and satin' where Sydney Harbour was 'enlivened with yachts and a diamanté-toothed shark'.[37] Here, the Sydney Opera House is an adornment, a miniaturised headdress atop a man pretending to be a middle-aged woman. McKee's miniature building-cum-hat is a playful celebration of the popular value of this place. Repurposing the form of the Sydney Opera House as a hat is the aesthetic inversion of seeing a scrum of nuns or crockery drying in a dish rack in the building's white monumental curved forms. The Sydney Opera House particularly lends itself to being a hat because of its sculptural composition that is best appreciated in the round, as well as its eye-catching silhouette, which is distinguishable even when highly abstracted. Surprisingly, there are many opera-house hats in addition to Dame Edna's (Figure 4.7). For example, Peter Morton's hat graced the cover of the *Women's Weekly* in July 1962, and is an example where the Sydney Opera House is a more formal inspiration.[38] Unlike the literal miniaturisation of the Opera House on McKee's Royal Ascot headdress, Morton's hat is an abstracted chic representation, featured on the front of a leading women's magazine.

There are contemporary examples too; in April 2008 a seemingly homemade 'Sydney Opera House fascinator' was listed on eBay for $85.00. The Sydney Opera House also appears as headwear, becoming hair styled into a 'mohawk', or a hat in the playful performances that people engage in at the building itself. While

Figure 4.6 Dame Edna's Ascot races hat.

Sources: left, John Timbers' photograph of Sydney Opera House hat worn by Barry Humphries as Dame Edna Everage, Ascot Ladies Day, 15 June 1976 (© John Timbers, 1976, 2004.024.006.005 (file ending 485) ('Materials') – Collection: Arts Centre Melbourne: Performing Arts Collection, Donated by the Sidney Meyer Fund in honour of Geoffrey Cohen, Trustee 1992–2003); right, photograph posted to Flickr.com of Dame Edna's 1976 hat which was exhibited in the Theatre and Performance Galleries of the Victoria and Albert Museum (© Phil Guest, 2015).

Figure 4.7 Hats: serious, handmade and performed.

Sources: left, 'The Opera House Hat' designed by Peter Morton featured on the 25 July issue of the Australian *Women's Weekly* magazine in 1962. Archives of the publication held in the Trove digital collection at the National Library of Australia (© Bauer Media Pty Limited/The Australian Women's Weekly, 1962); middle, 'Sydney Opera House Hat made from paper plates' (© www.laughingkidslearn.com, 2016); right, photograph posted to Flickr.com showing a performed-opera-hat, titled 'Brez and Tim share an opera house hat' (© Anna Oakley, 2008).

repurposing is a strategy for *critique* it is also implicated in practices that employ *making* representations as a form of cultural engagement with the Sydney Opera House. Representations can be interpreted in a number of ways. For example, 40 years after *The Other Taj Mahal* was published, Susan Giles, an artist, produced a series of sculptural works titled *Spliced Buildings* (Figure 4.8). In this series of paper models one is a hybrid form; part Taj Mahal, part Sydney Opera

Figure 4.8 Susan Giles: *Spliced Buildings*.

From the artwork series *Spliced Buildings* by Susan Giles. This piece is titled 'Taj Mahal and Sydney Opera House'. Archival paper, 17.5 × 19 × 8.5 inches (© Susan Giles, 2008. Photograph: Susan Giles).

House, as if two hollow models had been superimposed at an awkward angle into each other. The Taj Mahal in yellow, the Opera House in grey. In these paper sculptures Giles states that she is exploring the power of architecture in the mind and the 'metonymic representation of place'.[39] Giles' artwork is both a *critique* of these two iconic buildings, as well as a form of cultural engagement, where *making* (as opposed to writing) offers an alternative means to communicate ideas about, and become familiar with, the Sydney Opera House.

Each of these references and reinterpretations of the Sydney Opera House embody the idea that lauding or subverting this national symbol is a way of engaging with this place. At the same time as taking part in an embedded cultural practice, enacting the building-as-hat performance or envisioning yet another visual metaphor for the building are vernacular forms of creativity. These metaphors at times become so well known that they prompt further reinterpretations themselves.

A personal Opera House in every home

In 1972, the year before the Sydney Opera House officially opened, Eric Thake (1904–1982) produced a linocut depicting gleaming white plates in a dish rack to adorn his annual Christmas card. Thake was an Australian artist from Melbourne, who exhibited infrequently and worked mostly as a graphic artist. His work drew on surrealist art's dreamlike quality and was little known except within his social circle and amongst collectors and curators. Some of his most well-known works are from his annual Christmas cards, which were vehicles for his sharp wit and sense of humour, and were 'private statements intended for those who knew him'.[40] In the card designed for Christmas 1972, Thake created an image of dishes mimetically posed to reference Utzon's architectural masterpiece. He titled the card *An Opera House in Every Home* (Figure 4.9). This pun has become a popular visual metaphor for this building and is probably Thake's best-known image. The linocut is now widely reproduced on post-cards, aprons and tea towels, the 'Sydney Opera House as a dish-rack full of crockery' is a part of the visual rhetoric of this building.

On the surface it might appear that this work of art and the popular analogy it has inspired is an innocuous and trivial link to a work of architecture such as the Sydney Opera House. But it reveals how the building has been a site for critique, for participation through creative works and how certain images become embedded the public mind. Arguably, the tone of Thake's *An Opera House in Every Home* must be understood in the context of the ongoing rivalry between Sydney and Melbourne for cultural supremacy.[41] The launch of the competition for the design of the Sydney Opera House took place in the year after Melbourne had positioned itself on the world stage by hosting the 1956 Summer Olympic Games. The fantastic forms of the Opera House and the controversy over the years of the building's realisation certainly superseded the attention Melbourne received for the Summer Olympics. In light of this, Thake, a staunch Melburnian, made a clever pun on Sydney's almost completed cultural icon. The carefully arranged plates sit in an ordinary wire washing up rack evenly tilted to form the radial arrangement of the shells of the building. Their gleaming clean surfaces made shining by Thake's stark use of a single black ink to depict the scene. The washing-up water to the right is Sydney Harbour, gently lapping at the crockery-building and the scene even offers a certain distaste towards the architecture by the presence of a fly sullying clean

Figure 4.9 An Opera House in Every Home, original and copies.

Sources: top left, Eric Thake (Australia, b.1904, d.1982) *An Opera House in Every Home* 1972. Linocut, printed in black ink on white cartridge paper folded as card, 13.7 x 21.2 cm. (© Estate of Eric Thake, 1972 7.1973 – Collection: Art Gallery of New South Wales Gift of Hal Missingham 1973. Photograph AGNSW); top right, photograph posted on Flickr.com of dishes arranged in a washing-up rack to look like Thake's 1972 linocut (© James Prince, 2012); bottom, photomontage titled 'Opera Dishouse' referencing Thake's 1972 linocut which was produced as postcards by Avant Card and the Museum of Contemporary Art, Sydney (© Marco Berton, 2006).

dishes, drawing attention to the ordinary Australian experience. Thake's ironic Christmas card takes an international work of architecture that resides firmly in the masculine domain of high culture and concrete construction and swiftly draws it into the feminine realm of the domestic, the everyday experience and the personal connection with Australians.

Thake's linocut is a material object. Several of the prints made are held in the collections of various Australian and international cultural institutions.[42] However, the linocut is also an imagined metaphor that inspires further participation and creative social practice. References to Thake's image can be found online. Not simply its repetition on souvenirs, but rather as evidence of the way people make 'personal versions' of this scene as part of their everyday lives. The analogy between the Sydney Opera House and clean dishes in a dish rack has been repeated in various forms (Figure 4.9). Not only do people imagine the form of the building in completing their domestic chores, but contribute to the critique around the building's imagery by photographing these moments and sharing them online.

To illustrate the way in which Thake's visual analogy is implicated in the social value of the Sydney Opera House through participatory culture it is valuable to discuss an anecdotal blog entry. The fleeting reference to Thake's artwork by a young Australian mother abroad, offers an example of the relevance of this visual analogy to contemporary domestic life. On 11 November 2006, Lauren Purcell wrote:

with all the baths he's been getting he's probably cleaner than our crockery any-how. Which reminds me … there's a pile of dirty dishes in the kitchen waiting for me. A mummy's work is never done!! It's actually daddy's work in this house but they've been sitting there since Sunday and are starting to rival the Sydney Opera house [*sic*] for architectural ingenuity.[43]

The young mother describes the unruly havoc her son's illness is causing in her home, a situation most parents would relate to. The chaos of unexpected events, like childhood illnesses, could be likened to the difficulties faced by Utzon, Arups and subsequently by Hall, Todd and Littlemore in the realisation and construction of the Sydney Opera House. In this instance this internationally recognised and well-documented series of architectural events becomes the inspiration for a new interpretation of mess and disturbance to daily routine. Thake's visual analogy in *An Opera House in Every Home* offers a form of mediation between the sig-nificance of an architectural monument and the insignificance of a mother's daily caring for her children and home. Purcell uses the metaphor of domesticity, of femininity, simultaneously in opposition, and appropriation of the Sydney Opera House, at once distancing herself from the masculinity of its achievement (i.e. the notion of Utzon's genius) and drawing the building into her personal life. She com-ments on the structural ingenuity displayed by the precarious pile of dirty dishes, awaiting scullery.

The use of visual analogies for the building, like Thake's *An Opera House in Every Home*, is an expression of the relationship communities have with this place. The work of theorists, such as sociologist Ann Game and geographer Gillian Rose, can help reveal the way such moments as that described above are imbued with meaning. While their scholarship is not directed at heritage sites, their theoretical approach to the construction of meaning through subjective elements like memory, association and experience is an approach that embraces community attachment.

Game approaches the production of meaning by including emotion and experi-ence in the construction of sociological knowledge. In her book, *Undoing the Social*,[44] she critiques sociology's positivist position through deconstructive theory, while Rose draws on ethnography to understand the meaning of visual artefacts, and develop visual methodologies.[45] Game's deconstructive reading of sociology positions 'theory' as a writing practice, a story, a narrative or, in her words, a fiction. She argues that the dominant view, in which theory is seen as an abstract representation of the real, ignores or excludes affective qualities like memory and emotion and that the hegemonic view where empirical research is the only valid representation of reality, disregards the body and experience, in memory and association. Rose too emphasises the value of analys-ing visual material in an embodied manner as well as in its context. Theoretically aligned with Game, Rose sees meaning as a relational interaction between image and individual. For Rose, 'the significance of an object does not pre-exist its social life'.[46] Her anthropological approach uses the visual artefact to elicit the embodied meanings attributed by people. She continues:

> This [is a] performative understanding of the *co-constitution of image and observer* [which] thus demands a fine-grained analysis of how images and people relate to each other in specific times and places, producing each other in particular ways as they do so.[47]

The relationship between the young mother and the stack of plates is, like Rose asserts, 'co-constitutive'; the young mother is attributing meaning for the Sydney Opera House through her rendition of unclean crockery as an ingenious structure and Thake's visual analogy, of the Sydney Opera House as a dish rack full of crockery, gives her chaos some personal significance and homely comfort. In her blogpost describing the chaos of motherhood through the analogy of Thake's *An Opera House in Every Home*, the image co-constitutes her experience as a performance of critique, one that is embodied through the everyday rather than through more formal written means. She demonstrates the way Thake's analogy has value beyond the material linocut and has become a mental image associated with the Sydney Opera House, to such an extent that it can be relived through the ordinary act of washing dirty crockery. What is important to consider here is that while the act of critiquing can infer the building sublime or ridiculous, its main effect is the way such engagement and participation enables a form of appropriation at a personal level. Game's emphasis on subjective experiences, memories and associations as key to social meaning, in conjunction with Rose's argument for the co-constitution of image and observer, demonstrates how a visual analogy can mediate participation and individual expressions about significant places.

Conclusion

In describing telling and critiquing and proposing these as socio-visual practices of participatory culture, the chapter has provided evidence of the way in which representations mediate people's engagement with the Sydney Opera House, and by extension its social value. While many of these representations appear innocuous, their role in expressing people's connection with the building becomes exemplified under closer examination. The community of watchers for the Sydney Opera House Wikipedia article page demonstrates how the story of this building's realisation is a site for coming together and debating what qualifies to be included as significant, developing connections at a collective level. In contrast the observations of a young mother's everyday experience, which draws upon Eric Thake's subversive analogy of 'dishes in a washing-up rack' and the Sydney Opera House, demonstrates a much more personal moment. This aligns with the relational identity axis of van Dijck's conceptual tool, where the Sydney Opera House and by extension its representations are cultural touchstones through which identity is generated, maintained and expressed.

Notes

1 For example, dedicated monograph: Philip Drew (2001) *The Masterpiece: A Secret Life*. 2nd edn. South Yarra: Hardie Grant Books. Souvenir book: Michael Moy (2008) *Sydney Opera House: Idea to Icon*. Ashgrove: Alpha Orion Press. Travel guides: Ken Brass and Kirsty McKenzie (2005) *Eyewitness Travel Guides: Sydney*. London: Dorling Kindersley. Architectural tours: Eoghan Lewis (2000–2012, ongoing) 'Sydney Architecture Walks: Saw 2 Utzon and the Sydney Opera House' [Guided Walking Tour]. Sydney: Sydney Architecture Walks. Retrieved: 09/10/2012, from: www.sydneyarchitecture.org/pages/saw_TOUR_DESCRIPTIONS_main.html#saw2. Enthusiasts 'Sydneyoperahouse.Biz' (2013) Retrieved: 09/10/2012, from: www.sydneyoperahouse.biz/. Wikipedia 'Sydney Opera House' (2013) *Wikipedia*. Sydney Opera House website (2013) 'Sydney Opera House: House History'. Retrieved: 09/10/2012, from: www.sydneyoperahouse.com/about/house_history_landing. aspx. Wolanski Archives Paul Bentley (1998–2013 ongoing) 'The Sydney Opera House

Story'. Sydney: The Wolanski Foundation. Retrieved: 09/10/2012, from: www.twf.org.au/search/sohstory1.html.

2 Film. Play: George Bavinton (2006) *One Man's Vision: A Play in Two Acts and an Accompanying Exegesis*. MA thesis, Faculty of Creative Industries Queensland University of Technology. Opera: Alan John and Dennis Watkins (1995) 'The Eighth Wonder', Australian Opera.

3 Naomi Stead and Antony Moulis (2010) 'Sydney's Prometheus: Myth, Shame and Remediation at Joern Utzon's Sydney Opera House'. Presented at the *Imagining: Proceedings of the 27th Annual Conference of the Society of Architectural Historians, Australia and New Zealand (SAHANZ)*, University of Newcastle, Newcastle, New South Wales, Australia, 30 June–2 July. pp. 403–408. Drew, *The Masterpiece*, p. xii.

4 'Dane's Controversial Design Wins Opera House Contest' (1957) *Sydney Morning Herald*, 30 January, front page.

5 'Opera House Design Be a Lively Topic' (1957) *Sydney Morning Herald*, 2 February, p. 2.

6 Yeomans' book was reprinted in 1973. The other two monographs were by Michael Baume and Elias Duek-Cohen. The accounts portrayed were polemic and sought to either vilify Utzon or to redeem him. A few hundred untrimmed and unbound copies of Duek-Cohen's book were found in 1998, and were released with an additional introduction by Duek-Cohen and an addendum by Philip Drew, himself author of many books on the Opera House. John Yeomans (1968) *The Other Taj Mahal: What Happened to the Sydney Opera House*. London: Longmans, Green. Michael Baume and Peter Hall (1967) *The Sydney Opera House Affair*. Melbourne: Nelson. Elias Duek-Cohen (1967) *Utzon and the Sydney Opera House: Statement in the Public Interest*. Sydney: Morgan Pubs. Elias Duek-Cohen and Philip Drew (1998 [1967]) *Utzon and the Sydney Opera House: Statement in the Public Interest (with Additional Text by Philip Drew)*. Sydney: Morgan Pubs.

7 *The Eighth Wonder* was re-staged in 2000 to coincide with the Sydney 2000 Olympic Games and again in 2016.

8 Michael Halliwell (2004) 'A Comfortable Society: The 1950s and Opera in Australia'. *Australasian Drama Studies*, 45, pp. 11 and 25, respectively.

9 Lewis, 'Sydney Architecture Walks: Saw 2 Utzon and the Sydney Opera House'.

10 Lewis, 'Sydney Architecture Walks: Saw 2 Utzon and the Sydney Opera House'.

11 The author attended one of Lewis' walking tours in 2007.

12 Henry Jenkins (2006) *Fans, Bloggers, and Gamers: Exploring Participatory Culture*. New York: New York University Press, p. 1. Henry Jenkins (1988) '*Star Trek* Reread, Rerun, Rewritten: Fan Writing as Textual Poaching'. *Critical Studies in Mass Communications*, 5 (2), p. 103.

13 'Wikipedia:Statistics' (2016) *Wikipedia*.

14 Giles (2005) 'Internet Encyclopaedias Go Head to Head'. *Nature*, 438 (15 December).

15 'Sydney Opera House' (2016) *Wikipedia*.

16 Wikipedia membership is not a prerequisite to editing a page. Instead of showing the name of the member, Wikipedia records the IP address of the computer used to make the edit.

17 'Information for "Sydney Opera House"' (2016) *Wikipedia*.

18 'Pageviews Analysis: Sydney Opera House' (2016) *WikiMedia Tool Labs*. In contrast, the whole Wikipedia site received 245 million page views on average per day calculated over 90 days. 'Pageviews Analysis: Sydney Opera House'.

19 'WikiHistory: Sydney Opera House' (2016) *WikiMedia Tool Labs*.

20 The page with the most revisions was 'Wikipedia:Administrator intervention against vandalism'. George W. Bush ranked 50th in the list. These figures are dynamic and change daily. 'Wikipedia:Database Reports/Pages with the Most Revisions' (2016) *Wikipedia*.

21 'WikiHistory: Sydney Opera House'.

22 Twenty-nine users had made at least ten edits. The sum of their individual number of edits was 1,290. The sum of the top five users' edits was 610. 'WikiHistory: Sydney Opera House'.

23 Sabine Niederer and José van Dijck (2010) 'Wisdom of the Crowd or Technicity of Content? Wikipedia as a Sociotechnical System'. *New Media & Society*, 12 (8), p. 1372.

24 'Wikipedia:Manual of Style' (2016) *Wikipedia*.

25 Niederer and van Dijck, 'Wisdom of the Crowd or Technicity of Content?' p. 1375.

26 Niederer and van Dijck, 'Wisdom of the Crowd or Technicity of Content?'.

27 'Wikipedia:Verifiability' (2016) *Wikipedia*.

28 'Wikipedia:No Original Research' (2016) *Wikipedia*.

29 'Wikipedia:Neutral Point of View' (2016) *Wikipedia*.

30 'Talk:Sydney Opera House/Archive 1 (Popular Culture Section)' (2012) *Wikipedia*.

31 The Taj Mahal was inscribed in 1983, under Criterion (i). UNESCO (1983) 'Taj Mahal'. *World Heritage Centre*. Retrieved: 18/07/2012, from: http://whc.unesco.org/en/list/252/.

32 Leslie Sklair (2017) *The Icon Project: Architecture, Cities, and Capitalist Globalization*. New York: Oxford University Press.

33 Yeomans, *The Other Taj Mahal*, p. 3.

34 Letter titled: 'Looking to the Future' by Lynd Nathan of Killara. 'Opera House Design Be a Lively Topic', p. 2.

35 The *Sydney Morning Herald* was quoting member of the opposition Mr F.M. Hewitt. 'Opera House Like Taj Mahal: Opposition M.L.C.' (1962) *Sydney Morning Herald*, 12 September, p. 16.

36 For more on Tourism Studies and the architectural destinations see: D. Medina Lasansky and Brian D. McLaren (2004) *Architecture and Tourism: Perception, Performance and Place*. New York: Berg. John Urry (2002) *The Tourist Gaze*. 2nd edn. London: Sage. Dean MacCannell (1999) *The Tourist: A New Theory of the Leisure Class*. Berkeley: University of California Press.

37 Barry Humphries and Lorraine McKee (1976) 'Theatre Costume for Dame Edna Everage' [Hat]. Victoria and Albert Museum. Retrieved: 26/03/2013, from: http://collections.vam. ac.uk/item/O100914/theatre-costume-humphries-barry/.

38 Peter Morton (1962) 'Hat on the Cover of the Australian Women's Weekly on 25 July' [Hat]. Trove Digitised Newspapers and More, National Library of Australia. Retrieved: 26/12/2013, from: http://trove.nla.gov.au/ndp/del/page/4912887.

39 Steve Ruiz (2010) 'Susan Giles @ Kavi Gupta' [Blog]. Chicago Art Review. Retrieved: 30/09/2012, from: http://chicagoartreview.com/2010/02/24/susan-giles-kavi-gupta/. I corresponded by email with Susan Giles on 21/10/2011. I asked her for an artist's statement on the piece: 'A red Neuschwanstein Castle has settled on top of a green Cathedral of Notre-Dame. A lavender Himeji Castle has slid into the side of a brown Parthenon. An orange Big Ben has collided with a blue Leaning Tower of Pisa. Splice is a series of paper models of iconic buildings that have been spliced together to create an amalgam. Each model is made from a single, solid color of paper so that when it is merged with another building the elements of each remain visible. Reduced in detail and simplified in form, the models, though reductive versions of the original, are still so familiar that they are immediately recognizable. Through these combinations, my goal is to create an entirely new form while leaving the original architectural forms apparent. My work explores the clichés of tourism and often refers to the architecture that becomes a metonymic representation of place.'

40 Ron Radford, 'Forward' in Eric Thake (1978) *The Christmas Linocuts of Eric Thake, 1941–1975*. South Yarra: Croft Press, p. 12 (unpaginated).

41 Sandra Kaji-O'Grady (2006) 'Melbourne Versus Sydney'. *Architectural Theory Review*, 11 (1).

42 Copies of Thake's Christmas card *An Opera House in Every Home* are held in the National Gallery of Victoria, the State Library of Victoria, the National Gallery of Australia and the British Museum.

43 Lauren Purcell (2006) 'Tuesday 11th November', in *Little Swagman* (no longer publicly available).

44 Ann Game (1991) *Undoing the Social: Towards a Deconstructive Sociology*. Milton Keynes and Toronto: Open University Press and University of Toronto Press.

45 Gillian Rose (2007) *Visual Methodologies: An Introduction to the Interpretation of Visual Materials*. 2nd edn. London: Sage.

46 Rose, *Visual Methodologies*, p. 220.

47 Rose, *Visual Methodologies*, p. 220 (italics in original text, brackets – mine).

5 Mediating experience
Making and trading

That the Sydney Opera House is so widely replicated in so many different forms is a curious phenomenon. The building's iconic form features in the logos and visual branding of many non-associated organisations. While this use in the branding of other companies and organisations is not always authorised – the image and form of the building are both trademarked – it nonetheless offers evidence of the way it has become a commodity for *trading*.[1] The image of the building is also traded in other ways – on postage stamps or national symbols such as the Sydney 2000 Olympic logo. *Trading* the Sydney Opera House takes place at both personal and national levels and can be conceptualised as a form of participatory culture. The use of the building's form as a tradable commodity is also implicated in a second way that people participate with this building. The Sydney Opera House is also represented in the form of cakes, as salt and pepper shakers, a table lamp, hi-fi speakers, as evening gowns, costumes, napkins and tea cosies, Christmas tree ornaments, hairstyles and hats. These representations evidence *making* as a practice which can be expressed in the way some representations repurpose the Sydney Opera House, as a cake for example, or a hat. In the previous chapter, repurposing was used to exemplify the way some forms of participatory culture of the Sydney Opera House are centred on critique. Here, *making* representations uses one of two strategies – they either are miniature versions and therefore offer the maker an opportunity to understand and comprehend the building first-hand (Figure 5.1), or they derive their association with the Sydney Opera House through more formal means by developing and extending the visual language of the building (Figure 5.2).

More closely, Chapter 5 explores the participatory culture of the Sydney Opera House that took place in the *making* of a 1.3-ton Opera House cake as a promotional charity challenge for Australia Day 2011. Through this event the experience of the people involved is situated as an embodied practice; both within the tradition of cake making and of architecture. This is then followed by a description and analysis of another event, World Youth Day 2008, in which Qantas drew on the iconic value of the Sydney Opera House for its in-flight magazine. The Sydney Opera House frequently appears in advertising and on national branding. While *making* a Sydney Opera House cake can be aligned with van Dijck's third axis of embodiment, the use of the building's symbolic capital, that is *trading* on its value, is part of an embedded set of practices, ones which whilst commercial are forms of participation with the building which would not exist if it was not valued socially.

Figure 5.1 Repurposed miniatures: teapot, origami and chook (chicken) shed.

Sources: left, small single cup teapot manufactured by Fitz and Floyd in 2004 from their 'Around the World' pattern which includes other landmarks such as the Statue of Liberty and the Eiffel Tower as well as the Sydney Opera House; middle, photograph posted on Flickr.com by Yee depicting his design for an origami Sydney Opera House which sells as part of the Origami Architecture kits published by Tuttle (© Yee, www.yeesjob.com, 2010); right, the fabulous 'Sydney Brockera House' designed and made by Brendan Donohue and Wendy Harmer for the chooks at Narabeen North Public School (© Brendan Donohue and Wendy Harmer, 2009).

Figure 5.2 Repurposed language: speakers, campervan and jewellery.

Sources: left, conceptual design by Made by Makers titled 'Utzon Speakers' where iconic buildings were reframed (© Made by Makers, www.madebymakers.com, 2009); middle, Campervan inspired by the Sydney Opera House titled 'The Opera' (© Rob Vos, 2010); right, sterling silver earrings designed by Regitze Overgaard, made by Georg Jensen Silversmiths Ltd, Denmark, 1987–1998 (© Georg Jensen, 1987–1998. DS-1871-0002.jpg – Collection: Museum of Applied Arts and Sciences. Photograph: Ryan Hernandez).

Making: miniaturisation and derivation

Making a representation of something, such as the Sydney Opera House, involves a process of familiarisation. Regardless of whether it is facilitated by a commercial kit, or from first principles, *making* an opera-house-shaped-something demands attention to detail to ensure the outcome is recognisable to someone else. It involves spending time in a mental state of playful or creative attention, testing out methods, reflecting upon the result and considering how it matches with the original.[2] *Making* can be understood as a personal form of engagement as well as a commercial strategy that trades on the popularity of the building. Miniature replicas offer a means to apprehend the building, understand its geometric complexity and gain a bird's-eye view. In her book *On Longing*: *Narratives of the Miniature, the Gigantic, the Souvenir, the Collection*, Susan Stewart explores the significance of manipulations of scale. She argues that miniaturisation or enlargement are not innocuous strategies, but directly affect our physical apprehension and experience. Physical distortions, such as these, influence the way in which we know and remember the building; in the miniature we become gigantic, our bodies the landscape context for the Sydney Opera House.[3] Miniatures offer a means to incorporate the building into a personal sense of self, mediating between the full-scale reality of the building at Bennelong Point and desire for attachment to it. Like Ann Game and Gillian Rose she acknowledged the nuances of distinct experiences that are mediated through representations.

A giant cake

On Australia Day 2011 the ceremonial cutting of an edible Sydney Opera House constructed from 1.3 tons of chocolate mud-cake, ganache and fondant icing was broadcast to the nation by Channel 7. Cakes might seem an unlikely setting for participation with architecture. After all, cakes are popular edible concoctions and their decoration a fanciful pastime, while the Sydney Opera House is a cultural monument of great significance. However, the making of the gigantic cake was a more than $40,000 marketing stunt for Planet Cake, the Sydney-based cake-decorating company behind the project. The project was meticulously documented through photographs, videos and blog updates of the team's progress that were posted to social media sites, such as YouTube, Facebook and Blogger.[4] *Making* this giant cake also drew together a community of volunteers in an architectural endeavour where they were able to engage and reaffirm their special relationship with this place.

In September 2010 Planet Cake posted on its social media channels that it was seeking volunteers to help make the largest Sydney Opera House cake ever constructed.[5] The project was a culinary and architectural challenge due to the sheer size of the cake and the difficulty of replicating the form of the Sydney Opera House.[6] Paris Cutler, the owner of Planet Cake, wanted to shift perceptions of cake decorating as a hobbyist's endeavour into a professional artistic pursuit. Twenty self-funded volunteers were selected to participate in the project, hoping to gain valuable semi-professional experience. The history of cake and sugar-art reveals that these sweet treats have a long and rich history, both as objects of aesthetic pleasure and social and ritual importance.[7]

Cakes are central to rituals across the world. They are both confectionery and food and decorating them is not a new phenomenon. Wedding cakes have traditionally been tiered structures intricately decorated with hard icing that resembles lace,[8] while the 'subtleties' or 'sotelties' of the medieval court were elaborate constructions of 'spiced sugar paste, almond paste and quince jelly' that 'depicted landscapes and castles, decorated with people and animals'.[9] It was not until 1974, however, that Mary Douglas, a cultural anthropologist, first distinguished cakes as a subject for academic study.[10] She observed that the rituals enacted around wedding cakes were important aspects of cultural life. Cakes have a long history, and the making and consumption of cakes can be traced back to some of the earliest civilisations.[11] Interestingly, the sweet soft and spongy treat currently associated with the term 'cake' did not come into existence until the middle of the 18th century when baking powder was invented along with cake tins (or hoops as they were known) and ovens that could reliably keep an even temperature.[12] Earlier forms of cakes were 'flat rounds of crushed grain, moistened, compacted and cooked'.[13] The exact technical definition of 'cake' is uncertain, but they share a common role as centrepieces of celebrations and markers of important social occasions.

The Sydney Opera House cake was made over nine days.[14] It was an extremely large cake, a 1:50 scale replica similar to other replicas that can be found within theme parks, such as Legoland in California.[15] Utzon's working drawings had been enlarged and pinned up on a long blank wall in Planet Cake's premises, annotated, much like they might be in an architect's office during the development of a design scheme (Figure 5.3). The video documentation of the event shows people working together in a studio setting where some are assigned to laborious tasks such as kneading fondant icing, while others work outside on cutting out templates and sculpting the polystyrene sail-tips. A souvenir model, along with photographs of the Sydney Opera House, are scattered around the space and, like an architect's office where models from past

Figure 5.3 Photograph posted to Planet Cake's Facebook page (in 2011) showing the volume from which one row of 'sails' will be carved, with Utzon's drawings in the background.

Source: © Paris Cutler, Planet Cake, and Facebook Inc., 2011.

projects are displayed, iced cakes sit on the shelves lining the walls. While making cakes is a distinct practice from that of making buildings, the video documentation reveals the way in which participants perceive they are involved in a similar process.[16]

Cakes may appear to have little consequence for architecture, yet the videos documenting the Planet Cake challenge show that making cakes is a technical craft that requires sculptural skills not too distant from those of the architectural model maker. Volunteers were required to have a basic level of proficiency in decorating techniques developed in the 20th century.[17] Many of the volunteers had made smaller cakes, but none one that was 3.6 by 2.4 meters by 1.5 meters high. This presented new and unexpected compositional and structural problems that they had not faced before.[18] The process of making the cake appeared inclusive, yet the YouTube videos (Figure 5.4) revealed the hierarchy between the members of the group. Professional employees were in charge of the delicate and critical aspects of the cake, whilst the volunteers did more menial tasks such as kneading fondant icing, cutting cake, preparing chocolate ganache or assisting in preparing baseboards. While the premise of making the giant Sydney Opera House cake is collaboration, in reality the volunteers are labourers. Decisions on how to accomplish the task and its narrative are controlled by Cutler.

Participation in the field of architecture was theorised as early as 1969 by Sherry Arnstein, in her 'ladder of participation'. Here, participation is theorised in the context of public urban planning projects. Arnstein's 'ladder of participation' offers a nuanced way of reading the collaboration around the Opera House cake project.[19] She divides participation into three tiers: therapy and manipulation are classed as non-participation; placation, consultation and informing are classed as forms of participation that are tokenistic to

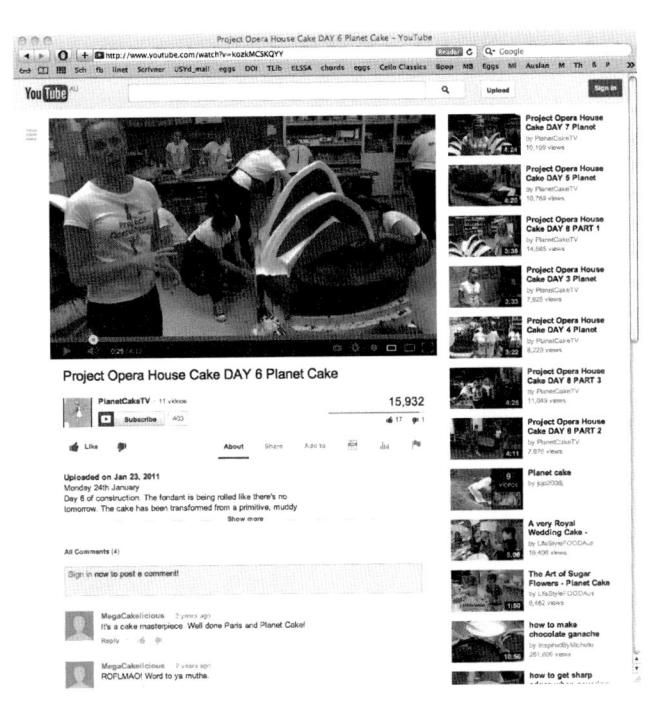

Figure 5.4 Day 6 documentation video posted to YouTube by Planet Cake.

Source: © Paris Cutler, Planet Cake, and YouTube, 2011.

different degrees; and only citizen control, delegate power and partnership are classed as true forms of participation that transfer control and power to the participants.[20] Viewed through this framework the volunteers are essentially being manipulated: they bring their skills, give their time, fund their expenses and provide manual labour in exchange for the opportunity to observe how the cake is constructed by the experts, and gain media exposure.

Whilst volunteers are not empowered in determining how the cake is made, its form or documentation, their experience is projected as an imaginary architectural experience. The cake-building is divided into three sections where each row of sails is set upon a plywood timber base on castor wheels and lined with a plan drawing at 1:50, with the forecourt at the front. Cutler compares the construction of the cake to architectural elements, describing the way the cake is built from layers of mud-cake with a chocolate ganache adhesive that 'sets like concrete'.[21] At this scale, the spongy structure of cake cannot support its own weight and therefore the cake requires an internal structure of black plastic-covered plywood boards and wooden dowel columns to avoid collapse. Using this method the massing volume of the cake is built up quickly in order to allow the form of the building to be carved. Cutler describes this process as 'exactly like building a house, so this is just putting it brick by brick by brick'.[22] Yet this additive and subtractive process has nothing in common with the way in which the Sydney Opera House was structurally realised. Instead, the framing of this culinary endeavour as architectural feat hints at the way in which participants see the process as a form of architectural engagement.

Decorating cakes is often considered the realm of 'blue haired ladies and frilly aprons', with the consequence that it is often under-valued as a frivolous luxury.[23] Like the dishes that are central to Eric Thake's *An Opera House in Every Home* analysed in the previous chapter, they challenge the masculine identity of the architectural profession.[24] Hilde Heynen observes that this gender bias underpins the cultural construction of the creative genius.[25] In the case of the Sydney Opera House, Utzon is both a recipient of the Prtizker Prize (2003) and his 'creative genius' is central to the 2007 UNESCO World Heritage inscription.[26] Heynen argues that this bias is a characteristic of the cultural system of merit in architecture, which necessitates the continuous production of role models that reinforce the importance of authorship.[27] This is significant as the volunteers, who were all women, were professionals; paramedics and occupational therapists, food technologists, flight attendants and educational support officers as well as some 'stay at home mothers'. Yet there is something subversive in the act of taking a national icon, such as the Sydney Opera House, and rendering it in cake. Not only does it shift the monumental value of the original building by drawing it into the realm of popular culture, but it makes something that is recognised as solid, concrete and imposing, into a shareable, ephemeral edible event. The act of producing the cake takes an object that represents masculine creativity and artistic genius and re-presents it within a feminine domestic frivolous context. Yet while the methods employed in the construction of the cake do not reflect the reality of making an edifice, the sheer size and scale of this cake means that it requires tools normally associated with building – saws, sandpaper and drills – which facilitates a space for participants to 'imagine' being the author and genius. Even though their participation is not autonomous it is personally significant for the *participants*. The experience was a unique opportunity that comes 'once in a lifetime'.

The heightened sense of artistic challenge is explained by expert decorator, Jean Michel, who states that while he has created and worked on some large and complex cakes during his 15 years as a professional cake decorator, 'this one just however is another ball game altogether, it really is something else'.[28] Towards the end of the fifth day of the project the form of the cake is at last recognisable as Utzon's masterpiece. The team of volunteers and staff have worked long hours to create a 1.5-meter-high chocolate-flavoured replica. They describe their sense of achievement and exclaim a 'new appreciation for the people who built this in the first place'.[29] To build a representation of the building is to come to grips with the building's complex spatial geometry and possibility of gaining some sense of the achievement that was felt by those who realised the actual edifice. While the volunteers, in terms of making a cake, might be participating at a low menial level according to Arnstein's ladder, as a group they are subverting the existing hegemony prevalent in the valuation of architecture within the discipline. The event, whilst at some level commercially driven, operates outside of the architectural paradigm implied within Arnstein's ladder. Even in her highest level of participation – citizen power – control was not given to this group at any stage. Unlike making real buildings, which requires some architectural expertise to ensure they are structurally sound, participation through representations of architecture enables groups with other creative skills to appropriate and remake works of creative genius, such as the Sydney Opera House, outside of the professional boundaries of the discipline. Participation in this context is not about the production of architecture, but rather it is an example of participatory culture.

On the morning of Australia Day 2011, Cutler describes just how excited she is to be revealing the completed cake. She invites the audience to admire the 3.6-meter-long, 1.5-meter-high cake, now glossy and finished with sugary people promenading around the building (Figure 5.5). She exclaims 'we did it! . . . just a group of ordinary people',[30]

Figure 5.5 Photograph from Planet Cake's blog showing the final outcome.

then confides that the real climax will be when the cake is cut and its ambiguous status as an edible or sculptural object is finally determined. Perhaps this is the allure of making inedible objects, such as buildings, from foodstuffs like cake and sugar.

Through the concept of participatory culture Planet Cake's Opera House project can be framed as an event with commercial and community motivation. Whilst this blurs established boundaries between the professional and the amateur, still embedded in architectural takes on participation, this phenomenon is explained by Jenkins as a 'convergence'. The increased flow of content in the new media landscape is both 'a top-down corporate driven process and a bottom-up consumer driven process. Corporate convergence coexists with grassroots convergence'.[31] Each of the members involved in making the giant cake is both a consumer and fan of the Sydney Opera House and a producer of its representation. By participating in the making of the architectural cake, individuals subvert the hegemony of the architectural genius, engage with the imagined architectural process and contribute to its popular value.

Opera-House-things

In contrast representations of the Sydney Opera House that are miniaturisations, derivations of the forms of the building, inspired by its visual language, are more often commercial in purpose. For example, the 'Utzon Speakers' designed in 2008 by the Danish design firm Made by Makers, are not miniature Opera Houses but instead reflect the stepped shells as the basic form for each speaker.[32] Another Danish collaboration, between Rob and Ingrid Vos and Axel Enthoven, produced a hybrid camper trailer named *The Opera*. The white stepped arches draw a connection with the architecture of the Sydney Opera House, a serendipitous part of the design process.[33] The speakers and the camper trailer are examples that extend the language of the white shells of the building. Another example, a pendant necklace from Sydney-based jewellery designer, Polli, picks up on the tiled pattern used to clad the concrete shells. Although the necklace is not explicitly associated with the Sydney Opera House, perhaps due to copyright and licensing restrictions, the pendant is described as composed of 'decorative abstract shapes' that are 'inspired by Sydney Harbour'.[34] Although each of these representations of the Sydney Opera House has a commercial imperative they nonetheless extend and reinterpret the formal visual associations with this place. Like the miniatures, these derivatives are examples of acts of creative engagement and participatory culture with the architecture of the Sydney Opera House. They facilitate apprehension and familiarity, creatively extend the visual rhetoric of this place, and contribute to its iconicity.

Making representations using a derivative strategy is scaffolded on the cultural capital of iconic works of architecture. It picks up on the symbolic charge that Terry Smith associates with such works of architecture where these places seem:

> to collect and summarise a set of supra-individual aspirations and actualities, differentiating itself thereby from the everydayness around it (even that which contains, in a lesser way, the same elements). At the same time it permits and encourages variations on and additions to these aspirations, making them (and it) seem actual, living, growing in significance. Symbolic sites, like symbolic objects and images (iconotypes) are, therefore, both summative and elaborative. Some may tend to be more one than the other. Either way, they increase their sacredness, if they are religious sites, or become sacral, if they are secular sites.[35]

Figure 5.6 Ordinary things made more valuable as merchandise.

Source: Corporate Cap $34.95, Notebook with pen $19.95, Golf Glove $39.95, Bag of Tees $4.95, Set of 3 Golf Balls $36.95, SOH Tote $29.95, SOH T Shirt $34.95, Pureform Tea Towel $14.95, SOH Mugs $24.95, Stick Pins (above) $7.95, Sail Magnets (below) from $12.95. All items were part of an earlier Sydney Opera House Corporate Gift Catalogue and were priced in AUD (Sydney Opera House trademark reproduced with permission of the Sydney Opera House Trust, photographer unknown, 2007).

This symbolic charge is a valuable commodity, one that is used to increase the value of otherwise ordinary objects. This is most clearly evidenced in branded items available in the souvenir shop at the Sydney Opera House. Here, caps, pens, even golf-balls are printed with an image of the building. It does not matter whether the image is figurative or abstract, but the addition of the image increases the value of the otherwise ordinary object by connecting it with the Sydney Opera House (Figure 5.6). Like representations made by deriving new forms from the architecture of the building, these ordinary objects are *trading* on the already invested symbolic charge connected with the building.

Trading on architecture

The Sydney Opera House features in logotypes, in advertisements and on stamps (Figure 5.7). The building's silhouette was central to the Sydney 2000 Olympic logo, the Sydney Writers Festival logo, and sports team logos, such as the Sydney Swans, the Sydney Roosters and the Sydney Kings. The building is also curiously implied in the branding of the Australasian College, a Sydney educational institute for hair and make-up tuition. These kinds of representations evidence the way the building is a means for commercial organisations to gain cultural capital, to draw upon the role of the building as an international symbol identified with Sydney and Australia, which can add prestige and legitimacy to their corporate image. However, the abstraction of the building in these logos varies; in the Sydney 2000 Olympic logo it is a multi-coloured dynamic ribbon, whereas in the Australasian College logo it is an awkward hand with sharp painted nails cantilevered off each sail. Trading on the highly recognisable form of the building is evident in its commercial appropriation in advertising and it becomes literally a form of currency when part of postage stamps (Figure 5.8). The stamps are a utilitarian celebration of Australian Modern Architecture, where the Sydney Opera House is the stamp with the highest value.[36] In advertising, the use of the building is more playful. The American Airlines advertisement brings two symbols together: New York is colloquially known as 'the Big Apple' and it is divided and positioned so as to give the form of the Sydney Opera House. The image presented is both New York and Sydney at once, intimately connected by the double metaphor. Commercial organisations engage with the Sydney Opera House by *trading* on its

Figure 5.7 Logos, brands and corporate identities.

Sources: left, Sydney Swans Football Club (© Sydney Swans Football Club, 2017); middle, Sydney Gay and Lesbian Mardi Gras logo (© Sydney Gay and Lesbian Mardi Gras Ltd, 2017); right, Editors NSW logo (© NSW branch of Institute of Professional Editors, 2017).

Figure 5.8 Stamps and advertisements.

Sources: left, $2.45 Sydney Opera House Stamp from the 2007 Modernist Australian Architecture Series (© Australian Postal Corporation, 2007); right, Competition entry for American Airlines advertisement titled 'Apples' by Pubio Santander Torrejón, Advertising School: Universidad Peruana de Ciencias Aplicadas, Lima, Peru. 2007 Finalist in the Student Categories | Magazine/Newspaper Advertisement of the New York Festivals World's Best TV & Films (© Publio Santander Torrejón, 2007).

existing familiarity and contributing to the frequent representation of the building in visual culture, positioning the Sydney Opera House a as locus for shared forms of cultural engagement and participatory culture at all levels.

Qantas and World Youth Day

Trading on the cultural capital of the Sydney Opera House is exemplified in the use of the building on the July 2008 in-flight Qantas magazine. The cover featured an aerial photograph of the building, with the headline 'Sydney for the masses: A city shines for World Youth Day'. The Opera House is photographed late in the day, the low angle of the sun from the west bleaching the white sails against the deep blue harbour. The building is a little distorted; perhaps by the use of a wide-angle lens which

Figure 5.9 Cover of Qantas in-flight magazine, July 2008 issue.

Source: Bauer Media Limited (previously ACP), 2008.

serves to bring the front corner of the podium almost out of the page. The building is displayed volumetrically, rather than as a classic silhouette, and from a vantage point that neatly disguises its architectural neighbours and displays a green backdrop of the Royal Botanic Gardens. The scene is expectant, empty and waiting; an expectant city awaiting the masses of World Youth Day. 'Sydney' – here represented by the Sydney Opera House – is offered up to the Catholic pilgrims en route to attend 'mass' conducted by Pope Benedict XVI. The magazine cover suggests that the focus of visitors will be on such spectacular icons, rather than the more nuanced corners of the city. The branding alliance between Qantas and the Sydney Opera House dates back as far as 1967, before the building was even complete. Here, in the in-flight magazine, it is used to simultaneously advertise a city, a national airline and a religious event. The Harbour Bridge, Sydney's 'other' icon, is deliberately excluded; the Sydney Opera House is essentially isolated from the city and ready for consumption.

At first glance one could argue that Qantas is merely 'reporting' the current affairs of July 2008. But magazines like this one are produced well in advance of their distribution in aircraft; the magazine has to pre-empt the upcoming events, potentially some months prior to the distribution of the magazine. The main events of World Youth Day were located at far less spectacular Sydney sites than the Opera House; including Barangaroo, the recently demolished industrial wharves at East Darling Harbour, and Randwick Racecourse, which was converted from a racetrack for the event. The Sydney Opera House was instead a setting for the 'live theatrical and devotional re-enactment of the last days of Jesus' life [which] took place in Sydney's spectacular harbour backdrop'.[37] The '*Sydney 2000*', the Papal 'boat-a-cade' would carry Pope Benedict XVI and his 500-strong entourage around the harbour as each stage of the religious re-enactment of the Stations of the Cross took place. The selection by Qantas of the Sydney Opera House as the image for this news feature in its in-flight magazine suggests that beyond simply reporting events, it was also reinforcing its strategic alliance with the Sydney Opera House Trust.[38]

The idea of *trading* on the cultural capital imbued in the image and architecture of the Sydney Opera House is part of, as Terry Smith argues, the 'symbolic exchanges between people, things, ideas, interest groups, and cultures that take predominantly visual form'.[39] The dissemination of architecture through images becomes a vehicle for negotiation and cultural exchange. This reframes architecture as having a value beyond its material function. Publications like the Qantas in-flight magazine can be understood as spaces for trading these values.

Beatriz Colomina explores how the value of contemporary architecture is formed and informed by its existence in mass media.[40] She argues that once architecture enters the realm of mass media, as a photograph, it simultaneously enters historical space. In the space of mass media images are more readily accessed and easily disseminated than the built object. In this way they are in fact more permanent and persistent as they can continue in circulation long after the built artefact is gone. Representations are usually considered lesser copies of the original built artefact, yet when representation is more permanent and pervasive than a building it 'literally dematerializes architecture'.[41] The relationship between architecture and mass media is not only beneficial to architecture, in expanding its realm of existence, but also serves to make representations of architecture a kind of commodity or currency that can be used, as Qantas does in this example, to create and reinforce national and cultural identities.

Figure 5.10 Jesus carries his cross, performed as part of the Stations of the Cross at Sydney Opera House forecourt during World Youth Day Sydney 2008 on 18 July 2008 in Sydney, Australia.

Source: photographs of the event posted to Flickr.com (© Christopher Chan, 2008).

Architecture has more conventionally been a spatial commodity, in which its exchange is tied to its housing function. Yet Smith's description of the 'iconomy' demonstrates how examples of images trading on well-known destinations or icons of architecture

> point to the existence of a larger structure of symbolic exchange at work in the world today, one in which the competition between visual images – well known in most cultures when it appears in commodity advertising, entertainment, urban planning, religious ritual, and political campaigning – has spread to saturate most of the ways in which peoples, nations, religions, even civilisations relate to each other, not simply at the level of stereotype but at the deepest levels of psyche and society.[42]

Both Smith and Colomina reframe architecture as an active participant in the cultural exchange of meaning. In the case of the Sydney Opera House, part of its value is its symbolic charge as a metonym for high culture, for Australian identity, for innovation, to name a few. It is this charge that enables organisations, such as Qantas, or even smaller local examples, to *trade* on the image of the building. Smith notes that the 'Opera House was a turning point in the entry of architecture into the growing global iconomy'.[43] The Sydney Opera House was not only commissioned to house performance venues, but also to complement the then other icon of Sydney, the Harbour Bridge and its glorious harbour setting. 'Sydney needed a symbol that would anchor the imagery of its competing attractions, tie them to a tangible entity, and thus draw tourists from everywhere'.[44] Part of the primary purpose of the Sydney Opera House was that it was to be an 'iconic image'.

Architecture is most often discussed in terms of its materiality, its fabric and its tangibility rather than as a currency for cultural negotiations or exchanges. Anna Klingmann's recent scholarship decouples the value of architecture from its materiality and grounds it through the experience it can provide the viewer:

> Once architecture is successfully linked to a series of values that is shared and understood by a larger audience, it is almost inevitable that the architecture exceeds its use value and becomes a catalyst for perceptual values and transformative experiences.[45]

Architecture, according to Klingmann, is no longer bounded by its geographical site, but exists beyond these boundaries it in the realm of mass media. As the example of the Qantas in-flight magazine demonstrates, one common way of engaging with the Sydney Opera House is to engage with it through images. The photograph is more than a pictorial depiction of the building, or a form of mundane exchange. The image is a tangible representation of the values, aspirations and ideas embedded within the social narratives of the Sydney Opera House. So, if architecture can now be constituted as an exchange of meaning, or as cultural currency, it brings to light why the Sydney Opera House operates so successfully as a kind of 'national brand'. Klingmann describes a brand as something much less tangible than a product, rather she argues it is 'an aura of meaning'.[46] And that architecture can benefit from conceiving of itself as a brand. She situates her discussion in Joseph Pine's and James Gilmore's era of the 'experience economy'[47] whereby businesses trade in experiences or events, and where the product is the memory produced. In the 'experience economy' a brand becomes 'transformative' to its participants. In the case of the Sydney Opera House, the brand-like quality of this building is not only tied to the organisation, but is augmented by significant cultural and historical events, like the story of its construction. As Klingmann notes:

> Social values and lifestyles, formerly defined by religion and nationhood, are increasingly transferred to the branding of products. In the search for identities people use brands as universal signifiers, because brands bring into play means of identification that transcend cultural, traditional, and local differences. In this regard, a brand signifies a kind of platonic ideal to identify a system of values that is shared in the minds of many people irrespective of their nationalities.[48]

There is something about the Sydney Opera House that promises this kind of transformation. Bound up in the narrative of its production are the social and political beliefs that have become part of its ethos, perhaps even its meaning. The building's expressive and romantic architectural form has become imbued with value and meaning for its society at large. The building's value is, arguably, more and more negotiated through its immaterial or intangible meanings and associations through representations in mass media and popular culture. These images operate like relics – that is, fragments that embody the essential qualities associated with this place. Like the religious pilgrimage for World Youth Day, described in the Qantas in-flight magazine, the Sydney Opera House promises a kind of personal change and transformation in association. Just like the way tourists circle the building focused on capturing their experiences as memories, the July 2008 Qantas in-flight magazine, 'mine-to-keep', is a relic and repository for the memories collected on that particular journey.

The Sydney Opera House exists in images, objects and myths, and its social value is embedded in its ability to be a cultural currency through which values and desires are bought and sold. In the 'experience economy' the value of architecture shifts from its function and its materiality to its transformative ability and its associated meanings. The architecture of the building becomes a tradable social commodity continuously negotiated and exchanged in the iconomy.

Conclusion

The representations examined here, a giant cake and cover photograph for an airline's in-flight magazine, among others, mediate engagements with the Sydney Opera House. Participation in making a giant cake offers an embodied experience for the volunteers, who reframe cake-making as both the design and construction of the building, drawing personal meanings through this activity and collectively challenging the notional boundaries of architecture. Both the making of the cake and the use of the photograph of the Sydney Opera House on the cover of Qantas' in-flight magazine are concrete examples of van Dijck's third axis, which proposes that mediated memories connect embodied experiences with embedded practices. In the case of the cake-making, the embodied experience is connected with the socially embedded traditions of decorating cakes, and in the case of the photograph of the Sydney Opera House on the magazine cover, the use of this building to symbolise Sydney becomes connected to the passengers' embodied experience during their flight. While these connections are not necessarily singular or discrete, van Dijck's mediated memories is useful. It helps to unpack how such forms of participatory culture transcend ideas of heritage singularly as built form and expand the ways in which social value can be evidenced.

Notes

1 Peter Black (2007) 'Photographing the Sydney Opera House (10 June)'. *Peter Black's Freedom to Differ*. Retrieved: 25/09/2012, from: www.freedomtodiffer.com/freedom_to_differ/2007/06/photographing_t.html; Bernard Lane (2014) 'Iconic Image of Opera House No Longer Public'. *The Australian*, 25 January. Retrieved: 15/07/2016, from: www.theaustralian.com.au/arts/iconic-image-of-opera-house-no-longer-public/story-e6frg8n6-1226810021279.

2 For more on making as a methodology see David Gauntlett: David Gauntlett and Peter Holzwarth (2006) 'Creative and Visual Methods for Exploring Identities', *Visual Studies*, 21 (1), pp. 82–91; David Gauntlett (2011) *Making Is Connecting: The Social Meaning of Creativity, from Diy and Knitting to Youtube and Web 2.0*. Cambridge: Polity Press; David Gauntlett (2007) *Creative Explorations: New Approaches to Identities and Audiences*. London: Routledge. For the value of seeing culture as practice rather than product see Richard Sennett and Craig Calhoun (eds) (2007) *Practising Culture*. London: Routledge, p. 5.

3 Susan Stewart (1984) *On Longing: Narratives of the Miniature, the Gigantic, the Souvenir, the Collection*. Baltimore: Johns Hopkins University Press, p. 70.

4 Paris Cutler (2011) 'Project Opera House Cake Day 1 Planet Cake'. *Planet Cake TV (YouTube Channel)*. Retrieved: 26/06/2013, from: www.youtube.com/watch?v=3t5Jwdbx6vI; Paris Cutler (2011) 'Beginning of Day 6 We Are Getting Somewhere!' *Planet Cake (Facebook)*. Retrieved: 26/06/2013, from: www.facebook.com/photo.php?fbid=491611001259&set=a.114530826259.107996.22942151259&type=1; Paris Cutler (2011) 'This Cake Really Might Just Work!', in *Planet Cake Update*.

5 Planet Cake was established in 2003, when Paris Cutler bought a declining cake business after resigning from her previous career as stockbroker and law student, and disappointment in her own lacklustre wedding cake.

6 Paris Cutler (2010) 'Worlds Largest Opera House Cake 2011', in *Planet Cake Update*.

7 Simon R. Charsley (1992) *Wedding Cakes and Cultural History*. London: Routledge; Nicola Humble (2010) *Cake: A Global History*, edited by Andrew F. Smith. London: Reaktion Books.

8 Charsley, *Wedding Cakes and Cultural History*, p. 13.

9 Humble, *Cake*, p. 25.

10 Charsley, *Wedding Cakes and Cultural History*, p. 1.

11 Humble, *Cake*, p. 10.

12 Humble, *Cake*, pp. 22–23.

13 Humble, *Cake*, p. 10.

14 Paris Cutler (2011) 'Project Opera House Cake Day 1 to 8 (Series of 10 Videos)'. *Planet Cake TV (YouTube Channel)*. Retrieved: 27/06/2013, from: www.youtube.com/user/PlanetCakeTV.

15 SilverSteel3000 (2011) 'Coast Cruise Pov Legoland Ca'. *YouTube* [Video]. Retrieved: 26/03/2013, from: www.youtube.com/watch?feature=player_embedded&v=At7xzRl2k_s.

16 Dana Cuff provides an excellent ethnography of the practice of architecture. Dana Cuff (1991) *Architecture: The Story Practice*. Cambridge, MA: MIT Press.

17 Joseph A. Lambeth (1980 [1934]) *Lambeth Method of Cake Decoration and Practical Pastries*. California: Continental Publications; Wilton (2013) 'History of Wilton'. *Wilton*. Retrieved: 26/06/2013, from: www.wilton.com/about/history.cfm. Charsley, *Wedding Cakes and Cultural History*.

18 Paris Cutler (2011) 'Project Opera House Cake Day 4 Planet Cake'. *Planet Cake TV (YouTube Channel)*. Retrieved: 26/06/2013, from: www.youtube.com/watch?v=hBxJrJy9UAc.

19 Sherry R. Arnstein (1969) 'A Ladder of Citizen Participation'. *Journal of the American Institute of Planners*, 35 (4).

20 Arnstein, 'A Ladder of Citizen Participation', p. 217 (Figure 2).

21 Paris Cutler (2011) 'Project Opera House Cake Day 6 Planet Cake'. *Planet Cake TV (YouTube Channel)*. Retrieved: 27/06/2013, from: www.youtube.com/watch?v=kozkMCSKQYY.

22 Paris Cutler (2011) 'Project Opera House Cake Day 3 Planet Cake'. *Planet Cake TV (YouTube Channel)*. Retrieved: 27/06/2013, from: www.youtube.com/watch?v=3PGZDV2KC7o.

23 Paris Cutler (2011) 'Project Opera House Cake Day 2 Planet Cake'. *Planet Cake TV (YouTube Channel)*. Retrieved: 27/06/2013, from: www.youtube.com/watch?v=23ILAflXrEI.

24 Bridget Fowler and Fiona Wilson (2004) 'Women Architects and Their Discontents'. *Sociology*, 38 (1).

25 Hilde Heynen (2012) 'Genius Gender and Architecture: The Star System as Exemplified in the Pritzker Prize'. *Architectural Theory Review*, 17 (2–3), p. 322.

26 Bill N. Lacy (2003) 'Jorn Utzon 2003 Laureate: Jury Citation'. *The Pritzker Architecture Prize*. Retrieved: 27/04/2013, from: www.pritzkerprize.com/2003/jury; Philip Goad, 'Jørn Utzon:

Pritzker Architecture Prize Laureate 2003', *Architecture Australia* 2003; Kenneth Frampton (2003) 'Jørn Utzon 2003 Laureate Essay: The Architecture of Jørn Utzon'. *Pritzker Prize Website*. Retrieved: 02/03/2014, from: www.pritzkerprize.com/sites/default/files/file_fields/field_files_inline/2003_essay.pdf; UNESCO (2007) 'Sydney Opera House'. *World Heritage Centre*. Retrieved: 26/02/2012, from: http://whc.unesco.org/en/list/166rev.

27 Heynen, 'Genius Gender and Architecture', p. 342.

28 Paris Cutler (2011) 'Project Opera House Cake Day 5 Planet Cake'. *Planet Cake TV (YouTube Channel)*. Retrieved: 27/06/2013, from: www.youtube.com/watch?v=LypQQyp6aFE.

29 Amanda Iesing. Cutler (2011) 'Project Opera House Cake Day 5 Planet Cake'. *Planet Cake TV (YouTube Channel)*.

30 Paris Cutler (2011) 'Project Opera House Cake Day 8 Part 1 Planet Cake'. *Planet Cake TV (YouTube Channel)*. Retrieved: 27/06/2013, from: www.youtube.com/watch?v=DQ7u2AYfBPI.

31 Henry Jenkins (2006) *Convergence Culture: Where Old and New Media Collide*. New York: New York University Press, p. 18.

32 Made by Makers (2010) 'Reframing – Three Days 20 Ideas'. Retrieved: 26/03/2013, from: www.madebymakers.dk/content/reframing-three-days-20-ideas.

33 Rob Vos, Ingrid Vos and Axel Enthoven (2008) 'The Opera'. Retrieved: 26/03/2013, from: www.ysin.co.uk/show/nl/content/3,19. Chris Fincham (2011) 'Opera Sails into Sydney'. Retrieved: 26/03/2013, from: www.caravancampingsales.com.au/news/2011/camping-trailers/opera-sails-into-sydney-26553.

34 Maja Rose and Tess Lloyd (circa 2010) 'Ss Sail Necklace'. Retrieved: 26/03/2013, from: www.polli.com.au/necklaces/ss-sail-necklace#.UGq8q5hzu4Q.

35 Terry Smith (2002) 'The Political Economy of Iconotypes and the Architecture of Destination: Uluru, the Sydney Opera House and the World Trade Center'. *Architectural Theory Review*, 7 (2), p. 5.

36 The other buildings in the series are the Academy of Science, Canberra, 50c, Former ICI House, Melbourne, 50c, and Council House, Perth, $1.00.

37 'World Youth Day' (2008). Retrieved from: www.wyd2008.org/index.php/en/wyd08_events (website no longer active).

38 Qantas is not currently a corporate sponsor.

39 Terry Smith (2006) *The Architecture of Aftermath*. London: The University of Chicago Press, p. 2.

40 Beatriz Colomina (1994) *Privacy and Publicity: Modern Architecture as Mass Media*. Cambridge, MA: The MIT Press.

41 Lucy Bowditch (1996) 'Privacy and Publicity: Modern Architecture as Mass Media by Beatriz Colomina' [Book Review]. *Afterimage*, 23 (5).

42 Smith, *The Architecture of Aftermath*, p. 5.

43 Smith, *The Architecture of Aftermath*, p. 35.

44 Smith, *The Architecture of Aftermath*, p. 37.

45 Anna Klingmann (2007) *Brandscapes*. Cambridge, MA: The MIT Press, p. 65.

46 Klingmann, *Brandscapes*, p. 55.

47 B. Joseph II Pine and James H. Gilmore (1999) *The Experience Economy: Work is Theatre & Every Business a Stage*. Boston: Harvard Business School Press.

48 Klingmann, *Brandscapes*, p. 55.

6 Mediating time
Visiting and capturing

Only a quarter of visitors to the Sydney Opera House attend performances. The other three-quarters come specifically to experience the building. Certain activities and artefacts structure such experiences. *Visiting* is preceded by guidebooks, tour bookings or simply viewing images of the destination prior to arrival. Once at the site the experience of visiting the Sydney Opera House is structured by moving around the building and frequently, by taking photographs or *capturing* the architecture. The experience of visiting is fleeting and, to commemorate and extend the experience, people often purchase souvenirs. This chapter explores examples of two forms of participatory culture, *visiting* and *capturing*. Visiting is explored in more depth through an analysis of the characteristics of souvenirs, not simply as representations but as performative artefacts that become repositories of memories, while capturing is explored through an observation of two groups on Flickr identified through the inclusion or exclusion of photographs of the Sydney Opera House. Through visiting and capturing the relationship between participatory cultures centred on taking photographs or acquiring souvenirs can be connected with van Dijck's second vertical axis of time. The photographs mediate the present experience in order to access it later, while the souvenirs can alter the present experience through their scalar operations. Inevitably, time becomes central to the motivation of these practices.

Visiting and capturing

Tourist objects, such as maps, guidebooks and souvenirs, are evidence of the importance of experiencing the building first-hand (Figure 6.1). Such direct experiences offer an opportunity to apprehend the building at full scale, to physically touch the building and gain a sense of its materiality uncensored by the constructing eye of representations. Whilst *visiting*, people move around the building, they touch it, they look up to the peaks of the sails and out to Sydney Harbour (Figure 6.2). The experiences attained by visiting are synonymous with particular ways of 'seeing'.[1] The late sociologist, John Urry, developed the notion of the 'tourist gaze', drawing on Michel Foucault's 'medical gaze', to encapsulate the scopic nature of such 'touristic experiences'. Urry proposes that this 'tourist gaze' is socially organised, constructed and regulated by the representations circulated in society by media organisations, government and travel industries. Its effect is to define the tourist's mode of vision; both in the sights tourists seek and the desire to reproduce them, usually, by taking their own photographs, that is, *capturing* their experience. Such experiences, while initially framed through 'the tourist', also apply to the way many local people also appreci-ate places like the Sydney Opera House. The scopic practices through which people apprehend the building also organises and constructs a visit. Urry's seminal concept of the 'tourist gaze' has been shifted and extended by scholars such as Jonas Larsen and Jørgen Ole Bærenholdt to include new understandings of the embodied perfor-mances that take place during visits to places.[2] People experience the building through movement, walking on the promenade, up close and from vantage points around the harbour. The camera, a familiar object, offers individuals a sense of familiarity, an important factor in encounters of 'difference'. The 'space of the camera', as revealed in the vast range of photographs taken at the Sydney Opera House and posted on Flickr, allows people to re-visualise the building through a familiar frame, thus closing the distance of objectification which has been generated and is regulated by the socially constructed 'tourist gaze'.

Creating representations through photography, *capturing*, offers visitors a means for accessing 'past embedded' cultural and social representations set up by tourist guidebooks and other media, whilst present at the site. The camera offers 'something to do' within the familiar space of the camera where it is an aid to apprehending the building. Photographs are a specific form of souvenir. Part of the motivation to take them is to have evidence of, and for, remembering and recollecting the experience. Their ubiquity and dominance as a mode of experiencing the Sydney Opera House demands focused exploration. Souvenirs, on the other hand, are objects that make tan-gible the ephemeral experience of a *visit* to the Sydney Opera House, in ways that are

Figure 6.1 Guidebooks, souvenirs and maps.

Sources: top left, leafing through the 2005 edition of the Dorling Kindersley Eyewitness Travel Guide for Sydney; top right, souvenir teaspoon collection; bottom, Sydney edition of PopOut Maps (© Compass Maps Ltd, 2017).

Figure 6.2 People looking and touching.

Sources: left, photograph posted to Flickr.com 'Team overlooking the Sydney Opera House' (© Ryan Baum, 2002); middle, photograph posted to Flickr.com showing visitors scattered over the southern steps absorbed in the act of looking (© Rachel Bell, www.rachelbell.com.au, 2011); bottom, Sydney edition of PopOut Maps (© Kevin Kin Soon Wong).

distinct from the photograph. They can be understood as more than 'markers' or signifiers of experiences, but rather as a 'static idealized blueprint of an experience'.[3] Whilst performances of photographic *capturing* structure experiences of *visiting*, souvenirs appropriate them and help people hold on to them. Souvenirs do more than simply trigger memories; they alter the physical relationship between building and visitor.[4]

Souvenirs and models

Many visitors to the Sydney Opera House come with the specific intent of experiencing its architecture. These experiences are often commemorated through souvenirs, a seemingly innocuous practice, but one which is highly revealing of the interrelations between the visitor's experience, the architecture of this place and the souvenir object itself. How participation with the building is mediated through 'tourist' artefacts such as souvenirs has generally been overlooked, with the exception of the work of Medina D. Lasansky and Brian D. McLaren.[5] The theorisation of the souvenir by Lisa Love and Nathaniel Kohn positions these usually insignificant trinkets as objects that are 'engaged, active, and fraught with possibilities'.[6] In order to explore how souvenirs can offer a form of engagement with architecture, it is essential to frame them as 'performative' objects. Love and Kohn's work on souvenirs tries to bridge the gap between the object as a representation and its meaning for the visitor, and consider the souvenir as more than a representation or an object for consumption. Examining souvenirs both as tourist artefacts and architectural representations reveals the tactics employed in the mediation of visitors' experiences to the Sydney Opera House and how such popular interactions with architectural representations are implicated in collective remembering.

In her essay 'The Souvenir: Messenger of the Extraordinary', Beverly Gordon defines the souvenir from a position which frames the tourist experience as being differentiated from the normal experience of everyday life:

> The universality of the souvenir can be understood in light of its underlying role or function. As an actual object, it concretises or make tangible what was otherwise only an intangible state. Its physical presence helps locate, define, and freeze in time a fleeting, transitory experience, and bring back into ordinary experience something of the quality of an extraordinary experience.[7]

Arguably, iconic architecture, such as the Sydney Opera House, prompts experiences for all that are somehow detached from the everyday. Anecdotal evidence suggests that even those who work at the building experience it with awe each day.[8] To analyse souvenirs, Gordon proposes a five-part taxonomy for souvenirs: picture images; pieces-of-rock; symbolic shorthand; markers; and local products. Her description of each category's underlying function allows for direct comparisons to be drawn with souvenirs of the Sydney Opera House. 'Picture images' are namely books, postcards and photographs that function through their figurative representation of the building and align with scopic regimes of travel. 'Local products' are regional produce or indigenous art and crafts and, in the case of the Sydney Opera House, are its performances, events and tours. 'Markers' are unrelated products which are linked to place by means of text, image or symbol – this type of souvenir is also connected to participatory culture founded on practices of *trading*, already discussed earlier. Such objects have no formal link to the Sydney Opera House, and could just as easily be branded by another destination. They are authenticated by the use of the official logo and graphic variants, 'markers' which are – in Gordon's words – 'in themselves have no reference to a particular place or event, but are inscribed with words [or symbols] which locate them in place and time'.[9] However, souvenirs, which function in Gordon's terms as 'symbolic shorthand', namely, manufactured products that evoke a coded message and 'pieces-of-rock' which are spolia or authentic fragments from the site provide examples through which to explore visitors' apprehension of architecture. The idea of miniatures as a way of exploring and manipulating the 'real' relationship between person and building is also a tactic employed in architectural practice.

Architects routinely use models (which are a form of miniature) as design tools. They use these to communicate the spatial experience of the building, and test physical aspects of an architectural proposal. Models are used to imagine the way one might move through the 'yet to be built' structure, in an analogous manner to the way the tourist perhaps uses the miniature building to experience or re-experience a visit to the Sydney Opera House. Models in architecture are, like souvenirs, little studied. As Mark Morris argues, models 'do not dominate discourse, they footnote it'.[10] The architectural qualities of the souvenir, as a kind of 'architectural model', 'extend [this] footnote [by] specifically targeting the model's relationship to size, scale and the effects of the miniature'.[11] Arguably, 'authentic fragments' employ analogous strategies to mediate a tangible and physical experiencing of architecture that is located towards the past or the future.

Souvenirs which function as 'symbolic shorthand' are all miniature versions of the building: mass-produced three-dimensional representations; a 'captured' Sydney Opera House, laser-etched inside a glass prism; snowdomes featuring a conglomeration of recognised architectural landmarks in Sydney atop an 'Opera House' base; salt and pepper shakers – one for each recital hall; Sydney-Opera-House-shaped soap and chocolates; an Opera-House-shaped light; an Opera-House-shaped gift box and miniature buildings made of pewter (Figure 6.3).

In contrast, the other souvenir is the ultimate metonym; literally a part of the building. In Gordon's terms, it is a 'piece-of-rock'. A shard from one of the tiles that clads the shells of the Sydney Opera House is suspended in glass, floating ethereally in the way architecture never can. Here, a strange scalar relationship is inscribed between the souvenir miniature building and this souvenir tile fragment. In the miniature building the Sydney Opera House is reduced to ornamental or toy-like dimensions, directly

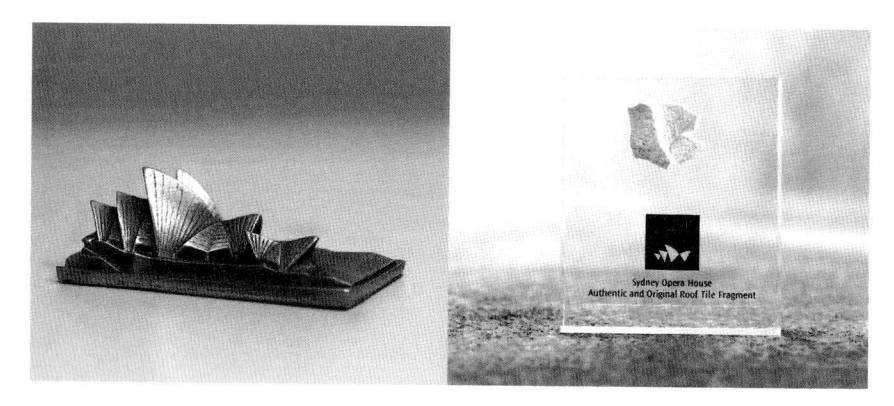

Figure 6.3 Miniature and fragment.

Sources: left, pewter miniature model produced by the Sydney Opera House Trust; right, souvenir fragment of a Sydney Opera House tile, AUD$135.00, from their Corporate Gift Catalogue (Sydney Opera House trademark reproduced with permission of the Sydney Opera House Trust, photographer unknown, 2007).

inverting the 'real' gigantic scale of the building and the visitor. This play on scale is not employed in the fragment of the tile. In this case the souvenir is at 1:1, the same scale as the actual edifice. Further, the fragment, in itself, is meaningless. As a sign or symbol of the building, it cannot be distinguished from an off-white ceramic shard, which might result from the breaking of a vase. Somehow it both questions and is founded upon its authenticity as spolia, as a piece of the Sydney Opera House. The fragment gains value in its removal and distinction from its destination. The heavy glass surround and officiating text and logo authenticate the souvenir. The miniature works by being the 'form' of the Sydney Opera House, but the fragment functions by being 'from' the Sydney Opera House.

These two souvenirs, a miniature building and a fragment of tile, function through manipulations of size and scale. Susan Stewart's scholarship on souvenirs argues that these manipulations are not innocuous; rather they directly affect our physical apprehension and experience of these objects. The physical distortion implicit in each type influences the way in which we remember the building, through the souvenir. In the miniature, Stewart asserts, we become gigantic, our bodies become the context, the landscape for the Sydney Opera House:

> The miniature offers us a transcendent vision which is known only through the visual. In approaching the miniature, our bodies erupt into a confusion of before unrealised surfaces. We are able to hold the miniature object within our hand, but our hand is no longer in proportion with its world; instead our hand becomes a form of undifferentiated landscape, the body a kind of background.[12]

The miniature version of the Sydney Opera House reduces the building to toy or ornamental dimensions, a direct inversion of the 'real' gigantic scale which the tourist experiences during their visit to this destination (Figure 6.4). This inversion functions to take the extraordinary experience of the visit into the ordinary realm of life 'back home'. The experience of walking around the building, in which the tourist apprehends

Figure 6.4 Scale and relationship.

Sources: left, photograph showing the miniature scale of a pewter miniature model produced by the Sydney Opera House Trust; right, photograph of the Sydney Opera House showing the way people play with scale (© Mary-Pierre Serveaux and Fabien Hoareau, 2005).

the building in a partial and enveloped way, is transformed into the realm of ordinary experience. Here, in the miniature, the tourist can see the complete view of the building. In the hands of the tourist, the miniature can be rotated, and moved to allow for a re-experiencing or reminiscence of the experience. Specific vantage points and events from the tourist's personal visit can be pointed out on the miniature, in this way making concrete the visitor's experience, through narrative, to family and friends, away and at home.

In architectural practice models are also used to experience the building in a predictive manner. In designing the Sydney Opera House, many models were built. Like the souvenir, the model can be whole or partial. And, like the souvenir, the model can incite anticipation or a 'kind of future experiencing' of the building through a miniature or partial model of the building at 1:1 scale. This brings to light the role that souvenirs and models play in mediating scale and time. The functions of the souvenir go beyond representing the building. The souvenir, like the model, facilitates the re-experience of architecture. However, this vicarious experience is not a direct simulacra of the event, rather it actively alters the apprehension of the building through its manipulation of physical relationship to the person. Further, this relationship, in these particular souvenirs, sets up the position or way in which this memory is experienced.

Olalquiaga's scholarship on the 'kitsch' object, and in particular her work on the souvenir, discusses the way memory is experienced through such objects.[13] She asserts that memory operates from two antithetical positions; remembrance and reminiscence. Memory that is reminiscence dissociates from the death or the intangibility of experience. The physical relationship engendered by representing the Sydney Opera House as a miniature activates this kind of nostalgic activity, by offering a way to apprehend the building and re-experience visiting still in the past. The miniature building, characterised by reminiscence, incites an active imagining of moving around the building, a dynamic and generative relationship through which to recall the architecture of the Sydney Opera House.

Olalquiaga presents remembrance as being anchored in the present. Memories as remembrance differ from reminiscence in that they acknowledge the feeling of loss at the obvious demise of the experience. Unlike reminiscence it does not erase, recreate

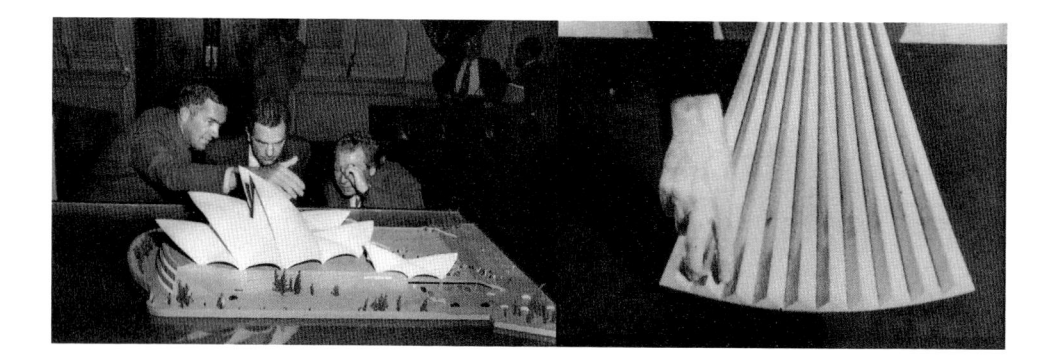

Figure 6.5 Architects working with complete and partial models of the Sydney Opera House.

Sources: left, 'Joern Utzon unpacking his model of the Sydney Opera House at Sydney Town Hall' (© State Library of NSW. IE1624918 Collection: State Library of NSW, 1957); right, 'Item 10: Jorn Utzon Sydney Opera House photographs: models of stage towers, ceilings, seating folded slabs and shells, ca. 1961' (© State Library of NSW and Jorn Utzon. IE959223 Collection: State Library of NSW, 1961).

and replay experience, but rather characterises the original experience as obsolete. The fragment evokes this type of memory experience. Although the tile fragment is in a sense a more authentic souvenir, its experience cannot be used to apprehend the building as a whole.

Models in architecture are also involved in the mediation of time. The model is described by Christian Hubert as an antecedent; 'the model purports to present architecture not re-present it'.[14] The architectural model, both as miniature and as fragment or part of a building, is always positioned in front; it precedes the architecture. However, as discussed previously, the model is also party to manipulations of scale, engaged to facilitate the physical apprehension by practitioners, clients and communities, of the 'yet to be built' edifice. In the documented development of the Sydney Opera House we can observe models which employ this temporal and physical mediation. Models which are miniatures generally explore the composition of the shells, their geometries, the relationship to the city and the experience of moving around the building. Models which explore the building through the fragment test the curved roof sections, present the articulation of the 'fan' structure of the shells, and display the geometric composition of their forms.

The use of the miniature and the fragment in architecture, in mediating the intrinsic physical and temporal distance of this activity, appears to function in an analogous manner to the way the souvenir is used to commemorate architectural experience. Like these souvenirs the model in architecture mediates scale and presence, making tangible the intangibility of experiencing the building in an 'other' time.

Souvenirs of the Sydney Opera House function by distorting time and scale in order to mediate experiences of the building. Although souvenirs are directed towards the past and models are directed towards the future, they can be seen as analogous; the souvenir is characterised by reminiscence and remembrance, the model by imagining and anticipation. Like models, souvenirs invert the 'real' scale between the tourist and the building. The diminution of the building into a pewter miniature or an architectural model enables people to experience the building as a whole. In this way the miniature aids in a holistic apprehension by both the architect and visitor.

The movement of walking around the building, in both cases, is re-enacted by turning the miniature in the landscape of the hand, reminiscing and imagining the experience though the souvenir. In the model, the architect is projecting this same movement and experience, seeing into the scaled model the future experience of the tourist. The fragment, whether the shard of tile from the roof of the Sydney Opera House, or partial architectural model at real scale, invokes an experience of the building in the present in real scale. This experience, however, is characterised by a state of remembrance or anticipation as it encompasses the state of the building in its demise or its state of gestation. Souvenirs, rather than being insignificant, and inaccurate representations, when understood as performative objects mediate participation with experiences of the Sydney Opera House across time.

Performances

Practices of *visiting* and *capturing* are not limited to the real site of the Sydney Opera House. In Legoland, California, a miniature replica of the Sydney Opera House has been constructed from the plastic toy LEGO bricks. Closely located to the replica is a miniature version of the Taj Mahal (they are only separated by Lions Gate Bridge).[15] While the Sydney Opera House LEGO kit is a souvenir that extends a visit to the Sydney Opera House into the personal domain of the home and thereby offers a means to become familiar through *making*, the miniature version on exhibition in California offers an alternative form of *visiting*. This phenomenon is not limited to Legoland theme parks, but is part of a wider cultural phenomenon of miniature cities or model parks. The proliferation of such places, some of which feature replicas of the Sydney Opera House, suggest that there is something important to be gained from both the authentic visit to the Sydney Opera House itself, and to the miniature replica in another country. The Sydney Opera House receives many visitors each year who come to see and photograph the building without attending a performance. Photographs posted publicly online, on sites such as Flickr, show people moving around the building, both on the promenade and from vantage points around the harbour. People touch the building, pretend to wear or hold the building, apprehend it and *capture* themselves in front of it.

Such performances occur also at miniature parks. Just as a trip on a ferry in Sydney Harbour is a way to view the Sydney Opera House, so too at Legoland, California, the 'Coast Cruise' can be boarded to take in the 'sights'. Curiously, individuals take photos of these miniatures, in the same way they take photos of the actual edifice; pretending to hold it or simply recording their presence near this landmark. Such touristic performances, evidenced by taking a photograph, are understood to be an 'embodied and creative performance "full of life" that produces memories, social relations and places'.[16] That such performances are enacted both around the original building, and around miniature replica souvenirs and those located in other countries, suggests that the practice of *visiting* is not limited to seeing and experiencing the building in Sydney, but rather is a way of engaging with the architecture of this place in ways that question architecture's authenticity.

Yet the participatory culture of the Sydney Opera House is not limited to the embodied practices of visiting the building. The photographs captured during these experiences (at the building, and at its replicas) are artefacts that become sites for exchange between individuals and communities on sites such as Flickr.

Figure 6.6 Performing at the Sydney Opera House.

Sources: left, photograph posted on Flickr.com showing how people seek to capture images that demonstrate a sense of closeness with the Sydney Opera House (© Summer, 2010); right, like the photograph posted on Flickr.com on the left, this one shows how people seek to capture images that demonstrate a sense of closeness regardless of whether it is the real or a miniature copy the Sydney Opera House (© Eunah Kim, 2006).

Photosharing on Flickr

Flickr was one of the first participatory media platforms and was launched in February 2004. The photosharing website grew quickly; by 2005 it hosted almost eight million images and by 2006 177 million.[17] At last count in 2011 it was estimated that Flickr hosted six billion images.[18] There are over 77 million registered Flickr members; it is a public repository of personal photography covering almost every imaginable subject utilised by over 90 million users each month.[19] Between 2008 and 2012, Flickr's prominence as an example of participatory media waned as other image-based platforms, such as Instagram, became established, and platforms such as Twitter and Facebook expanded their services to include the sharing of photographs.[20] Even so, Flickr continues to be a site for cultural research.

Photographs on Flickr can be explored in several ways; by tag descriptions, via Flickr's ranking algorithms ('interestingness' or 'relevance'), by geographical location, by group, or by date of contribution.[21] On Flickr, members can form and come together through groups where they can submit photographs to the group's 'pool' (archive or collection). Members can comment on individual photographs in the pool, or post comments in the group's discussion thread. Groups are self-organised communities that form around photographic contributions.

By 2012, there were almost 200,000 photographs and 175 groups on Flickr associated with the Sydney Opera House.[22] The focus in this part of the chapter is on the photographic contributions and online interactions of two groups associated with the Sydney Opera House: a group that goes by the same name – '*Sydney Opera House*' – and another as a counterpoint called '*Sydney-alt*'. In 2008 *Sydney Opera House* had over 600 members and more than 2,000 photos in its pool. In comparison, *Sydney-alt* had over 460 members and almost 6,000 photographic contributions.[23] Each group is governed by guidelines that describe the kinds of photographic contributions sought. Members can join public groups, or may need an invitation from an existing member. Both of the groups observed use the Sydney Opera House in their definitions of their identities: the guidelines for *Sydney Opera House* state 'the Sydney Opera House needs to be the main subject of photos submitted to this group, and needs to

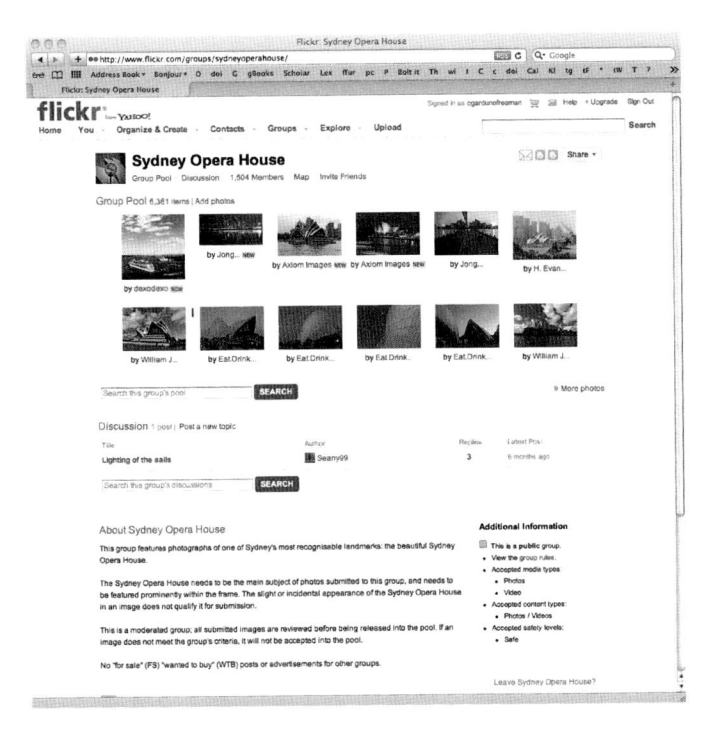

Figure 6.7 Flickr group: Sydney Opera House.

Source: screengrab from Flickr.com of the Sydney Opera House group, 2006–2017. (© Yahoo, Flickr and members of 'Sydney Opera House' group, 2012).

be featured prominently within the frame'.[24] In contrast the guidelines for *Sydney-alt* state the group 'celebrates and records the alternative side of Sydney life and scenery' and warns 'shots of the Bridge and Opera House will probably be deleted on sight'.[25] The two groups have adopted mutually exclusive curatorial strategies centred on the inclusion or exclusion of the Sydney Opera House (see Figures 6.7 and 6.8).

Groups on Flickr have been characterised in two ways: a community of people where individuals are connected by exchanging photographs, or as a kind of communal archive where members simply deposit photographs and the group is a technological repository of images. Empirical work on groups reveals a small number of very active users own the majority of photographs on Flickr, nonetheless, half of the site's members contribute at least one photograph to a group.[26] Although contribution is unevenly distributed, Flickr's function as a place to share in groups is a primary feature of this media platform where the social interactions and negotiations that occur through the exchange and sharing of photographs is the reward for participation. Nicholas Pissard and Christopher Prieur consider the social relationships of groups to see if Flickr is more akin to a photographic archive or a social media site and conclude that thematic groups tend to focus on geographical locations, while social groups are more likely to be based on abstract themes.[27] Under these parameters *Sydney Opera House* might be classified as a thematic group (in 2009 it had no discussions) and *Sydney-alt* as a social group (in 2009 it had 198 discussion threads).[28] However, Pissard and Prieur's study ignores the possibility

Figure 6.8 Flickr group: Sydney-alt.

Source: screengrab from Flickr.com of the Sydney Opera House group, 2006–2017. (© Yahoo, Flickr and members of 'Sydney-alt' group, 2012).

that group interactions can be enacted through images, not just centred on them. They assume that conversations or social interactions only occur in a textual form, and overlook the potential of images as a discursive site and medium of social negotiation.

On Flickr, participatory culture is enacted through photosharing, which is an extension of the embodied experience of taking photographs (Figure 6.9).[29] The photographs document individual experiences and sharing these images via computer or cameraphones is an extension of popular photographic engagements with this place. Richard Chalfen proposes that amateur photography entails more than the automated making of images; personal photographs serve to reinforce social relations.[30] The photographic practices that precede photosharing are some of the ways in which people negotiate their sense of identity and document their personal experiences to be remembered and shared with others at a later date.[31]

Photos that are shared can be memory artefacts or intended as a form of communication. As José van Dijck argues, this has implications, as:

> When pictures become a visual language conveyed through the channel of a communication medium, the value of individual pictures decreases while the general significance of visual communication increases. A thousand pictures sent over the phone may now be worth a single word: 'see!' Taking, sending and receiving photographs is a real-time experience and, like spoken words, image exchanges are not meant to be archived (Van House et al., 2005). Because of their abundance, these photographs gain value as 'moments', while losing value as mementoes.[32]

Figure 6.9 Performing photography.

Sources: left, photograph posted on Flickr.com showing people's photographic performances on the steps of the Sydney Opera House (©Mark Jones, 2007); right, photograph posted on Flickr.com of people on the harbour taking photographs of the Sydney Opera House (©Jeremy Keith, 2006).

Prior to platforms like Flickr, personal photographs were stored privately, only to be shared among family and friends.[33] Now, photosharing practices extend their value in the public realm. Flickr groups offer extensions to these traditional kinds of sharing and modes of communication. The viewing and sharing of photographs through groups such as *Sydney Opera House* and *Sydney-alt* is examined next, to investigate how these practices are ways in which existing sharing practices are extended around discursive social interactions that are associated with the Sydney Opera House.

Flickr structures the experience of group photosharing in three ways; it provides real-time visual updates; it presents photographs individually in order of contribution; and it presents them en masse as thumbnails. Photographs on Flickr are displayed in real time. Members' individual home pages are refreshed with current thumbnail images of each new contribution to the group pool (Figure 6.10). This means that each time a member opens their home page, they are able to see the current contributions to the groups to which they belong. Like receiving a photograph on a mobile phone, it allows members to stay up-to-date with the latest group activity. The real-time distribution of these images on Flickr makes them more like messages than memory artefacts. The images appear as a continual reminder of the dynamic nature of their communities; like tuning into the group's visual conversation. Van Dijck and Van House's observation on the communicative role of photographs counters Pissard and Prieur's assumption that only textual discussions indicate social interaction in groups. Photographs gain communicative value by being contributed to groups; just as the cameraphone photograph becomes a message in being sent. Visual contributions make the group an active social space rather than an archive, regardless of the discussions that take a textual form.

On the group's home page, visitors can view the photographs in the group's pool as a slideshow or as a page of thumbnails (Figure 6.11 and 6.12). These presentation

Figure 6.10 Real-time updates from Sydney Opera House group as displayed on author's
home page.

Source: screengrab of author's updates from an earlier interface, no longer available (© Yahoo, Flickr and
members of 'Sydney Opera House' group, 2009).

modes offer different types of interactions with the photographs in a group's pool.
Viewing the photographs as a slideshow presents the collection one image at a time, in
chronological order of submission. In this case, new contributions supplant older ones,
and the narrative moves from the present to the past, with events such as the Vivid
Luminous Festival creating a cluster of identifiable images.[34] Although the submissions
to the group are initially curated by the group's guidelines, the slideshow is a serendipitous sequence and representation of the building. The photographs are not organised
like an exhibition, where narrative or categorisation orders the viewer's experience. In
slideshow mode, typical silhouettes of the Sydney Opera House are followed by tightly
cropped details of the tiled surfaces of the roof forms; flat, slightly-out-of-focus snapshots follow spectacular sunsets that proclaim their author's technical skill. As one
representation of the Sydney Opera House is overlaid by the next, each contribution

Figure 6.11 Slideshow mode showing photograph from Sydney Opera House group pool.

Source: screengrab of one member's photograph in 'slideshow mode' (© Yahoo, Flickr and Scott
Henry, 2009).

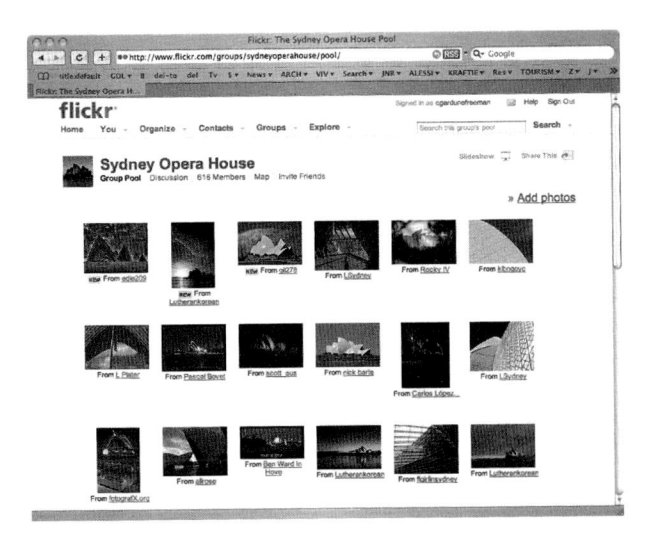

Figure 6.12 Thumbnail mode showing group pool from Sydney Opera House.

Source: screengrab of the way members' images were displayed some years earlier. This has been updated to present images in a 'tiled format' but it still operates in a very similar way (Yahoo, Flickr and members of 'Sydney Opera House' group, 2009).

asserts itself against the previous one. The knowledge that a member of the Flickr community has contributed each image of the Sydney Opera House means the slideshow can be read as a series of moments or experiences.

In contrast, exploring photographs through a group's 'photo pool' page (Figure 6.12) arranges thumbnails in a grid; approximately 30 small images, each underlined with the member's name. These thumbnails are linked to members' accounts where each photograph is presented on its own page. Here any Flickr member may offer feedback or comments (Figure 6.13). As opposed to the sequential viewing of the photographs in slideshow mode, seeing them laid out en masse gives a composite view of the group's collection. It facilitates comparison between the images and allows both similarities and differences to be observed.[35] Elizabeth Chaplin argues that viewing images in this way creates 'a micro-world whose visual coherence is such that we acquire an understanding of that society and its ethos which is not straightforwardly a function of verbal conventions'.[36] This collective representation of the Sydney Opera House, curated by the group's set of guidelines, offers a collective view, in which it is possible to discern common perspectives and experiences, as well as to observe images that appear unique.

The sequential contributions of photographs in *Sydney Opera House* work together to build a comprehensive picture of the Sydney Opera House, whilst the thumbnail views of the group's photographs offer a more complex and collective understanding. At the same time the contributions serve to connect members with each other in a collective project by sharing the experience of photographing the same building. The photographs, as structured by Flickr's viewing through slideshows, thumbnails and in real-time updates serve to enable an ongoing dynamic visual discourse that frames an understanding of the Sydney Opera House.

Figure 6.13 Individual mode from Sydney Opera House group pool.

Source: screengrab of the way member's images are displayed individually. (© Yahoo, Flickr and Jong Soo (Peter) Lee, 2009).

Generative communities

The technological structure of Flickr extends photosharing into a vehicle through which new audiences and communities are formed. The emergence of the two groups under analysis here, *Sydney Opera House* and *Sydney-alt*, will now be examined to show how these discursive negotiations, coupled with Flickr's group function, extend and refine the audiences of the Sydney Opera House. Andrew Miller and W. Keith Edwards find two major types of users on Flickr. One is an infrequent participant who shares within their existing social networks.[37] The second – 'Snaprs' – are more active participants who embrace Flickr as a public space by making all their photographs publicly accessible across the internet. Snaprs are also more active in discussion threads – spaces for debate that provide the impetus for the formation of new groups. What emerges through these discussions is that *Sydney Opera House* and its antithesis *Sydney-alt* were the result of discussions in an older group called *Sydney, Australia*. In this older group members critiqued the use of the Sydney Opera House as a symbol for Sydney; they described it as clichéd. This led to a discussion on what *should* represent Sydney (and by extension Australia). This discussion around the curation of online photographs became a generative process that led to two new public formations: *Sydney Opera House* and *Sydney-alt*. Snaprs' negotiation of their collective identity by defining the group's visual criteria spurs new interconnected social groupings.

In 2008, when this research was conducted, all of the discussion threads in *Sydney Opera House* were advertisements, except for one titled 'Buildings based on the Sydney Opera House'. This thread generated many responses (Figure 6.14), and exemplifies the role that Snaprs play in defining groups, and the role dissonance plays in the formation of new groups. Flickr groups are politically structured; members participate, moderators assist and administrators govern the group by removing photographs or posts that fall outside the stipulated guidelines. In the thread depicted, one member, 'yewenyi', proposes that photographs of buildings that look similar to the Sydney Opera House be allowed in the group. Yewenyi illustrates this by posting his own photograph of an opera-house-shaped structure on JiuJiang Road in Shanghai, China. 'Xenedis', the administrator of *Sydney Opera House*, rejects this idea. He replies this group 'is for photos of the *one and only* Sydney Opera House. :-)' (original emphasis).[38] This outright rejection is interesting as two other images in the group's pool are not photographs of the building, but photographs of representations. The first depicts a stylised drawing of the Sydney Opera House that has been printed on a shirt designed under the fashion label Mambo. The second is a photograph of watermelon pieces arranged to allude to the building's form (Figure 6.15). The inclusion of these representations, whilst yewenyi's is rejected, is perhaps related to the fact that his representation is an architectural object. It appears that the representation *of architecture* is acceptable, but not representation *through architecture*. The reproduced building is somehow construed as an inauthentic version of the Opera House, whilst the representations are an homage to it. Yewenyi responds to this rejection by threatening to form a new group called 'Not the Sydney Opera House' to accommodate representations of the Sydney Opera House. Although such a group has never been established, it does demonstrate the way in which discourse on the visual criteria of submissions is closely linked with the formation of new groups. Negotiations of inclusion and exclusion serve to draw together some members whilst excluding others. Like all social formations, audiences and communities,

Figure 6.14 Sydney Opera House group discussion thread.

Source: 'Buildings Based on the Sydney Opera House' (Yahoo, Flickr and members of 'Sydney Opera House' group, 2006).

Flickr groups are political. However Flickr's self-organising structure encourages new formations by allowing any member to establish a public group. On Flickr, these discussions are generative.

Although *Sydney Opera House* and *Sydney-alt* are defined by the inclusion and exclusion of photographs of the Sydney Opera House respectively, these two groups share members. Further, their photographic pools are not entirely exclusive; within *Sydney-alt*'s pool of 6,000 contributions there are at least 33 photographs of the Sydney Opera House.[39] Photographs that seemed to contravene the curatorial guidelines of the group have not 'been deleted on sight'. This suggests that it is the group's imagined sense of communal identity (rather than their visual one) that support their presentation as a cohesive group. Interestingly, the negotiations between members around issues of identity linked to the Sydney Opera House are what led to the formation of these Flickr groups.

The discussion threads reveal that both 'Xenedis' (administrator of *Sydney Opera House*) and 'Naddsy' (administrator of *Sydney-alt*) are also administrators in a third group, known as *Sydney, Australia*. This third group has over 2,500 members and more than 24,000 photographic contributions. In a discussion within *Sydney, Australia* titled 'Administration Roles for all', Xenedis proposes that an image of the Sydney Opera House or the Sydney Harbour Bridge be the group's identifying 'icon'.[40] On Flickr, members and groups can represent themselves with a thumbnail image. These thumbnail images, so commonplace now that they have become invisible, proliferate the digital space. They are visual identifiers for software, files and online identities. *Sydney, Australia* rejects both these landmarks as suitable representations for the group's icon. They consider these to be clichéd symbols for Sydney, and refer Xenedis to an earlier discussion titled 'Two Sydney groups. . . . .why?'[41] In this earlier discussion Naddsy asks why there are two groups on the subject of Sydney, which

Figure 6.15 Other representations of the Sydney Opera House in group pool.

Sources: left, photograph posted on Flickr.com and contributed to 'Sydney Opera House' group of watermelons arranged titled 'Sydney Melon House' (© Patrick Boland, 2006); right, a photograph was posted on Flickr.com and contributed to 'Sydney Opera House' group of Reg Mombassa's illustration featured on a Mambo shirt titled 'Lost Weekend' from the 1996 Loud Shirt Series (© Reg Mombassa, 1996).

incites responses on the visual parameters of the group. They agree to exclude Sydney's famous icons in lieu of a more 'real' (or authentic) representation of Sydney leading to the proposal of several new groups. What is revealed is the complex attachment and significance of individuals and groups to the Sydney Opera House. The formation of new groups is a strategy to control the abundant contribution of photographs of the building to existing groups associated with Australia. On the one hand, this place is revered and admired, but its liberal use as an icon for Sydney, and by extension for Sydney-siders, clashes with a more complex and nuanced sense of the way these communities identify with Sydney.

Here on Flickr, outside of formal institutions, such complex relationships to the Sydney Opera House are able to co-exist. The visual association between the building and the city of Sydney impacts on the sense of identity of members of *Sydney, Australia*. Such a blunt association with the building is deemed too clichéd and expected to be symbolic of a group of people. To do so would imply that these groups are unthinking and uncritical, rather than recognising that although people do have affection for the Sydney Opera House, this sentiment is critical and discursive.

The participatory culture on Flickr demonstrates the way in which audiences are critically engaged with the symbolic value of the Sydney Opera House. Their discussion and generation of new groups where alternative views on the Sydney Opera House can be articulated reveals the way in which audience-communities participate in generating and disseminating representations of this place. On Flickr, the socio-visual value of the Sydney Opera House is a currency for social negotiations, enacted through the sharing of representations, therefore framing the building as a place for experience, and a place around which to structure creative photographic practices.

Conclusion

Unlike the previous two chapters that focused on the way in which representations mediate participation and engagement with the Sydney Opera House in other places, this chapter explored how representations mediate experiences with the building itself across time. These exemplify the way time is implicated, as van Dijck's model describes, in the use of such representations to mediate experience and memory. The activity of taking photographs structures and authorises a way of looking at the architecture, with the premise that these images (regardless of their quality) offer a way to re-engage with the experience at a later time. The exploration of Flickr demonstrates how participatory media extends these uses into the public realm where conversation and discussion takes place not only about photographs but through them. In contrast, the exploration of souvenirs of the Sydney Opera House, through the miniature and fragment, shows how such performances that take place at the building are extended post factum within the personal realm. The souvenirs offer a means to re-engage with the embodied experience of visiting, in a similar way to that enabled by making a giant Sydney Opera House cake. The souvenirs also trade on the symbolic value of the building, as does the Wikipedia article page and the practice of critique exemplified in the young mother's personal reference to Eric Thake's *An Opera House in Every Home*.

The descriptions and detailed explorations of the six practices using examples of representations in the collection can be understood as instantiations of van Dijck's mediated memories. The Wikipedia article and Thake's analogy of the building with dishes in a washing-up rack mediate personal and collective identities. The making of a giant Sydney Opera House cake and the symbolic use of the building in the Qantas in-flight magazine touch on embodied and embedded practices. The performativity of souvenirs and the use of photographs on Flickr are all ways in which particular forms of participation with the Sydney Opera House enable the mediation of the past, the present and the future. This is not to say that these are the only aspects which each of these representations exemplifies, but rather that van Dijck's tool connects each of these to participatory culture and demonstrates how it is enabled and mediated by them. It offers a way to describe in more nuanced detail the complexity of socio-visual value as evidenced through a collection of representations that mediate experience, time and identity.

Notes

1 John Urry (2002) *The Tourist Gaze*. 2nd edn. London: Sage.
2 Jørgen Ole Bærenholdt, Jørgen Ole, Jonas Larsen, John Urry and Michael Haldrup (2003) *Performing Tourist Places*. Aldershot: Ashgate.
3 Celeste Olalquiaga (1999) *The Artificial Kingdom: A Treasury of the Kitsch Experience*. London: Bloomsbury, p. 70.
4 Susan Stewart (1984) *On Longing: Narratives of the Miniature, the Gigantic, the Souvenir, the Collection*. Baltimore: Johns Hopkins University Press.
5 D. Medina Lasansky and Brian D. McLaren (2004) *Architecture and Tourism: Perception, Performance and Place*. New York: Berg.
6 Lisa Love and Nathaniel Kohn (2001) 'This, That, and the Other: Fraught Possibilities of the Souvenir'. *Text and Performance Quarterly*, 21 (1), p. 50.
7 Beverly Gordon (1986) 'The Souvenir: Messenger of the Extraordinary'. *The Journal of Popular Culture*, 20 (3), p. 135.
8 Conversations with performers, staff and locals with the author over the course of research for this book.
9 Gordon, 'The Souvenir', p. 142.
10 Mark Morris (2006) *Models: Architecture and the Miniature*. England: Wiley-Academy, p. 7.
11 Morris, *Models*, p. 7.
12 Stewart, *On Longing*, p. 70.
13 Olalquiaga, *The Artificial Kingdom*.
14 Christian Hubert (1981) 'The Ruins of Representation'. In *Idea as Model*, edited by Kenneth Frampton and Silvia Kolbowski. New York: Rizzoli, p. 17.
15 The co-location of the Sydney Opera House and the Taj Mahal was observed by viewing YouTube videos of the 'Coast Cruise' at Legoland, California. SilverSteel3000 (2011) 'Coast Cruise Pov Legoland Ca'. *YouTube* [Video]. Retrieved: 26/03/2013, from: www.youtube.com/watch?feature=player_embedded&v=At7xzRl2k_s.
16 Bærenholdt *et al.*, *Performing Tourist Places*, p. 69.
17 John Naughton (2008) 'How Flickr Developed into a Classic Web 2.0 Success'. *Guardian*, 9 March. Retrieved: 06/09/2012, from: www.guardian.co.uk/media/2008/mar/09/web20.internet.
18 Kay Kremerskothen (2011) '6,000,000,000'. *Flickr Blog*, 4 August. Retrieved: 17/07/2012, from: http://blog.flickr.net/en/2011/08/04/6000000000/.
19 Markus Spiering (2012) 'We Want You to Grow Big Things at Flickr (Aka We're Hiring!)'. *Flickr Blog*, 12 June. Retrieved: 17/07/2012, from: http://blog.flickr.net/en/2012/06/06/we-want-you-to-grow-big-things-at-flickr-aka-were-hiring/.
20 Jenise Uehara Henrikson (2011) 'The Growth of Social Media: An Infographic'. *Search Engine Journal*. Retrieved: 27/04/2013, from: www.searchenginejournal.com/the-growth-of-social-media-an-infographic/32788/#5TbsKmFDH811DJ69.99; Melissa Fach, 'The Content Omniverse', *Search Engine Journal*, 10 August 2012.
21 Flickr (2012) 'Explore'. Retrieved: 17/07/2012, from: www.flickr.com/explore/.

22 A search performed by the author on 7 November 2008 showed 81,333 photographs tagged 'sydney', 'opera' and 'house'. The same search in July 2012 retrieved 197,825 photographs. A search for groups using the same terms retrieved 87 examples in 2008 and 175 in 2012. In 2016 this has grown to 275,835, demonstrating the shift away from the platform.

23 Figures given from the author's observations of the group *Sydney Opera House* and *Sydney-alt* (quotations added to distinguish groups from the building itself). Figures given are approximate for years 2008/2009. *Sydney Opera Hou*se now has over 1,400 members and almost 6,000 images in its pool, whilst *Sydney-alt* has 787 members but over 14,000 photographs contributed. The uneven growth is interesting, where even though the membership of *Sydney Opera House* and *Sydney-alt* have both doubled, the image pool of *Sydney Opera House* has not increased at the same rate, revealing the different approaches between these two communities. *Sydney-alt* members contribute much more frequently than those of *Sydney Opera House.*

24 'Flickr Group: Sydney Opera House' (2006–2013) *Flickr.* Retrieved: 27/02/2013, from: www.flickr.com/groups/sydneyoperahouse/.

25 'Flickr Group: Sydney-Alt' (2006–2012) *Flickr* [Photosharing Group]. Retrieved: 27/02/2013, from: www.flickr.com/groups/33606562@N00/.

26 Radu-Andrei Negoescu and Daniel Gatica-Perez (2008) 'Analyzing Flickr Groups'. Presented at the *CIVR'08 - International Conference on Content-Based Image and Video Retrieval*, Niagara Falls, Ontario, Canada, 7–9 July. Retrieved: 29/07/2009, from: www.idiap. ch/~negora/GroupWebPage/res/civr2696-negoescu.pdf.

27 Nicolas Pissard and Christopher Prieur (2007). 'Thematic Vs. Social Networks in Web 2.0 Communities: A Case Study on Flickr Groups'. Presented at the *Institut National de Recherche en Informatique et en Automatique (INRIA) HAL-CCSD*. Retrieved: 21/11/2008, from: http://hal.inria.fr/docs/00/17/69/54/PDF/42-algotel-flickr.pdf.

28 Administrators can delete discussion threads. This group had seven discussion threads in December 2008, but these have now all been deleted since the appointment of a new administrator.

29 The idea of tourist photography as a cultural practice is well established in the work of John Urry, Jonas Larsen and Jørgen Ole Bærenholdt *et al.*, and the idea of tourism and performance is explored in D. Median Lasansky and Brian D. McLaren's volume on architecture and tourism. Urry, *The Tourist Gaze*; Jonas Larsen (2004) *Performing Tourist Photography*. PhD thesis, Department of Geography and International Development Studies, Roskilde University, Denmark; Jonas Larsen (2005) 'Families Seen Sightseeing: Performativity of Tourist Photography'. *Space and Culture*, 8 (4), pp. 416–434; Bærenholdt *et al.*, *Performing Tourist Places*; Lasansky and McLaren, *Architecture and Tourism*.

30 Richard Chalfen (2002) 'Snapshots 'R' Us: The Evidentiary Problematic of Home Media'. *Visual Studies*, 17 (2), pp. 141–149; Richard Chalfen (2006) 'Can You See Me Now? Problems in the Study of Camera-Phone Use in the US and Japan'. Presented at the *Eyes on the City, International Visual Sociology Association Conference*, Urbino, Italy, 3–5 July.

31 Nancy Van House (2009) 'Collocated Photo Sharing, Story-Telling, and the Performance of Self'. *International Journal of Human-Computer Studies*, 67 (12), pp. 1073–1086.

32 José van Dijck (2008) 'Digital Photography: Communication, Identity, Memory'. *Visual Communication*, 7 (1), p. 62; Nancy Van House, Marc Davis and Morgan Ames (2005) 'The Uses of Personal Networked Digital Imaging: An Empirical Study of Cameraphone Photos and Sharing'. Presented at the *CHI'05 Conference on Human Factors in Computing Systems*, New York, Association of Computing Machinery.

33 Van House, 'Collocated Photo Sharing', pp. 1073–1086; José van Dijck (2005) 'From Shoebox to Performative Agent: The Computer as Personal Memory Machine'. *New Media & Society*, 7 (3), pp. 311–332.

34 *Vivid Sydney* is an annual winter festival of light, music and ideas. *Luminous* is part of this festival presented by the Sydney Opera House, where the sails of the building are dynamically animated through a lighting performance.

35 Brenda Danet and Tamar Katriel (1994) 'No Two Alike: Play and Aesthetics in Collecting'. In *Interpreting Objects and Collections*, edited by Susan M. Pearce. London: Routledge, pp. 253–277.

36 Elizabeth Chaplin (1994) *Sociology and Visual Representation*. London: Routledge, p. 212.

37 Andrew D. Miller and W. Keith Edwards (2007) 'Give and Take: A Study of Consumer Photo-Sharing Culture and Practice'. Presented at the *CHI 2007*, San Jose, CA, 28 April–3 May. Retrieved: 27/04/2013, from: www.cc.gatech.edu/~keith/pubs/chi2007-photosharing.pdf.

38 'Buildings Based on the Sydney Opera House' (2006) *Flickr* [Discussion Thread in Photosharing Group: Sydney Opera House]. 26 February. Removed.

39 Search performed by the author on 27 January 2009.

40 'Administration Roles for All' (2006) *Flickr* [Discussion Thread in Photosharing Group: Sydney, Australia]. 16 February. Removed.

41 'Two Sydney Groups…Why?' (2006) *Flickr* [Discussion Thread in Photosharing Group: Sydney, Australia]. 14 January. Removed.

7 Entangled significance
Personal tributes

On 30 November 2008, Australia awoke to news that Jørn Utzon, the architect of the Sydney Opera House, had died at 90 years of age. Utzon had been unwell and had 'succumbed to a heart attack, while asleep at home in Denmark on Saturday'.[1] Reports recounted Utzon's life and described his most famed building, the Sydney Opera House, largely ignoring the rest of his architectural oeuvre, which includes the National Assembly of Kuwait (1982), a church in Bagsvaerd, Denmark, his own house in Majorca and several other housing projects. Instead, reports recalled

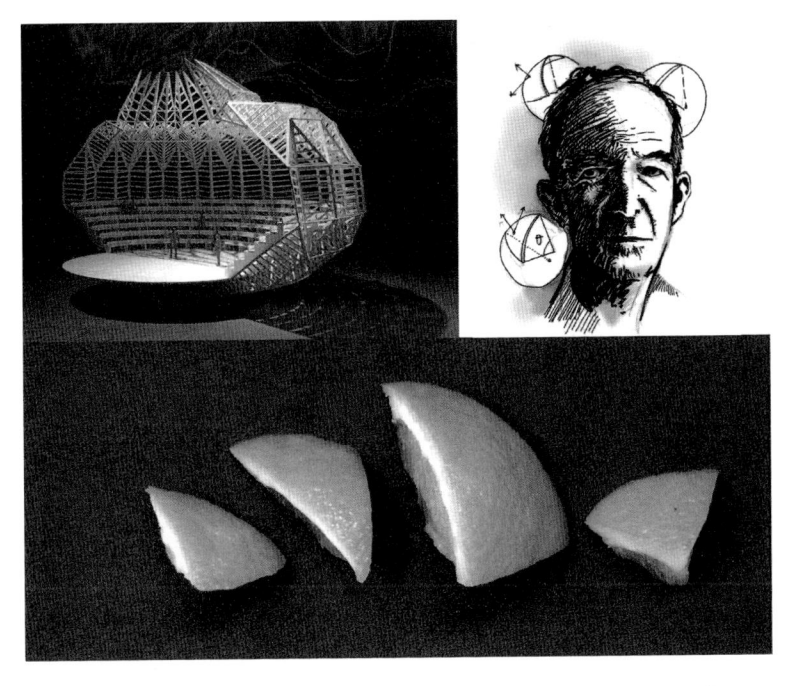

Figure 7.1 Public expression prompted by Utzon's death on participatory media.

Sources: top left, posted on Flickr.com of a model of Jorn Utzon's unbuilt subterranean Jeita Grotto Theatre, Lebanon, 1968, in recognition of Utzon's death (© Seier+Seier, 2008); top right, drawing of Utzon and his ideas to mark Utzon's death at 90 years of age (© Ibai Gandiaga Perez de Albeniz, 2009); bottom, photograph referencing the mythical moment Utzon found the solution to the modular construction of the shells when beholding an orange, posted on Flickr.com when Utzon died on November 2008. (©martin8th/Flickr, 2008).

the controversy that arose during the construction of the Sydney Opera House, Utzon's failure to meet deadlines and budgets, the strained political circumstances that led to his resignation and the national sense of loss connected to the knowl-edge that Utzon's complete vision for the building would forever remain unrealised. At the same time, reports reassured readers that Utzon was no longer bitter about the events of the past, and that there had been a reconciliation, facilitated by his re-appointment as architect of the Sydney Opera House and the World Heritage inscription in the previous year.[2]

Utzon's death was a sorrowful event for those closely connected with the architect and for the general public, who felt that he was synonymous with the Sydney Opera House. As with any kind of loss, the value of what is gone is felt intensely at the time of such an event.[3] The upsurge of emotion around Utzon's death and his role and treatment around the Sydney Opera House was evident on participatory media sites. People posted the news on Facebook, shared news articles and commented on photo-graphs in order to express their sentiment and sense of loss of the building's architect (Figure 7.1). Public expression through participatory forms of media at this time was an opportunity to research a further example of the building's social value and explore how José van Dijck's mediated memories could be a conceptual tool coupled with con-tent analysis. Building on the discussion of the previous three chapters that explored particular forms of participation through the schema of practices – *telling, critiquing, making, trading, visiting* and *capturing* – this chapter develops a creative analysis of a set of personal tributes posted in response to Utzon's death.

The death of the architect

On the day of Utzon's death the flags of the Harbour Bridge flew at half-mast and the lighting on the Sydney Opera House was dimmed between 8:30 and 9:30 p.m. as a sign of national respect, and in honour of his contribution to Australia.[4] Politicians, executives, major performing arts companies, historians, writers and artists all paid tribute to Utzon, lauding him as a visionary and the Opera House as his gift to Australians.[5] Kim Williams, Chairman of the Sydney Opera House Trust, stated that Utzon:

> was an architectural and creative genius who gave Australia and the world a great gift [and that the] Sydney Opera House is core to our national cultural identity and a source of great pride to all Australians. It has become the most globally recognised symbol of our country.[6]

Kevin Rudd, the prime minister at the time, called upon the nation to join him in cel-ebrating Utzon's legacy.[7] In the days that followed Utzon's death, 'the Sydney Opera House . . . received thousands of emails commemorating the life of its architect, Joern Utzon'.[8] This surge of public sentiment prompted the management of the Sydney Opera House (the Sydney Opera House Trust) to provide an online space for people to make a public tribute within the Sydney Opera House website.[9] The site, where hundreds of people posted their own personal tributes to Utzon and to the Sydney Opera House, is an example of participatory culture that resides within the institution, and forms the focus of the next part of this book's analysis.

Myth and Utzon

The tributes offered at the time of Utzon's death are the focus of a paper presented by Naomi Stead and Anthony Moulis in 2010.[10] In 'Sydney's Prometheus: Myth, Representation and Remediation at Joern Utzon's Sydney Opera House', Stead and Moulis describe the way in which Utzon and the story of the Sydney Opera House have become mythologised in popular culture. In doing so they recognise that the 'broader social and cultural significance of the building do not only reside in the "truth" of its architectural history'.[11] The authors are more interested in the public perception of the building and analyse this by drawing on obituaries and tributes that were published in newspapers and professional journals, as well as less conventional sources such as blog entries and the personal tributes on the Utzon Memorial Website.

Stead and Moulis' analysis of the obituaries reveals the retrospective public sense of guilt about Utzon's treatment during the construction of the Sydney Opera House. They argue that there is a sense of loss at his passing because reconciliation with the architect can now never be enacted. Woven into this public guilt is the theme of tragedy, where Utzon, the protagonist hero, is framed as an 'artist amongst the philistines'. Stead and Moulis demonstrate that this mythologising dates back to the time of Utzon's resignation.

Although the paper by Stead and Moulis is closely aligned with the following analysis of the personal tributes on the Utzon Memorial Website, their focus is on the deployment of myth as a counterpoint to architectural history. In particular, they note that such universals were part of the agenda of the third generation of Modernist architects who employed primitive architectures as tools for universal forms. Although Stead and Moulis cite two of the personal tributes, these support their overall argument regarding the myth of the building and Utzon, rather than, as is the aim here, to understand the tributes as an example of participatory culture implicated in the manifestation of the building's iconic value.

In the weeks that followed Utzon's death, over 700 personal tributes were posted on the *Jørn Utzon State Memorial Website (Utzon Memorial)* (Figure 7.2).[12] Two-thirds of the contributors identified nationally as Australian, others identified through their profession, mostly architects or musicians. But contributions were also received from as far afield as Denmark, the United Kingdom, the United States, France, Germany, Spain, Canada, Hong Kong, Malaysia, Kenya, Iceland, Nepal and Colombia. The interest, both nationally and internationally, demonstrates the widespread significance of the Sydney Opera House. In particular, it evidences the way in which people connect Utzon so immediately with this work of architecture. The Utzon Memorial Website is the only dedicated site that employed participatory media to engage with audiences at the time of Utzon's death, though it is no longer accessible.

Interestingly, a tribute page also existed on the website of the Utzon Centre, which was the last building designed by Utzon in collaboration with his son, Kim. It is located in Aalborg and was intended as a meeting space for architecture students to discuss their ideas, rather than to immortalise Utzon. There are exhibition spaces and other public facilities as part of the complex. The centre is managed and run by Aalborg University and promotes research on the significance of Utzon's oeuvre. On the website at the time of Utzon's death only three public tributes were included, along with links to two newspaper obituaries. No personal tributes were hosted at the time.[13]

Figure 7.2 Screengrab of the Utzon Memorial Website page with personal tributes posted.

Source: screengrab of the Utzon tributes website, no longer available (© Sydney Opera House Trust, 2009).

Another important observation was that memorial websites were not set up in relationship to Utzon's other works, such as the Church at Bagsvaerd or the Kuwait National Assembly Building, important buildings in their own right, aside from the Sydney Opera House.

The personal tributes on the Utzon Memorial Website are revealing of the personal and intimate relationship people feel they have with this place. Many recounted special moments experienced at the Sydney Opera House, or memories of visiting, or simply regretted Utzon's passing in relation to his contribution to the discipline of architecture. The tributes demonstrated how people feel love for the building; delight at the experience it affords; regret for the way Utzon was treated; and the identity that the building gives Sydney. The messages vary; some are short conventional statements offering condolences. Others are lengthy pieces of prose that merge personal memories with the story of the Sydney Opera House, demonstrating the way in which the place entwines in the everyday lived experience of its local and international communities.

The website organised the tributes chronologically in order of contribution with most recent first. The tributes were searchable by name and nationality. Contributing a tribute was all that was required to participate. Unlike other social media platforms, the Utzon Memorial Website did not require individuals to sign up as members or offer a service, like the sharing of photographs on Flickr or hosting a blog on Blogger or WordPress or becoming a watcher on Wikipedia. However, interaction on the site is implied in the participants' acts of posting and browsing the tributes already contributed. In this sense, the Utzon Memorial Website does not conform to Howard Rheingold's criteria for *participatory media*, but rather can be understood as an instance of *participatory culture*.[14] The website might be understood as a primitive form of participatory media; while it does not offer peer-to-peer communication, it presents individual contributions as a community of the Sydney Opera House that are creative and engaged. On this site individuals articulate their personal sentiment and connections with the Sydney Opera House through the socially embedded practice of offering a tribute. The tributes are a collective expression of the socio-visual value of the Sydney Opera House. Further, because this website exists as part of the official Sydney Opera House website, it exemplifies Henry Jenkins' concept of media convergence,[15] where institutions incorporate new media to engage with audiences and communities.

The personal tributes on the Utzon Memorial Website are accompanied by more formal representations; official tributes, a message from the Utzon family, Utzon's biography, the building's history and the programme for the State Memorial held four months after his death.[16] In addition, the online tributes were a means of obtaining tickets to the State Memorial held for Utzon. This celebration of Utzon's life featured performances by Australia's premier performing arts groups and ceremonial speeches by officials and the Utzon family.[17] One online tribute would have the honour of being selected and read at the memorial service, which was broadcast nationally on the Australian Broadcasting Corporation (ABC) television and radio network.

The creation of the online tributes was an institutional response to the emotion demonstrated by members of the public in the wake of Utzon's death. What is a tribute? Why were people motivated to write them? After all, these individuals did not personally know Utzon, and the Sydney Opera House itself had not been destroyed.

Online memorials

Offering a tribute is a personal act that is part of cultural practices associated with death, grief and bereavement in many cultures. Tributes are distinct from obituaries, which are public announcements of the death of a person. Obituaries describe the deceased person's life and achievements. In contrast, tributes are individual demonstrations of sorrow, gratitude, affection and thanks offered at the occasion of death, to someone held in high esteem.[18]

The use of websites as memorials was already well established in 2008 when the Sydney Opera House launched the *Utzon Memorial*.[19] Other memorial sites are more akin to 'virtual cemeteries', where individuals acquire a space to memorialise a loved one. The Utzon Memorial Website is more like an online guestbook, except that here, instead of the messages remaining private after the rituals of death have occurred, the tributes remain public.[20] Although the tributes are limited in their ability to facilitate ongoing forms of participatory culture they do evidence participation in response to Utzon's death.

Psychologists Brian de Vries and Pamela Roberts suggest that online forms of memorialisation operate in three ways; they help maintain or create a connection with the deceased, they strengthen existing relationships and are sites for the generation of new communities.[21] The act of writing and posting an online tribute can be understood as a means of articulating a personal connection with Utzon and with others by participating in a socially embedded practice.[22] Similarly, contributing to and then reading (or vice versa) entries in the Utzon Memorial Website is a way of participating in communal commemoration. Further, the role of the tributes as a means for obtaining tickets to the State Memorial, meant they were literally a means for an embodied form of 'coming together' as an audience in the Sydney Opera House Concert Hall.

The Utzon Memorial Website was a place for the unofficial expression of public sentiment triggered by an historic event. The messages contributed in the tributes were not only directed to Utzon, but also to the Sydney Opera House. Writing a tribute can be formulaic and simply follow conventions – such as 'sorry for your loss' – but it can also be an opportunity to express significance – about Utzon and the Sydney Opera House. Although these aspects can be perceived by reading the tributes online, the limitations of the website in terms of people's ability to self-organise mean that their analysis required a different approach.

Sentiment

The most straightforward method of organising the tributes for analysis was via their textual content. The aim was to reveal the strong emotional connections people have with the Sydney Opera House. Using content analysis, which measures word frequency, to derive words associated with strong emotions was a means for organising the tributes, which could then be analysed in a more contextualised way.

There are several publicly available software tools for content analysis.[23] Wordle was used to understand the overall word frequency of the tributes posted to the Utzon Memorial Website (Figure 7.3 and 7.4). Once the most frequent words, such as Sydney Opera House and Utzon, were removed from the visualisation, the word cloud revealed emotive words around which more complex visualisations could be constructed for detailed analysis. The results from Wordle are shown in Figure 7.3, where the word-map demonstrates how some words, such as Sydney, opera, house, Utzon and Australia appear most frequently in the entire body of tributes. This is what might be expected considering the subject and aim of these contributions. However, Wordle allows for a more refined approach where these terms can be removed to reveal a more fine-grained representation of the tributes associated with the Sydney Opera House, Australia and Utzon. The word-map in Figure 7.4 reveals more descriptive terms, such as magnificent,

Figure 7.3 Utzon tributes Wordle.

Source: screengrab of the full text sourced from the tributes and processed through Jonathan Feinberg wordmapping website Wordle available at www.wordle.net.

Figure 7.4 Utzon tributes Wordle with high frequency words removed.

Source: screengrab of the full text sourced from the tributes, processed through Jonathan Feinberg wordmapping website Wordle available at www.wordle.net with high frequency words removed.

beautiful, great and amazing. The word 'thank' dominates, while other less expected terms such as spirit, proud, see and visit appear in between the larger more frequent words. Interestingly, two clear emotions, love and sad, are made visible. These are sentiments and offer a means for the investigation of the attachment people have for this place.

The word love appeared 72 times. In contrast, the word sad appeared 29 times and the word sadness 10 times, saddened 6 times and sadly 9 times. All sentences that contained the word love were grouped together. The same process was applied to sentences that contained the word sad, sadness, saddened or sadly. The sentences were then grouped thematically. The results of this process are illustrated in Figure 7.5 and 7.6.

I love the Sydney Opera House.
I love her as though she is mine alone!
most beautiful building in Sydney and we love it.
I, like all Austalian love the opera house.
We love the Opera House and all it represents.
....I truly hope he knew just how all Australians love his Opera House....."
It is since then that I have this love affair with this most special and amazing building.
(we all love it!)"
I took a cruise of the harbour and fell in love with Opera House and the Sydney Harbour.
I love the legacy you left us.

love for the edifice itself
I love walking up to it, past it and around it and remind myself never to...
our magnificent harbour and I love the sight of it as I drive across our Harbour Bridge.
I still love walking up the stairs of that magnificent building.
We love going there to listen to opera, singing in the mass choir
I love walking up to it and exploring all of its angles.

love for the experience of visiting the edifice
....architecture 'an art, and an expression of love' as he did."
His talent, passion and love for architecture have blessed us
nobleness to pour such a great amount of love and passion into an architectural form.
A proposal to never forget, gentle and kind love in a place I always remember and imagine forever

the edifice as an expression of love
love of song and dance and being creative, love of beautiful buildings love of the ocean, love of sailing
daily inspiration and proving that love can conquer logistics.
your generosity and continuing to love Australia.
Thank you for your love

the edifice as an example of Utzon's love towards architecture
I feel love for the man who imagined it and made it real for us all.
Love him or hate him, irrespective the world has lost a true genius.
I love what you have done for us.
we unashamedly say that we love you, for bestowing upon us the greatest gift
With admiration and love"
Thank you Love.and Light"
With love and respect"
Thank you Warmest wishes and love"

love for Utzon
I first encountered this global icon in 1996, & was rendered speechless. While periodicals & journals provide startling detail, nothing quite prepares you for the first in-person encounter. With increasing familiarity, I have come to love her as one would an intimate friend, & yet it she has retained that mystical ability, I am still at a loss for words when in her company."
The real voyage of discovery consists not in seeking new landscapes but in having new eyes."
-Marcel Proust
With extreme gratitude AE Dunn.

Figure 7.5 Typographic map: love.

I am very sad to hear of the death of Jorn.

my deepest gratitude and sadness to the Utzon family for a man who transcended Sydney, our nation

to his family on this very sad occasion but also for the opportunities he gave to all Australians and visitors

It is with sadness that I hear of the loss of one of the world's visionary designers.

A very sad day for Australia as one of our national treasures has passed away.

We all feel immensely sad at the loss, yet proud that we have played a small role in the success

Mr Utzon's passing has left me sad and reflective on his wonderful contribution to the cultural life of Sydney.

Your insights will be sadly missed , but we will never forget your legacy to our culture and our mindset

such a wonderful man. Sadness for his loved ones however the happiness of his memorable legacy.

saddness and legacy of Utzon

I think it was very sad the way Joern Utzon was treated by the NSW government

Initially awe and admiration, then sadness, always sadness, for the way its brilliant creator was treated .

Though sad that Mr Utzon withdrew, we are lucky it survived.

I've always felt sad Utzon never got to see the opera house in real life.

It was dreadfully sad that Jorn Utzon did not see the spectacular building he had created.

vision and talent, and it is a great sadness that he never got to see his masterpiece.

What a sad affair to se such a magnificent piece of architecture, unsighted by its father.

However I was saddened to learn of its troubled history during construction

it is with great sadness that Utzon himself didn't come back again and get the public apology

I remember the reasons Utzon sadly left before his Opera House was finished.

I'm sad that you will now never see the interior that you had designed

....It saddens me that Jorn Utzon never got to touch his masterpeice, he was a genius

It will remain a sad story forever, than Jorn Utzon never came back to h i s opera...

sad tragedy that Utzon never returned

I sit here with tears in my eyes, saddened that such a wonderfully talented man has left us

It saddens me greatly to hear this morning of Jorn Utsons passing.

It is a sad day, but also a day of celebration of the life of a man

"Truly a sad day.

I was greatly saddened by his passing

proud Dane it was very sad to hear of Mr Jorgen Utzons death.

It was with great sadness that I heard the passing of Jørn Utzon, Sydney's dearest friend.

I am very sad to hear of the passing of such a talented man who has given so much

What a sad day

So sad to hear of Mr Utzon's passing

loss and sadness that Utzon died

54
sad

Utzon's inspirational Sydney Opera House was virtually responsible for the late 20th century development of this country's Performing Arts and Tourism industries. Without this House there would not be what we have today. His work here created untold numbers of opportunities for hundreds of thousands of arts workers, patrons and real and virtual visitors who have been elated by the poetry of his vision and of who I am merely one. I thank him for the joy his work has brought me: from being at its opening by the Queen, (when his presence was so sadly missed) through years working with companies performing there and now simply from just looking at it and walking in and around it. His work elsewhere demonstrates this was no isolated instance of genius and the users of those buildings too salute him at his passing. RIP Joern. My sympathy to your family."
Kate Williams,
Cremorne

Figure 7.6 Typographic map: sad.

The significance of these typographic maps is the way in which they reveal individuals' intimate and emotive connections with the Sydney Opera House. In keeping with the personal nature of a tribute, the expressions are often in the first person and describe a relationship: with this building, its story, or with Utzon, its architect.

In analysing these texts five broad themes emerged in relation to the word 'love'. The Sydney Opera House is an object of affection. People assert their strong emotional attachment toward this place by stating that they feel love for the building. People also express love for the experience of visiting the building, both close-up walking around the exterior or attending a performance or afar from the Harbour Bridge, Taronga Zoo or Sydney Harbour. The Sydney Opera House is also recognised as an expression of love; from Utzon to Australia and more specifically from Utzon to architecture. Finally people also express love for Utzon's contribution to the Sydney Opera House. Tributes that use the word love are primarily about the Sydney Opera House, and those that do include a reference to Utzon, do so in terms of his contribution to the building, to Australia or to the discipline of architecture.

In contrast, the themes that arise around the words sad, sadness, saddened, and sadly all are in direct reference to Utzon: the legacy he left in the Sydney Opera House, the tragedy embodied in his resignation and permanent departure from Australia, and simply sadness at the news of his death. Unlike the statements that use the word love, these statements demonstrate the connection that people feel with Utzon in terms of the story of the building's realisation. As Stead and Moulis' analysis of Utzon's mythical status reveals, the public sense of guilt surrounding Utzon's treatment is still a prominent association with the building.

How do the tributes evidence a participatory culture of the Sydney Opera House? How can these personal contributions be understood as evidencing socio-visual value? Writing a tribute is a way of articulating a particular relationship. By making a tangible representation of this relationship, through text, or through photography, it can be argued that we make a relationship tangible. Death is a time of loss. Often this loss prompts us to articulate the significance of the deceased through public rituals, such as funerals and memorials. Joyce Walker describes this as exigency – an urgent need to form connections; both with the deceased and with those still alive. Her research on online memorials notes that these sites capture private and public expression around historical events and are spaces where multiple narratives and perspectives are entwined.[24] Understood from this perspective, the tributes, as artefacts, are evidence of a public desire to articulate the significance of the Sydney Opera House, through textual representation.

The tributes can be understood as articulations of the relationships that people have with the Sydney Opera House, triggered by the intertwined association of Utzon and the building. Articulating this significance involves the remembering of experiences and important occasions associated with this place. Georges Teitler's tribute recalls his memories of his migration to Sydney and the Sydney Opera House as a place for special occasions, an aspect he has passed on to his daughter:

> When I migrated to Australia exactly 48 years before this memorial function, the foundation of the Opera House were already in place. I saw it then rising until in 1973 it was complete. My wife and I took our then seven year old daughter to the first concert which took place even before the official [sic] opening by H.M. The Queen. I instilled in my daughter: When the Opera House will celebrate its 75th anniversary, you may be the only person alive having experienced the opening![25]

Like many of the tributes, Georges Teitler's creates a direct relationship by stating he migrated '48 years before this memorial', at a time when the Sydney Opera House was under construction. He describes moments from his own life and intertwines these with moments in the building's history, recalling from the past and projecting into the future when his daughter will (hopefully) be able to celebrate the building's 75th anniversary. Georges Teitler's tribute exemplifies how the Sydney Opera House is a touchstone both temporal and geographic against which personal biographies are constructed and familial relations are reinforced.

The typographic maps of the terms love and sad are revealing of the way the Sydney Opera House mediates personal and social relationships and conceptions of the past, present and future for people. Sentiment for this place is intermingled with its value as a locus around which these issues can be negotiated. To explore the significance of such online and offline sentiment, mediated memories is employed as a conceptual tool to analyse the tributes. In this way, practices of participatory culture can be explored for the way they mediate relationships, time and experience. It observes the way in which these statements evidence the way the Sydney Opera House mediates relational, temporal and embodied aspects of everyday life and social value.

Three axes of participatory culture

In earlier chapters, van Dijck's conceptual tool of mediated memories was used to explain how participatory culture was significant in terms that align with the aims of heritage, particularly social value. In the chapters that explore the participatory culture of the Sydney Opera House, the three axes of van Dijck's conceptual tool can be evidenced as central to the socio-visual practices proposed as a way of organising and analysing the collection of representations. The practices of *telling* and *critiquing* were explored in more detail through instances of collective participation on Wikipedia and personal participation in a blogpost about washing up dishes. The practices of *making* and *trading* demonstrated the way in which practices of participatory culture are carried out through both embodied and embedded instances. These two practices were explored through the creation of a giant architectural cake and the value of association through a religious event. The mediation of time through representations was explored through the practices of *visiting* and *capturing*, where miniature souvenirs and spolia purchased in the present enable experiences in the future and the act of photosharing on Flickr is a way of re-negotiating aspects of the past. From these examples it is possible to see how the representations found online are not simply visual material that can be read for its content, but rather that it must also be understood from its interpreted context of production and reception.[26] It is also clear that conceiving of participatory culture as a central way in which social value is generated, transmitted and maintained disrupts the notion that the significance is embedded within the material fabric of the building. It also raises questions around how social values can be conserved as part of heritage listing, when they appear to cross the existing divisions of tangible, intangible and digital heritage. Participatory culture evidences social value as a networked form of heritage. This issue will be taken up in the next chapter.

This chapter proposes to explore how van Dijck's tool offers a way to analyse practices of participatory culture within the online tributes offered at the time of Utzon's death. Following the analysis of the tributes using the terms 'love' and 'sad', van Dijck's tool, mediated memories, is used to further investigate how a participatory activity such as posting a tribute could have a role in mediating relationships, temporality and embodiment. By searching the content analysis from Wordle for frequent terms that correlated to van Dijck's relational, temporal and embodied axes, a further six typographic maps were created. Frequent terms drawn from the content analysis were used to classify statements from the tributes in line with the axes in mediated memories: relational (personal and collective); temporal (past and future); and embodiment (embedded and embodied). Key to the analysis was to select the terms that appeared most frequently but that also connected the contributor of the tribute with the Sydney Opera House. These terms are abstract and focus on the relationship being expressed rather than the content of the tribute. In this way, the analysis is based on the connection first and then points to more concrete objects that are implicated in these connections.[27] Figure 7.7 is a diagram that attaches the selected term to each of van Dijck's axes and illustrates how they also connect with practices of participation as understood from the discussion in Chapters 4, 5 and 6.

The terms 'my' and 'people' respectively were selected to explore the relational axis. 'My' mediates a personal sense of self and a collective identity (Figure 7.8). Personal connections to the Sydney Opera House were about seeing the building, having a sense of intimacy, memories of performances attended, memories of working on the building's realisation and sympathy for the family at Utzon's passing:

> My wife and I were married and held our reception at the Opera House, so many years ago ... My soul as others has found a place to sing in this magical space ... My father worked on the building.[28]

Personal connections demonstrate the way in which social value is demonstrably intimate and emotional. The descriptions were of experiences and small, personally significant (often familial) connections, as opposed to those usually acknowledged

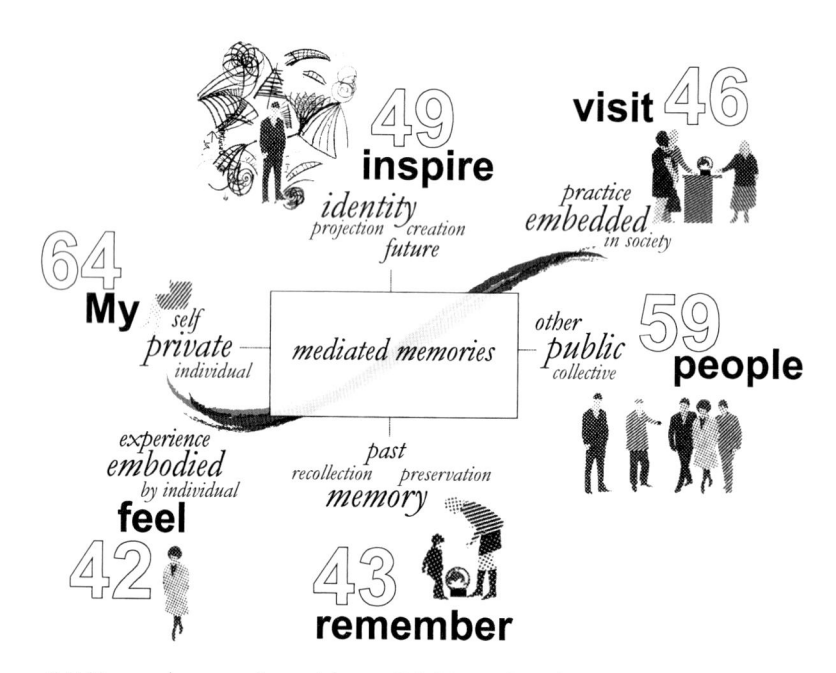

Figure 7.7 Terms that correlate with van Dijck's mediated memories.

in the historical accounts of the building. There was also the display of empathy extended to Utzon's relatives for the real loss of a family member who was surely cherished, not only as a grand architectural figure, but simply as a father, grand-father or uncle.

My childhood dream was to see the Sydney Opera House.
My siblings and I are of migrant parents and the Opera House symbolised
My spirit has been uplifted by the shape and beauty of your work
My first glimpse of the Opera House was thru the May mist from the deck
My first vision of the City was been the Sydney Opera House.
My heart lifts whenever I see the Opera House - from all angles, in all seasons,
My first "assignment" I set myself was to photograph the Opera House

seeing the opera house

My mother and father came across Jørn whilst shopping (I think)
My only wish was that you were allowed to finish the amazing design.
My name is Peter Coleman and I was born the year the opera house was finished
when my daughter was born my Husband bought me a peice of roof tile
My wife and I were married and held our reception at the Opera House

intimate and personal connections

My husband took his mother to the opening of the Opera House.
"My husband and I are from two different countries,
My family and I have enjoyed immensely being at Opera House concerts,
My daughter has performed on it's stage

memories of performances

My brother in law at the time did some contracting work on the air conditioning
My husband, as a young architect, was hired by Ove Arap
My first job was working for Ove Arup & Partners as a secretary in 1959.
My uncle Bill Lambert built the model of the Opera House

working on the project

My soul as others has found a place to sing in this magical space
My Grandma thought it was all so wonderful and I feel so proud
My partner and I share a love of this building and secretly treat it as "ours";
My husband and I are both Architects and we have been greatly inspired
My tribute to a great architect who stayed true to his vision.
My sincere sympathy go out to his family at this time. Vale…Jorn Utzon."
My familly and I thank you.
My sympathies to his family and friends."
My sympathy to your family."
My condolances"

sympathy to Utzon's family

My mother, Enid Morrison, was one of the earliest female Computer Operators. Computer operator did I hear you say? Well that's what they called them in the 1960's. My mother worked for Ove Arup & Partners in their head office in London as a Computer Operator, having travelled to England from Rhodesia in 1961.

We may never have been here in Australia if it wasn't for Joern and his magnificent structure.

My mother died at 65yrs old, about a month before Joern Utzon, so I would be honoured to go in her place to the State Memorial, which is being held to celebrate the man that gave us so much.
I often wonder if he ever realised the depth of his gift. Thank you.
Lorna Morrison.

Figure 7.8 Typographic map: my.

At a collective level, the term 'people' was connected to descriptions of the world-wide community of the Sydney Opera House and its significance as a gift to Australia that represented the value of art and dreams (Figure 7.9). These kinds of connections with the Sydney Opera House are more frequently rehearsed in the literature on the building, but here in these statements their centrality as a form of social cohesion is evidenced. Annika Edsberg posted that the building is 'cherished as both a cultural icon for the Australian people and significantly as a modern expression of hope + creativity for all the world'.[29] The relational axes reveal social values through which we recognise both personal and collective present-day experiences of the building

Now i go overseas and when people discover I am from Sydney, they say 'Oh the place with the Opera House',
delighted that many millions of other people who visit take it into their hearts too.
you have given Australia and its people and those that visit our city.
enriching the lives of the Australian people the Australian nation.
Thankyou Jorn for giving the people of australia such a magnificient building to welcome overseas visitors...
wonderful man and his gift to the people of Australia and the rest of the world!"

community of people of the world

a cultural icon for the Australian people and significantly as a modern expression of hope + creativity
singer and hero entertaining people who were constructing something so beautiful for the people of Sydney
Opera House, a treasure of the people and sublime legacy of its creative visionary.
architecture you have build for the people of Australia.

gift for the people of Australia and the World.

People flock to see it and to be part of it.
It is a very special place and it lets people enjoy it.
memories Opera House brings to the people....to the world!
joy, pride and wonderment to people who experienced his architecture.
a long way for most people, but well worth the effort when we get the chance to stare

people come to see it

Thank you, Mr Utzon, for giving people like me, such a beautiful and inspiring sight, as the Sydney Opera House.
I sit next to people who have come from all over the world and, as we rehearse
Your iconic gift has enabled the people of australia to lift their standards both in performance and ...

for people it represents the value of art

Few people ever achieve this level of greatness."
observing the expressions of people seeing it for the first time, remembering my first time.
an icon for the people of Sydney and the world. His memory will live on in the Opera House."
the Opera House synonomous in people's minds with Sydney - a far cry from the previous image of kangaroos
You dared to dream for the people of this far flung city.

dared to dream

a great building, the material, the people, the tormented processes, the disappointments...
in his lifetime there were people who affected a reconciliation and ensured that the future
Jorn Utzon is one of the key people who helped formed the direction of my life and career.

a community who realised the work

You gave us a symphony in architecture. You inspired the imagination of the world, and you gave every Sydneysider a masterpiece that will live in our hearts forever. With this unique and spectacular building you have achieved immortality - for yourself and for the city of Sydney - and we will hold you close to our hearts forevermore, and be proud and vociferous in acclaiming you an honorary Australian.
Saying thank you just doesn't seem enough, and so we unashamedly say that we love you, for bestowing upon us the greatest gift that Australia has ever been given. Quite simply, there is no other building anywhere in the world that comes close to matching its unequivocal beauty and conceptual symbolism.
Like all great artists, your brilliance will shine brighter with the passing of time, and your creation will be a tribute to your genius so long as humans live.
The people of Sydney, and the people all over the world who are visionaries and pursuers of the impossible, will never forget you."
Barry John McGrath.

Figure 7.9 Typographic map: people.

as well as the building's significance as a representation of the efforts of those who worked to realise the project more than 50 years ago.

The Sydney Opera House serves to inspire people in interesting ways; to be a better person, to be creative as an artist, designer or architect, or more collectively as inspiration for the world as a community. The temporal axis was explored through the terms 'inspire' and 'remember' (Figures 7.10 and 7.11). Inspiration is a projective sentiment; it is about what could be, what is potential and as-yet-unrealised. In this sense the term

creative Antipodean souls inspired to wonder at such nobility of purpose.
makeup artist and continue to be inspired by the Opera House as well as the incrdible works of Lin Utzon
That one man can inspire so much in an individual, [and no doubt in thousands of individuals]
I am inspired by his creative vision and integrity ."
Jorn Utzon you inspired me as a child.
it's beauty awes and inspires me still.
architect, 73 years old and still inspired by Utzon's work
Your wonderful building inspires us and all who view it.
vision in creating a building that inspires everyone that sees it and works in it.
full sails of the Opera House I feel inspired to give more of myself to my fellow travellers in this world.
this incredible piece of art, it inspires and tell me that this opera house and Sydney Harbour
and uniqueness never fails to inspire me.
I always feel revived and inspired by sharing the experience in such a wonderful building.
It lifts my spirits and inspires me every single time.
that invariably lifts the spirit and inspires wonder.
The power to move, change and inspire.

inspiration to be a better person

masterpiece will continue to inspire great artists, visitors, employees and residents
Opera House is a structure that inspires the arts world, a city and a nation.
we have been greatly inspired by the passion, foresight and ingenuity that you
Your Opera House inspired me to follow the path of architecture. Your magnificent design inspires
This great man's vision inspired countless generations of young architects, from far and abroad
His spirit also inspire many Chinese architects.
Utzon inspired me to be a better designer

inspiration to be an artist, architect, designer, creative

changed so many lives, inspired so many individuals and brought joy and happiness
since it opened and continue to be inspired by the creative ideas of Jorn Utzon in this wonderful performance space.
You inspired the imagination of the world
Sydney is enriched and inspired each day by this tangible proof of the genius of the man who conceived it
An inspired idea from an inspired man, and Sydney Harbour will never the same without it.
This is really a tribute to a gentle, inspired man,whose contribution to our cultural life in Sydney has been unique,
your absolute best, these are all inspired by this this singularly unmatchable gift to a nation
- thank you, Master for your inspired gift to Australia and the World, for generations to awe and enjoy!

inspiration for the world

Jorn Utzon you inspired me as a child. I remember with great affection, the buiding of the Sydney Opera House. As an adult it has become a symbol of Australia. Your Sydney Opera House is an inspiration to me, my children and grandchildren - it symbolises Australia and its independence, its beauty, its future thinking.
Thank you Jorn - you will always be remembered"
Carole Mules.

Figure 7.10 Typographic map: inspire.

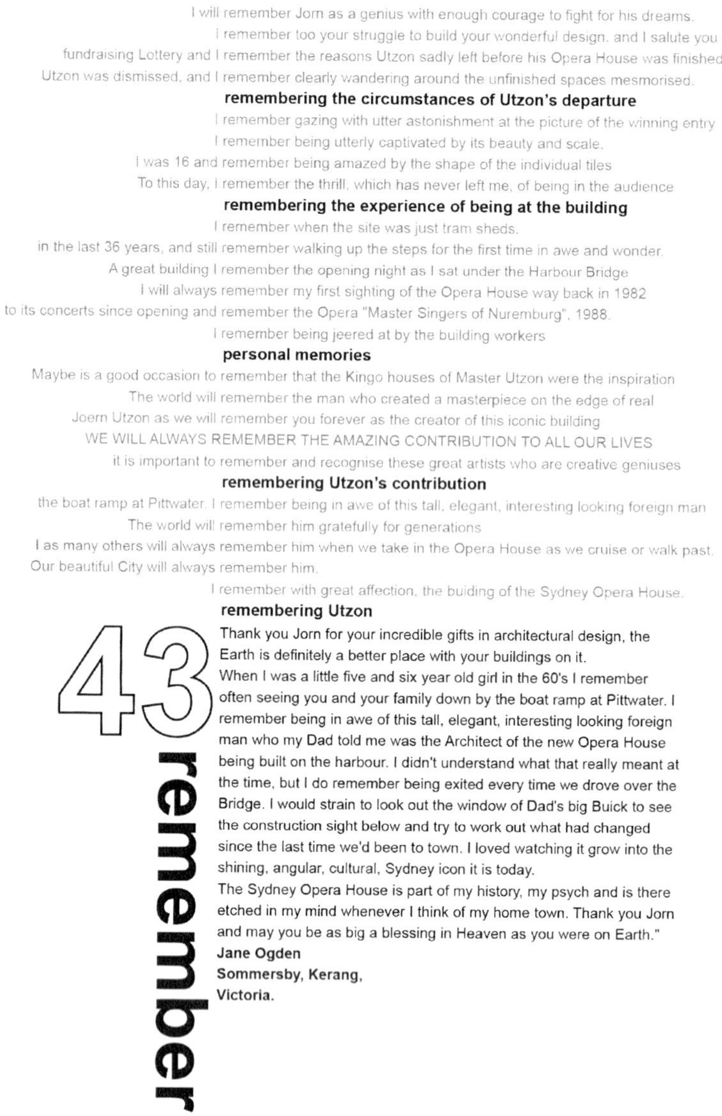

I will remember Jorn as a genius with enough courage to fight for his dreams.
I remember too your struggle to build your wonderful design. and I salute you now
fundraising Lottery and I remember the reasons Utzon sadly left before his Opera House was finished
Utzon was dismissed, and I remember clearly wandering around the unfinished spaces mesmorised.
remembering the circumstances of Utzon's departure
I remember gazing with utter astonishment at the picture of the winning entry
I remember being utterly captivated by its beauty and scale.
I was 16 and remember being amazed by the shape of the individual tiles
To this day, I remember the thrill, which has never left me, of being in the audience
remembering the experience of being at the building
I remember when the site was just tram sheds.
in the last 36 years, and still remember walking up the steps for the first time in awe and wonder.
A great building I remember the opening night as I sat under the Harbour Bridge
I will always remember my first sighting of the Opera House way back in 1982
to its concerts since opening and remember the Opera "Master Singers of Nuremburg", 1988.
I remember being jeered at by the building workers
personal memories
Maybe is a good occasion to remember that the Kingo houses of Master Utzon were the inspiration
The world will remember the man who created a masterpiece on the edge of real
Joern Utzon as we will remember you forever as the creator of this iconic building
WE WILL ALWAYS REMEMBER THE AMAZING CONTRIBUTION TO ALL OUR LIVES
it is important to remember and recognise these great artists who are creative geniuses
remembering Utzon's contribution
the boat ramp at Pittwater. I remember being in awe of this tall, elegant, interesting looking foreign man
The world will remember him gratefully for generations
I as many others will always remember him when we take in the Opera House as we cruise or walk past.
Our beautiful City will always remember him.
I remember with great affection, the buiding of the Sydney Opera House.
remembering Utzon
Thank you Jorn for your incredible gifts in architectural design, the
Earth is definitely a better place with your buildings on it.
When I was a little five and six year old girl in the 60's I remember
often seeing you and your family down by the boat ramp at Pittwater. I
remember being in awe of this tall, elegant, interesting looking foreign
man who my Dad told me was the Architect of the new Opera House
being built on the harbour. I didn't understand what that really meant at
the time, but I do remember being exited every time we drove over the
Bridge. I would strain to look out the window of Dad's big Buick to see
the construction sight below and try to work out what had changed
since the last time we'd been to town. I loved watching it grow into the
shining, angular, cultural, Sydney icon it is today.
The Sydney Opera House is part of my history, my psych and is there
etched in my mind whenever I think of my home town. Thank you Jorn
and may you be as big a blessing in Heaven as you were on Earth."
Jane Ogden
Sommersby, Kerang,
Victoria.

Figure 7.11 Typographic map: remember.

offers a sense of the way the Sydney Opera House as a building and as an object of social value mediates the future. This was observed in what Paul posted: 'Jørn Utzon created a magical building that invariably lifts the spirit and inspires wonder.'[30] The sentiment expressed in the tributes in the statements using the term 'inspire' describe a sense of possibility which connects individuals with a future time when such potentials are realised.

Remembering is more clearly descriptive of the way in which the Sydney Opera House, like the souvenirs, enables people to remember important occasions at a personal and collective level. Margaret Armour posted: 'A great building I remember the opening night as I sat under the Harbour Bridge and enjoyed the Esky of food and the spectacle.'[31] People anchor personal memories in this place; they remember their experiences here. The experiences described are both everyday moments that become heightened memories. The opening night is a collective moment experienced at a personal level. Similarly, people recalled their first visit or a particular concert that was significant. They also remember Utzon, his contribution to the building and departure from the project in 1966. Ann Lomas posted 'we remember your pain and your passion, your genius and your gift to us of our Sydney Opera House!'[32] Remembering, like inspiration, operates in both personal and collective ways.

The axis of embodiment was explored through the terms 'feel' and 'visit' (Figures 7.12 and 7.13). Posting a tribute is both a personal experience, an opportunity to express connections alongside emotions of grief and loss. But it is simultaneously a culturally embedded practice; to not offer a tribute is to ignore the achievements the positives the person has offered during their life. The notion that a building can engender feelings is central to assessing social value. This is exemplified in Nick Bradt's post where he stated that 'the opera house is a very special building, much more than bricks and concrete – you can feel it when youre [*sic*] there!'[33] People feel uplifted by the Sydney Opera House, and share these feelings in order to be part of a community. At the same time, empathy was felt for Utzon, particularly in relation to the difficulties he faced during the building's construction. Sue Patchett stated: 'we all feel a sense of guilt, shame or anger that Jorn Utzon did not finish his masterpiece but we will never forget him and he will always be part of Australian history for time immemorial'.[34] People embody experiences and value and feel their effects at an individual level.

Another embedded practice is a visit to the Sydney Opera House. This was also recognised as an occasion that created connections, not just with other fellow visitors or the broader community of the Sydney Opera House, but with Denmark and more broadly the 'world'. The experience of visiting was described by Jennifer Callaghan and John Piccles as both sublime and prosaic:

> it never ceases to impress with its beauty and majesty no matter how often you visit it ... ever since I've first visit it, every week I cant stop sketching it, as it moves with the sun and the water and is never the same experience for me.[35]
>
> I visit every theatre and hall regularly as part of my cultural life and I share it with every visitor ... as a Sydney-sider I never fail to get a thrill each time I see or visit the Opera House.[36]

Individuals described the experience of visiting as an occasion to be remembered as well as part of their everyday lives. The Sydney Opera House is framed as spectacular in both circumstances, where details in the way the light falls on the forms continues to be noticed; as if the building is never a background, but always an object to be experienced.

Exploring the tributes using van Dijck's concept of mediated memories revealed shared themes across the analytical categories, some of which were not discovered in the initial analysis of sentiment using the terms 'love' and 'sad'. The findings from the second stage of analysis through mediated memories were cross-referenced to the findings from the initial analysis of sentiment. Whilst negative sentiments around Utzon's

I feel love for the man who imagined it and made it real for us all.
I amost feel that Jorn Utzon was born marked for the task that spoiled him for any other.
We all feel a sense of guilt, shame or anger that Jorn Utzon did not finish his masterpiece
A joy that I can still feel in seeing the finished work.
New South Welchman, I still feel ashamed of the way we treated him.
visionaries should feel proud.
which made us feel closer to this remarkable man
(Utzon's birthplace), I feel priviledged to be one of very few to have had Jørn Utzon as a central influence
May his critics feel justifiably guilty, whilst embracing the sight and sounds of the Opera House!!!

feel empathy for Utzon

I appreciate its beauty and feel joy, as I do when I see a perfectly constructed spider-web
, Sydneysiders can't help but feel better when they glimpse the sails – from any angle.
Sydney Explorers, and I feel privileged to see the Opera House from the four corners every day
Sydney Opera House I feel special just like this building is.
bricks and concrete - you can feel it when youre there!
Because of our shared Birthday, I feel a special affinity for the Opera House, and Utzon will forever be special
all of my life and still feel a tingling thrill whenever I see that most magical and majestic of sculptures.
Twenty years later, I still feel the same each and every time I visit this magnificent masterpiece
I still feel uplifted whenever I go there. Thank you, Jørn Utzon.
It makes me feel special because it is SO special.
I always feel revived and inspired by sharing the experience in such a wonderful building.

feel uplifted by the building

"I feel a deep personal loss, even though I have never met Mr. Utzon.
I feel sad today on hearing of the death of Jorn Utzon
We all feel immensely sad at the loss, yet proud that we have played a small role
hardly express the sorrow I feel for his passing away.
always makes me feel I've come home."

feel loss at Utzon's passing

I feel priveleged to be an Australian to have this magnificent building grace our country.
I feel an amazing bond with the development of this building
We feel so privileged in our lifetime to have seen the transformation of the Bennelong Point
Now a Sydney-sider myself, I feel a great gratitude to Jørn Utzon for a true architectural wonder in our city.
all 'Sydneysiders' feel today on hear of Jorn Utzon's passing.
Aussies we feel we really own it, it is part of us."
building in the world to which I feel more attracted
full sails of the Opera House I feel inspired to give more of myself to my fellow travellers in this world.
at the end of the 1960s, I feel my life in Sydney has developed alongside the Opera House.
allows Sydney residents to feel proud of this cultural venue.
some of us wearen't Aussies feel like your tribute is a world legacy.

feeling of community

Thank you Mr Utzon. I have visited the Sydney Opera House many times since my first Christmas concert and each time I feel very special. It makes me feel special because it is SO special. Your design is so beautiful and fresh.It really suits the Harbour. Each day I walk on the Harbour Bridge I admire the Opera House and I love to watch her sails glow in the twilight.You have designed something that people from all over the world travel to see. That is very special.Thanks again for giving me something SO special.
Katie Haywood.
Australia

Figure 7.12 Typographic map: feel.

death were evident in individual statements of a personal nature as well as memories that recalled the historical events of the building's realisation, positive sentiments were frequently reframed in terms of experience and the building's role as a representation of Utzon's love for Australia and for architecture. Contributions that recognised the building's symbolic value expressed this in terms of its role as a gift to an international community of people. The value of the Sydney Opera House was understood

I will visit Denmark in 2010 and will pay my repects to him there.

creative minds continue to visit the Utzon centre to celebrate and learn about the important mark

he was not persuaded to visit the finished edifice which is his and our legacy.

its people and those that visit our city.

revered by those who live and visit Sydney.

national connections through Utzon

Many of us are dreaming to visit the Sydney Opera House.

Opera and Concert Halls and every visit is thrilling for me.

I gasp at its beauty and every visit for a performance is joyful and uplifting.

majesty no matter how often you visit it.

feel the same each and every time I visit this magnificent masterpiece.

ideas for the pageant I would often visit the Opera House, touch it and look at it from various angles.

enriched by all who perform and visit.

Ever since I've first visit it, every week I cant stop sketching it, as it moves with the sun

No matter how many times I visit the Opera House, it never fails both to humble me by its grandeur

Every occasion we visit be it theatre, concert, children's activity or merely to enjoy the view

A visit to the Opera House or simply a glimpse of its beauty

I would visit your building when I was unemployed and feeling down in Sydney.

sublime visitng

After my very first visit I was captivated , my soul sated and eager to return

I'm still so looking forward to my visit to Opera House every time.

I visit every theatre and hall regularly as part of my cultural life

I could visit it every day if I wanted to...thousands of others pay huge sums

I visit it at least once a fortnight and everytime I do I think how blessed I am

Every time I visit Sydney, I am drawn to the magnificent Opera House.

The Opera House is a place we can visit over our lifetimes, a place that effects us in a different way each time.

to get a thrill each time I see or visit the Opera House.

hardship does not allow me to visit and see much of what on show in the Opera House

such a pleasure every time I visit Circular Quay.

I remember him when ever I visit it.

millions of other people who visit take it into their hearts too.

with the massed choir and visit it often for cultural nourishment.

I have been to Sydney 16 times, no visit is complete without travelling downtown and seeing Utzon's inspirational

the Sydney Opera House is a MUST visit.

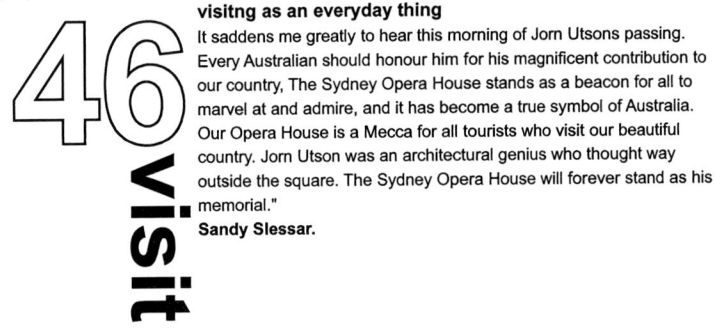

visitng as an everyday thing

It saddens me greatly to hear this morning of Jorn Utsons passing. Every Australian should honour him for his magnificent contribution to our country, The Sydney Opera House stands as a beacon for all to marvel at and admire, and it has become a true symbol of Australia. Our Opera House is a Mecca for all tourists who visit our beautiful country. Jorn Utson was an architectural genius who thought way outside the square. The Sydney Opera House will forever stand as his memorial."
Sandy Slessar.

Figure 7.13 Typographic map: visit.

as generative; an inspiration for other creative endeavours that require individuals to 'dream'. At the same time the place was a significant anchor for personal memories both of experiences and autobiographical events in people's lives.

Posting a tribute is a complex practice as it requires individuals to reflect and then articulate the reasons why a person, and in this case a building, is significant to them (Figure 7.14). This involves remembering times at this place and projecting forward to imagine how it will be a significant place in the future. Such reflective

Figure 7.14 Writing a tribute: a reflective practice.

acts are described in terms of personal and collective significance demonstrating how these are not separate but co-constituted. Embedded practices, such as writing and offering a tribute, or indeed taking photographs and sharing them, are ways of embodying the significance of places. This instance of participatory culture reveals the socio-visual value of the Sydney Opera House as a place for aesthetic experience, an inspirational symbol for creative endeavours and a site through which to embed autobiographical memories. Whilst Utzon is remembered in terms of the difficulties of the realisation of the Sydney Opera House and the sense of loss felt at his incomplete vision, the building itself is described in terms of its possibilities as a locus for community, for experiences and for artistic creation. The tributes are significant because they emerge in response to the sense of loss felt in relation to Utzon's death. The tributes seek to articulate individuals' moments of significance that are associated around the building. They demonstrate the way in which the audience of the Sydney Opera House draws the building into their everyday lives and uses it as a locus or touchstone around which memories, projections and events can be measured. This example of participatory culture as embraced by the institution of the Sydney Opera House evidences the strong sense of attachment felt with the place.

Conclusion

Participatory culture underpins much of the new online media environs and the way these technologies enable groups and individuals to come together online. It also reveals how the new media landscape is creating a convergence between individual contributions, such as those representations analysed in Chapters 4, 5 and 6, and those prompted by commercial organisations and institutions, such as those analysed here. Understood through these practices, the community of the Sydney Opera House is not a clearly bound group of people, but instead is revealed as broad and contingent, connected in both direct and indirect ways and maintained through practices that are both material, embodied and ephemeral.

Notes

1 Paola Totaro (2008) 'Joern Utzon Dead'. *Sydney Morning Herald*, 30 November. Retrieved: 29/11/2012, from: www.smh.com.au/articles/2008/11/30/1227979814647.html.

2 'Opera House Architect Dies at 90' (2008) *ABC News*, 30 November. Retrieved: 29/03/2013, from: www.abc.net.au/news/stories/2008/11/30/2433437.htm.

3 Several theories explore value in relation to ownership and loss in the field of psychology, including the Endowment Effect and the Familiarity Effect and association through Classical Conditioning. These are efforts to theorise the phenomenon whereby the value and sense of loss is heightened when a valued object or person is under threat, or lost, beyond what might have been perceived at a different time.

4 'Opera House Lights to Be Dimmed in Utzon Tribute' (2008) *Sydney Morning Herald*, 30 November. Retrieved: 28/11/2011, from: www.smh.com.au/news/world/opera-house-lights-to-be-dimmed/2008/11/30/1227979817473.html.

5 Public tributes from the following people were published on the Utzon Memorial Website: The Hon. Nathan Rees, MP Premier NSW, the Hon. Kevin Rudd, MP Prime Minister, Kim Williams, AM Chairman of Sydney Opera House Trust, Libby Christie, Managing Director, Sydney Symphony, David McAllister, Artistic Director, The Australian Ballet, Rob Brookman, General Manager, Sydney Theatre Company, Trevor Green, Managing Director, Melbourne Symphony Orchestra, Paul Brandling, Vice President and Managing Director, Hewlett-Packard. 'Jørn Utzon Tributes (Official)'. *Sydney Opera House: Jorn Utzon*. Retrieved: 27/04/2013, from: http://jornutzon.sydneyoperahouse.com/Tributes.aspx?m=official.

 Notable architectural and design authorities offered tributes to Utzon worldwide. Architectural critic and director of the Design Museum London, Deyan Sudjic, also made a public tribute in the UK newspaper the *Guardian*. Deyan Sudjic (2008) 'Obituary Jørn Utzon'. *Guardian*, 1 December. Retrieved: 29/11/2012, from: www.guardian.co.uk/artanddesign/2008/dec/01/architecture-denmark-j-oslash-rn-utzon., as did architectural historian Denis Sharp, in the *Independent*. Denis Sharp (2008) 'Jorn Utzon: Award-Winning Architect Who Designed the Sydney Opera House'. *Independent*, 3 December. Retrieved: 27/04/2013, from: www.independent.co.uk/news/obituaries/jorn-utzon-awardwinning-architect-who-designed-the-sydney-opera-house-1048763.html. In the United States, architectural critic Fred A. Bernstein wrote an obituary in the *New York Times*. Fred A. Bernstein (2008) 'Jorn Utzon, 90, Dies; Created Sydney Opera House'. *New York Times*, 30 November. Retrieved: 27/02/2014, from: www.nytimes.com/2008/11/30/arts/design/30utzon.htm?pagewanted=print. In Australia, architectural historian Philip Drew, author of several books and journal articles on the Sydney Opera House and architectural writer, Davina Jackson, published tributes. Philip Drew (2008) 'Opera House Is Utzon's Legacy'. *The Australian*, 1 December. Retrieved: 27/02/2014, from: www.theaustralian.com.au/arts/opera-house-is-utzons-legacy/story-e6frg8n6-1111118184942; Davina Jackson (2008) 'Joern Oberg Utzon Dies Aged 90'. *The Australian*, 1 December. Retrieved: 27/02/2014, from: www.theaustralian.com.au/arts/naive-perfectionist/story-e6frg8n6-1111118183743. Australian writer David Malouf and architecture critic Elizabeth Farrelly also published tributes. David Malouf (2009) 'How an Angel at Bennelong Point Gave Sydney Its Spirit'. *Sydney Morning Herald*, 25 March. Retrieved: 29/11/2012, from: www.smh.com.au/opinion/how-an-angel-at-bennelong-point-gave-sydney-its-spirit-20090324-98sa.html; Elizabeth Farrelly (2008) 'Obituary: High Noon at Bennelong Point'. *Sydney Morning Herald*, 1 December. Retrieved: 29/11/2012, from: www.smh.com.au/news/national/high-noon-at-bennelong-point/2008/11/30/1227979845045.html?page=fullpage.

6 Ashleigh Wilson (2008) 'Sydney Opera House Architect Joern Utzon Dies'. *The Australian*, 30 November. Retrieved: 29/03/2013, from: www.theaustralian.com.au/news/sydney-opera-house-architect-dies/story-e6frg6to-1111118181028.

7 Wilson, 'Sydney Opera House Architect Joern Utzon Dies'.

8 'Utzon Tributes Flood Opera House Website' (2008) *ABC News*, 1 December. Retrieved: 27/04/2013, from: www.abc.net.au/news/stories/2008/12/01/2434041.htm?section=australia.

9 Richard Evans was the Chief Executive Officer at the time. In 2012 Louise Herron took over this position.

10 Naomi Stead and Antony Moulis (2010) 'Sydney's Prometheus: Myth, Shame and Remediation at Joern Utzon's Sydney Opera House'. Presented at the *Imagining: Proceedings*

of the 27th Annual Conference of the Society of Architectural Historians, Australia and New Zealand (SAHANZ), University of Newcastle, Newcastle, New South Wales, Australia, 30 June–2 July, pp. 403–404.

11 Stead and Moulis, 'Sydney's Prometheus', p. 404.

12 'Jørn Utzon Tributes (Official)'. *Sydney Opera House: Jorn Utzon.*

13 'Tribute to Joern Utzon'. *Utzon Centre.* Retrieved: 29/11/2012, from: www.utzoncenter.dk/en/joern_utzon/tribute_02/tribute.htm.

14 Howard Rheingold (2008) 'Using Participatory Media and Public Voice to Encourage Civic Engagement'. In *Civic Life Online: Learning How Digital Media Can Engage Youth*, edited by W. Lance Bennett. Cambridge, MA: The MIT Press.

15 Henry Jenkins (2006) *Convergence Culture: Where Old and New Media Collide.* New York: New York University Press.

16 The State Memorial was held on 25 March 2009. 'Sydney Opera House: Jørn Utzon'. Retrieved: 11/09/2012, from: http://jornutzon.sydneyoperahouse.com/home.htm.

17 Companies who participated were: Sydney Symphony, Opera Australia, the Australian Ballet, Sydney Theatre Company, Bell Shakespeare Company, Bangarra Dance Theatre, and Neil Finn of the band Crowded House. People who spoke were: Sydney Opera House Trust Chairman, Kim Williams, Chief Executive Officer Richard Evans and Minister for the Environment, Heritage and the Arts Peter Garret, Artistic Director of the Australian Ballet David McAllister, John Bell of the Bell Shakespeare Company, Co-artistic Director of the Sydney Theatre Company Cate Blanchett, the Utzon Family and Lorna Morrison on behalf of the people. 'Memorial Program'. *Sydney Opera House: Jørn Utzon.* Retrieved: 11/09/2012, from: http://jornutzon.sydneyoperahouse.com/memorial.htm.

18 'Tribute, N.'. In *The New Shorter Oxford English Dictionary*, edited by Leslie Brown. Vol. 2. Oxford: Clarendon Press, p. 1b; 'Obituary, N. And Adj.'. In *The New Shorter Oxford English Dictionary*, edited by Leslie Brown. Vol. 2. Oxford: Clarendon Press, p. 2.

19 Tim Hutchings cites *The World Wide Cemetery* in Canada and *Web Healing* in the United States as examples that existed in 1995. Pamela Roberts notes the *Virtual Memorial Garden* existed as early as 1999. The World Wide Cemetery (www.cemetery.org), Web Healing (www.webhealing.org), Virtual Memorial Garden (www.virtualmemorialgarden.net). Tim Hutchings (2012) 'Wiring Death: Dying Grieving and Remembering on the Internet'. In *Emotion, Identity and Death: Mortality across the Disciplines*, edited by Douglas J. Davies and Chang-Wok Park. Surrey: Ashgate, p. 48; Brian de Vries and Pamela Roberts (2004) 'Introduction'. *Omega: Journal of Death and Dying*, 49 (1), pp. 1–3.

20 The Sydney Opera House provided a physical book for members of the public who wished to pay tribute to Jørn Utzon at the Sydney Opera House from Monday 1 December to Sunday 7 December between 10 a.m. and 7 p.m., which was then sent to the Utzon family. This was as well as the online space for public tributes hosted on the Sydney Opera House website (2008) '2008 Corporate Media Release – Sydney Opera House Pays Tribute to Jørn Utzon'. Retrieved: 01/08/2012, from: www.sydneyoperahouse.com/08CorporateMediaRelease_JornUtzon.aspx.

21 Brian de Vries and Pamela Roberts (2004) 'The Living and the Dead: Community in the Virtual Cemetery'. *Omega: Journal of Death and Dying*, 49 (1), pp. 57–76.

22 Joyce Walker (2007) 'Narratives in the Database: Memorializing September 11th Online'. *Computers and Composition*, 24 (2), pp. 121–153.

23 For example, the software used to organise the tributes, *Wordle*, is a free publicly available service that performs simple word based content analysis. Word Clouds are a quick visual way of comprehending a long body of text, such as the tributes on the *Utzon Memorial*. Wordle offers several controls, such as removing high frequency words (such as 'the' and 'and'), layout parameters, or font selection or colour scheme. The word counts generated by Wordle are also available to users. 'Word Clouds' are popular online tools that create visual representations, where word frequency is translated into visual prominence through size, colour or font. These representations can be formatted using different orientations, colour or typographic schemes. To perform this content analysis textual copies were made of all the tributes and these were processed through the website *Wordle.net*. Developed by Jonathan Feinberg, Wordle is not the only word cloud service available online, others include TagCrowd, Tagxedo, Worditout, ToCloud. Each service uses their own analytical

algorithm for calculating frequency, but generally the patterns remain similar. Although it might appear that these websites are inaccurate or unreliable, Carmel McNaught and Paul Lam demonstrates that Wordle and other Word Cloud sites broadly correlate with more accurate methods However, McNaught and Lam caution against a simplistic reading of Wordle diagrams as it decontextualises terms, and neglects the semantics of phrases and clauses. For example, 'not convenient' will contribute to the frequency of convenient. For this reason, Wordle was used as a means for organisation of the content, rather than as a tool for analysis. 'Wordle'. Retrieved from: www.wordle.net/; Carmel McNaught and Paul Lam (2010) 'Using Wordle as a Supplementary Research Tool'. *The Qualitative Report*, 15 (3), pp. 630–643.

24 Walker, 'Narratives in the Database'.
25 Georges Teitler (2009) *Utzon Memorial Website* [Tribute to Jørn Utzon]. Sydney Opera House. Retrieved: 12/03/2013, from: http://jornutzon.sydneyoperahouse.com/Tributes.aspx.
26 Gillian Rose (2007) *Visual Methodologies: An Introduction to the Interpretation of Visual Materials*. 2nd edn. London: Sage.
27 It is possible to consider this form of content analysis aligned with approaches in research on sentiment analysis.
28 Steve McCarthy (2009) *Utzon Memorial Website* [Tribute to Jørn Utzon]. Sydney Opera House. Retrieved: 12/03/2013, from: http://jornutzon.sydneyoperahouse.com/Tributes.aspx; Diane McQueen (2009) *Utzon Memorial Website* [Tribute to Jørn Utzon]. Sydney Opera House. Retrieved: 12/03/2013, from: http://jornutzon.sydneyoperahouse.com/Tributes. aspx; Linda Briggs (2009) *Utzon Memorial Website* [Tribute to Jørn Utzon]. Sydney Opera House. Retrieved: 12/03/2013, from: http://jornutzon.sydneyoperahouse.com/Tributes.aspx.
29 Annika Edsberg (2009) *Utzon Memorial Website* [Tribute to Jørn Utzon]. Sydney Opera House. Retrieved: 12/03/2013, from: http://jornutzon.sydneyoperahouse.com/Tributes.aspx.
30 Paul (2009) *Utzon Memorial Website* [Tribute to Jørn Utzon]. Sydney Opera House. Retrieved: 12/03/2013, from: http://jornutzon.sydneyoperahouse.com/Tributes.aspx.
31 Margaret Armour (2009) *Utzon Memorial Website* [Tribute to Jørn Utzon]. Sydney Opera House. Retrieved: 12/03/2013, from: http://jornutzon.sydneyoperahouse.com/Tributes.aspx.
32 Ann Lomas (2009) *Utzon Memorial Website* [Tribute to Jørn Utzon]. Sydney Opera House. Retrieved: 12/03/2013, from: http://jornutzon.sydneyoperahouse.com/Tributes.aspx.
33 Nick Bradt (2009) *Utzon Memorial Website* [Tribute to Jørn Utzon]. Sydney Opera House. Retrieved: 12/03/2013, from: http://jornutzon.sydneyoperahouse.com/Tributes.aspx.
34 Sue Pattchett (2009) *Utzon Memorial Website* [Tribute to Jørn Utzon]. Sydney Opera House. Retrieved: 12/03/2013, from: http://jornutzon.sydneyoperahouse.com/Tributes.aspx.
35 Jennifer Callaghan (2009) *Utzon Memorial Website* [Tribute to Jørn Utzon]. Sydney Opera House. Retrieved: 12/03/2013, from: http://jornutzon.sydneyoperahouse.com/Tributes.aspx; and Julio Brenes B. (2009) *Utzon Memorial Website* [Tribute to Jørn Utzon]. Sydney Opera House. Retrieved: 12/03/2013, from: http://jornutzon.sydneyoperahouse.com/Tributes.aspx.
36 John Piccles (2009) *Utzon Memorial Website* [Tribute to Jørn Utzon]. Sydney Opera House. Retrieved: 12/03/2013, from: http://jornutzon.sydneyoperahouse.com/Tributes.aspx; and Pervin Young (2009) *Utzon Memorial Website* [Tribute to Jørn Utzon]. Sydney Opera House. Retrieved: 12/03/2013, from: http://jornutzon.sydneyoperahouse.com/Tributes.aspx.

8 Recognising networked significance in heritage

How can socio-visual value, its manifestation in participatory culture and entangled significance be recognised within UNESCO's existing suite of heritage instruments? The first three chapters of the book considered the way the Sydney Opera House had been inscribed for its iconic value and that this was both evidenced in the building's aesthetic value and its social value. A series of representations were collected online and analysed as evidence of participatory culture. Importantly, the way such representations mediate time, embodiment and relationships was proposed through Jose van Dijck's model of mediated memories. In Chapters 4–6, the representations were explored as examples of practices of participatory culture revealing the way van Dijck's three axes offered insights into the value of these ephemeral acts. In Chapter 7, these axes demonstrate the entangled way social significance is embedded across various forms of culture. Here, the discussion returns to existing heritage instruments to consider how current legal instruments might recognise the ways in which the social value of the Sydney Opera House is generated, maintained and shared. Specifically, the discussion investigates Criterion (vi) from the *World Heritage Convention*, the *Digital Heritage Charter* and the *Intangible Heritage Convention* to conclude that heritage frameworks are yet to offer a straightforward means to recognise the social value of World Heritage sites at an international level.

The first part of this chapter explores how the *World Heritage Convention* attempts to account for the value of places in terms of memory and identity. This investigation finds that the use of these values for inscription is highly contested. The second part of the chapter explores how UNESCO's other heritage instruments, namely the *Digital Heritage Charter* and the *Intangible Heritage Convention*, are more able to account for socio-visual value as manifest online in participatory culture. The chapter then explores how representations and participatory culture manifest socio-visual value, but only for the contingent communities that occur in relation to world-famous iconic sites.

Socio-visual value and Criterion (vi)

Chapter 2 analysed the 2007 inscription of the Sydney Opera House as a World Heritage site. The chapter focused specifically on its outstanding universal value as a 'world-famous iconic building' to open up larger questions about the relationship of the building's iconic status and its social value, namely socio-visual value. This value as evidenced through the findings of Chapter 4, 5, 6 and 7 is embodied in the practices that comprise the participatory culture of the Sydney Opera House and is implicated in individuals' and groups' sense of identity and shared memories. Representations are both a means for, and sites at which people engage with the building. How might these findings be recognised within World Heritage?

Social values such as memory and identity are defined as associative values within the World Heritage programme. Therefore, places can only be inscribed for such values through Criterion (vi). The *Operational Guidelines* state that a property is considered to have outstanding universal value under Criterion (vi) if it is:

> directly or tangibly associated with events or living traditions, with ideas, or with beliefs, with artistic and literary works of outstanding universal significance. (The Committee considers that this Criterion should preferably be used in conjunction with other criteria).[1]

The *Operational Guidelines* do not explicitly state what values can be inscribed under each criterion. However, Criterion (vi) is the only one that recognises associative values, that is, values that are not directly evident or embodied by the site itself. As has been demonstrated, socio-visual value, alongside other intangible values like memory and identity, is not evidenced by examining the building fabric of the Sydney Opera House or the grounds on which it is situated. Rather, such values are manifest in people's present-day engagements with the building and with each other. Telling the story of the building or describing its silhouette as analogous to a nun's cornette are ways in which the building is ever-present in popular culture. Creative engagements, such as designing an opera-house costume, or at a national level, representing the building on a postage stamp, both describe and contribute to the building's iconic status. At an experiential level, visiting the building in person and recording such visits through personal photographs that depict the building both as a sublime sculpture and foreshortened as a hat are ways in which the building is significant, both socially and aesthetically. Can these practices, as manifestations of memory and identity, be recognised through Criterion (vi)? Would this be a means for including these practices as part of the World Heritage inscription of the Sydney Opera House?

While Criterion (vi) facilitates the inscription of sites to the World Heritage List whose values are evident through their connection to other significant forms or aspects of culture, its use for the inscription of sites as World Heritage has been problematic. Take, for example, a place listed because, as a site of war atrocities, it has become part of a culture's collective memory, or alternatively a landscape that is significant because it has been the subject of outstanding works of art. The degree of separation between the site to be inscribed and the form of culture which makes it significant (i.e. the atrocities or the work of art) means that the value of a site can change even if the fabric of the place is being conserved. For World Heritage status to be maintained, a site's outstanding universal value must too be preserved. If the reason for inscription is because of a site's association with atrocities or with the value of an artwork, maintaining the site through conservation plans will not necessarily maintain these values. The debate around the interpretation and application of Criterion (vi) highlights the difficulties in using socially defined evidence for inscription,[2] because it is often enlisted as a means for recognising subjective and mutable values. The *Operational Guidelines* around the autonomous use of Criterion (vi) for inscription has been modified many times over the 40-year life of the World Heritage programme.[3] Presently, the World Heritage Committee recommends this criterion be used in conjunction with other criteria.

Socio-visual value is not directly evidenced in the architectural fabric of the Sydney Opera House, rather it is manifest in the participatory culture that is associated with the building. Unlike its value as a work of architecture and engineering that is attributed to the building by academic experts, socio-visual value develops in association with communities and audiences. Criterion (vi) states that events or living traditions, ideas and beliefs and artistic and literary works must be of 'outstanding universal significance' and that the site must be integral to the association for this criterion to be employed.[4] Yet the activities that people engage in and around the Sydney Opera House, and additionally, the representations that are integral to these activities, are not themselves of outstanding universal value. On the contrary, the many representations of the Sydney Opera House collected and categorised are amateur, often kitsch, popular representations, that are distinct from professional examples, such as the seminal black-and-white photography of the Sydney Opera House by Australian photographer Max Dupain or the obituary by acclaimed Australian writer, David Malouf. Whilst these later examples were included in the collection as implicated in the widespread and frequent representation of the Sydney Opera House in visual culture, individually these works are not of outstanding universal value either. Implicit in the condition of Criterion (vi) is an assumption that only places recognised by *outstanding artists* are 'worthy of World Heritage status' but 'not if they inspire thousands of non "consecrated" amateurs to paint [or represent] the same scene'.[5] The definition of socio-visual value, as the attachment that communities and audiences have around the aesthetic value of the Sydney Opera House, means that this value does not meet the condition of 'outstanding artists' required in the use of Criterion (vi). Further, socio-visual value as evidenced in participatory culture emerges out of the practices and traditions that are part of present-day culture. For socio-visual value to be maintained, as is required by the World Heritage listing, the participatory culture in which socio-visual value is embodied would also need to be maintained. Olwen Beazley, whose focus is the use and application of Criterion (vi), describes how the separation between the site and its reason for inscription through association with another example of culture is problematic in the context of World Heritage. Beazley contends that there is an inherent contradiction in attempting to maintain forms of culture that have subjective and mutable values through the *World Heritage Convention*, because they are difficult to document, maintain and evidence.

Beazley demonstrates how the values inscribed under Criterion (vi) are often slippery in her analysis of Auschwitz-Birkenau and the Hiroshima Peace Memorial, two sites inscribed through autonomous use of this criterion. She argues that this is problematic because World Heritage endorses and fixes a singular account of such places, where their meanings and values are often highly contested.[6] Beazley argues that such a strategy is founded on the idea of 'locational authenticity' as characteristic of 'modern societies' compulsion to locate memory in place'.[7] There is an assumption that subjective values, such as memory and identity and by extension socio-visual value, can be maintained through physical places. The idea that memory is locational is affirmed by Pierre Nora's assertion, cited by Beazley, that 'memory relies entirely on the materiality of the trace'.[8] While materiality and place are associated with memory, Nora's assertion does not acknowledge that memory is also co-constituted by *practices*.

José van Dijck's exploration of memory in relation to digital manifestations argues that personal memory items, such as diaries and photographs, structure these activities as much as they are means to capture memories. Memory slips between place and practice and the technologies by which these are made physically tangible. So, while memory can be located in place, it is also embedded in practices and representations.

In the case of the Sydney Opera House and its socio-visual value, the stories, memories and associations that people have with this place are ways in which the building is significant. As argued in Chapter 2, the building's socio-visual value is critical to its recognition as a world-famous iconic building. Whether such a subjective value can be preserved, is perhaps secondary to the more important question of whether this value can be recognised at an international level. Although inscription is a means to ensure the conservation of places by their State Parties, World Heritage is also a political structure that defines what forms of culture constitute heritage, and further which values should be recognised. The recognition of socio-visual value is worthy because it elevates the social value of the Sydney Opera House to the same level of importance as its architectural and engineering value. This is in keeping with the broader movement in heritage to acknowledge the significance of places, not only in expert terms, but also at a community level, and the desire evidenced in the nomination dossier for the 2007 inscription to acknowledge the popular value of the building. Criterion (vi) cannot recognise non-expert values such as socio-visual value. It is also unable to account for subjective values, such as memory and identity. Because of the *World Heritage Convention*'s reliance on stable values, it is also unable to recognise the embodiment of socio-visual value, participatory culture, as this is a living form of culture, which cannot be directly maintained through conservation of the built fabric of the Sydney Opera House.

If socio-visual value and participatory culture cannot be straightforwardly inscribed through the World Heritage programme, how else might this be recognised as heritage? Perhaps these cultural manifestations are better recognised as digital or intangible forms of heritage? The next part of the chapter explores how the *Digital Heritage Charter* and the *Intangible Heritage Convention* are alternative vehicles for recognising this part of the iconic value of the Sydney Opera House.

Why UNESCO's *Digital Heritage Charter* is obsolete

Much of the early discussion on digital technologies and heritage emerged from research around museums and cultural heritage institutions, before the advent of participatory media, social media or Web 2.0.[9] In this early research, digital technologies were characterised as virtual versions of tangible artefacts that could extend the remit of the museum. Heritage institutions became concerned that the rapid development and uptake of digital technologies would render these digital artefacts obsolete and inaccessible in the future, unless active measures were taken to ensure their preservation.[10]

In response to this situation UNESCO adopted the 2003 *Charter on the Preservation of Digital Heritage* (*Digital Heritage Charter*). The charter, unlike the *World Heritage Convention*, is not a legal instrument, but is better described as soft policy, essentially a 'best practice guide' produced by UNESCO as a way of providing a moral imperative to its members to put these aims into practice. The charter recognises that digital heritage has distinctly different characteristics to physical objects and places, and acknowledges digital heritage as a form of culture in its own right, equal, rather than inferior to, their material (and in some cases original) counterparts. Fiona Cameron takes up the issue of the digital artefact as a copy in a chapter titled 'Beyond the Cult of the Replicant: Museums and Historical Digital Objects – Traditional Concerns, New Discourses'.[11] Here, Cameron notes that authorities such as Walter Benjamin and more recently Jean Baudrillard argue that the copy, replica or simulacrum subverts and threatens the distinct meaning of the original and the 'real' copy (Benjamin) and the simulacrum (Baudrillard). Rather than defining digital artefacts as unimportant copies of original heritage artefacts, the *Digital Heritage Charter* defines digital forms of culture as significant on their own terms. The charter is evidence of the move to broaden the definition of heritage from those forms of culture, such as buildings and material artefacts that have been traditionally recognised as heritage, to include immaterial forms of culture. Although the charter marks this willingness, its lack of legal status and its articulation of digital artefacts as 'things' or 'entities' to be managed, preserved, collected and archived, makes it obsolete in an online environment that is characterised by media platforms founded on social communication and participatory culture. The charter does not recognise the activities and engagements that are associated and enabled by digital artefacts such as social media platforms.

Article 1 of the *Digital Heritage Charter* states:

> The digital heritage consists of unique resources of human knowledge and expression. It embraces cultural, educational, scientific and administrative resources, as well as technical, legal, medical and other kinds of information created digitally, or converted into digital form from existing analogue resources. Where resources are 'born digital', there is no other format but the digital object.
>
> Digital materials include texts, databases, still and moving images, audio, graphics, software and web pages, among a wide and growing range of formats. They are frequently ephemeral, and require purposeful production, maintenance and management to be retained.[12]

Cameron argues that the *Digital Heritage Charter* evidences the way in which 'digital cultural materials have been inducted uncritically into the wider accelerated global process of heritagization'.[13] Cameron argues that the uses and practices of the digital object must be 'understood as part of the broader heritage complex' that is political, social and cultural.[14] In other words digital artefacts are not simply virtual versions of the tangible; they must be considered forms of culture in their own right, and understood as artefacts and cultural processes implicated in wider culture, not just in the online realm. Situated more broadly, they have the potential to reveal continuities and transformations afforded by the technological shifts enabled by new media technologies and new perspectives on heritage as a cultural process.

Yola de Lusenet suggests that the limitations of the *Digital Heritage Charter* can be countered by thinking of digital activities and representations through the concept of intangible heritage.[15] Lusenet argues that this convention offers a means to understand the 'practices, expressions and representations' that underpin participatory media as forms of cultural heritage. The advent of user-based content that rose with Web 2.0 has increasingly revealed common ground between digital and intangible forms of culture. Kate Hennessy finds that digital technologies 'have become normative tools and economically viable resources for the documentation and preservation of intangible cultural heritage'.[16] She argues that the ubiquity of these tools demand that we consider not only how they interface with their analogue counterparts, but also consider how digitisation and its implied and tangible accessibility integrates with the principles of community ownership embedded in the *Intangible Heritage Convention*. Just as digital technologies are employed in the service of tangible forms of culture, so too they are employed and integrated as transformative media to promote and document intangible heritage practices.[17]

Intangible Heritage Convention

The *Intangible Heritage Convention* has been heralded as a counterpoint to the *World Heritage Convention* by authorities such as Laurajane Smith.[18] The convention offers a formal means for the recognition of non-material forms of heritage that are often the manifestations of Indigenous people and cultural practices from non-Western countries. Prior to the adoption of this convention in 2003, no legal or organisational framework existed for the recognition of intangible forms of culture such as language, performing arts, social rituals and practices, traditional forms of knowledge and craftsmanship.[19] According to Smith, the convention 'marks a significant intervention into international debate about the nature and value of cultural heritage' by recognising that non-material forms of culture are as significant as the material forms already recognised.[20] Although the convention does not directly address digital artefacts, its broader definition of heritage offers scope for recognising participatory culture that is facilitated by online technologies.

The definition of heritage embodied within the *Intangible Heritage Convention* is useful because it embraces the very characteristics of socio-visual value and participatory culture that are problematic within World Heritage. The convention defines heritage as:

> the practices, representations, expressions, knowledge, skills – as well as the instruments, objects, artefacts and cultural spaces associated therewith – that communities, groups and, in some cases, individuals recognize as part of their cultural heritage. This intangible cultural heritage, transmitted from generation to generation, is constantly recreated by communities and groups in response to their environment, their interaction with nature and their history, and provides them with a sense of identity and continuity, thus promoting respect for cultural diversity and human creativity.[21]

The *Intangible Heritage Convention* specifically recognises immaterial or living forms of culture (social practices, language, skills) as the manifestations of subjective and mutable values such as memory and identity. Further it is not dependent on definitions of outstanding universal value, rather, intangible heritage is defined by its *social value* for communities in fostering a sense of continuity and tradition. The *Intangible Heritage Convention* is still in its infancy; support organisations and experts, theoretical literature, case studies and preservation practices, such as those that support the World Heritage programme, are still in the process of being established.[22] Currently there are 391 elements inscribed as Intangible Heritage. Examples of inscribed elements include French cuisine and needle lace making as well as Peruvian sung prayers, Korean tightrope walking, Chinese calligraphy and paper cut crafts.[23]

The protection of non-material forms of culture was first attempted through the UNESCO *Recommendation on the Safeguarding of Traditional Culture and Folklore, 1989*, which sought to address the impact of industrialisation and mass media were having on traditional patterns of culture.[24] D. Fairchild Ruggles and Helaine Silverman state that the recommendation was found to be ineffectual.[25] Korea's Living Treasures Program, which followed in 1993, was, according to Smith, the 'first time that skills and knowledge were placed as a focus point of preservation'.[26] By 1998 UNESCO had proposed the *Proclamation of Masterpieces of the Oral and Intangible Heritage*, the precedent for the *Intangible Heritage Convention*. The proclamation was adopted two years later.[27]

The *Intangible Heritage Convention* follows the same structure as the *World Heritage Convention*. State Parties to the convention can nominate elements of intangible heritage drawn from their tentative lists, and these are assessed by *The Intergovernmental Committee for the Safeguarding of Intangible Cultural Heritage (Intangible Heritage Committee)*. The *Intangible Heritage Convention* is interpreted through the *Operational Directive*, which is regularly revised and updated to reflect current ideas.[28] Elements of intangible heritage can be inscribed onto one of the two lists: the *Representative List of the Intangible Cultural Heritage of Humanity* (whose aim is to demonstrate the diversity of intangible heritage and to increase awareness of its value), or the *List of Intangible Cultural Heritage in Need of Urgent Safeguarding* (which is intended to assist in gathering support for elements whose existence is under threat).[29] Although the *Intangible Heritage Convention* has been critiqued for its similarity to the World Heritage programme, it nonetheless embodies a radical redefinition of heritage. The convention's focus on cultural processes, such as practices, representations, expressions, knowledge and skills, rather than material artefacts and built monuments, widens the remit of culture that can be formally recognised as heritage.

The discourse on intangible heritage is still emerging. This early body of academic research has mainly focused on issues arising from the definition of heritage promoted by the convention, its implications and historical antecedents.[30] The application of the convention is at an early stage and not yet well theorised. Because intangible heritage is 'embodied in people rather than inanimate objects',[31] 'the question of the meanings and values . . . becomes vastly complex'.[32] Like the problems faced in relation to social value (within the Australian discourse), its articulation, research and theorisation remains difficult. Discussions on intangible heritage often draw from many fields that intersect with its definition, including: heritage studies, identity, memory, performativity and interpretation.[33] Further, while the convention represents an important step in the broader recognition of socially based value, it has also been characterised as an instrument which simply sits beside existing documents.

Participatory culture, and therefore socio-visual value, manifests in tangible and intangible ways, more readily defined as practices, expressions and representations that are recognised as heritage within the *Intangible Heritage Convention*. A key structure of the convention is that 'elements' of intangible heritage, as they are termed, are inscribed in relation to the communities for whom they are significant. As they are different to sites of World Heritage, elements of Intangible Heritage are not subject to substantiation by expert opinion. The convention recognises that the value of these practices is not in their historical accuracy (for they may change), but for their role in reinforcing existing social relationships and providing continuity of identity for these groups of people. Intangible Heritage embraces the mutable character of social values as embodied by living forms of culture, and offers an alternative means of recognition to the problems in achieving this through the *World Heritage Convention*'s Criterion (vi).

The *Intangible Heritage Convention* does not identify specific values that must be preserved to maintain inscription, in the way the *World Heritage Convention* does. Rather it seeks to protect living practices so that they remain meaningful to communities. In this way, the *Intangible Heritage Convention* is able to embrace contested meanings, dissonant perspectives. Practices, such as those interpreted through the representations of the Sydney Opera House, can be understood as forms of heritage through the definition embodied by the *Intangible Heritage Convention*. Such practices reveal the fluid and dynamic social interactions of identity and memory that occur through and around representations. Practices of participatory culture, such as *telling, critiquing, making, trading, visiting* and *capturing*, are ways in which people express and maintain the personal and collective cultural meanings that have become attached to the Sydney Opera House, and where these are negotiated and extended online.

Representations of buildings, such as the Sydney Opera House, offer a means to evidence the social value of iconic works of architecture. The particularity of this relationship is explored in the next part of the chapter, to demonstrate that such an online method of analysis is specific to iconic places and their widespread contingent global communities.

The contingent communities of iconic sites

Participatory culture is unlike the practices that are recognised through the *Intangible Heritage Convention*, as it is founded on the notion that audience-communities are responding to a form of culture, such as a television programme, or a building, such as the Sydney Opera House. Practices, expressions and representations recognised as Intangible Heritage are not responses to forms of culture, but rather are autonomous forms of culture themselves, and their communities are geographically, culturally or spiritually defined, much like those described in relation to the Australian concept of social value.[34] The analysis of the representations of the Sydney Opera House finds the building's community (as defined through the representations posted online) is much more contingent than the definitions proposed in the literature on social value. The community of the Sydney Opera House evidenced online is more aligned with Benedict Anderson's concept of 'imagined communities' where belonging is a mental rather than a geographical, cultural or spiritual construct.[35] Anderson's seminal concept acknowledges that our individual sense of being part of a community is generated not only through direct engagement with other members, but by our imagined sense of belonging. Building on Anderson's idea of an imagined sense of community, Michael Warner has proposed in *Publics and Counterpublics* that social formations, such as those conceptualised through the term participatory culture, emerge in relation to 'texts'.[36] Warner uses the term 'publics' to describe these social entities, a term more usually associated with ideas of politics, citizenship and society. Warner embraces the notion that audiences and communities are complex and multifarious social entities and argues against solely investigating these entities empirically. He argues for interpretive approaches that embrace these entities as animated, dynamic and multileveled, where each text or building works to co-constitute an audience-community-public:

Each time we address a public ... we draw on what seems like simple common sense. If we did not have a practical sense of what publics are, if we could not unself-consciously take them for granted as really existing and addressable social entities, we could not produce most of the books or films or broadcasts or journals that make up so much of our culture; we could not conduct elections or indeed imagine ourselves as members of nations or movements. Yet publics exist only by virtue of their imagining. They are a kind of fiction that has taken on life, and very potent life at that.[37]

Warner's observation, that communities come into being in response to forms of culture such as films, books, and here, buildings, describes a different kind of social entity than that embodied within the *Intangible Heritage Convention*. Yet while the community described through the analysis of the representations may not necessarily fit with the definitions in the convention, the representations and practices outlined in the previous chapters demonstrate the role of these in negotiating identity and memory for this contingent group of people, organisations and institutions.

Are these communities that have formed in response to the Sydney Opera House unique? Or are these contingent audience-community-publics also in existence around other iconic places? Do practices, such as those interpreted from the representations of the Sydney Opera House, occur around other iconic sites? To explore whether this is the case, a search for similar representations was carried out for six other iconic sites, of which four are also inscribed on the World Heritage List.

Representations of iconic sites

Christina Cameron raised the connection between the World Heritage List and iconicity in her 2005 paper on the use of the term 'outstanding universal value'.[38] In this paper, Cameron notes that in the early years of the *World Heritage Convention*, many of the sites inscribed were listed through an interpretation of outstanding universal value as the 'best of the best', understood as iconic sites, versus 'representative of the best', where several sites can be exemplars of a particular kind of property. Cameron defines iconic sites as those which 'transcend cultural affiliation . . . are unique and widely known' and notes that iconic sites dominated listings in the first five years of the operation of the convention (1978–1982), perhaps because they did not require comparative evaluation as they were considered unique and famous by the advisory bodies.[39] Cameron's description of iconic places accords with those of Terry Smith, Leslie Sklair and Richard Weston, discussed in relation to the inscription of the Sydney Opera House for its outstanding universal value as a world-famous iconic building. Over the following decade four other global icons were inscribed as World Heritage sites. These, as well as the Sydney Opera House, have all been inscribed under Criterion (i), a masterpiece of human creative genius, as well as Criterion (vi), with the exception of the Taj Mahal:

  1983 – Taj Mahal, India. Criterion (i).[40]
  1984 – Statue of Liberty, United States of America. Criteria (i) and (vi).[41]
  1987 – Piazza del Duomo, Pisa (Tower of Pisa), Italy. Criteria (i), (ii), (iv) and (vi).[42]
  1991 – Paris, Banks of the Seine (Eiffel Tower), France. Criteria (i), (ii) and (iv).[43]

In Figure 8.1–8.5, these four well-known iconic World Heritage sites, as well as two further examples of iconic works of architecture, were used as comparisons to discover whether their representations also evidenced the practices of participatory culture inspired by the Sydney Opera House. The two further examples in the visual comparison, Frank Lloyd Wright's Solomon R. Guggenheim Museum in New York, and Frank Gehry's Guggenheim Museum in Bilbao were both included in the comparative analysis in the nomination dossier for the Sydney Opera House.[44] Notably, Wright's Guggenheim is already included in a tentative nomination put forward in 2008 and 2016 by the United States that seeks to recognise this building as part of a nomination of the architect's oeuvre, both of which were unsuccessful. Gehry's Guggenheim is yet to be considered for nomination, but perhaps this is because it was only completed in 1997.

Figure 8.1 Comparison of representations of iconic places: cakes.

Figure 8.2 Comparison of representations of iconic places: costumes.

Whilst the search categories were drawn from the results of the analysis of the Sydney Opera House, the comparison reveals that representations can be found with relative ease for all the examples, except the Guggenheim Museum, Bilbao. The categories were selected to reveal connections to practices of *telling, critiquing, making, trading, visiting* and *capturing*. The categories included: cakes, costumes and clothing, salt and pepper shakers, LEGO models and kits, tourist photographs, detail photographs, snowdomes, postage stamps, photoshopped images, advertisements and works of art. Such types of representations are unique to iconic places, such as those exemplified in the comparison. Whilst some types of representations exist for less globally acclaimed works of architecture, such as photographs on Flickr of the Olympic Park Railway Station by Australian architects Hassell Studio,[45] the wide

Figure 8.3 Comparison of representations of iconic places: architectural details.

variety of examples evidenced in the comparison in Figures 8.1–8.5 only appear in relation to iconic World Heritage sites. Representations do evidence the socio-visual value iconic works of architecture, but this socio-visual value is associated with the broad contingent communities of world-famous places. Could this be recognised as an intangible heritage of the global community of the Sydney Opera House?

The privileging of tangible over intangible heritage

The recognition of intangible heritage that is inspired by World Heritage is problematic because of the way the *Intangible Heritage Convention* explicitly articulates its

Figure 8.4 Comparison of representations of iconic places: tourist souvenirs.

relationship to the *World Heritage Convention*. The *Intangible Heritage Convention* states that nothing may be interpreted as:

> altering the status or diminishing the level of protection under the 1972 Convention concerning the Protection of the World Cultural and Natural Heritage of World Heritage properties with which an item of the intangible cultural heritage is directly associated.[46]

This implies that no form of intangible heritage may impinge on the values upheld by inscription of the World Heritage List. If the participatory culture of the Sydney Opera House were to be recognised as an element of intangible heritage, such practices could

Figure 8.5 Comparison of representations of iconic places: stamps.

conflict with the conservation strategies and policies in place as part of the World Heritage inscription. For example, taking photographs and posting them on Flickr is on one hand a creative pastime, but their formal publication and commercialisation must be sanctioned by the Sydney Opera House Trust to protect sponsors' association with the building as a brand.[47] Within the collection of representations gathered to ascertain whether they can reveal socio-visual value there are many instances where the Sydney Opera House is used as a vehicle for commercial gain; souvenirs, opera-house wedding cakes, clothing, and theme parks for example. The practice of making such representations, like the sale of the photograph, could be argued to impinge on the value of the image of the building as articulated in the World Heritage inscription.

The practices of participatory culture, as evidenced through online representations of the Sydney Opera House reveal the problems that arise from the division of heritage into discrete categories of tangible (World Heritage), intangible and digital. The UNESCO suite of heritage conventions and charters fails to recognise the way in which culture is expressed and made significant through different mediums; from architecture to taking photographs or building a model out of LEGO and posting these online. Anthropologist Barbara Kirchenblatt-Gimblett recognises that although these divisions are historically founded, they are somewhat arbitrary; culture is slippery, both material and immaterial. Kirchenblatt-Gimblett states that intangible heritage 'is not only embodied, but also inseparable from the material and social world of persons'.[48] This view is echoed in the work of media scholar José van Dijck, whose research around mediated memories and digital artefacts states:

> to understand the digital as immaterial is as erroneous as the idea of analogue mediated objects being static reminders of past experience. Layers of code are definitely material, even if this materiality is different from the analogue objects that we are used to and that are still very much part of our personal cultural memory.[49]

Although van Dijck's conceptual tool, *mediated memories*, is not about heritage, it serves as a theoretical model for it nonetheless. Unlike UNESCO's *World Heritage Convention*, *Intangible Heritage Convention* and *Digital Heritage Charter*, which divide forms of culture into various heritage subsets, van Dijck's tool articulates their interconnection, bringing the tangible, the intangible and the digital into one space where their dynamic and fluid relationship can be explained. Conceiving of heritage from this perspective the representations and their practices, both online and offline, as the participatory culture of the Sydney Opera House, evidence the socio-visual value of this World Heritage site. Van Dijck's articulation of representational forms (digital or analogue) as technologies dissolves the distinctions created by UNESCO's conventions and charters and their emphasis on material form. She observes that 'we cannot separate the individual psyche from culture' and that this '[prompts] the integration of psychological and cognitive perspectives into cultural theory'.[50] Rather than reinforce the idea that online interactions are virtual, van Dijck offers a reminder that these experiences also occur through physical objects and encounters, that they mediate the future and the past to offer an individual and collective sense of continuity and connect embedded social practices with personal experiences and meanings.

Conclusion

Participatory culture and the representations that arise from it evidence the socio-visual value of the Sydney Opera House. These cultural phenomena are also revealing of the inadequacies of the existing UNESCO suite of heritage instruments to account for the way that people make iconic places significant. Over the 40 years of the implementation of the *World Heritage Convention*, the recognition of associative values embodied in intangible practices, such as socio-visual value and participatory culture, has been widely contested. It remains a problematic task within an instrument that is founded on the premise that heritage is inherently material. Newer instruments, such as the *Intangible Heritage Convention*, offer more appropriate means for the recognition of mutable and subjective values, such as socio-visual value (memory and identity) and intangible forms of culture, such as participatory culture. However, this is not straightforward. Representations evidence socio-visual value, but only for the contingent communities associated with iconic works of architectures. Further, the *Intangible Heritage Convention*'s subservience to the *World Heritage Convention* means that some of the practices that comprise the building's participatory culture could be construed as infringing on the building's inscribed values. Yet the social value of the Sydney Opera House does not reside only in the building, the practices of its audience-community, or the representations. As van Dijck's integrated model for the significance of analogue and digital memory artefacts suggests, the social significance of the Sydney Opera House exists in the interconnections between the tangible, intangible and digital examples of culture examined in this book. *Mediated memories* offers a way to explain online and offline practices, the representations implicated in these, and the manner in which people express and represent the social significance of the Sydney Opera House at a personal and collective level. More broadly it offers both a model for a more integrated way of understanding heritage and a critique of the current divisions within UNESCO's suite of instruments.

Notes

1 UNESCO Intergovernmental Committee for the Protection of the World Cultural and Natural Heritage, Paris (2011) *Operational Guidelines for the Implementation of the World Heritage Convention*. Retrieved: 26/11/2012, from: http://whc.unesco.org/archive/opguide11-en.pdf. Paragraph 77(vi).
2 Jukka Jokilehto (2008) *The World Heritage List: What Is Ouv? Defining the Outstanding Universal Value of Cultural World Heritage Properties*. Paris: ICOMOS, p. 32.
3 See footnote 34 in Chapter 3. For a more detailed report on the use of this criterion see the following UNESCO 2001 report cited. Olwen Beazley (2009) 'Protecting Intangible Heritage Values through the World Heritage Convention?' *Historic Environment*, 22 (3), p. 8; Jokilehto, *The World Heritage List*, p. 32; UNESCO (2001) *Information Document: Analysis of the Application of Cultural Criterion (Vi)*. Retrieved: 27/04/2013, from: http://whc.unesco.org/uploads/events/documents/event-827-9.pdf.
4 UNESCO (2012) *Report of the International World Heritage Expert Meeting on Criterion (Vi) and Associative Values (Warsaw, Poland, 28–30 March 2012)*. Paris. Retrieved: 11/04/2012, from: http://whc.unesco.org/en/news/866/. Paragraph 13.
5 Olwen Beazley (2004) 'Inspirational Landscapes as World Heritage: Problems of Identification and Management'. Presented at the *World Heritage Cultural and Ecological Landscapes, US ICOMOS*, Natchitoches, Louisiana, 25–27 March. Retrieved: 28/03/2011, from: www.usicomos.org/symp/archive/2004/docs/beazley-4780, p. 7.
6 For more detailed analysis of Criterion (vi) see: Beazley, 'Protecting Intangible Heritage Values through the World Heritage Convention?'; Olwen Beazley (2006) *Drawing a Line around a Shadow? Including Associative, Intangible Cultural Heritage Values on the World Heritage List*. PhD thesis, Australian National University. Work on Hiroshima appears in: Olwen Beazley (2010) 'Politics and Power: The Hiroshima Peace Memorial (Genbaku Dome) as World Heritage'. In *Heritage and Globalisation*, edited by Colin Long and Sophia Labadi. London: Routledge, pp. 45–66; Olwen Beazley (2009) 'A Paradox of Peace: The Hiroshima Peace Memorial (Genbaku Dome) as World Heritage'. In *A Fearsome Heritage: Diverse Legacies of the Cold War*, edited by John Schofield and Wayne Cocroft. Vol. 50. London: Left Coast Press, pp. 33–50.
7 Beazley is quoting the work of William S.F. Miles. Beazley, 'Protecting Intangible Heritage Values through the World Heritage Convention?' p. 12; William S. F. Miles (2002)

'Auschwitz: Museum Interpretation and Darker Tourism'. *Annals of Tourism Research*, 29, pp. 1175–1178. Beazley also draws on important scholarship on memory by Pierre Nora, Andreas Huyssen and Alois Riegl.

8 Pierre Nora (2007 [1989]) 'Between Memory and History: Les Lieux De Mémoire'. In *Cultural Heritage: Critical Concepts in Media and Cultural Studies*, vol. 2, edited by Laurajane Smith.. London: Routledge, p. 295.

9 See for example Fiona Cameron and Sarah Kenderine (2007) *Theorizing Digital Cultural Heritage*. Cambridge, MA: The MIT Press; Yehuda Kalay, Thomas Kvan and Janice Affleck (2008) *New Heritage: New Media and Cultural Heritage*. New York: Routledge.

10 The Charter on the Preservation of Digital Heritage was adopted in October. It was preceded by a set of guidelines on the preservation of digital heritage prepared by the National Library of Australia. UNESCO (2003) *Charter on the Preservation of the Digital Heritage*. Retrieved: 11/04/2011, from: http://portal.unesco.org/en/ev.php-URL_ID=17721&URL_DO=DO_TOPIC&URL_SECTION=201.html; National Library of Australia (2003) *Guidelines for the Preservation of Digital Heritage*. Information Society Division: UNESCO. Retrieved: 18/07/2012, from: http://unesdoc.unesco.org/images/0013/001300/130071e.pdf; Yola de Lusenet (2007) 'Tending the Garden or Harvesting the Fields: Digital Preservation and the UNESCO Charter on the Preservation of the Digital Heritage'. *Library Trends*, 56 (1), pp. 164–182.

11 Fiona Cameron (2007) 'Beyond the Cult of the Replicant: Museums and Historical Digital Objects – Traditional Concerns, New Discourses'. In *Theorizing Digital Cultural Heritage*, edited by Fiona Cameron and Sarah Kenderine. Cambridge, MA: The MIT Press, pp. 49–75.

12 UNESCO (2003) *Charter on the Preservation of the Digital Heritage*, Article 1.

13 Fiona Cameron (2008) 'The Politics of Heritage Authorship: The Case of Digital Heritage Collections'. In *New Heritage: New Media and Cultural Heritage*, edited by Yehuda Kalay, Thomas Kvan and Janice Affleck. New York: Routledge, p. 170.

14 Cameron, 'Beyond the Cult of the Replicant', p. 50.

15 Lusenet, 'Tending the Garden or Harvesting the Fields'.

16 Kate Hennessy (2012) 'From Intangible Expression to Digital Cultural Heritage'. In *Safeguarding Intangible Cultural Heritage*, edited by Michelle L. Stefano, Peter Davis and Gerard Corsane. Woodbridge: The Boydell Press, p. 38.

17 Hennessy, 'From Intangible Expression to Digital Cultural Heritage', pp. 33–46.

18 Laurajane Smith (2006) *Uses of Heritage*. London: Routledge, p. 3.

19 UNESCO (2012) 'Working Towards a Convention'. *Intangible Cultural Heritage* [Website]. Retrieved: 19/07/2012, from: www.unesco.org/culture/ich/index.php?lg=en&pg=00004; UNESCO (2003) *Convention for the Safeguarding of the Intangible Cultural Heritage*, 32nd Session: The General Conference of the United Nations Educational, Scientific and Cultural Organization. Paris. Retrieved: 29/11/2010, from: www.unesco.org/culture/ich/index.php?lg=en&pg=00022. Preamble.

20 Laurajane Smith and Natsuko Akagawa (2009) *Intangible Heritage*, edited by William Logan and Laurajane Smith. London: Routledge, p. 1.

21 UNESCO (2003) *Convention for the Safeguarding of the Intangible Cultural Heritage*, Article 2.

22 Three edited collections were published in 2009, plus another in 2012. In addition, the National Folk Museum of Korea has published the *International Journal of Intangible Heritage* since 2006 (www.ijih.org) and ICOMOS formed an International Committee on Intangible Cultural Heritage in 2005, however this still operates under the main organisation. D. Fairchild Ruggles and Helaine Silverman (2009) *Intangible Heritage Embodied*. London: Springer; Smith and Akagawa, *Intangible Heritage*; Sérgio Lira and Rogério Amoêda (2009) *Constructing Intangible Heritage*. Barcelos: Green Lines Institute; Michelle L. Stefano, Peter Davis and Gerard Corsane (2012) *Safeguarding Intangible Cultural Heritage*. Woodbridge: The Boydell Press; ICOMOS (2012) 'Homepage'. *International Committee on Intangible Cultural Heritage (ICICH)*. Retrieved: 22/07/2012, from: http://icich.icomos.org/index.html.

23 Elements counted inscribed between 2008 and 2016. The first were inscribed in 2008 when the elements from the convention's predecessor, the *Proclamation of the Masterpieces of the Oral and Intangible Heritage of Humanity, 2001*, were transferred. As at 22 August 2016 the Representative List has inscribed 336 elements, the Urgent Safeguarding List has inscribed 43 and the Register of Best Safeguarding Practices has inscribed 12. For further information on each of these examples. UNESCO (2012) 'Intangible Heritage Lists'. *Intangible Cultural Heritage* [Website]. Retrieved: 19/07/2012, from: www.unesco.org/culture/ich/index.php?lg=en&pg=00011&multinational=3&display1=inscriptionID#tabs.

24 UNESCO (1989) *Recommendation on the Safeguarding of Traditional Culture and Folklore,* 25th Session: The General Conference of the United Nations Educational, Scientific and Cultural Organization, UNESCO, Paris. Retrieved: 11/04/2011, from: http://portal.unesco.org/en/ev.php-URL_ID=13141&URL_DO=DO_TOPIC&URL_SECTION=201.html.

25 Fairchild Ruggles and Silverman, *Intangible Heritage Embodied*, p. 8.

26 Smith is citing Janet Blake here. Smith and Akagawa, *Intangible Heritage*, p. 107; Janet Blake (2001) *Developing a New Standard-Setting Instrument for the Safeguarding of Intangible Heritage: Elements for Consideration*. Paris: UNESCO. Retrieved: 29/08/2012, from: http://unesdoc.unesco.org/images/0012/001237/123744e.pdf, p. 45.

27 UNESCO (2001) *Proclamation of the Masterpieces of the Oral and Intangible Heritage of Humanity (2001–2005)*. Retrieved: 30/03/2013, from: www.unesco.org/culture/ich/index.php?lg=en&pg=00103.

28 The Operational Directives were adopted in June 2008, and were revised in 2010 and 2012. UNESCO (2012) 'Operational Directives for the Implementation of the Convention for the Safeguarding of the Intangible Heritage (2012)'. *Intangible Cultural Heritage*. Retrieved: 19/07/2012, from: www.unesco.org/culture/ich/index.php?lg=en&pg=00026; UNESCO Intergovernmental Committee for the Protection of the World Cultural and Natural Heritage, Paris (2012) *Operational Guidelines for the Implementation of the World Heritage Convention*. Retrieved: 26/11/2012, from: http://whc.unesco.org/archive/opguide12-en.pdf.

29 There is an additional list, which recognises best-practice in the safeguarding of Intangible Heritage. It is the register of 'Programmes, projects and activities for the safeguarding of intangible cultural heritage considered to best reflect the principles and objectives of the Convention'. UNESCO (2012) 'Intangible Heritage Lists'. Intangible Cultural Heritage [Website].

30 See, for example, Janet Blake and William Logan. Janet Blake (2007) *Safeguarding Intangible Cultural Heritage: Challenges and Approaches*. Builth Wells, UK: Institute of Art and Law; William Logan (2007) 'Closing Pandora's Box: Human Rights Conundrums in Cultural Heritage Protection'. In *Cultural Heritage and Human Rights*, edited by D. Fairchild Ruggles and Helaine Silverman. New York: Springer, pp. 33–52.

31 Logan, 'Closing Pandora's Box', p. 33.

32 Fairchild Ruggles and Silverman, *Intangible Heritage Embodied*, p. 1.

33 See, for example, publications by Tim Benton or Anthony Jackson and Jenny Kidd on memory and performativity: Tim Benton (2010) *Understanding Heritage and Memory*. Manchester: Manchester University Press; Anthony Jackson and Jenny Kidd (2011) *Performing Heritage: Research, Practice and Innovation in Museum Theatre and Live Interpretation*. Manchester: Manchester University Press; Brian Graham and Peter Howard (2008) *The Ashgate Research Companion to Heritage and Identity*. Hampshire: Ashgate. Or Brian Graham and Peter Howard on identity: Graham and Howard, *The Ashgate Research Companion to Heritage and Identity*.

34 Australian Government (2009) *Guidelines for the Assessment of Places for the National Heritage List*. Canberra: Australia Heritage Council & Department of the Environment, Water, Heritage and the Arts, p. 43.

35 Benedict Anderson (1991) *Imagined Communities: Reflections on the Origin and Spread of Nationalism*. London: Verso.

36 Michael Warner (2002) *Publics and Counterpublics*. New York: Zone Books. Elena Loizidou (2003) 'Publics and Counterpublics, by Michael Warner' [Book Review]. *Space and Culture*, 6 (1), p. 77.

37 Warner, *Publics and Counterpublics*, p. 8.
38 Christina Cameron (2008 [2005]) 'Evolution of the Application of "Outstanding Universal Value" for Cultural and Natural Heritage'. In *The World Heritage List: What Is Ouv? Defining the Outstanding Universal Value of Cultural World Heritage Properties*, edited by Jukka Jokilehto. Paris: ICOMOS, pp. 71–74.
39 Cameron, 'Evolution of the Application of "Outstanding Universal Value" for Cultural and Natural Heritage', p. 71.
40 UNESCO (1983) 'Taj Mahal'. *World Heritage Centre*. Retrieved: 18/07/2012, from: http://whc.unesco.org/en/list/252/.
41 UNESCO (1984) 'Statue of Liberty'. *World Heritage Centre*. Retrieved: 31/03/2013, from: http://whc.unesco.org/en/list/307.
42 UNESCO (1987) 'Piazza Del Duomo, Pisa'. *World Heritage Centre*. Retrieved: 31/03/2013, from: http://whc.unesco.org/en/list/395.
43 UNESCO (1991) 'Banks of the River Seine'. *World Heritage Centre*. Retrieved: 18/07/2012, from: http://whc.unesco.org/en/list/600/.
44 Australian Government (2006) *Sydney Opera House: Nomination by the Government of Australia for Inscription on the World Heritage List*. Canberra: Department of Environment and Heritage and NSW Heritage Office. Retrieved: 28/11/2012, from: http://whc.unesco.org/uploads/nominations/166rev.pdf, pp. 46–52.
45 A search on Flickr on 31/03/2013 returned 4,170 images of Olympic Park Station, Sydney, whilst it returned 206,054 images of the Sydney Opera House.
46 UNESCO (2003) *Convention for the Safeguarding of the Intangible Cultural Heritage*, Article 3(a)
47 The Sydney Opera House Trust has specific sponsor agreements with commercial entities, such as Google, MasterCard and Range Rover among others, that gives these corporations the right to advertise their association with this performing arts venue. In one particular case, the management of the Sydney Opera House prevented an amateur photographer from selling his image to a stock photography site, on the grounds that there was no formal agreement. On 27 May 2007 Simon Phipps posted to his blog the recent issues he had encountered in selling his amateur photograph of the Sydney Opera House to online commercial photography site iStockphoto. Proud of this photo, he did not expect to earn much from this endeavour. Instead he hoped to gain personal satisfaction from others deeming his image worthy of purchase. Phipps was surprised when he received a lengthy response from Caroline Ang, Corporate Counsel of the Sydney Opera House, stating that iStockphoto could not accept his photograph because the Sydney Opera House Trust 'vigorously protects the commercial exploitation of its intellectual property and does not approve use of the Sydney Opera House brand in commercial contexts where there is no association between the relevant business and Sydney Opera House'. Law academic Peter Black analysed the legal implications of the response offered to Phipps by the Sydney Opera House Trust. Although the organisation 'welcomes visitors to the Sydney Opera House precinct to photograph, film or video images for personal use only' it objects to the commercial use of such visual depictions on the basis that it might suggest or imply an association between the purchaser of this image and the Sydney Opera House Trust, and in this way breach the Australian Trade Practices Act, 1974 (Cth). The Sydney Opera House Trust reserves the privilege of 'brand association' for 'sponsors of a certain value'. Black observes that the Corporate Counsel of the Sydney Opera House are rather vague in their definition of 'intellectual property' by citing that taking a photograph of a building is not a breach of copyright law. Black states: 'See <u>Section 66</u> of the *Copyright Act 1968* <u>(Cth)</u>: The <u>copyright</u> in a <u>building</u> or a model of a <u>building</u> is not infringed by the making of a painting, <u>drawing,</u> <u>engraving</u> or <u>photograph</u> of the <u>building</u> or model or by the inclusion of the <u>building</u> or model in a <u>cinematograph film</u> or in a <u>television broadcast</u>.' Peter Black (2007) 'Photographing the Sydney Opera House (10 June)'. *Peter Black's Freedom to Differ*. Retrieved: 25/09/2012, from: www.freedomtodiffer.com/freedom_to_differ/2007/06/photographing_t.html. Further, Black goes on to argue that the organisation's claim, that an implied association between the Sydney Opera House and a non-sponsoring corporate entity would be a breach of the Australian *Trade Practices Act, 1974 (Commonwealth of Australia)* for being 'misleading' or 'deceptive', is ambiguously defined in the Act and essentially untested in the court of law. Some

of this information was sourced in conversation with Maria Sykes, April/May 2009. Sydney Opera House (2012) 'Sydney Opera House Current Partners – Corporate Sponsors'. Retrieved: 25/09/2012, from: www.sydneyoperahouse.com/support/current partners/corporate_sponsors.aspx. Bruce Livingstone (2012) 'Homepage'. *iStockphoto*. Retrieved: 30/11/2012, from: www.istockphoto.com/. Black (2007) 'Photographing the Sydney Opera House (10 June)'. *Peter Black's Freedom to Differ*.

48 Barbara Kirshenblatt-Gimblett (2004) 'Intangible Heritage as Metacultural Production'. *Museum International*, 56 (221–222), p. 60.

49 José van Dijck (2007). *Mediated Memories in the Digital Age*. Stanford: Stanford University Press, p. 47.

50 van Dijck, *Mediated Memories in the Digital Age*, p. 23.

Bibliography

'Administration Roles for All' (2006) *Flickr* [Discussion Thread in Photosharing Group: Sydney, Australia]. 16 February. Removed.

Ahmad, Yahaya (2006) 'The Scope and Definitions of Heritage: From Tangible to Intangible'. *International Journal of Heritage Studies*, 12 (3), pp. 292–300. doi: 10.1080/13527250600604639.

Alasuutari, Pertti (1999) 'Introduction: Three Phases of Reception Studies'. In *Rethinking the Media Audience: The New Agenda*. London: Sage, pp. 1–21.

Allen, Matthew (2009) 'Tim O'Reilly and Web 2.0: The Economics of Memetic Liberty and Control'. *Communication, Politics and Culture*, 42 (2), pp. 6–23.

Allen, Stan, and Diana Agrest (2000) *Practice: Architecture, Technique and Representation*. Amsterdam: Gordon and Breach.

Anderson, Benedict (1991) *Imagined Communities: Reflections on the Origin and Spread of Nationalism*. London: Verso.

Anderson, Max, and Pierre Cochrane (1989) *Julius Poole & Gibson: The First Eighty Years from Tote to Cad*. Sydney: Julius Poole & Gibson.

Ang, Ien (1985) *Watching Dallas: Soap Opera and the Melodramatic Imagination*. Translated by Della Couling. London: Routledge.

APP (2007) 'Opera House Wins Top Status'. *The Age*, 28 June. Retrieved: 26/06/2012, from: http://news.theage.com.au/national/opera-house-wins-top-status-20070628-kxi.html.

Armour, Margaret (2009) *Utzon Memorial Website* [Tribute to Jørn Utzon]. Sydney Opera House. Retrieved: 12/03/2013, from: http://jornutzon.sydneyoperahouse.com/Tributes.aspx.

Arnstein, Sherry R. (1969) 'A Ladder of Citizen Participation'. *Journal of the American Institute of Planners*, 35 (4), pp. 216–224.

'Arts and Crafts' (1962) *Sydney Morning Herald*, 11 April, p. 6.

Askew, Marc (2010) 'The Magic List of Global Status: UNESCO, World Heritage and the Agenda of States'. In *Heritage and Globalisation*. Edited by Sophia Labadi and Colin Long. London: Routledge, pp. 19–44.

'Assessing Social Values: Communities and Experts – a Workshop Held by Australia ICOMOS' (1996) Sydney.

Australian Bureau of Statistics (2011) 'Population Change in Greater Sydney'. Retrieved: 10/03/2013, from: www.abs.gov.au/ausstats/abs@.nsf/Products/3218.0~2011~Main+Features~New+South+Wales?OpenDocument - PARALINK1.

Australian Government (1955) *Sydney Opera House: The Brown Book* [Online Gallery], NSW Government State Records. Retrieved: 27/06/2012, from: http://gallery.records.nsw.gov.au/index.php/galleries/sydney-opera-house/sydney-opera-house-the-brown-book/.

Australian Government (1975) *Australian Heritage Commission Act 1975*. Retrieved: 31/12/2015, from: www.austlii.edu.au/au/legis/cth/num_act/ahca1975311/.

Australian Government (1980) *Nomination of the Sydney Opera House in Its Harbour Setting with the Sydney Harbour Bridge and the Surrounding Waterways of Sydney Harbour from*

Bradley's Head to Mcmahon's Point for Inclusion in the World Heritage List [Unpublished report submitted to the UNESCO World Heritage Committee in 1981 (Withdrawn)]. Canberra: Australian Heritage Commission.

Australian Government (1996) *Sydney Opera House in Its Harbour Setting* [Unpublished and unsubmitted World Heritage Nomination by the Government of Australia, Principal Consultant and Editor Joan Domicelj]. Glebe: Historic Houses Trust of NSW for the Commonwealth Department of the Environment, Sport and Territories and NSW Department of Urban Affairs and Planning.

Australian Government (1999) *Environment Protection and Biodiversity Conservation Act 1999*. Retrieved: 31/12/2015, from: www.austlii.edu.au/au/legis/cth/consol_act/epabca1999588/.

Australian Government (2003) *Australian Heritage Council Act 2003*. Retrieved: 31/12/2015, from: www.austlii.edu.au/au/legis/cth/consol_act/ahca2003262/.

Australian Government (2005) 'Place Details: Sydney Opera House, 2 Circular Quay East, Sydney, Nsw, Australia'. *Department of Sustainability, Environment, Water, Population and Communities*. Australian Heritage Database. Retrieved: 13/03/2013, from: www.environment. gov.au/cgi-bin/ahdb/search.pl?mode=place_detail;place_id=105738.

Australian Government (2006) *Sydney Opera House: Nomination by the Government of Australia for Inscription on the World Heritage List*. Canberra: Department of Environment and Heritage and NSW Heritage Office. Retrieved: 28/11/2012, from: http://whc.unesco. org/uploads/nominations/166rev.pdf.

Australian Government (2009) *Guidelines for the Assessment of Places for the National Heritage List*. Canberra: Australia Heritage Council & Department of the Environment, Water, Heritage and the Arts.

Australian Government (2012) 'Register of the National Estate – Archive'. *Department of Environment* [Federal government department information portal]. Canberra. Retrieved: 31/12/2015, from: www.environment.gov.au/topics/heritage/heritage-places/register-national-estate.

Australian Government (2016) 'Australia's National Heritage List'. Department of the Environment. Retrieved: 08/04/2016, from: www.environment.gov.au/heritage/places/national-heritage-list.

Awan, Nishat, Tatjana Schneider and Jeremy Till (2011) *Spatial Agency: Other Ways of Doing Architecture*. New York: Routledge.

Bærenholdt, Jørgen Ole, Jonas Larsen, John Urry and Michael Haldrup (2003) *Performing Tourist Places*. Aldershot: Ashgate.

Baudrillard, Jean (1994) *Simulacra and Simulation*. Ann Arbor: University of Michigan Press.

Baume, Michael, and Peter Hall (1967) *The Sydney Opera House Affair*. Melbourne: Nelson.

Bavinton, George (2006) *One Man's Vision: A Play in Two Acts and an Accompanying Exegesis*. Unpublished MA thesis, Faculty of Creative Industries Queensland University of Technology. Retrieved from: http://eprints.qut.edu.au/16311/3/George_Bavinton_Exegesis. pdf, http://eprints.qut.edu.au/16311/2/George_Bavinton_%2D_One_Man's_Vision.pdf.

Beazley, Olwen (2004) 'Inspirational Landscapes as World Heritage: Problems of Identification and Management'. Presented at the *World Heritage Cultural and Ecological Landscapes, US ICOMOS*, Natchitoches, Louisiana, 25–27 March. Retrieved: 28/03/2011, from: www. usicomos.org/symp/archive/2004/docs/beazley-4780.

Beazley, Olwen (2006) *Drawing a Line around a Shadow? Including Associative, Intangible Cultural Heritage Values on the World Heritage List*. Unpublished PhD thesis, Australian National University.

Beazley, Olwen (2009) 'A Paradox of Peace: The Hiroshima Peace Memorial (Genbaku Dome) as World Heritage'. In *A Fearsome Heritage: Diverse Legacies of the Cold War*. Edited by John Schofield and Wayne Cocroft. Vol. 50. London: Left Coast Press, pp. 33–50.

Beazley, Olwen (2009) 'Protecting Intangible Heritage Values through the World Heritage Convention?' *Historic Environment*, 22 (3), pp. 8–13.

Beazley, Olwen (2010) 'Politics and Power: The Hiroshima Peace Memorial (Genbaku Dome) as World Heritage'. In *Heritage and Globalisation*. Edited by Colin Long and Sophia Labadi. London: Routledge, pp. 45–66.

Beazley, Olwen, and Harriet Deacon (2007) 'The Safeguarding of Intangible Heritage Values under the World Heritage Convention: Auschwitz, Hiroshima and Robben Island'. In *Safeguarding Intangible Cultural Heritage: Challenges and Approaches*. Edited by Janet Blake. Builth Wells: Institute of Art and Law, pp. 93–107.

Beck, Haig (1995) 'Social and Aesthetic Values: New Assessment Methodologies for Involving the Community'. *In Place: A Cultural Heritage Bulletin*, 1, pp. 15–18.

Bennett, Tony, Lawrence Grossberg and Meaghan Morris (2009) *New Keywords: A Revised Vocabulary of Culture and Society*. Oxford: Blackwell.

Bentley, Paul (1998–2013 ongoing) 'The Sydney Opera House Story'. Sydney: The Wolanski Foundation. Retrieved: 09/10/2012, from: www.twf.org.au/search/sohstory1.html.

Benton, Tim (2010) *Understanding Heritage and Memory*. Manchester: Manchester University Press.

Bernstein, Fred A. (2008) 'Jorn Utzon, 90, Dies; Created Sydney Opera House'. *New York Times*, 30 November. Retrieved: 27/02/2014, from: www.nytimes.com/2008/11/30/arts/design/30utzon.htm?pagewanted=print.

Black, Peter (2007) 'Photographing the Sydney Opera House (10 June)'. *Peter Black's Freedom to Differ*. Retrieved: 25/09/2012, from: www.freedomtodiffer.com/freedom_to_differ/2007/06/photographing_t.html.

Blair, Sandy, and Marilyn Truscott (1988) *Places of Social Significance*. Australian Heritage Commission.

Blake, Janet (2000) 'On Defining the Cultural Heritage'. *International and Comparative Law Quarterly*, 49 (1), pp. 61–85. doi: 10.1017/S002058930006396X.

Blake, Janet (2001) *Developing a New Standard-Setting Instrument for the Safeguarding of Intangible Heritage: Elements for Consideration*. Paris: UNESCO. Retrieved: 29/08/2012, from: http://unesdoc.unesco.org/images/0012/001237/123744e.pdf.

Blake, Janet (2007). *Safeguarding Intangible Cultural Heritage: Challenges and Approaches*. Builth Wells, UK: Institute of Art and Law.

Borges, Jorge Luis (1965) 'The Analytical Language of John Wilkins (El Idioma Analítico De John Wilkins)'. In *Other Inquisitions 1937–1952*. Translated by Ruth L.C. Simms. Austin: University of Texas Press, pp. 101–150.

Bowditch, Lucy (1996) 'Privacy and Publicity: Modern Architecture as Mass Media by Beatriz Colomina' [Book Review]. *Afterimage*, 23 (5), pp. 19–20.

Bradt, Nick (2009) *Utzon Memorial Website* [Tribute to Jørn Utzon]. Sydney Opera House. Retrieved: 12/03/2013, from: http://jornutzon.sydneyoperahouse.com/Tributes.aspx.

Brass, Ken and Kirsty McKenzie (2005) *Eyewitness Travel Guides: Sydney*. London: Dorling Kindersley.

Brenes B., Julio (2009) *Utzon Memorial Website* [Tribute to Jørn Utzon]. Sydney Opera House. Retrieved: 12/03/2013, from: http://jornutzon.sydneyoperahouse.com/Tributes.aspx.

Briggs, Linda (2009) *Utzon Memorial Website* [Tribute to Jørn Utzon]. Sydney Opera House. Retrieved: 12/03/2013, from: http://jornutzon.sydneyoperahouse.com/Tributes.aspx.

Brooks, Graham (1992) 'Australia's Methodology for Conserving Cultural Heritage'. *Places*, 8 (1), pp. 84–88.

'Buildings Based on the Sydney Opera House' (2006) *Flickr* [Discussion Thread in Photosharing Group: Sydney Opera House]. 26 February. Removed.

Byrne, Denis, Helen Brayshaw and Tracy Ireland (2003) *Social Significance: A Discussion Paper*. Sydney: Research Unit, Cultural Heritage Division, NSW National Parks and Wildlife Service. Retrieved: 07/10/2010, from: www.environment.nsw.gov.au/resources/cultureheritage/SocialSignificance.pdf.

Callaghan, Jennifer (2009) *Utzon Memorial Website* [Tribute to Jørn Utzon]. Sydney Opera House. Retrieved: 12/03/2013, from: http://jornutzon.sydneyoperahouse.com/Tributes.aspx.

Cameron, Christina (2008 [2005]) 'Evolution of the Application of "Outstanding Universal Value" for Cultural and Natural Heritage'. In *The World Heritage List: What Is Ouv? Defining the Outstanding Universal Value of Cultural World Heritage Properties*. Edited by Jukka Jokilehto. Paris: ICOMOS, pp. 71–74.

Cameron, Fiona (2007) 'Beyond the Cult of the Replicant: Museums and Historical Digital Objects – Traditional Concerns, New Discourses'. In *Theorizing Digital Cultural Heritage*. Edited by Fiona Cameron and Sarah Kenderdine. Cambridge, MA: The MIT Press, pp. 49–75.

Cameron, Fiona (2008) 'Object-Oriented Democracies: Conceptualising Museum Collections in Networks'. *Museum Management and Curatorship*, 23 (3), pp. 229–243. doi: 10.1080/09647770802233807.

Cameron, Fiona (2008). 'The Politics of Heritage Authorship: The Case of Digital Heritage Collections'. In *New Heritage: New Media and Cultural Heritage*. Edited by Yehuda Kalay, Thomas Kvan and Janice Affleck. New York: Routledge.

Cameron, Fiona, and Sarah Kenderdine (2007) *Theorizing Digital Cultural Heritage*. Cambridge, MA: The MIT Press.

Cameron, Fiona, and Sarah Mengler (2009) 'Complexity, Transdisciplinarity and Museum Collections Documentation: Emergent Metaphors for a Complex World'. *Journal of Material Culture*, 14 (2), pp. 189–218. doi: 10.1177/1359183509103061.

Campbell, Brett. 'Sydney Opera House Mosaic Dining Table'. *Brett Campbell Mosaics*. Retrieved: 03/08/2012, from: www.mosaics.com.au/Sydney-Opera-House-mosaics-art-table.html.

Canning, Shaun, and Dirk Spenneman (2001) 'Contested Space: Social Value and the Assessment of Cultural Significance in New South Wales, Australia'. In *Heritage Landscapes: Understanding Place and Communities*. Edited by Maria Cotter, Bill Boyd and Jane Gardiner. Lismore: Southern Cross University Press, pp. 457–468.

Chalfen, Richard (2002) 'Snapshots 'R' Us: The Evidentiary Problematic of Home Media'. *Visual Studies*, 17 (2), pp. 141–149. doi: 10.1080/1472586022000032215.

Chalfen, Richard (2006) 'Can You See Me Now? Problems in the Study of Camera-Phone Use in the Us and Japan'. Presented at the *Eyes on the City, International Visual Sociology Association Conference*, Urbino, Italy, 3–5 July.

Chaplin, Elizabeth (1994) *Sociology and Visual Representation*. London: Routledge.

Charsley, Simon R. (1992) *Wedding Cakes and Cultural History*. London: Routledge.

Cheshire, Ben, Greg Hassall and Kieran Ricketts (2015) 'ABC Australian Story: The Man Who Fixed the "Plain Illegal" Sydney Opera House'. Retrieved: 15/03/2016, from: www. abc.net.au/news/2016-01-31/peter-hall-architect-who-fixed-opera-house-after-utzon-de parted/7127160.

Clarke, Annie, and Chris Johnston (2003) 'Time, Memory, Place and Land: Social Meaning and Heritage Conservation in Australia'. Presented at the *Proceedings of the International Scientific Symposium Place, Memory, Meaning Preserving Intangible Values in Monuments and Sites*, Victoria Falls, Zimbabwe, 27–31 October 2003. Retrieved: 13/11/2007, from: www.international.icomos.org/victoriafalls2003/papers/B3-7 - Johnston.pdf.

Cleere, Henry (2001) 'The Uneasy Bedfellows: Universality and Cultural Heritage'. In *Destruction and Conservation of Cultural Property*. Edited by Robert Layton, Peter G. Stone and Edward Thomas. London: Routledge, pp. 22–29.

Colomina, Beatriz (1994) *Privacy and Publicity: Modern Architecture as Mass Media*. Cambridge, MA: The MIT Press.

Colomina, Beatriz (1999) 'The Private Site of Public Memory'. *The Journal of Architecture*, 4 (4), pp. 337–360. doi: 10.1080/136023699373747.

Colomina, Beatriz (2002) 'Architectureproduction'. In *This Is Not Architecture: Media Constructions*. Edited by Kester Rattenbury. New York: Routledge, pp. 207–221.

Colomina, Beatriz, and Joan Ockman (1988) *Architectureproduction*. New York: Princeton Architectural Press.

Connell, John (2000) *Sydney: The Emergence of a World City*. Melbourne: Oxford University Press.

Council of Europe (2005) *Council of Europe Framework Convention on the Value of Cultural Heritage for Society (Faro Convention)*. Retrieved: 01/03/2013, from: http://conventions. coe.int/Treaty/en/Treaties/Html/199.htm.

Cresswell, Tim (2005) *Place: A Short Introduction*. Malden: Blackwell.

Crouch, David (2010) 'The Perpetual Performance of Heritage'. In *Culture, Heritage and Representation: Perspectives on Visuality and the Past*. Edited by Emma Waterton and Steve Watson. Surrey: Ashgate, pp. 57–72.

Cuff, Dana (1991) *Architecture: The Story Practice*. Cambridge, MA: The MIT Press.

Curtis, William J.R. (1987) *Modern Architecture since 1900*. 2nd edn. Oxford: Phaidon.

Cutler, Paris (2010) 'Worlds Largest Opera House Cake 2011'. In *Planet Cake Update*. Retrieved: 25/06/2013, from: http://planetcakeupdate.blogspot.com.au/2010/09/worlds-largest-opera-house-cake-2011.html.

Cutler, Paris (2011) 'Beginning of Day 6 We Are Getting Somewhere!' *Planet Cake (Facebook)*. Retrieved: 26/06/2013, from: www.facebook.com/photo.php?fbid=491611001259&set=a.1 14530826259.107996.22942151259&type=1.

Cutler, Paris (2011) 'Project Opera House Cake Day 1 Planet Cake'. *Planet Cake TV (YouTube Channel)*. Retrieved: 26/06/2013, from: www.youtube.com/watch?v=3t5Jwdbx6vI.

Cutler, Paris (2011) 'Project Opera House Cake Day 1 to 8 (Series of 10 Videos)'. *Planet Cake TV (YouTube Channel)*. Retrieved: 27/06/2013, from: www.youtube.com/user/ PlanetCakeTV.

Cutler, Paris (2011) 'Project Opera House Cake Day 2 Planet Cake'. *Planet Cake TV (YouTube Channel)*. Retrieved: 27/06/2013, from: www.youtube.com/watch?v=23ILAflXrEI.

Cutler, Paris (2011) 'Project Opera House Cake Day 3 Planet Cake'. *Planet Cake TV (YouTube Channel)*. Retrieved: 27/06/2013, from: www.youtube.com/watch?v=3PGZDV2KC7o.

Cutler, Paris (2011) 'Project Opera House Cake Day 4 Planet Cake'. *Planet Cake TV (YouTube Channel)*. Retrieved: 26/06/2013, from: www.youtube.com/watch?v=hBxJrJy9UAc.

Cutler, Paris (2011) 'Project Opera House Cake Day 5 Planet Cake'. *Planet Cake TV (YouTube Channel)*. Retrieved: 27/06/2013, from: www.youtube.com/watch?v=LypQQyp6aFE.

Cutler, Paris (2011) 'Project Opera House Cake Day 6 Planet Cake'. *Planet Cake TV (YouTube Channel)*. Retrieved: 27/06/2013, from: www.youtube.com/watch?v=kozkMCSKQYY.

Cutler, Paris (2011) 'Project Opera House Cake Day 8 Part 1 Planet Cake'. *Planet Cake TV (YouTube Channel)*. Retrieved: 27/06/2013, from: www.youtube.com/watch?v=DQ7u2AYfBPI.

Cutler, Paris (2011) 'This Cake Really Might Just Work!' In *Planet Cake Update*. Retrieved: 26/06/2013, from: http://planetcakeupdate.blogspot.com.au/2011/01/this-cake-really-just-might-actually.html.

'Dane's Controversial Design Wins Opera House Contest' (1957) *Sydney Morning Herald*, 30 January, front page.

Danet, Brenda, and Tamar Katriel (1994) 'No Two Alike: Play and Aesthetics in Collecting'. In *Interpreting Objects and Collections*. Edited by Susan M. Pearce. London: Routledge, pp. 253–277.

Darvill, Timothy (1995) 'Value Systems in Archaeology'. In *Managing Archaeology*. Edited by Malcolm A. Cooper, John Carman, Anthony Firth and David Wheatley. London: Taylor & Francis, pp. 40–50.

de Groot, Jerome (2010) 'Historiography and Virtuality'. In *Culture, Heritage and Representation*. Edited by Emma Waterton and Steve Watson. Surrey: Ashgate, pp. 91–104.

de Vries, Brian, and Pamela Roberts (2004) 'Introduction'. *Omega: Journal of Death and Dying*, 49 (1), pp. 1–3. doi: 10.2190/XR23-NDBN-UUM8-FALQ.

de Vries, Brian, and Pamela Roberts (2004) 'The Living and the Dead: Community in the Virtual Cemetery'. *Omega: Journal of Death and Dying*, 49 (1), pp. 57–76. doi: 10.2190/D41T-YFNN-109K-WR4C.

Delwiche, Aaron, and Jennifer Jacobs Henderson (2012) *The Participatory Cultures Handbook*. New York: Routledge.

Delwiche, Aaron, and Jennifer Jacobs Henderson (2013) *The Participatory Cultures Handbook*. New York: Routledge.

Di Giovine, Michael A. (2009) *The Heritage-Scape: UNESCO, World Heritage, and Tourism*. Lanham: Lexington Books.

Doust, Sam (2012) 'Bennelong Point: Indigenous Heritage'. *The Opera House Project, the Story of an Australian Icon* [Online Multimedia Documentary]. ABC Innovation and Sydney Opera House Trust. Retrieved: 27/11/2012, from: http://theoperahouseproject.com/ - !/bennelong-point.

Dovey, Kim (2009) *Becoming Places: Urbanism/Architecture/Identity/Power*. London: Routledge.

Drew, Philip (1972) *Third Generation: The Changing Meaning of Architecture*. London: Pall Mall Press.

Drew, Philip (1995) *Sydney Opera House: Jorn Utzon*. London: Phaidon Press.

Drew, Philip (2001) *The Masterpiece: A Secret Life*. 2nd edn. South Yarra: Hardie Grant Books.

Drew, Philip (2007) 'Romanticism Revisited: Jørn Utzon's Sydney Opera House'. *Architectural Theory Review*, 12 (2), pp. 121–145. doi: 10.1080/13264820701730868.

Drew, Philip (2008) 'Opera House Is Utzon's Legacy'. *The Australian*, 1 December. Retrieved: 27/02/2014, from: www.theaustralian.com.au/arts/opera-house-is-utzons-legacy/story-e6frg8n6-1111118184942.

Drexler, Arthur, and Wilder Green (1959) *Architecture and Imagery – Four New Buildings* [Exhibition Catalogue]. New York: MOMA.

Drexler, Arthur, and Wilder Green (1959) 'Architecture and Imagery – Four New Buildings'. *Museum of Modern Art* [Press Release]. MOMA, 10 February. Retrieved: 27/11/2012, from: www.moma.org/docs/press_archives/2448/releases/MOMA_1959_0014.pdf?2010.

Duek-Cohen, Elias (1967) *Utzon and the Sydney Opera House: Statement in the Public Interest*. Sydney: Morgan Pubs.

Duek-Cohen, Elias, and Philip Drew (1998 [1967]) *Utzon and the Sydney Opera House: Statement in the Public Interest (with Additional Text by Philip Drew)*. Sydney: Morgan Pubs.

Dunster, David (1996) *Arups on Engineering*. London: Ernst & Sohn.

Edsberg, Annika (2009) *Utzon Memorial Website* [Tribute to Jørn Utzon]. Sydney Opera House. Retrieved: 12/03/2013, from: http://jornutzon.sydneyoperahouse.com/Tributes.aspx.

Evans, Robin (1997) *Translations from Drawing to Building and Other Essays*. London: Architectural Association.

Faber, Tobias, Dennis Sharp and Christian Norberg-Schulz (1991) 'Jørn Utzon: Special Issue'. *World Architecture*, 15, pp. 32–35.

Fach, Melissa (2012) 'The Content Omniverse'. *Search Engine Journal*, 10 August. Retrieved: 25/11/2012, from: www.searchenginejournal.com/the-content-omniverse-infographic/47182/.

Fairchild Ruggles, D., and Helaine Silverman (2009) *Intangible Heritage Embodied*. London: Springer.

Farrelly, Elizabeth (2008) 'Obituary: High Noon at Bennelong Point'. *Sydney Morning Herald*, 1 December. Retrieved: 29/11/2012, from: www.smh.com.au/news/national/high-noon-at-bennelong-point/2008/11/30/1227979845045.html?page=fullpage.

Farrelly, Elizabeth (2010) 'Reviewing the Performance'. *Sydney Morning Herald*, 11 June. Retrieved: 18/05/2011, from: www.smh.com.au/entertainment/books/reviewing-the-performance-20100611-y2oi.html.

Farrelly, Elizabeth (2014) 'Frank Gehry's UTS Building Is No Opera House'. *Sydney Morning Herald*, 13 January. Retrieved: 06/01/2016, from: www.smh.com.au/comment/frank-gehrys-uts-building-is-no-opera-house-20140709-zt144.html - ixzz3wRZaPioR.

Feinberg, Jonathan (2013) 'Wordle'. Retrieved from: www.wordle.net/.

Ferguson, Simon (2007) 'Opera House Has Heritage'. *Daily Telegraph*, 28 June, p. 15.

Fincham, Chris (2011) 'Opera Sails into Sydney'. Retrieved: 26/03/2013, from: www.caravan campingsales.com.au/news/2011/camping-trailers/opera-sails-into-sydney-26553.

Fiske, John (1989) *Understanding Popular Culture*. Boston: Unwin Hyman.

Flickr (2012) 'Explore'. Retrieved: 17/07/2012, from: www.flickr.com/explore/.

Flickr (2012) 'Welcome to Flickr'. Retrieved: 17/07/2012, from: www.flickr.com/.

'Flickr Group: Sydney Opera House' (2006–2013) *Flickr*. Retrieved: 27/02/2013, from: www.flickr.com/groups/sydneyoperahouse/.

'Flickr Group: Sydney-Alt' (2006–2012) *Flickr* [Photosharing Group]. Retrieved: 27/02/2013, from: www.flickr.com/groups/33606562@N00/.

Foucault, Michel (2003 [1966]) *The Order of Things: An Archaeology of the Human Sciences*. London: Routledge.

Fowler, Bridget, and Fiona Wilson (2004) 'Women Architects and Their Discontents'. *Sociology*, 38 (1), pp. 101–109. doi: 10.1177/0038038504039363.

Frampton, Kenneth (2003) 'Jørn Utzon 2003 Laureate Essay: The Architecture of Jørn Utzon'. *Pritzker Prize Website*. Retrieved: 02/03/2014, from: www.pritzkerprize.com/sites/default/files/file_fields/field_files_inline/2003_essay.pdf.

Frampton, Kenneth, and John Cava (1995) *Studies in Tectonic Culture: The Poetics of Construction in Nineteenth and Twentieth Century Architecture*. Cambridge, MA: The MIT Press.

Francioni, Francesco (2008) 'The 1972 World Heritage Convention: An Introduction'. In *The 1972 World Heritage Convention: A Commentary*. Edited by Francesco Francioni and Federico Lenzerini. Oxford: Oxford University Press, pp. 3–7.

Game, Ann (1991) *Undoing the Social: Towards a Deconstructive Sociology*. Milton Keynes and Toronto: Open University Press and University of Toronto Press.

Gauntlett, David (2007) *Creative Explorations: New Approaches to Identities and Audiences*. London: Routledge.

Gauntlett, David (2011). *Making Is Connecting: The Social Meaning of Creativity, from Diy and Knitting to Youtube and Web 2.0*. Cambridge: Polity Press.

Gauntlett, David, and Peter Holzwarth (2006) 'Creative and Visual Methods for Exploring Identities'. *Visual Studies*, 21 (1), pp. 82–91. doi: 10.1080/14725860600613261.

Georgiades, Theodore Peter (1993) *Utzon's Unseen Work: A Search to Discover the Design Intentions of Jørn Utzon for the Interior Auditoria of the Sydney Opera House*. Unpublished Bachelor of Architecture thesis, School of Architecture, University of Technology, Sydney.

Giaccardi, Elisa (ed.) (2012) *Heritage and Social Media: Understanding Heritage in a Participatory Culture*. Edited by Elisa Giaccardi. London: Routledge.

Giaccardi, Elisa (2012) 'Introduction: Reframing Heritage in a Participatory Culture'. In *Heritage and Social Media: Understanding Heritage in a Participatory Culture*. Edited by Elisa Giaccardi. London: Routledge, pp. 1–10.

Giaccardi, Elisa, and Ole Sejer Iversen (2010) 'Workshop: Heritage Enquiries a Designerly Approach to Human Values'. Presented at the *Designing Interactive Systems*, Aarhus, Denmark, 16–20 August. Retrieved: 24/09/2012, from: www.dis2010.org/index.php?Workshops+at+DIS+2010.

Giedion, Sigfried (1965) 'Jørn Utzon and the Third Generation: Three Works by Jørn Utzon – a New Chapter of Space Time and Architecture'. *Zodiac*, 14, pp. 36–47.

Gilbert, Jack (2009) 'Dsc_0184' [Digital Photograph]. Retrieved from: www.flickr.com/photos/jack89/3213184608/.

Giles (2005) 'Internet Encyclopaedias Go Head to Head'. *Nature*, 438 (15 December), pp. 900–901.

Gilling, Ronald A. (2002) 'Utzon, the Institute and the Sydney Opera House: A Narrative of How the Resignation Affected the Profession and the Part Played by the Royal Australian Institute of Architects, 2002'. Mitchell Library. Retrieved: 26/04/2013, from: http://acms.sl.nsw.gov.au/item/itemDetailPaged.aspx?itemID=441836.

Gitelman, Lisa (2006) *Always Already New: Media, History, and the Data of Culture.* Cambridge, MA: The MIT Press.

Goad, Philip (1997) 'An Appeal for Modernism: Sigfried Giedion and the Sydney Opera House'. *Fabrications*, 8, pp. 129–145.

Goad, Philip (2003) 'Jørn Utzon: Pritzker Architecture Prize Laureate 2003'. *Architecture Australia*, 92 (3), pp. 27–28.

Goad, Philip (2005) 'Unpublished Written Statement Commissioned for the World Heritage Nomination for Sydney Opera House'.

Gombrich, Ernst Hans (1972). *Symbolic Images*. London: Phaidon.

'Google Images Search Using the Terms Sydney, Opera and House' (2012) [Screenshot]. Google Images. Retrieved from: http://images.google.com.au/search?num=10&hl=en&safe=active&site=&tbm=isch&source=hp&biw=1881&bih=922&q=sydney+opera+house&oq=sydney+opera+house&gs_l=img.3..0l10.2856.5019.0.5152.18.9.0.6.6.0.246.1021.0j2j3.5.0...0.0...1ac.1.jZ45caN9ooc.

Gordon, Beverly (1986) 'The Souvenir: Messenger of the Extraordinary'. *The Journal of Popular Culture*, 20 (3), pp. 135–146. doi: 10.1111/j.0022-3840.1986.2003_135.x.

Graham, Brian, and Peter Howard (2008) *The Ashgate Research Companion to Heritage and Identity*. Hampshire: Ashgate.

Hale, Patricia, and Susan Macdonald (2005) 'The Sydney Opera House, an Evolving Icon'. *Journal of Architectural Conservation*, 11 (2), pp. 7–21.

Hall, Michael C. (2006) 'Implementing the World Heritage Convention: What Happens after Listing?' In *Managing World Heritage Sites*. Oxford: Butterworth-Heinemann, pp. 20–34.

Hall, Stuart (1973) *Encoding and Decoding in the Television Discourse*. Birmingham: Centre for Contemporary Cultural Studies.

Hall, Stuart (1997) *Representation: Cultural Representations and Signifying Practices*. London: Sage, in association with The Open University.

Hall, Stuart (2007 [1999]) 'Whose Heritage? Un-Settling "the Heritage", Re-Imagining the Post-Nation'. In *Cultural Heritage: Critical Concepts in Media and Cultural Studies*. Edited by Laurajane Smith. Vol. 2. London: Routledge, pp. 87–100.

Halliwell, Michael (2004) 'A Comfortable Society: The 1950s and Opera in Australia'. *Australasian Drama Studies*, 45, pp. 10–29.

Harvey, David C. (2007 [2001]) 'Heritage Pasts and Heritage Presents: Temporality, Meaning and the Scope of Heritage Studies'. In *Cultural Heritage: Critical Concepts in Media and Cultural Studies*. Edited by Laurajane Smith. Vol. 1. London: Routledge, pp. 25–44.

Harvey, David C. (2008) 'The History of Heritage'. In *The Ashgate Research Companion to Heritage and Identity*. Edited by Brian Graham and Peter Howard. Hampshire: Ashgate, pp. 19–36.

Hayden, Dolores (1997) *The Power of Place: Urban Landscapes as Public History*. London: The MIT Press.

'Headlines: New South Wales' (1996) *Architecture Australia*, 85 (6), p. 20. May/June. Retrieved: 24/11/2012, from: www.architecturemedia.com/aa/aaissue.php?issueid=199605&article=3&typeon=1&highlight=headlines.

Helmer-Petersen, Keld, and Jørn Utzon (1959) 'A New Personality: Jørn Utzon'. *Zodiac*, 5, pp. 70–105.

Hennessy, Kate (2012) 'From Intangible Expression to Digital Cultural Heritage'. In *Safeguarding Intangible Cultural Heritage*. Edited by Michelle L. Stefano, Peter Davis and Gerard Corsane. Woodbridge: The Boydell Press, pp. 33–46.

Herman, Morton (1955) 'Interpret Own Age: Plea to Architects'. *Sydney Morning Herald*, 5 July, p. 11.

Heynen, Hilde (2012) 'Genius Gender and Architecture: The Star System as Exemplified in the Pritzker Prize'. *Architectural Theory Review*, 17 (2–3), pp. 331–345.

Hinkson, Melinda (2002) 'Exploring "Aboriginal" Sites in Sydney: A Shifting Politics of Place?' *Aboriginal History*, 26, pp. 62–77.

Hobsbawm, Eric J. (1983) 'Mass-Producing Traditions: Europe, 1870–1914'. In *The Invention of Tradition*. Edited by Eric J. Hobsbawm and Terence O. Ranger. Cambridge: Cambridge University Press, pp. 279–280.

Hodder, Ian (1985) 'Postprocessual Archaeology'. *Advances in Archaeological Method and Theory*, 8, pp. 1–26.

Holgate, Alan (1986) *The Art in Structural Design*. New York: Oxford University Press.

Hubble, Ava (1983) *The Sydney Opera House: More Than Meets the Eye*. Sydney: Lansdown Press.

Hubble, Ava (1988) *The Strange Case of Eugene Goossens and Other Tales from the Opera House*. Sydney: Collins.

Hubert, Christian (1981) 'The Ruins of Representation'. In *Idea as Model*. Edited by Kenneth Frampton and Silvia Kolbowski. New York: Rizzoli.

Humble, Nicola (2010) *Cake: A Global History*. Edited by Andrew F. Smith. London: Reaktion Books.

Humphries, Barry, and Lorraine McKee (1976) 'Theatre Costume for Dame Edna Everage' [Hat]. Victoria and Albert Museum. Retrieved: 26/03/2013, from: http://collections.vam. ac.uk/item/O100914/theatre-costume-humphries-barry/.

Hutchings, Tim (2012) 'Wiring Death: Dying Grieving and Remembering on the Internet'. In *Emotion, Identity and Death: Mortality across the Disciplines*. Edited by Douglas J. Davies and Chang-Wok Park. Surrey: Ashgate, pp. 43–58.

ICCROM (2013) 'International Centre for the Study of the Preservation and Restoration of Cultural Property (ICCROM)'. Retrieved: 25/04/2013, from: www.iccrom.org/.

ICOMOS (1964) *Venice Charter*. Retrieved: 31/12/2015, from: www.icomos.org/charters/ venice_e.pdf.

ICOMOS (1994) *Nara Document on Authenticity*. Retrieved: 26/04/2013, from: www.icomos. org/charters/nara-e.pdf.

ICOMOS (2011) 'International Council on Monuments and Sites (ICOMOS)'. Retrieved: 26/06/2012, from: www.icomos.org/en/.

ICOMOS (2012) 'Homepage'. *International Committee on Intangible Cultural Heritage (ICICH)*. Retrieved: 22/07/2012, from: http://icich.icomos.org/index.html.

ICOMOS Australia (1984) *Guidelines to the Burra Charter: Cultural Significance.*

ICOMOS Australia (1999). *The Burra Charter: The Australia ICOMOS Charter for Places of Cultural Significance 1999*. Retrieved: 31/12/2015, from: http://australia.icomos.org/ publications/burra-charter-practice-notes/burra-charter-archival-documents/.

ICOMOS Australia (2013). *The Burra Charter: The Australia ICOMOS Charter for Places of Cultural Significance 2013*. Retrieved: 31/12/2015, from: http://australia.icomos.org/ publications/charters/.

'Icon, N.' (1993) *The New Shorter Oxford English Dictionary*. Edited by Leslie Brown. Vol. 2. Oxford: Clarendon Press, p. 1302.

'Information for "Sydney Opera House"' (2016) *Wikipedia*. Retrieved: 02/10/2012, from: https:// en.wikipedia.org/w/index.php?title=Sydney_Opera_House&action=info-mw-pageinfo-watchers.

IUCN (2002) *Australian Natural Heritage Charter*. Retrieved: 31/12/2015, from: www. environment.gov.au/system/files/resources/56de3d0a-7301-47e2-8c7c-9e064627a1ae/files/ australian-natural-heritage-charter.pdf.

IUCN (2013) 'International Union for Conservation of Nature and Natural Resources (IUCN)'. Retrieved: 24/04/2013, from: www.iucn.org/.

Jackson, Anthony, and Jenny Kidd (2011) *Performing Heritage: Research, Practice and Innovation in Museum Theatre and Live Interpretation*. Manchester: Manchester University Press.

Jackson, Davina (2008) 'Joern Oberg Utzon Dies Aged 90'. *The Australian*, 1 December. Retrieved: 27/02/2014, from: www.theaustralian.com.au/arts/naive-perfectionist/story-e6frg8n6-1111118183743.

Jencks, Charles (1973) *Modern Movements in Architecture*. Garden City: Anchor Press.

Jencks, Charles (1977) *The Language of Post-Modern Architecture*. New York: Rizzoli.

Jencks, Charles (1981) 'Introduction'. In *The Language of Post-Modern Architecture*. New York: Rizzoli.

Jencks, Charles (1984) *The Language of Post-Modern Architecture*. 4th edn. London: Academy Editions.

Jencks, Charles (2005). *The Iconic Building*. New York: Rizzoli.

Jenkins, Henry (1988) '*Star Trek* Reread, Rerun, Rewritten: Fan Writing as Textual Poaching'. *Critical Studies in Mass Communications*, 5 (2), pp. 85–107. doi: 10.1080/1529 5038809366691.

Jenkins, Henry (2006) *Convergence Culture: Where Old and New Media Collide*. New York: New York University Press.

Jenkins, Henry (2006). *Fans, Bloggers, and Gamers: Exploring Participatory Culture*. New York: New York University Press.

Jenkins, Henry, and David Thorburn (2004) *Democracy and New Media*. Cambridge, MA: The MIT Press.

Jenkins, Paul, and Lesley Forsyth (eds) (2010) *Architecture, Participation and Society*. New York: Routledge.

John, Alan, and Dennis Watkins (1995) 'The Eighth Wonder' [Opera – Libretto and Score]. Australian Opera.

Johnston, Chris (1992) *What Is Social Value? A Discussion Paper*. Canberra: Australian Government Publishing Service.

Johnston, Chris (1992) 'Whose Views Count? Achieving Community Support for Landscape Conservation'. *Historic Environment*, 7 (2), pp. 33–37.

Johnston, Chris (1996). 'Corner Shops and Well-Trodden Ways'. In *Assessing Social Values: Communities and Experts – a Workshop Held by Australia ICOMOS*. Canberra: Australian Heritage Commission, pp. 8–11.

Johnston, Chris (2006) *An Integrated Approach to Environment and Heritage Issues*. 2006 Australia State of the Environment Committee. Retrieved: 31/12/2015, from: www.environment.gov.au/system/files/pages/38cc94e0-6c03-41b2-af5d-c73a8268e6c9/files/heritage.pdf.

Johnston, Chris (2012) 'Swimming Upstream, with Crocodiles: Social Value and the Prevailing Heritage Discourse'. Presented at the *ACT and Region Annual Australian Heritage Partnership Symposium. Valuing Heritage: Advocating for Community Attachment in Planning*, Canberra, 28 July.

Johnston, Chris, and Annie Clarke (2001) *Taking Action: Involving People in Local Heritage Places Part of the Heritage and Community: Theory and Practice Project*. Australian National University, Environment Australia, Context Pty Ltd. Retrieved: 26/04/2013, from: http://contextpl.com.au/static/pdf/taking_action_guide.pdf.

Johnston, Chris, Lorraine Cairnes and Kathy Eyles (2006) *An Integrated Approach to Environment and Heritage Issues*. Retrieved: 26/11/2012, from: http://laptop.deh.gov.au/soe/2006/publications/integrative/heritage/pubs/heritage.pdf.

Johnston, Chris, Libby Riches, Ann McGregor and Kristal Buckley (2003) *Inspirational Landscapes*. Canberra: Australian Heritage Commission.

Johnston, Chris, Libby Riches, Ann McGregor and Kristal Buckley (2003) 'Inspirational Landscapes. Volume 3: Overview of the on-Line Conference Inspirational Landscape – Heritage Places? (6 – 7 Nov 02)'. Canberra: Australian Heritage Commission.

Johnston, Chris, Libby Riches, Ann McGregor and Kristal Buckley (2003) 'Inspirational Landscapes. Volume 4: Assessment Method Report'. Canberra, ACT: Australian Heritage Commission.

Jokilehto, Jukka (1986). *A History of Architectural Conservation: The Contribution of English, French, German and Italian Thought Towards an International Approach to the Conservation of Property*. Unpublished PhD thesis, Institute of Advanced Architectural Studies, University of York.

Jokilehto, Jukka (1998) 'International Trends in Historic Preservation: From Ancient Monuments to Living Cultures'. *APT Bulletin, Historic Structure Reports (1997)*, 29 (3/4), pp. 17–19.

Jokilehto, Jukka (2002) 'Great Sites of Modern Architecture'. *World Heritage*, 25, pp. 4–21.

Jokilehto, Jukka (2005 [1999]) *A History of Architectural Conservation*. Oxford: Elsevier Butterworth-Heinemann.

Jokilehto, Jukka (2008) *The World Heritage List: What Is Ouv? Defining the Outstanding Universal Value of Cultural World Heritage Properties*. Paris: ICOMOS.

Jones, Paul R. (2006) *The Sociology of Architecture: Constructing Identities*. Liverpool: Liverpool University Press.

Jones, Peter (2006) *Ove Arup: Masterbuilder of the Twentieth Century*. New Haven: Yale University Press.

Jones, Peter Blundell, Doina Petrescu and Jeremy Till (eds) (2005) *Architecture and Participation*. New York: Taylor & Francis.

Jones-Garmil, Katherine (1997) *The Wired Museum*. Washington, DC: American Association of Museums.

'Jørn Utzon Tributes (Official)' (2008) *Sydney Opera House: Jorn Utzon*. Retrieved: 27/04/2013, from: http://jornutzon.sydneyoperahouse.com/Tributes.aspx?m=official.

Kaji-O'Grady, Sandra (2006) 'Melbourne Versus Sydney'. *Architectural Theory Review*, 11 (1), pp. 60–72. doi: 10.1080/13264820609478556.

Kalay, Yehuda, Thomas Kvan and Janice Affleck (2008) *New Heritage: New Media and Cultural Heritage*. New York: Routledge.

Keating, Paul (2011) 'Building a Masterpiece: The Sydney Opera House. Sydney 10 August 2006'. In *After Words: The Post-Prime Ministerial Speeches*. Crows Nest: Allen & Unwin, pp. 3–9.

Keen, Andrew (2007) *The Cult of the Amateur: How Today's Internet Is Killing Our Culture*. 1st edn. New York: Doubleday.

Kharbanda, Om Prakash, and Jeffrey K. Pinto (1996) *What Made Gertie Gallop? Lessons from Project Failures*. New York: Van Nostrand Reinhold.

Kirshenblatt-Gimblett, Barbara (2004) 'Intangible Heritage as Metacultural Production'. *Museum International*, 56 (221–222), pp. 56–65. doi: 10.1111/j.1350-0775.2004.00458.x.

Klingmann, Anna (2007) *Brandscapes*. Cambridge, MA: The MIT Press.

Kremerskothen, Kay (2011) '6,000,000,000'. *Flickr Blog*, 4 August. Retrieved: 17/07/2012, from: http://blog.flickr.net/en/2011/08/04/6000000000/.

Labadi, Sophia (2007) 'Representations of the Nation and Cultural Diversity in Discourses on World Heritage'. *Journal of Social Archaeology*, 7 (2), pp. 147–170. doi: 10.1177/1469605307077466.

Labadi, Sophia, and Colin Long (eds) (2010) *Heritage and Globalisation*. Edited by William Logan and Laurajane Smith. London: Routledge.

Lacy, Bill N. (2003) 'Jorn Utzon 2003 Laureate: Jury Citation'. *The Pritzker Architecture Prize*. Retrieved: 27/04/2013, from: www.pritzkerprize.com/2003/jury.

Lambeth, Joseph A. (1980 [1934]) *Lambeth Method of Cake Decoration and Practical Pastries*. California: Continental Publications.

Landorf, Chris (2011) 'Evaluating Social Sustainability in Historic Urban Environments'. *International Journal of Heritage Studies*, 17 (5), pp. 463–477. doi: 10.1080/13527258. 2011.563788.

Landorf, Chris (2011) 'Measuring the Social Value of Heritage: A Framework Based on the Evaluation of Sustainable Development'. Presented at the *Audience: Proceedings of the 28th Annual Conference of the Society of Architectural Historians, Australia and New Zealand*, State Library of Queensland, Brisbane, Queensland, Australia, 7–10 July.

Lane, Bernard (2014) 'Iconic Image of Opera House No Longer Public'. *The Australian*, 25 January. Retrieved: 15/07/2016, from: www.theaustralian.com.au/arts/iconic-image-of-opera-house-no-longer-public/story-e6frg8n6-1226810021279.

Larsen, Jonas (2004) *Performing Tourist Photography*. Unpublished PhD thesis, Department of Geography and International Development Studies, Roskilde University, Denmark. Retrieved: 26/0/2013, from: http://rudar.ruc.dk/bitstream/1800/788/1/Performing_tourist_photography.pdf.

Larsen, Jonas (2005) 'Families Seen Sightseeing: Performativity of Tourist Photography'. *Space and Culture*, 8 (4), pp. 416–434. doi: 10.1177/1206331205279354.

Larson, Magali Sarfatti (1994) 'Architectural Competitions as Discursive Events'. *Theory and Society*, 23 (4), pp. 469–504.

Lasansky, D. Medina, and Brian D. McLaren (2004). *Architecture and Tourism: Perception, Performance and Place*. New York: Berg.

'Letters to Editor' (1955) *Sydney Morning Herald*, 6 August, p. 2.

Lewis, Eoghan (2000–2012, ongoing) 'Sydney Architecture Walks: Saw 2 Utzon and the Sydney Opera House' [Guided Walking Tour]. Sydney: Sydney Architecture Walks. Retrieved: 09/10/2012, from: www.sydneyarchitecture.org/pages/saw_TOUR_DESCRIPTIONS_main. html - saw2.

Lewis, Peter (2007) 'Opera House Makes World Heritage List'. *ABC News*, 28 June. Retrieved: 26/06/2012, from: www.abc.net.au/news/2007-06-28/opera-house-makes-world-heritage-list/83814.

Lira, Sérgio, and Rogério Amoêda (2009) *Constructing Intangible Heritage*. Barcelos: Green Lines Institute.

Livingstone, Bruce (2012) 'Homepage'. *iStockphoto*. Retrieved: 30/11/2012, from: www. istockphoto.com/.

Lixinski, Lucas (2008) '"Spaces of Normativity" World Heritage and the Heritage of the World – Book Review; F. Francioni and F. Lenzerini, the 1972 World Heritage Convention: A Commentary' [Book Review]. *European Journal of Legal Studies*, 2 (1), pp. 371–386.

Logan, William (2007) 'Closing Pandora's Box: Human Rights Conundrums in Cultural Heritage Protection'. In *Cultural Heritage and Human Rights*. Edited by D. Fairchild Ruggles and Helaine Silverman. New York: Springer, pp. 33–52.

Loizidou, Elena (2003) 'Publics and Counterpublics, by Michael Warner' [Book Review] *Space and Culture*, 6 (1), pp. 77–78. doi: 10.1177/1206331202238964.

Lomas, Ann (2009) *Utzon Memorial Website* [Tribute to Jørn Utzon]. Sydney Opera House. Retrieved: 12/03/2013, from: http://jornutzon.sydneyoperahouse.com/Tributes.aspx.

Long, Colin, and Sophia Labadi (2010) 'Introduction'. In *Heritage and Globalisation*. Edited by Sophia Labadi and Colin Long. London: Routledge, pp. 1–16.

Love, Lisa, and Nathaniel Kohn (2001) 'This, That, and the Other: Fraught Possibilities of the Souvenir'. *Text and Performance Quarterly*, 21 (1), pp. 47–63. doi: 10.1080/10462930128121.

Love, Lisa L., and Peter S. Sheldon (1998) 'Souvenirs: Messengers of Meaning'. Presented at the *Advances in Consumer Research*, Provo UT. Retrieved: 26/04/2013, from: www.acrwebsite. org/volumes/display.asp?id=8149.

Lowenthal, David (1998) *The Heritage Crusade and the Spoils of History*. Cambridge: Cambridge University Press.

Lusenet, Yola de (2007) 'Tending the Garden or Harvesting the Fields: Digital Preservation and the UNESCO Charter on the Preservation of the Digital Heritage'. *Library Trends*, 56 (1), pp. 164–182.

MacCannell, Dean (1999) *The Tourist: A New Theory of the Leisure Class*. Berkeley: University of California Press.

Macdonald, Susan (2009) 'Materiality, Monumentality and Modernism: Continuing Challenges in Conserving Twentieth-Century Places'. Presented at the *(Un)Loved Modern: Conservation of 20th Century Heritage Conference*, Sydney, NSW, 7–10 July 2009.

Made by Makers (2010) 'Reframing – Three Days 20 Ideas'. Retrieved: 26/03/2013, from: www.madebymakers.dk/content/reframing-three-days-20-ideas.

Malouf, David (2009) 'How an Angel at Bennelong Point Gave Sydney Its Spirit'. *Sydney Morning Herald*, 25 March. Retrieved: 29/11/2012, from: www.smh.com.au/opinion/how-an-angel-at-bennelong-point-gave-sydney-its-spirit-20090324-98sa.html.

Malpas, Jeff (2008) 'New Media, Cultural Heritage and the Sense of Place: Mapping the Conceptual Ground'. *International Journal of Heritage Studies*, 14 (3), pp. 197–209. doi: 10.1080/13527250801953652.

'Masterpiece for All Mankind' (2007) *Hobart Mercury*, 29 June, p. 5.

McCarthy, John, and Peter Wright (2004) *Technology as Experience*. Cambridge, MA: The MIT Press.

McCarthy, Steve (2009) *Utzon Memorial Website* [Tribute to Jørn Utzon]. Sydney Opera House. Retrieved: 12/03/2013, from: http://jornutzon.sydneyoperahouse.com/Tributes.aspx.

McMichael, Nancy (1990) *Snowdomes*. New York: Abbeville Press.

McNaught, Carmel, and Paul Lam (2010) 'Using Wordle as a Supplementary Research Tool'. *The Qualitative Report*, 15 (3), pp. 630–643.

McQueen, Diane (2009) *Utzon Memorial Website* [Tribute to Jørn Utzon]. Sydney Opera House. Retrieved: 12/03/2013, from: http://jornutzon.sydneyoperahouse.com/Tributes.aspx.

Mikami, Yuzo, and Osamu Murai (2001) *Utzon's Sphere: Sydney Opera House: How It Was Designed and Built*. Tokyo: Shokokusha.

Miles, William S.F. (2002) 'Auschwitz: Museum Interpretation and Darker Tourism'. *Annals of Tourism Research*, 29, pp. 1175–1178.

Miller, Andrew D., and W. Keith Edwards (2007) 'Give and Take: A Study of Consumer Photo-Sharing Culture and Practice'. Presented at the *CHI 2007*, San Jose, CA, 28 April–3 May. Retrieved: 27/04/2013, from: www.cc.gatech.edu/~keith/pubs/chi2007-photosharing.pdf.

Mitchell, William J. Thomas (1986) *Iconology: Image, Text, Ideology*. Chicago: University of Chicago Press.

Molnar, Georges (1957) 'Candela: Authority on Shapes'. *Sydney Morning Herald*, 23 March, p. 11.

Morgan, Joyce (2007) 'Opera House Wins Top Status'. *Sydney Morning Herald*, 28 June. Retrieved: 26/06/2012, from: www.smh.com.au/news/travel/opera-house-wins-top-status/2007/06/28/1182624058781.html.

Morris, Mark (2006) *Models: Architecture and the Miniature*. England: Wiley-Academy.

Morris, William (2007 [1877]) 'Manifesto of the Society for the Protection of Ancient Buildings (Spab)'. In *Cultural Heritage: Critical Concepts in Media and Cultural Studies*. Edited by Laurajane Smith. Vol. 1. London: Routledge, pp. 111–113.

Morton, Peter (1962) 'Hat on the Cover of the Australian Women's Weekly on 25 July' [Hat]. Trove Digitised Newspapers and More, National Library of Australia. Retrieved: 26/12/2013, from: http://trove.nla.gov.au/ndp/del/page/4912887.

Moy, Michael (2008) *Sydney Opera House: Idea to Icon*. Ashgrove: Alpha Orion Press.

Munjeri, Dawson (2004) 'Tangible and Intangible Heritage: From Difference to Convergence'. *Museum International*, 56 (1–2), pp. 12–20. doi: 10.1111/j.1350-0775.2004.00453.x.

Murray, Peter (2004) *The Saga of the Sydney Opera House: The Dramatic Story of the Design and Construction of the Icon of Modern Australia*. New York: Spon Press.

National Library of Australia (2003) *Guidelines for the Preservation of Digital Heritage*. Information Society Division: UNESCO. Retrieved: 18/07/2012, from: http://unesdoc.unesco.org/images/0013/001300/130071e.pdf.

National Library of Australia (2013) 'Picture Australia (Now Trove)'. National Library of Australia. Retrieved: 19/03/2013, from: http://trove.nla.gov.au/general/australian-pictures-in-trove.

Naughton, John (2008) 'How Flickr Developed into a Classic Web 2.0 Success'. *Guardian*, 9 March. Retrieved: 06/09/2012, from: www.guardian.co.uk/media/2008/mar/09/web20.internet.

Negoescu, Radu-Andrei, and Daniel Gatica-Perez (2008) 'Analyzing Flickr Groups'. Presented at the *CIVR'08 – International Conference on Content-Based Image and Video Retrieval*, Niagara Falls, Ontario, Canada, 7–9 July. Retrieved: 29/07/2009, from: www.idiap.ch/~negora/GroupWebPage/res/civr2696-negoescu.pdf.

Niederer, Sabine, and José van Dijck (2010) 'Wisdom of the Crowd or Technicity of Content? Wikipedia as a Sociotechnical System'. *New Media & Society*, 12 (8), pp. 1368–1387. doi: 10.1177/1461444810365297.

Nobis, Philip. 'Unseen Utzon'. *YouTube* [Animation of Original Interiors of the Sydney Opera House as Designed by Jørn Utzon, between July 1965 and February 1966]. Retrieved: 02/07/2012, from: www.youtube.com/watch?v=aU6oQpHfDz8.

Nobis, Philip (1994) *Utzon's Interiors for the Sydney Opera House: The Design Development of the Major and Minor Hall 1958–1966*. Unpublished Bachelor of Architecture thesis, University of Technology, Sydney, Australia.

Nobis, Philip, and John Murphy (1994) 'Unseen Utzon' [Exhibition]. Sydney Opera House and NSW State Library, 1 November.

Nora, Pierre (2007 [1989]) 'Between Memory and History: Les Lieux De Mémoire'. In *Cultural Heritage: Critical Concepts in Media and Cultural Studies*. Edited by Laurajane Smith. Vol. 2. London: Routledge, pp. 289–306.

Norberg-Schulz, Christian (1996) 'The Sydney Opera House: International Comparison, an Evaluation of Its Position in the History of Modern Architecture'. In *Sydney Opera House in Its Harbour Setting, Unpublished World Heritage Nomination by the Government of Australia*. Edited by Government of Australia. Glebe: Historic Houses Trust of NSW for the Commonwealth Department of the Environment, Sport and Territories and NSW Department of Urban Affairs, pp. 161–173.

Norberg-Schulz, Christian (1996 [1976]) 'The Phenomenon of Place'. In *Theorizing a New Agenda for Architecture: An Anthology of Architectural Theory 1965–1995*. Edited by Kate Nesbitt. New York: Princeton Architectural Press, pp. 412–428.

Norberg-Schulz, Christian and Yukio Futagawa (1980) 'Jørn Utzon: Sydney Opera House, Sydney, Australia, 1957–73'. *Global Architecture*, 54, pp. 54–58.

Norberg-Schulz, Christian, Jørn Utzon and Yukio Futagawa (1980) *Sydney Opera House: Sydney, Australia, 1957–73*. Tokyo: A.D.A. Edita.

NSW Government (1955) *An International Competition for a National Opera House at Bennelong Point, Sydney, New South Wales, Australia: Conditions and Program (Brown Book)*. Sydney: Booklet printed by A.H. Pettifer, Government Printer.

NSW Government (2012) 'Archives in Brief 28: A Brief History of the Sydney Opera House'. *NSW Government State Records*. Retrieved: 26/10/2012, from: www.records.nsw.gov.au/state-archives/guides-and-finding-aids/archives-in-brief/archives-in-brief-28.

Nutt, John (2006) 'Constructing a Legacy: Technological Innovation and Achievements'. In *Building a Masterpiece: The Sydney Opera House*. Edited by Anne Watson. Aldershot: Lund Humphries, pp. 104–121.

O'Reilly, Tim (2005) 'What Is Web 2.0: Design Patterns and Business Models for the Next Generation of Software'. Retrieved: 27/09/2007, from: www.oreillynet.com/lpt/a/6228.

'Obituary, N. And Adj.' (1993) In *The New Shorter Oxford English Dictionary*. Edited by Leslie Brown. Vol. 2. Oxford: Clarendon Press, p. 1964.

Olalquiaga, Celeste (1999) *The Artificial Kingdom: A Treasury of the Kitsch Experience*. London: Bloomsbury.

'Opera House Architect Dies at 90' (2008) *ABC News*, 30 November. Retrieved: 29/03/2013, from: www.abc.net.au/news/stories/2008/11/30/2433437.htm.

'Opera House Design Be a Lively Topic' (1957) *Sydney Morning Herald*, 2 February, p. 2.

'Opera House Gets a Standing Ovation' (2007) *Geelong Advertiser*, 29 June, p. 16.

'Opera House Lights to Be Dimmed in Utzon Tribute' (2008) *Sydney Morning Herald*, 30 November. Retrieved: 28/11/2011, from: www.smh.com.au/news/world/opera-house-lights-to-be-dimmed/2008/11/30/1227979817473.html.

'Opera House Like Taj Mahal: Opposition M.L.C.' (1962) *Sydney Morning Herald*, 12 September, p. 16.

'Pagerank' (2012) *Wikipedia*. Retrieved: 03/08/2012, from: http://en.wikipedia.org/wiki/PageRank.

'Pageviews Analysis: Sydney Opera House' (2016) *WikiMedia Tool Labs*. Retrieved: 09/06/2016, from: https://tools.wmflabs.org/pageviews/?project=en.wikipedia.org&platform=all-access&agent=all-agents&range=latest-90&pages=Sydney_Opera_House.

Parliament of New South Wales (1998) *Sydney Opera House World Heritage Listing*. Retrieved: 27/11/2012, from: www.parliament.nsw.gov.au/prod/parlment/hansart.nsf/V3Key/LA19980506030.

Pattchett, Sue (2009) *Utzon Memorial Website* [Tribute to Jørn Utzon]. Sydney Opera House. Retrieved: 12/03/2013, from: http://jornutzon.sydneyoperahouse.com/Tributes.aspx.

Paul (2009) *Utzon Memorial Website* [Tribute to Jørn Utzon]. Sydney Opera House. Retrieved: 12/03/2013, from: http://jornutzon.sydneyoperahouse.com/Tributes.aspx.

Perez, Andy (2009) 'Flickr Member Rxnmontage: Obligatory Opera House Photo' [Digital Photograph]. Retrieved from: www.flickr.com/photos/ifiwerethekingoftheforest/3934591625/.

Piccles, John (2009) *Utzon Memorial Website* [Tribute to Jørn Utzon]. Sydney Opera House. Retrieved: 12/03/2013, from: http://jornutzon.sydneyoperahouse.com/Tributes.aspx.

Pine, B. Joseph II, and James H. Gilmore (1999) *The Experience Economy: Work Is Theatre & Every Business a Stage*. Boston: Harvard Business School Press.

Pissard, Nicolas, and Christopher Prieur (2007) 'Thematic Vs. Social Networks in Web 2.0 Communities: A Case Study on Flickr Groups'. Presented at the *Institut National de Recherche en Informatique et en Automatique (INRIA) HAL-CCSD*. Retrieved: 21/11/2008, from: http://hal.inria.fr/docs/00/17/69/54/PDF/42-algotel-flickr.pdf.

'Poetry or Pastry? Argument on Opera House Plans' (1957) *Sydney Morning Herald*, 30 January, p. 3.

Powerhouse Museum (2012) 'Homepage'. Retrieved: 19/07/2012, from: www.powerhousemuseum.com/.

'Praise for Opera Move' (1955) *Sydney Morning Herald*, 22 May, p. 3.

Proudfoot, Peter (1997) 'Operatic Recitative: Nomination of Sydney Opera House in Its Harbour Setting for Inscription on the World Heritage List by the Government of Australia, 1996'. *Fabrications*, 8, pp. 153–155.

Purcell, Lauren (2006) 'Tuesday 11th November'. In *Little Swagman*. Retrieved from: http://littleswagman.blogspot.com/2006/11/for-frantic-masses.html. No longer publicly available.

Rand, Erica (2005) *The Ellis Island Snow Globe*. Durham, NC: Duke University Press.

Rattenbury, Kester (2002) 'Introduction'. In *This Is Not Architecture: Media Constructions*. Edited by Kester Rattenbury. New York: Routledge, pp. xxi–xxiv.

Rattenbury, Kester (2002) *This Is Not Architecture: Media Constructions*. New York: Routledge.

Rheingold, Howard (2008) 'Using Participatory Media and Public Voice to Encourage Civic Engagement'. In *Civic Life Online: Learning How Digital Media Can Engage Youth*. Edited by W. Lance Bennett. Cambridge, MA: The MIT Press, pp. 97–118.

Rice, Peter (1989) 'A Celebration of the Life and Work of Ove Arup'. *RSA Journal*, pp. 425–437.

Riegl, Alois (2007 [1903]) 'The Modern Cult of Monuments: Its Character and Its Origin'. In *Cultural Heritage: Critical Concepts in Media and Cultural Studies*. Edited by Laurajane Smith. Translated by Kurt W. Foster and Diane Ghirardo in 1982 from German. Vol. 1. London: Routledge, pp. 114–142.

Rimini, Mario Gabriele Roberto (2010) *Iconic Lands: Wilderness as a Reservation Criterion for World Heritage*. Unpublished PhD, Institute of Environmental Studies, University of New South Wales, Sydney.

Rose, Gillian (2007) *Visual Methodologies: An Introduction to the Interpretation of Visual Materials*. 2nd edn. London: Sage.

Rose, Maja, and Tess Lloyd (circa 2010) 'Ss Sail Necklace'. Retrieved: 26/03/2013, from: www.polli.com.au/necklaces/ss-sail-necklace -.UGq8q5hzu4Q.

Ruiz, Steve (2010) 'Susan Giles @ Kavi Gupta' [Blog]. Chicago Art Review. Retrieved: 30/09/2012, from: http://chicagoartreview.com/2010/02/24/susan-giles-kavi-gupta/.

Russell, Jim, and Chris Johnston (2005) 'Community and Cultural Values: The Upper Mersey Valley and the Tasmanian Wilderness World Heritage Area'. *Historic Environment*, 18 (2), pp. 39–42.

Saunders, Alan, Philip Drew, Sylvia Lawson, Dennis Watkins, Anne Watson and Alan John (2006) 'By Design: Writing the House' [Radio Broadcast]. Sydney: ABC Radio National, 3 June. Retrieved: 23/11/2012, from: www.abc.net.au/radionational/programs/bydesign/writing-the-house/3326266.

Seligmann, Ari D. (2008) *Architectural Publicity in the Age of Globalization*. Unpublished PhD thesis, Architecture and Urban Design, University of California Los Angeles.

Sennett, Richard, and Craig Calhoun (eds) (2007) *Practising Culture*. London: Routledge.

Sharp, Denis (2008) 'Jorn Utzon: Award-Winning Architect Who Designed the Sydney Opera House'. *Independent*, 3 December. Retrieved: 27/04/2013, from: www.independent.co.uk/news/obituaries/jorn-utzon-awardwinning-architect-who-designed-the-sydney-opera-house-1048763.html.

Sharp, Dennis (1991) *The Illustrated Dictionary of Architects and Architecture*. London: Headline.

Sharp, Dennis (2005) 'Unpublished Written Statement Commissioned for the World Heritage Nomination for Sydney Opera House'.

ShotsbyGun.com (2005) 'Sydney Opera House'. *Flickr*. Retrieved: 03/08/2012, from: www.flickr.com/photos/gunsydney/176222797/.

SilverSteel3000 (2011) 'Coast Cruise Pov Legoland Ca'. *YouTube* [Video]. Retrieved: 26/03/2013, from: www.youtube.com/watch?feature=player_embedded&v=At7xzRl2k_s.

Sim, James (1983) *The Sydney Opera House*. Sydney: View Productions.

Simes, Ric, John O'Mahony, Frank Farrall, Kate Huggins and David Redhill (2013) *How Do You Value an Icon? The Sydney Opera House: Economic, Cultural and Digital Value*. Edited by Deloitte. Sydney: Deloitte.

Sklair, Leslie (2011) 'Iconic Architecture and Urban, National, and Global Identities'. In *Cities & Sovereignty: Identity Politics in Urban Spaces*. Edited by Diane E. Davis and Nora Libertun De Duren. Bloomington: Indiana University Press, pp. 179–195.

Sklair, Leslie (2017) *The Icon Project: Architecture, Cities, and Capitalist Globalization*. New York: Oxford University Press.

Smith, Laurajane (2006) *Uses of Heritage*. London: Routledge.

Smith, Laurajane (ed.) (2007) *Cultural Heritage: Critical Concepts in Media and Cultural Studies*. 4 vols. London: Routledge.

Smith, Laurajane (2007) 'General Introduction'. In *Cultural Heritage: Critical Concepts in Media and Cultural Studies*. London: Routledge, pp. 1–21.

Smith, Laurajane, and Natsuko Akagawa (2009) *Intangible Heritage*. Edited by William Logan and Laurajane Smith. London: Routledge.

Smith, Michael Pomeroy (1984) *Sydney Opera House: How It Was Built and Why It Is So*. Sydney: Collins.

Smith, Terry (2002) 'The Political Economy of Iconotypes and the Architecture of Destination: Uluru, the Sydney Opera House and the World Trade Center'. *Architectural Theory Review*, 7 (2), pp. 1–43. doi: 10.1080/13264820209478455.

Smith, Terry (2003) 'The Dialectics of Disappearance: Architectural Iconotypes between Clashing Cultures'. *Critical Quarterly*, 45 (1–2), pp. 33–51. doi: 10.1111/1467-8705.00470.

Smith, Terry (2006) *The Architecture of Aftermath*. London: The University of Chicago Press.

Smith, Terry (2008) 'Spectacle Architecture before and after the Aftermath: Situating the Sydney Experience'. In *Architecture between Spectacle and Use*. Edited by Anthony Vidler. Williamstown: Sterling and Francine Clark Art Institute, pp. 3–24.

Spearritt, Peter (1999) *Sydney's Century: A History*. 1st edn. Sydney: UNSW Press.

Spiering, Markus (2012) 'We Want You to Grow Big Things at Flickr (Aka We're Hiring!)'. *Flickr Blog*, 12 June. Retrieved: 17/07/2012, from: http://blog.flickr.net/en/2012/06/06/we-want-you-to-grow-big-things-at-flickr-aka-were-hiring/.

Stead, Naomi, and Cristina Garduño Freeman (2013) 'Architecture and "the Act of Receiving, or the Fact of Being Received": Introduction to a Special Issue on Reception'. *Architectural Theory Review*, 18 (3), pp. 267–271.

Stead, Naomi, and Antony Moulis (2010) 'Sydney's Prometheus: Myth, Shame and Remediation at Joern Utzon's Sydney Opera House'. Presented at the *Imagining: Proceedings of the 27th Annual Conference of the Society of Architectural Historians, Australia and New Zealand (SAHANZ)*, University of Newcastle, Newcastle, New South Wales, Australia, 30 June–2 July.

Stefano, Michelle L., Peter Davis and Gerard Corsane (2012) *Safeguarding Intangible Cultural Heritage*. Woodbridge: The Boydell Press.

Stevens, Garry (2002) *The Favoured Circle: The Social Foundations of Architectural Distinction*. Cambridge, MA: The MIT Press.

Stewart, Susan (1984) *On Longing: Narratives of the Miniature, the Gigantic, the Souvenir, the Collection*. Baltimore: Johns Hopkins University Press.

Sudjic, Deyan (2005) *The Edifice Complex: How the Rich and Powerful Shape the World*. New York: Penguin Press.

Sudjic, Deyan (2008) 'Obituary Jørn Utzon'. *Guardian*, 1 December. Retrieved: 29/11/2012, from: www.guardian.co.uk/artanddesign/2008/dec/01/architecture-denmark-j-oslash-rn-utzon.

'Sydney Opera House' (2013) *Wikipedia*. Retrieved: 26/03/2013, from: http://en.wikipedia.org/wiki/Sydney_Opera_House.

'Sydney Opera House' (2016) *Wikipedia*. Retrieved: 26/03/2013, from: http://en.wikipedia.org/wiki/Sydney_Opera_House.

Sydney Opera House (2008) '2008 Corporate Media Release – Sydney Opera House Pays Tribute to Jørn Utzon'. Retrieved: 01/08/2012, from: www.sydneyoperahouse.com/08CorporateMediaRelease_JornUtzon.aspx.

Sydney Opera House (2011) *Sydney Opera House Annual Report 2010/11: Imagination Lives Inside*. Sydney. Retrieved: 07/06/2012, from: www.sydneyoperahouse.com/uploadedFiles/About_Us_(new_nav)/Sydney_Opera_House/Annual_Report/Annual Report 2011.pdf.

Sydney Opera House (2012) 'Photo Gallery'. Retrieved: 03/08/2012, from: www.sydneyoperahouse.com/about/media/photo_gallery.aspx.

Sydney Opera House (2012) 'Sydney Opera House Current Partners – Corporate Sponsors'. Retrieved: 25/09/2012, from: www.sydneyoperahouse.com/support/currentpartners/corporate_sponsors.aspx.

Sydney Opera House (2012) 'Sydney Opera House: Jørn Utzon'. Retrieved: 11/09/2012, from: http://jornutzon.sydneyoperahouse.com/home.htm.

Sydney Opera House (2013) 'Homepage' [Screenshot]. Retrieved from: www.sydneyoperahouse.com/homepage.aspx.

Sydney Opera House (2013) 'Sydney Opera House as a Member of Facebook'. *Facebook* [Screenshot]. Retrieved from: www.facebook.com/sydneyoperahouse?fref=ts.

Sydney Opera House (2013) 'Sydney Opera House as a Member of Twitter'. *Twitter* [Screenshot]. Retrieved from: https://twitter.com/SydOperaHouse.

Sydney Opera House (2013) 'Sydney Opera House as a Member of Youtube'. *YouTube* [Screenshot]. Retrieved from: www.youtube.com/user/sydneyoperahouse.

Sydney Opera House (2013) 'Sydney Opera House Photo Gallery' [Screenshot]. Retrieved from: www.sydneyoperahouse.com/about/media/photo_gallery.aspx.

Sydney Opera House (2013) 'Sydney Opera House: House History'. Retrieved: 09/10/2012, from: www.sydneyoperahouse.com/about/house_history_landing.aspx.

Sydney Opera House (circa 2007) 'World Heritage Listing' [Website]. Retrieved: 26/11/2012, from: www.sydneyoperahouse.com/the_building/world_heritage.aspx.

Sydney Opera House Trust (2012) 'Memorial Program'. *Sydney Opera House: Jørn Utzon.* Retrieved: 11/09/2012, from: http://jornutzon.sydneyoperahouse.com/memorial.htm.

'Sydneyoperahouse.Biz' (2013) Retrieved: 09/10/2012, from: www.sydneyoperahouse.biz/.

Sykes, Jill (1993) *Sydney Opera House: From the Outside In.* Pymble: Playbill.

Taffs, David (2006) 'Computers and the Opera House: Pioneering a New Technology'. In *Building a Masterpiece: The Sydney Opera House.* Edited by Anne Watson. Aldershot: Lund Humphries, pp. 84–103.

'Talk:Sydney Opera House/Archive 1 (Popular Culture Section)' (2012) *Wikipedia.* Retrieved: 02/10/2012, from: http://en.wikipedia.org/wiki/Talk:Sydney_Opera_House/Archive_1 - Popular_culture_section.

Tapscott, Don, and Anthony D. Williams (2006) *Wikinomics: How Mass Collaboration Changes Everything.* New York: Portfolio.

Taylor, Ken (1999) 'Reconciling Aesthetic Value and Social Value: Dilemmas of Interpretation and Application'. *APT Bulletin, Landscape Preservation Comes of Age*, 30 (1), pp. 51–55.

Teitler, Georges (2009) *Utzon Memorial Website* [Tribute to Jørn Utzon]. Sydney Opera House. Retrieved: 12/03/2013, from: http://jornutzon.sydneyoperahouse.com/Tributes.aspx.

Thake, Eric (1978) *The Christmas Linocuts of Eric Thake, 1941–1975.* South Yarra: Croft Press.

Tilden, Freeman (1977) *Interpreting Our Heritage.* Chapel Hill: University of North Carolina Press.

Tombesi, Paolo (2005) 'Iconic Public Buildings as Sites of Technological Innovation'. *Harvard Design Magazine*, 21, pp. 1–5.

Tombesi, Paolo, and Andrew Martel (2005) 'Vessels of Expression and Flows of Innovation on the Connection between Toilets and Architecture'. *Journal of Architectural Education*, 59 (2), pp. 43–52. doi: 10.1111/j.1531-314X.2005.00015.x.

Totaro, Paola (2008) 'Joern Utzon Dead'. *Sydney Morning Herald*, 30 November. Retrieved: 29/11/2012, from: www.smh.com.au/articles/2008/11/30/1227979814647.html.

'Tribute to Joern Utzon' (circa 2008) *Utzon Centre.* Retrieved: 29/11/2012, from: www.utzon center.dk/en/joern_utzon/tribute_02/tribute.htm.

'Tribute, N.' (1993) In *The New Shorter Oxford English Dictionary.* Edited by Leslie Brown. Vol. 2. Oxford: Clarendon Press, p. 3388.

Truscott, Marilyn (2003) 'Intangible Values as Heritage in Australia'. Presented at the *Proceedings of the International Scientific Symposium Place, Memory, Meaning Preserving Intangible Values in Monuments and Sites*, Victoria Falls, Zimbabwe, 27–31 October. Retrieved: 10/07/2012, from: www.international.icomos.org/victoriafalls2003/truscott_eng.htm.

Tuan, Yi-Fu (1975) 'Place: An Experiential Perspective'. *Geographical Review*, 65 (2), pp. 151–165.

'Two Sydney Groups ...Why?' (2006) *Flickr* [Discussion Thread in Photosharing Group: Sydney, Australia]. 14 January. Removed.

Uehara Henrikson, Jenise (2011) 'The Growth of Social Media: An Infographic'. *Search Engine Journal.* Retrieved: 27/04/2013, from: www.searchenginejournal.com/the-growth-of-social-media-an-infographic/32788/ - 5TbsKmFDH811DJ69.99.

UNESCO. 'Global Strategy'. *World Heritage Centre* [Website]. Retrieved: 27/04/2013, from: http://whc.unesco.org/en/globalstrategy.

UNESCO. 'The Operational Guidelines for the Implementation of the World Heritage Convention'. *World Heritage Centre* [Website]. Retrieved: 26/11/2012, from: http://whc. unesco.org/en/guidelines.

UNESCO. 'State Parties: Ratification Status'. *World Heritage Centre* [Website]. Retrieved: 31/12/2015, from: http://whc.unesco.org/en/statesparties/.

UNESCO. 'UNESCO: Culture'. *World Heritage Centre* [Website]. Retrieved: 26/06/2012, from: www.unesco.org/new/en/culture.

UNESCO (1972) *Convention Concerning the Protection of the World Cultural and Natural Heritage.* Retrieved: 26/11/2012, from: http://whc.unesco.org/archive/convention-en.pdf.

UNESCO (1981) 'Bureau of the World Heritage Committee, Fifth Session, Paris, 4–7 May 1981: Report of the Rapporteur'. *World Heritage Centre.* Retrieved: 27/11/2012, from: http://whc.unesco.org/archive/1981/cc-81-conf002-4e.pdf.

UNESCO (1983) 'Taj Mahal'. *World Heritage Centre.* Retrieved: 18/07/2012, from: http://whc.unesco.org/en/list/252/.

UNESCO (1984) 'Statue of Liberty'. *World Heritage Centre.* Retrieved: 31/03/2013, from: http://whc.unesco.org/en/list/307.

UNESCO (1987) 'Piazza Del Duomo, Pisa'. *World Heritage Centre.* Retrieved: 31/03/2013, from: http://whc.unesco.org/en/list/395.

UNESCO (1989) *Recommendation on the Safeguarding of Traditional Culture and Folklore,* 25th Session: The General Conference of the United Nations Educational, Scientific and Cultural Organization, UNESCO, Paris. Retrieved: 11/04/2011, from: http://portal.unesco.org/en/ev.php-URL_ID=13141&URL_DO=DO_TOPIC&URL_SECTION=201.html.

UNESCO (1991) 'Banks of the River Seine'. *World Heritage Centre.* Retrieved: 18/07/2012, from: http://whc.unesco.org/en/list/600/.

UNESCO (2001). *Information Document: Analysis of the Application of Cultural Criterion (Vi).* Retrieved: 27/04/2013, from: http://whc.unesco.org/uploads/events/documents/event-827-9.pdf.

UNESCO (2001) *Proclamation of the Masterpieces of the Oral and Intangible Heritage of Humanity (2001–2005).* Retrieved: 30/03/2013, from: www.unesco.org/culture/ich/index.php?lg=en&pg=00103.

UNESCO (2003) *Charter on the Preservation of the Digital Heritage.* Retrieved: 11/04/2011, from: http://portal.unesco.org/en/ev.php-URL_ID=17721&URL_DO=DO_TOPIC&URL_SECTION=201.html.

UNESCO (2003) *Convention for the Safeguarding of the Intangible Cultural Heritage,* 32nd Session: The General Conference of the United Nations Educational, Scientific and Cultural Organization. Paris. Retrieved: 29/11/2010, from: www.unesco.org/culture/ich/index.php?lg=en&pg=00022.

UNESCO (2003) *Identification and Documentation of Modern Heritage: World Heritage Papers 5,* World Heritage Centre. Retrieved: 11/04/2012, from: www.whitr-ap.org/themes/69/userfiles/download/2012/3/5/f8psqtlnnavqjro.pdf.

UNESCO (2007) 'Sydney Opera House'. *World Heritage Centre.* Retrieved: 26/06/2012, from: http://whc.unesco.org/en/list/166rev.

UNESCO (2007) 'Sydney Opera House (Australia) No 166 Rev: Advisory Body Evaluation'. *World Heritage Centre.* Retrieved: 27/04/2013, from: http://whc.unesco.org/archive/advisory_body_evaluation/166rev.pdf.

UNESCO (2007) 'Twenty-Two New Sites Inscribed on Unesco's World Heritage List, and One Deleted During Committee Meeting in Christchurch'. *World Heritage Centre.* Retrieved: 26/06/2012, from: http://whc.unesco.org/en/news/365.

UNESCO (2011) 'Member States'. *UNESCO* [Website]. Retrieved: 31/12/2015, from: http://en.unesco.org/countries/member-states.

UNESCO (2011). *Preparing World Heritage Nominations (Second Edition).* World Heritage Centre. Retrieved: 27/04/2013, from: http://whc.unesco.org/uploads/activities/documents/activity-643-1.pdf.

UNESCO (2012) 'Intangible Heritage Lists'. *Intangible Cultural Heritage* [Website]. Retrieved: 19/07/2012, from: www.unesco.org/culture/ich/index.php?lg=en&pg=00011&multinational=3&display1=inscriptionID - tabs.

UNESCO (2012) 'Operational Directives for the Implementation of the Convention for the Safeguarding of the Intangible Heritage (2012)'. *Intangible Cultural Heritage*. Retrieved: 19/07/2012, from: www.unesco.org/culture/ich/index.php?lg=en&pg=00026.

UNESCO (2012) *Report of the International World Heritage Expert Meeting on Criterion (Vi) and Associative Values (Warsaw, Poland, 28–30 March 2012)*. Paris. Retrieved: 11/04/2012, from: http://whc.unesco.org/en/news/866/.

UNESCO (2012) 'Working Towards a Convention'. *Intangible Cultural Heritage* [Website]. Retrieved: 19/07/2012, from: www.unesco.org/culture/ich/index.php?lg=en&pg=00004.

UNESCO Intergovernmental Committee for the Protection of the World Cultural and Natural Heritage, Paris (1980) *Operational Guidelines for the Implementation of the World Heritage Convention*. Retrieved: 26/11/2012, from: http://whc.unesco.org/archive/opguide80.pdf.

UNESCO Intergovernmental Committee for the Protection of the World Cultural and Natural Heritage, Paris (1999) *Operational Guidelines for the Implementation of the World Heritage Convention*. Retrieved: 26/11/2012, from: http://whc.unesco.org/archive/opguide99.pdf.

UNESCO Intergovernmental Committee for the Protection of the World Cultural and Natural Heritage, Paris (2008) *Operational Guidelines for the Implementation of the World Heritage Convention*. Retrieved: 26/11/2012, from: http://whc.unesco.org/archive/opguide08-en.pdf.

UNESCO Intergovernmental Committee for the Protection of the World Cultural and Natural Heritage, Paris (2011) *Operational Guidelines for the Implementation of the World Heritage Convention*. Retrieved: 26/11/2012, from: http://whc.unesco.org/archive/opguide11-en.pdf.

UNESCO Intergovernmental Committee for the Protection of the World Cultural and Natural Heritage, Paris (2012) *Operational Guidelines for the Implementation of the World Heritage Convention*. Retrieved: 26/11/2012, from: http://whc.unesco.org/archive/opguide12-en.pdf.

UNESCO Intergovernmental Committee for the Protection of the World Cultural and Natural Heritage, Paris (2015) *Operational Guidelines for the Implementation of the World Heritage Convention*. Retrieved: 01/01/2016, from: http://whc.unesco.org/document/137843.

Urry, John (2002) *The Tourist Gaze*. 2nd edn. London: Sage.

Urry, John (2007 [1990]) 'Gazing on History'. In *Cultural Heritage: Critical Concepts in Media and Cultural Studies*. Edited by Laurajane Smith. Vol. 3. London: Routledge, pp. 306–338.

Urry, John (2007 [1996]) 'How Societies Remember the Past'. In *Cultural Heritage: Critical Concepts in Media and Cultural Studies*. Edited by Laurajane Smith. Vol. 2. London: Routledge, pp. 188–205.

Utzon, Jørn (1956–1967) 'Jorn Utzon Sydney Opera House Collection, 1956–1967'. *State Library of NSW*. Retrieved: 02/07/2012, from: http://acms.sl.nsw.gov.au/item/itemdetail paged.aspx?itemid=41166.

Utzon, Jørn (1958) 'Longitudinal Section through Major Hall. Sydney Opera House – Red Book. Nrs 12707 [Sz107]'. *Digital Gallery: Sydney Opera House – The Red Book* [Presentation Drawings Uploaded to Website]. State Records of NSW. Retrieved from: http://gallery. records.nsw.gov.au/index.php/galleries/sydney-opera-house/sydney-opera-house-the-red-book/.

Utzon, Jørn (1962) 'Platforms and Plateaus: Ideas of a Danish Architect'. *Zodiac*, 10, pp. 112–140.

Utzon, Jørn (1962) *The Yellow Book: Sydney National Opera House* [39 Plans for the Sydney Opera House by Jørn Utzon with Others Including Consultants Ove Arup & Partners]. Sydney: State Records of NSW. Retrieved: 27/04/2013, from: http://gallery.records.nsw.gov. au/index.php/galleries/sydney-opera-house/sydney-opera-house-the-yellow-book/.

Utzon, Jørn, and Sydney Opera House Trust (2002). *Utzon Design Principles*. Sydney. Retrieved: 27/04/2013, from: http://sohweb.cdnl.sydneyoperahouse.com/uploadedFiles/About_Us/ The_Building/Content_AboutUs_UtzonDesignPrinciples.pdf.

'Utzon Tributes Flood Opera House Website' (2008) *ABC News*, 1 December. Retrieved: 27/04/2013, from: www.abc.net.au/news/stories/2008/12/01/2434041.htm?section=australia.

Uzzell, David (2007 [1998]) 'Interpreting Our Heritage: A Theoretical Interpretation'. In *Cultural Heritage: Critical Concepts in Media and Cultural Studies*. Edited by Laurajane Smith. Vol. 4. London: Routledge, pp. 74–84.

van Dijck, José (2005) 'From Shoebox to Performative Agent: The Computer as Personal Memory Machine'. *New Media & Society*, 7 (3), pp. 311–332. doi: 10.1177/1461444805050765.

van Dijck, José (2007) *Mediated Memories in the Digital Age*. Stanford: Stanford University Press.

van Dijck, José (2008) 'Digital Photography: Communication, Identity, Memory'. *Visual Communication*, 7 (1), pp. 57–76. doi: 10.1177/1470357207084865.

van Dijck, José (2010) 'Search Engines and the Production of Academic Knowledge'. *International Journal of Cultural Studies*, 13 (6), pp. 574–592. doi: 10.1177/1367877910376582.

Van House, Nancy (2009) 'Collocated Photo Sharing, Story-Telling, and the Performance of Self'. *International Journal of Human-Computer Studies*, 67 (12), pp. 1073–1086. doi: 10.1016/j.ijhcs.2009.09.003.

Van House, Nancy, Marc Davis and Morgan Ames (2005) 'The Uses of Personal Networked Digital Imaging: An Empirical Study of Cameraphone Photos and Sharing'. Presented at the *CHI'05 Conference on Human Factors in Computing Systems*, New York, Association of Computing Machinery. doi: 10.1145/1056808.1057039.

Vardoulakis, Dimitris (2009) 'Between Logos and Icons: Notes Towards a Transfigurative Culture'. *Empedocles: European Journal for the Philosophy of Communication*, 1 (2), pp. 175–186. doi: 10.1386/ejpc.1.2.175_1.

Vecco, Marilena (2010) 'A Definition of Cultural Heritage: From the Tangible to the Intangible'. *Journal of Cultural Heritage*, 11 (3), pp. 321–324. doi: 10.1016/j.culher.2010.01.006.

Voase, Richard (2010) 'Visualising the Past: Baudrillard, Intensities of the Hyper-Real and the Erosion of Historicity'. In *Culture, Heritage and Representation*. Edited by Emma Waterton and Steve Watson. Surrey: Ashgate, pp. 105–123.

Vos, Rob, Ingrid Vos and Axel Enthoven (2008) 'The Opera'. Retrieved: 26/03/2013, from: www.ysin.co.uk/show/nl/content/3,19.

Walker, Joyce (2007) 'Narratives in the Database: Memorializing September 11th Online'. *Computers and Composition*, 24 (2), pp. 121–153.

Walker, Meredith (1998) *Protecting the Social Value of Public Places*. ACT: Australian Council of National Trusts.

Walker, Meredith, Chris Johnston and Carmel Boyce (1986) *Heritage Issues and Strategies: Western Region Cultural Heritage Study*. Braybrook: Melbourne Western Region Commission.

Warner, Michael (2002) *Publics and Counterpublics*. New York: Zone Books.

Waterton, Emma (2010) 'The Advent of Digital Technologies and the Idea of Community'. *Museum Management and Curatorship*, 25 (1), pp. 5–11. doi: 10.1080/09647770903529038.

Waterton, Emma, and Laurajane Smith (2010) 'The Recognition and Misrecognition of Community Heritage'. *International Journal of Heritage Studies*, 16 (1–2), pp. 4–15. doi: 10.1080/13527250903441671.

Waterton, Emma, Laurajane Smith and Gary Campbell (2006) 'The Utility of Discourse Analysis to Heritage Studies: The Burra Charter and Social Inclusion'. *International Journal of Heritage Studies*, 12 (4), pp. 339–355. doi: 10.1080/13527250600727000.

Watson, Anne (2006) *Building a Masterpiece: The Sydney Opera House*. Aldershot: Lund Humphries.

Watson, Anne (2006) 'An Opera House for Sydney: Genesis and Conclusion of a Competition'. In *Building a Masterpiece: The Sydney Opera House*. Edited by Anne Watson. Aldershot: Lund Humphries, pp. 38–55.

Watson, Anne (2012) 'Divided Loyalties: Peter Hall, Philip Parsons and the Dilemma of Utzon's Return'. *Fabrications*, 22 (2), pp. 164–185. doi: 10.1080/10331867.2012.733160.

Watson, Anne (2013) *Peter Hall and the Sydney Opera House: The 'Lost' Years 1966–70*. Sydney: Sydney University.

Watson, Steve, and Emma Waterton (2010) 'Introduction: A Visual Heritage'. In *Culture, Heritage and Representation: Perspectives on Visuality and the Past*. Edited by Emma Waterton and Steve Watson. Surrey: Ashgate, pp. 1–16.

Webber, Peter (2013) *The Phantom of the Opera House*. Boorowa: Watermark Press.

Weston, Richard (2002) *Utzon: Inspiration, Vision, Architecture*. Hellerupis: Edition Bløndal.

Weston, Richard (2006) 'Monumental Appeal: Reflections on the Sydney Opera House'. In *Building a Masterpiece: The Sydney Opera House*. Edited by Anne Watson. Aldershot: Lund Humphries, pp. 20–37.

'WikiHistory: Sydney Opera House' (2016) *WikiMedia Tool Labs*. Retrieved: 09/06/2016, from: https://tools.wmflabs.org/xtools/wikihistory/wh.php?page_title=Sydney_Opera_House.

'Wikipedia:Database Reports/Pages with the Most Revisions' (2016) *Wikipedia*. Retrieved: 09/06/2016, from: https://en.wikipedia.org/wiki/Wikipedia:Database_reports/Pages_with_the_most_revisions.

'Wikipedia:Manual of Style' (2016) *Wikipedia*. Retrieved: 12/06/2016, from: https://en.wikipedia.org/wiki/Wikipedia:Manual_of_Style.

'Wikipedia:Neutral Point of View' (2016) *Wikipedia*. Retrieved: 13/06/2016, from: https://en.wikipedia.org/wiki/Wikipedia:Neutral_point_of_view.

'Wikipedia:No Original Research' (2016) *Wikipedia*. Retrieved: 13/06/2016, from: https://en.wikipedia.org/wiki/Wikipedia:No_original_research.

'Wikipedia:Statistics' (2016) *Wikipedia*. Retrieved: 09/06/2016, from: https://en.wikipedia.org/wiki/Wikipedia:Statistics.

'Wikipedia:Verifiability' (2016) *Wikipedia*. Retrieved: 13/06/2016, from: https://en.wikipedia.org/wiki/Wikipedia:Verifiability.

Wilson, Ashleigh (2008) 'Sydney Opera House Architect Joern Utzon Dies'. *The Australian*, 30 November. Retrieved: 29/03/2013, from: www.theaustralian.com.au/news/sydney-opera-house-architect-dies/story-e6frg6to-1111118181028.

Wilton (2013) 'History of Wilton'. *Wilton*. Retrieved: 26/06/2013, from: www.wilton.com/about/history.cfm.

Woolley, Ken (2010) *Reviewing the Performance*. Boorowa: The Watermark Press.

'World Youth Day' (2008) Retrieved from: www.wyd2008.org/index.php/en/wyd08_events.

Yeomans, John (1968) *The Other Taj Mahal: What Happened to the Sydney Opera House*. London: Longmans, Green.

Young, Gregory (1996) 'Cultural Mapping: Capturing Social Value, Challenging Silence'. In *Assessing Social Values: Communities and Experts – a Workshop Held by Australia ICOMOS*. Canberra: Australian Heritage Commission, pp. 12–17.

Young, Pervin (2009) *Utzon Memorial Website* [Tribute to Jørn Utzon]. Sydney Opera House. Retrieved: 12/03/2013, from: http://jornutzon.sydneyoperahouse.com/Tributes.aspx.

Zunz, Jack (1988) 'Sydney Revisited'. *The Arup Journal*, 23, pp. 2–11.

Image credits and URLs

Figure I.1 Representations of the Sydney Opera House

TOP LEFT: Cristina Garduño Freeman.
TOP RIGHT: Heather Baird, www.sprinklebakes.com, 2010. www.sprinklebakes.com/2010/05/sydney-opera-house-opera-cake.html.
BOTTOM LEFT: Jennifer Fortwengler, 2008. www.flickr.com/photos/problemgirl/3103954988/.
BOTTOM RIGHT: Mary-Pierre Serveaux and Fabien Hoareau, 2005.

Figure I.2 Results from Flickr search

TOP LEFT: Laurie Wilson, 2011. www.flickr.com/photos/lsydney/5502133254/.
TOP MIDDLE: Denise Penney, 2007. www.flickr.com/photos/denny5277/400234043/.
TOP RIGHT: Nick Richards, 2006. www.flickr.com/photos/43295534@N00/253632571/.
BOTTOM LEFT: Anthony Agius, 2007. www.flickr.com/photos/aagius/395225106/.
BOTTOM MIDDLE: Thomas Rotte, 2014. www.flickr.com/photos/101372578@N07/14554715457/.
BOTTOM RIGHT: Jimmy Harris, 2006. www.flickr.com/photos/jimmyharris/114536865/.

Figure 2.1 Defacing the sails

LEFT: Deborah Pitt, 2006. www.flickr.com/photos/89724473@N00/147170358/.
MIDDLE: Chris Adkins, 2005. www.flickr.com/photos/c23gooey/49224917/.
RIGHT: Cristina Garduño Freeman.

Figure 3.1 The ubiquity of the Sydney Opera House according to Richard Weston

LEFT: Cristina Garduño Freeman.
MIDDLE: Sydney Opera House trademark reproduced with permission of the Sydney Opera House Trust, photographer unknown, 2007.
RIGHT: Wilmot Harvey, 2017. www.wilmotharvey.com.au/miscellaneous_2.html.

Figure 3.3 A photograph and a serviette

LEFT: Andy Perez, 2009. www.flickr.com/photos/ifiwerethekingoftheforest/3934591625/.
RIGHT: Jack Gilbert, 2009. www.flickr.com/photos/jack89/3213184608/.

Figure 3.4 Mitchell's family of images

William J. Thomas Mitchell (1986) *Iconology: Image, Text, Ideology*. Chicago: University of Chicago Press, p. 10.

Figure 3.7 Order of reality (real pieces of the Sydney Opera House)

LEFT: Cristina Garduño Freeman.
MIDDLE: Wayne Lorentz/Artefaqs, 2013. www.chicagoarchitecture.org/2013/03/05/pictures-of-all-149-rocks-stuck-on-the-tribune-tower/tribune-tower-rock-sydney-opera-house-sydney-australia/.
RIGHT: Sydney Opera House trademark reproduced with permission of the Sydney Opera House Trust, photographer unknown, 2007.

Figure 3.8 1st order: reflection of reality (photographs on Flickr.com of the Sydney Opera House)

LEFT: Jim Robinson, 2006. www.flickr.com/photos/no_fixed_address/268942294/.
MIDDLE: David Moggs, 2006. www.flickr.com/photos/moggsy/308439343/.
RIGHT: Jong Soo (Peter) Lee, 2009. www.flickr.com/photos/lutherankorean/3213767434/.

Figure 3.9 2nd order: denatures reality (things in the shape of the Sydney Opera House)

LEFT: Cristina Garduño Freeman.
MIDDLE: Livia Cheng, Chamelle Photography, 2009. www.flickr.com/photos/supercamel/3280696110/.
RIGHT: Bauer Media Pty Limited/The Australian Women's Weekly, 1962. http://nla.gov.au/nla.news-page4912887.

Figure 3.10 2nd order: absence of a reality (artefacts that preceded the realisation of the Sydney Opera House)

LEFT: Unknown. IE868656 Collection: State Library of NSW. http://archival.sl.nsw.gov.au/Details/archive/110072076.
MIDDLE: State Library of New South Wales and Max Dupain and Associates, 1964. IE976912 - Collection: State Library of NSW. http://archival.sl.nsw.gov.au/Details/archive/110036989.
RIGHT: Arup/Utzon, 1961-1965 2003 34 1 1 – Collection: Museum of Applied Arts and Sciences. Photograph: Alison Brennan. https://ma.as/12037.

Figure 3.11 3rd order: associative relationship (things inspired by the form of the Sydney Opera House)

LEFT: Jenny Lamy, approx. 2009.
MIDDLE: James Prince, 2012. www.flickr.com/photos/onthestreetphotography/8354510189/.
RIGHT: Rob Vos, 2010. www.robvosdesign.com/images/gallery/opera_in_nature_robvosdesign.jpg.

Figure 3.12 4th order: simulacra (buildings that are like the Sydney Opera House)

LEFT: Brian Yap, 1992. www.flickr.com/photos/yewenyi/2215433169/.
MIDDLE: Travis Wise, 2014. www.flickr.com/photos/photographingtravis/15842497231/in/photolistq8W
WtZ6ixdwiqtisCM6w6g2MqbTiBB9LYFEJ7uqbjp915biQ27DU7eYyYA2T5fUV6ixaLX8t27E
38sY64v2ZkKhhcB9jRb9Uqkoa6ixcbD9Uqk6BfNmMdWdtm2mUajKeXq6ix9z48gN3vQq6QHS53K2ob
C9Uqkir3K2oTG3JX5Rc6rPD5UaCnPWLEKvsZ6h6ZNZrbNsEhpRH14eboGj6T94tALD5xXNh7w9dg
WbuGZdX5iXPva6eXcGehqKJ6zonh3MXnBSaN1eiCwQWDvnD4g2LA8DPc3rmkX7eT.
RIGHT: James Scantlebury, 2014. www.flickr.com/photos/jamesscantlebury/14617900357/.

Figure 3.16 Rose's sites of meaning for images

Drawing by Cristina Garduño Freeman based on Gillian Rose (2007) *Visual Methodologies: An Introduction to the Interpretation of Visual Materials*. London: Sage, p. 13.

Figure 3.18 Mediated memories by José van Dijck

José van Dijck (2007) *Mediated Memories in the Digital Age*. Stanford: Stanford University Press, p. 50.

Figure 3.19 Homemade hat and commercial snowdome

LEFT: www.laughingkidslearn.com, 2016. http://laughingkidslearn.com/sydney-opera-house-hat-made-from-paper-plates/.
RIGHT: Cristina Garduño Freeman.

Figure 3.20 Scanned pages from *The Red Book* in a digital gallery

Jørn Utzon, 1958. NRS 12707 [SZ107] – Collection: State Records of NSW, 2017. http://gallery.records.nsw.gov.au/index.php/galleries/sydney-opera-house/sydney-opera-house-the-red-book/.

Figure 4.1 Critiquing: flowers, sails, clouds, dishes, nuns and turtles copulating

TOP LEFT: Luke Olsen, 2007. www.flickr.com/photos/9474425@N07/980054313.
TOP MIDDLE: Darren Cox, 2007. www.flickr.com/photos/global-wandering/1355089599/.

TOP RIGHT: Árný Jóhanns, 2006. www.flickr.com/photos/arny_johanns/138411057/.
BOTTOM LEFT: Nathalie-Margaux Jouenne, 2008. www.flickr.com/photos/margauxrainbaux/304
0010616/.
BOTTOM MIDDLE: Architecture in Australia, 1974. http://architectureinaustralia.com/issues/1974-
architecture-in-australia-vol63-no1-february/.
BOTTOM RIGHT: © Estate of Eric Thake, 1972 7.1973 – Collection: Art Gallery of New South Wales
Gift of Hal Missingham 1973. Photograph AGNSW. www.artgallery.nsw.gov.au/collection/works/7.1973/.

Figure 4.2 Telling: books, operas and tours

LEFT: Cristina Garduño Freeman.
MIDDLE: Cristina Garduño Freeman.
RIGHT: Craig Bentley Smith, 2006. www.flickr.com/photos/superciliousness/288227009/.

Figure 4.3 Wikipedia's Sydney Opera House page

Wikipedia, 2016. http://en.wikipedia.org/wiki/Sydney_Opera_House.

Figure 4.4 Why was my popular culture section deleted?

Wikipedia, 2012. http://en.wikipedia.org/wiki/Talk:Sydney_Opera_House/Archive_1#Popular_culture_
section.

Figure 4.5 The Sydney Opera House and the Taj Mahal

LEFT: Jim Robinson, 2006. www.flickr.com/photos/no_fixed_address/268942294/.
RIGHT: Linda Ross, 2017. www.flickr.com/photos/superciliousness/288227009/.

Figure 4.6 Dame Edna's Ascot races hat

LEFT: John Timbers, 1976, 2004.024.006.005 (file ending 485) ('Materials') – Collection: Arts Centre
Melbourne: Performing Arts Collection, Donated by the Sidney Meyer Fund in honour of Geoffrey
Cohen, Trustee 1992–2003. https://performingartscollection.wordpress.com/2011/11/03/ladies-day-at-the-
races-1976/.
RIGHT: Phil Guest, 2015. www.flickr.com/photos/philip-rosie/22436985714/in/photolist-9imLnB-9WHjM3-
jLZ6RT-p2Tyoh-s1XxnB-AbFqah-f5e9L8-6v5jkc.

Figure 4.7 Hats: serious, handmade and performed

LEFT: Bauer Media Pty Limited/The Australian Women's Weekly, 1962. http://nla.gov.au/nla.news-
page4912887.
MIDDLE: www.laughingkidslearn.com, 2016. http://laughingkidslearn.com/sydney-opera-house-hat-
made-from-paper-plates/.
RIGHT: Anna Oakley, 2008. www.flickr.com/photos/98675081@N00/2430875522/.

Figure 4.8 Susan Giles: *Spliced Buildings*

Susan Giles, 2008. http://susangiles.net/wp-content/uploads/2015/02/TajMahalSydney.jpg.

Figure 4.9 An Opera House in Every Home, original and copies

LEFT: Bauer Media Pty Limited/The Australian Women's Weekly, 1962. http://nla.gov.au/nla.news-
page4912887.
MIDDLE: James Prince, 2012. www.flickr.com/photos/onthestreetphotography/8354510189/.
RIGHT: Marco Berton, 2006. www.bertonwithanee.com/art3c1.html.

Figure 5.1 Repurposed miniatures: teapot, origami and chook (chicken) shed

LEFT: Cristina Garduño Freeman.
MIDDLE: © Yee, www.yeesjob.com, 2010. www.flickr.com/photos/69729787@N00/5517858924/.
RIGHT: Brendan Donohue and Wendy Harmer, 2009. http://blogs.abc.net.au/nsw/2009/03/sydney-opera-
ho.html.

Figure 5.2 Repurposed language: speakers, campervan and jewellery

LEFT: Made by Makers, www.madebymakers.com, 2009. www.flickr.com/photos/madebymakers/301
9222844/.
MIDDLE: Rob Vos, 2010. www.robvosdesign.com/images/gallery/opera_in_nature_robvosdesign.jpg.
RIGHT: © Georg Jensen, 1987–1998. DS-1871-0002.jpg – Collection: Museum of Applied Arts and
Sciences. Photograph: Ryan Hernandez. https://ma.as/467754.

Figure 5.3 Photograph posted to Planet Cake's Facebook page showing the volume from
which one row of 'sails' will be carved, with Utzon's drawings in the background

Paris Cutler, Planet Cake, and Facebook Inc., 2011. www.facebook.com/PlanetCake/photos/a.114530826
259.107996.22942151259/489992741259/?type=3&theater.

Figure 5.4 Day 6 documentation video posted to YouTube by Planet Cake.

Paris Cutler, Planet Cake, and YouTube, 2011. www.youtube.com/watch?v=kozkMCSKQYY

Figure 5.5 Photograph from Planet Cake's blog showing the final outcome

Paris Cutler and Planet Cake, 2011. http://planetcakeupdate.blogspot.com.au/2011/01/holy-cow-it-actually-
worked.html.

Figure 5.6 Ordinary things made more valuable as merchandise

Sydney Opera House trademark reproduced with permission of the Sydney Opera House Trust, photographer
unknown, 2007.

Figure 5.7 Logos, brands and corporate identities

LEFT: Sydney Swans Football Club, 2017. www.sydneyswans.com.au.
MIDDLE: Sydney Gay and Lesbian Mardi Gras Ltd, 2017. www.mardigras.org.au.
RIGHT: NSW branch of Institute of Professional Editors, 2017. www.editorsnsw.com.

Figure 5.8 Stamps and advertisements

LEFT: Sydney Swans Football Club, 2017. www.sydneyswans.com.au.
RIGHT: Publio Santander T., 2007. https://adsoftheworld.com/media/print/american_airlines_apple also
www.newyorkfestivals.com/tvfilm/main.php?p=3,1&wp=info&id=314527.

Figure 5.9 Cover of Qantas in-flight magazine, July 2008 issue

Bauer Media Limited (previously ACP), 2008.

Figure 5.10 Jesus carries his cross, performed as part of the Stations of the Cross at Sydney Opera
House forecourt during World Youth Day Sydney 2008 on 18 July 2008 in Sydney, Australia

TOP: Christopher Chan, 2008. www.flickr.com/photos/chanc/2680245221/.
MIDDLE: Christopher Chan, 2008. www.flickr.com/photos/chanc/2679730108/.
BOTTOM: Christopher Chan, 2008. www.flickr.com/photos/chanc/2683632239/.

Figure 6.1 Guidebooks, souvenirs and maps

LEFT: Cristina Garduño Freeman.
MIDDLE: Cristina Garduño Freeman.
RIGHT: Compass Maps Ltd, 2017. http://popoutproducts.com/retail/popout-city-maps/.

Figure 6.2 People looking and touching

LEFT: Ryan Baum, 2002. www.flickr.com/photos/rbaum/293651039/.
MIDDLE: Rachel Bell, www.rachelbell.com.au, 2011. www.flickr.com/photos/rachelbell2010/5351846114/.
RIGHT: Kevin Kin Soon Wong.

Figure 6.3 Miniature and fragment

LEFT: Cristina Garduño Freeman.
RIGHT: Sydney Opera House trademark reproduced with permission of the Sydney Opera House Trust, photographer unknown, 2007.

Figure 6.4 Scale and relationship

LEFT: Cristina Garduño Freeman.
RIGHT: Mary-Pierre Serveaux and Fabien Hoareau, 2005.

Figure 6.5 Architects working with complete and partial models of the Sydney Opera House

LEFT: State Library of NSW, 1957.
RIGHT: State Library of NSW and Jorn Utzon. IE959223 Collection: State Library of NSW, 1961. http://digital.sl.nsw.gov.au/delivery/DeliveryManagerServlet?dps_pid=FL960214&embedded=true&toolbar=false.

Figure 6.6 Performing at the Sydney Opera House

LEFT: Summer, 2010. www.flickr.com/photos/sweetsummertime/4288666682/.
RIGHT: Eunah Kim, 2006. www.flickr.com/photos/dmsk999/2717236038/.

Figure 6.7 Flickr group: Sydney Opera House

Yahoo, Flickr and members of 'Sydney Opera House' group, 2012. www.flickr. com/groups/sydneyoperahouse/.

Figure 6.8 Flickr group: Sydney-alt

Yahoo, Flickr and members of 'Sydney-alt' group, 2012. www.flickr.com/groups/33606562@N00/.

Figure 6.9 Performing photography

LEFT: Mark Jones, 2007. www.flickr.com/photos/31243004@N02/4649731983/.
RIGHT: Jeremy Keith, 2006. www.flickr.com/photos/adactio/257923247/.

Figure 6.10 Real-time updates from Sydney Opera House group as displayed on author's home page

Yahoo, Flickr and members of 'Sydney Opera House' group, 2009.

Figure 6.11 Slideshow mode showing photograph from Sydney Opera House group pool

Yahoo, Flickr and Scott Henry, 2009. www.flickr.com/photos/20719570@N04/3457980106/.

Figure 6.12 Thumbnail mode showing group pool from Sydney Opera House

Yahoo, Flickr and members of 'Sydney Opera House' group, 2009.

Figure 6.13 Individual mode from Sydney Opera House group pool

Yahoo, Flickr and Jong Soo (Peter) Lee, 2009. www.flickr.com/photos/lutherankorean/3207850764/in/pool-sydneyoperahouse.

Figure 6.14 Sydney Opera House group discussion thread

Yahoo, Flickr and members of 'Sydney Opera House' group, 2009.

Figure 6.15 Other representations of the Sydney Opera House in group pool

LEFT: Patrick Boland, 2005. www.flickr.com/photos/patrickboland/109610311/in/photolist-aFMjX-ouk
Sub-4oaNco-hfyXYU-cDzBYN-hfyXLj-owtfjX-r6JTZV-owkmxw.
RIGHT: Reg Momabassa 1996.

Figure 7.1 Public expression prompted by Utzon's death on participatory media

LEFT: Seier+Seier, 2008. www.flickr.com/photos/seier/3069164260/.
RIGHT: Ibai Gandiaga Perez de Albeniz, 2009. www.flickr.com/photos/ibai/3364385033/.
BOTTOM: martin8th/Flickr, 2008. www.flickr.com/photos/martin8th/3079103323/.

Figure 7.2 Screengrab of the Utzon Memorial Website page with personal tributes posted

Sydney Opera House Trust, 2009.

Index

over intangible heritage 186–7; socio-visual value and Criterion (vi) 11, 174–7
World Heritage inscription 1, 4–5, 19, 25, 34; inscription for its value as a world-famous iconic building 5, 35–41; nomination documents 43–6; significance of for the Opera House 14, 19–23; unsuccessful attempts 19–20, 22, 38
World Youth Day 2008 113, 123–7
Wright, F.L. 183–4

Xenedis 145, 146

Yeomans, J. 98, 103
yewenyi 145
young mother's blog 108–9, 110
YouTube 75

Taylor & Francis eBooks

Helping you to choose the right eBooks for your Library

Add Routledge titles to your library's digital collection today. Taylor and Francis ebooks contains over 50,000 titles in the Humanities, Social Sciences, Behavioural Sciences, Built Environment and Law.

Choose from a range of subject packages or create your own!

Benefits for you

- » Free MARC records
- » COUNTER-compliant usage statistics
- » Flexible purchase and pricing options
- » All titles DRM-free.

Benefits for your user

- » Off-site, anytime access via Athens or referring URL
- » Print or copy pages or chapters
- » Full content search
- » Bookmark, highlight and annotate text
- » Access to thousands of pages of quality research at the click of a button.

REQUEST YOUR **FREE** INSTITUTIONAL TRIAL TODAY

Free Trials Available
We offer free trials to qualifying academic, corporate and government customers.

eCollections – Choose from over 30 subject eCollections, including:

Archaeology	Language Learning
Architecture	Law
Asian Studies	Literature
Business & Management	Media & Communication
Classical Studies	Middle East Studies
Construction	Music
Creative & Media Arts	Philosophy
Criminology & Criminal Justice	Planning
Economics	Politics
Education	Psychology & Mental Health
Energy	Religion
Engineering	Security
English Language & Linguistics	Social Work
Environment & Sustainability	Sociology
Geography	Sport
Health Studies	Theatre & Performance
History	Tourism, Hospitality & Events

For more information, pricing enquiries or to order a free trial, please contact your local sales team:
www.tandfebooks.com/page/sales